The coloured boxes show the extents and page numbers for all maps in this Road Atlas.
The box colours correspond to the maps' page trim colours, representing different scales and types of map.

W9-ANW-589

1:3,000,000 maps
Cover the entire country. Essential for long-distance road touring and route-planning.

1:1,500,000 maps
Cover the popular Queensland coast and around the cities of Perth and Adelaide, giving increased coverage for short-distance road touring.

1:1,250,000 maps
Cover the whole of Tasmania, at a scale suitable for discovering the island State.

1:1,000,000 maps
Cover the south-east coast of Australia from Brisbane to South Australia at a scale ideal for journeys on and off the beaten track.

Fraser Is **33**

Feature maps
Areas of special interest shown in greater detail for in-depth exploration.

Perth **113**

City maps
Everything you'll need to discover all the State and Territory capital cities and the national capital, Canberra.

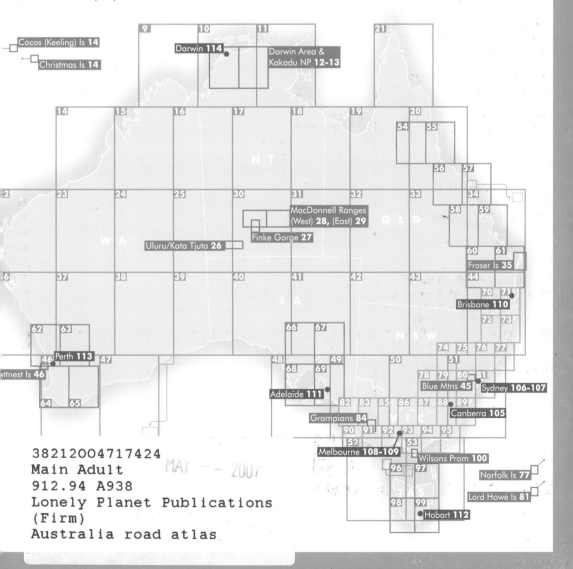

Cocos (Keeling) Is **14**

Christmas Is **14**

Darwin **114**

Darwin Area & Kakadu NP **12-13**

N T

MacDonnell Ranges (West) **28**, (East) **29**

Finke Gorge **27**

Uluru/Kata Tjuta **26**

W A

Q L D

Fraser Is **35**

Brisbane **110**

S A

N S W

V I C

Perth **113**

ttnest Is **46**

Adelaide **111**

Grampians **84**

Blue Mtns **45**

Sydney **106-107**

Canberra **105**

Melbourne **108-109**

Wilsons Prom **100**

Norfolk Is **77**

Lord Howe Is **81**

T A S

Hobart **112**

ELEVATION

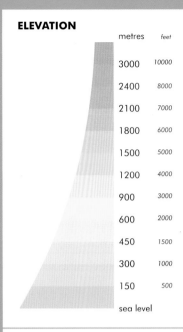

metres	feet
3000	10000
2400	8000
2100	7000
1800	6000
1500	5000
1200	4000
900	3000
600	2000
450	1500
300	1000
150	500
sea level	

BOUNDARIES

State Boundary
Limites del'Etat
Landesgrenze
Frontera del Estado

National Park
Parc National
Nationalpark
Parque Nacional

State Park, other parks
Parc d'Etat, autres parcs
staatlicher Park, andere Parks
Parques Regionales, otros parques

Marine Park
Parc Maritime
Marine Park
Parque Marino

Aboriginal Land
Territoire Aborigène
Eingeborenenland
Tierra Aborígenes

Military/Prohibited Area
Zone Militaire/Interdite
Militär-/Spergebiet
Zona Militar/Prohibida

Fence
Clôture
Zaun
Valla

TRANSPORTATION

Freeway
Autoroute
Autobahn
Autovía

Freeway under construction
Autoroute en construction
Autobahn in Bau
Autovía en construccion

Primary Road
Route Principale
Fernstraße
Carretera Principal

Secondary Road
Route Secondaire
Nebenstraße
Carretera Secundaria

Other roads
Autres Routes
Übrige Straße
Otras Carreteras

4WD Track
Sentier
Fahrspur
Senda

Unsealed Roads
Route non bitumée
unversiegelte Straße
Carretera sin Asfaltar

25 **Distance in Kilometres**
Distance en Kilomètres
Entfernung in Kilometern
Distancia en Kilómetros

Railway
Voie de chemin de fer
Eisenbahn
Ferrocarril

Freight Railway
Train de marchandises
Güterzug
Ferrocarril de mercancías

Ferry Route; Ferry Terminal
Route de ferry; Terminal du ferry
Fährroute; Fähranlegestelle
Transbordador; Estación Marítima

13 A300 44 **Route Numbers**
Numéro de Route
Straße Nummer
Número de Autopista

NATURAL FEATURES

River
Fleuve
Fluß
Rio

Creek, Irrigation Channel
Ruisseau; Canal d'irrigation
Flußarm; Bewässerungskanal
Riachuelo; Acequia

Intermittent River or Creek
Rivière, ruisseau intermittent
zeitweise wasserführender Fluß oder Bach
Rio o Riachuelo Intermitente

Lake; Intermittent Lake
Lac; Lac intermittent
See; zeitweise wasserführender
Lago; Lago Intermitente

Spring; Waterfall
Source; Cascades
Quelle; Wasserfall
Manantial; Catarata

Reef
Récife
Riff
Arrecife

Swamp
Marais
Sumpf
Pantano

Mount Werong **Mountain**
Montagne
Berg
Montaña

Pass
Col
Paß
Desfiladero

Cliff
Falaise
Klippe, Steilabbruch
Acantilado

Gardens; Lookout
Jardins; Point de Vue
Gärten; Aussicht
Jardines; Mirador

**For map features on the City Maps
in this Atlas (pp 105-114), please
refer to the City Map Legend p104.**

POPULATION

• Durham Ox	0 - 750
• Murrumbateman	750 - 2,000
○ Castlemaine	2,000 - 7,500
○ **Devonport**	7,500 - 25,000
○ **Toowoomba**	25,000 - 100,000
○ **Newcastle**	100,000 - 750,000
○ **Brisbane**	> 750,000

✪ National Capital
Capitale
Hauptstadt
Capital

○ **Perth** State Capital
Capital d'Etat
Landeshauptstadt
Capital del Estado

Urban Area
Zone urbanisée
Stadtgebiet
Zona Urbana

▪ *Aurukun* Aboriginal Community
Communauté aborigène
Eingeborenengemeinde
Comunidad Aborigenes

▪ *Clifton Downs* Farmhouse, Homestead
Ferme, exploitation agricole
Gutshaus, Siedlungsstätte
Casa de Labranza, Granja

MAP LINES

Latitude/Longitude
Latitude/Longitude
Breitengrad/Längengrad
Latitud/ Longitud

Tropics
Tropiques
Tropen
Los Trópicos

Gridlines
Grille
Gitternetzlinien
Barras

SYMBOLS

✈ ✈ Airport; Airfield
Aéroport; Aérodrome
Flughafen; Flugplatz
Aeropuerto; Pista de Aterrizaje

🐦 Bird Sanctuary
Rèserve d'oiseaux
Vogelschutzgebiet
Reserva Ornitológica

⌂ Cave
Grotte
Höhle
Cueva

ℹ Information Centre
Centre d'information
Informationszentrum
Centro de Información

✖ Mine
Mine
Mine
Mina

National Park
Parc National
Nationalpark
Parque Nacional

Ruins
Ruines
Ruinen
Ruinas

Ski Field; Cross-Country Skiing
Domaine Skiable; Ski de randonnée
Skipiste; Skilanglaufstrecke
Campo para esquiar; Esqui de Fondo

Wine Region
Domaine viticole
Weinanbaugebiet
Región vinícola

🏖 Beach
Plage
Strand
Playa

⛺ Camping Ground
Terrain de Camping
Zeltplatz
Camping

Diving Site
Site de plongée
Tauchplatz
Zona de Buceo

Lighthouse
Phare
Leuchtturm
Faro

Monument, Cairn
Monument
Denkmal
Monumento

● Point of Interest
Curiosités
Sehenswerter Ort
Punto de Interés

Shipwreck
Épave
Schiffbruch
Naufragio

Surf Beach
Surf
Surfstrand
Playa de Surf

Zoo
Jardine Zoologique
Zoo
Parque Zoológico

USING THIS ROAD ATLAS

Map 84

Extents of Larger Scale Map, with Page No.
Renvoi sur une carte à plus grande échelle
Ausdehnung von Karten größeren Maßstabs mit Seitenzahl
Extensiones de mapa a escala mayor con número de página

Adjoining Map Indicator
Repère indiquant la présence d'une carte adjacente
Anzeiger angrenzender Karten
Indicador de Mapa Colindante

▲39▲

No Adjoining Map
Pas de carte adjacente
keine angrenzende Karte
Sin Mapa Colindante

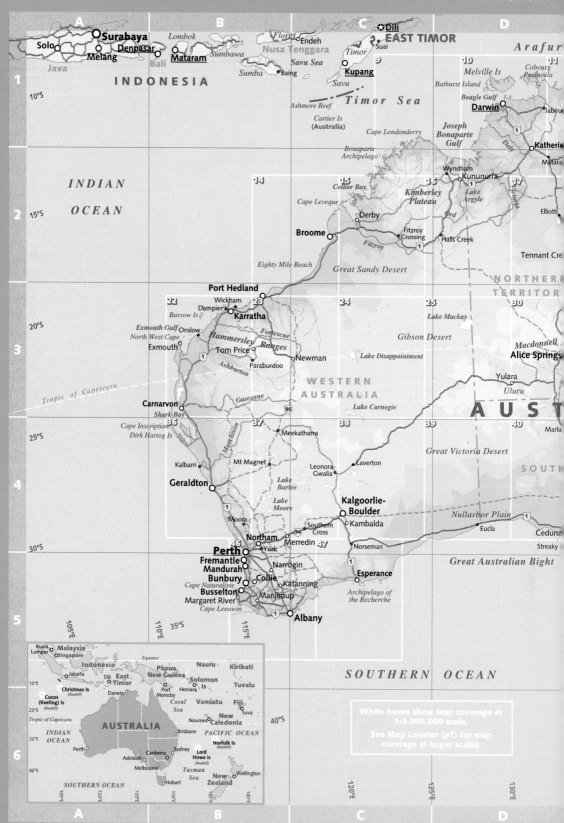

INDONESIA

Solo   Surabaya   Lombok   *Flores*   Endeh   ◈ Dili   **EAST TIMOR**   *Arafur*
Melang   Denpasar   Mataram   *Sumbawa*   *Sumba*   Baing   *Savu Sea*   Suai   9
Java   *Bali*   *Nusa Tenggara*   *Timor*   Kupang

Melville Is   *Cobourg Peninsula*
Bathurst Island

10°S   **INDONESIA**

Ashmore Reef   *Timor Sea*   Beagle Gulf   **Darwin**   Jabiru
Cartier Is (Australia)   *Cape Londonderry*   *Joseph Bonaparte Gulf*   **Katheri**

INDIAN   *Bonaparte Archipelago*   Wyndham   *Matara*
OCEAN   13   *Collier Bay*   15   16   Kununurra   17
Cape Leveque   *Kimberley Plateau*   Lake Argyle   Elliott
15°S   Derby   *Ord*
Cape Leveque   Fitzroy Crossing   Halls Creek

Broome   *Fitzroy*   Tennant Cre

Eighty Mile Beach   *Great Sandy Desert*   **NORTHER**
TERRITOR

Port Hedland   Wickham   22   23   24   25   30
Barrow Is   Dampier   **Karratha**   Lake Mackay
20°S   *Exmouth Gulf*   Onslow   *Hammersley*   *Gibson Desert*   *Macdonnell*
North West Cape   Tom Price   *Ranges*   Lake Disappointment   **Alice Springs**
Exmouth   Paraburdoo   Newman
Ashburton   Yulara
Tropic of Capricorn   **WESTERN**   *Uluru*
Carnarvon   *Gascoyne*   **AUSTRALIA**   **A U S T**
Shark Bay   95   Lake Carnegie   Marla
Cape Inscription   36   37   38   39   40
Dirk Hartog Is   Meekatharra   **SOUTH**
25°S   Kalbarri   *Great Victoria Desert*
Mt Magnet   Leonora-Gwalia   Laverton
Murchison   *Lake Barlee*
Geraldton   Lake Moore   **Kalgoorlie-Boulder**   *Nullarbor Plain*   Ceduna
Moora   Kambalda   Eucla
94   Southern Cross   Streaky
Northam   Merredin   Norseman
30°S   York   *Great Australian Bight*
Perth   47
Fremantle   Narrogin   **Esperance**
Mandurah
Bunbury   Collie   Katanning
Cape Naturaliste   **Busselton**   Manjimup   *Archipelago of the Recherche*
Margaret River
Cape Leeuwin   **Albany**

SOUTHERN OCEAN

105°E   110°E   35°S   115°E   120°E   125°E   130°E

Inset map:

Kuala Lumpur   **Malaysia**   Singapore   *Equator*   Nauru   **Kiribati**
Indonesia   **Papua New Guinea**   **Solomon Is**   **Tuvalu**
Jakarta   Dili   **East Timor**   Port Moresby   Honiara
Christmas Is (Austrl)   Darwin   *Coral Sea*   **Vanuatu**   **Fiji**
Cocos (Keeling) Is (Austrl)   Noumea   Suva
Tropic of Capricorn   **New Caledonia**
INDIAN OCEAN   **AUSTRALIA**   Brisbane   *PACIFIC OCEAN*
Perth   Norfolk Is (Austrl)
Adelaide   Canberra   Sydney   Lord Howe Is (Austrl)
Melbourne   *Tasman Sea*   **New Zealand**   Wellington
Hobart
SOUTHERN OCEAN

105°E   120°E   135°E   150°E   165°E   180°E

White boxes show map coverage at 1:3,000,000 scale.

See Map Locator (p1) for map coverage at larger scales.

A   B   C   D

250   500 km
150   300 mi

E   F   G   H

Daru

Torres Strait
Thursday
Island
Torres Strait Is
Cape York

Port Moresby

PAPUA
NEW GUINEA

Solomon Sea

Gizo

SOLOMON
ISLANDS

Alotau

D'Entrecasteaux
Islands

Louisiade
Archipelago

Guadalcanal

10°S   1

Wessel Is

Nhulunbuy
Cape Arnhem

Weipa

Groote Eylandt
Alyangula

Gulf of
Carpentaria

Cape York
Peninsula

Cape Melville   *Osprey Reef*

Coral Sea Islands Territory

Willis Group

Lihou Reefs

Coral Sea

15°S   2

Borroloola

Burketown

Mornington
Is

Normanton

Cooktown

Port Douglas
Mareeba   **Cairns**
Atherton   **Innisfail**
Tully
Hinchinbrook I
Ingham
Townsville
Ayr

Marion Reef

Îles Chesterfield
(Fr)

20°S

Mt Isa   Cloncurry

Hughenden

Charters
Towers

Collinsville

Bowen
Airlie Beach
Whitsunday Is
Proserpine

QUEENSLAND

Winton

Moranbah

Mackay
Sarina

Northumberland
Is   Swains
Reef

Saumarez
Reef

Boulia

Longreach

Barcaldine

Clermont

Middlemount

Wreck Reef

Cato Is

Simpson Desert
Birdsville

Emerald

Yeppoon
Rockhampton
Gladstone

Biloela

Tropic of Capricorn

Oodnadatta

Charleville

Quilpie

Roma

Chinchilla

Hervey Bay

Bundaberg
Sandy Cape
Fraser Is
Maryborough
Gympie
Noosa Heads
Maroochydore

25°S

SOUTH

Cunnamulla

St George

Dalby

Toowoomba
Warwick

Brisbane
Surfers Paradise
Tweed Heads
Byron Bay

PACIFIC

Goondiwindi

Moree

Walgett

Bourke

Narrabri

Lismore
Inverell

Ballina

Grafton
Armidale   **Coffs Harbour**

OCEAN

Lord Howe Is

30°S

Broken Hill

Cobar   Nyngan

Gunnedah

Tamworth

Kempsey
Port Macquarie
Taree
Forster
Nelsons Bay

Quorn
Peterborough

Ivanhoe

Parkes

Dubbo   Maitland

Whyalla   Port Pirie

Clare
Gawler

Mildura

Griffith

Orange
Cowra
Narrandera   Katoomba
Goulburn

Bathurst

Newcastle
Gosford

SYDNEY

Tasman Sea

35°S

Adelaide
Murray
Bridge
Victor Harbor

Swan Hill
Deniliquin
Echuca

Hay

Wagga
Wagga   Albury

Canberra
Batemans Bay
Narooma
Bega

Naracoorte

Horsham

Bendigo
Shepparton

Sale
Bairnsdale

VICTORIA

Mt Gambier

Portland
Warrnambool

Ararat
Ballarat

MELBOURNE

Geelong   Morwell

Cape Otway

Wilsons Promontory

King Is   *Bass Strait*   *Flinders Is*

Smithton

Burnie
Devonport
Launceston

Queenstown

TASMANIA

Lake Gordon

Hobart

Bruny Is
South East Cape

40°S   6

140°E   145°E   150°E   155°E   160°E   165°E

E   F   G   H

Distance is measured in kilometres and assumes travel on the most direct route using main roads and highways.

See also Trip Maps on pages 101-103.

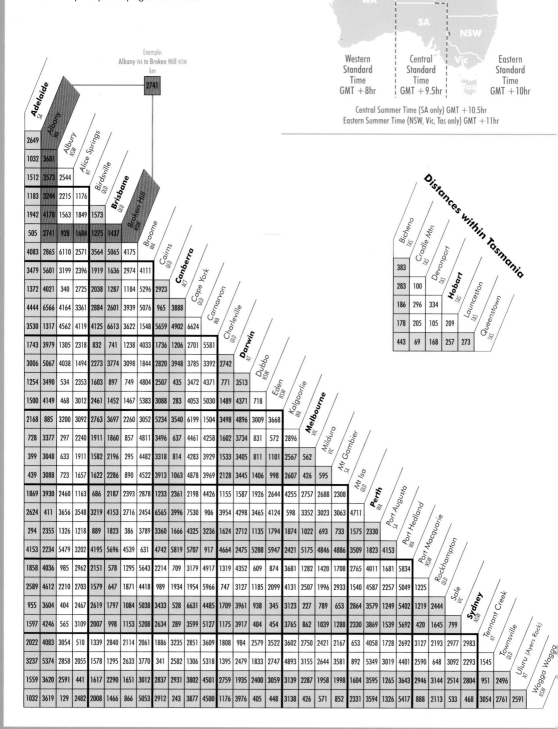

Western Standard Time GMT +8hr

Central Standard Time GMT +9.5hr

Eastern Standard Time GMT +10hr

Central Summer Time (SA only) GMT +10.5hr
Eastern Summer Time (NSW, Vic, Tas only) GMT +11hr

Example:
Albany WA to Broken Hill NSW
km
2741

Australia's climate varies immensely from the tropical north to the temperate south. In the far north, it's the monsoon belt where there are just two seasons – hot and wet, and hot and dry. The centre of the continent is arid – hot and dry during the day, but often bitterly cold at night. Further south is more temperate, Victoria and southern NSW have snowfields and Tasmanians know the true definition of cold!

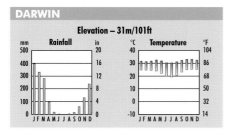

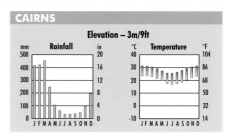

Tropical

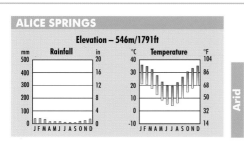

Arid

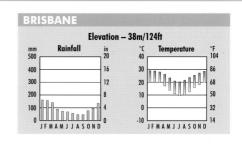

Sub Tropical

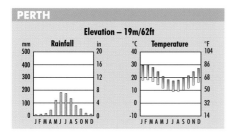

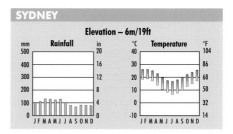

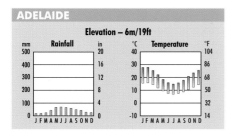

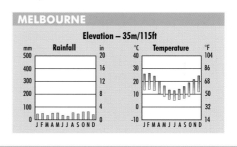

Temperate

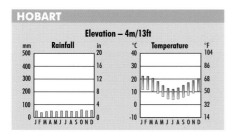

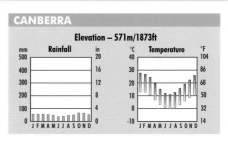

Cool Temperate

Road Rules

Driving in Australia holds few real surprises. Australians drive on the left-hand side of the road just like in the UK, Japan and most countries in south and east Asia and the Pacific. An important road rule is 'give way to right' - if an intersection is unmarked (unusual), you must give way to vehicles entering the intersection from your right. The general speed limit in built-up areas is 60km/h (50km/h in some states) and on the highway it's usually 100 or 110km/h. In the Northern Territory there is no speed limit outside of built-up areas, although you might still be booked for driving at a 'speed inappropriate to the prevailing conditions' (for instance, 160km/h at dawn/dusk/night). The police have radar guns and speed cameras and are very fond of using them in hidden locations.

All new cars in Australia have seat belts back and front and if your seat has one you're required to wear it - you're likely to get fined if you don't. Small children must be buckled into an approved safety seat.

Drink driving is a real problem. Serious attempts are being made to reduce the resulting road toll - random breath tests are not uncommon in built-up areas. If you're caught with a blood-alcohol level of more than 0.05% be prepared for a hefty fine and the loss of your licence.

To be safe, pick up a copy of the state's road rules at any police station.

Road Conditions

The majority of major roads in Australia are sealed and dual lane, but you don't have to travel very far off the beaten track to find yourself on dirt roads.

The northern wet season occurs somewhere between November and May. Once the wet sets in, tracks can become bottomless mud, dry creeks become raging torrents and low-lying areas are flooded. Vast areas can be cut off for weeks at a time.

Signposting along the major routes is usually adequate, but you'll still need your Road Atlas if you want to explore in any detail. When asking for directions, remember that most roads are known by their names rather than their official route numbers.

Fuel

Service stations generally stock diesel, super and unleaded fuel. Liquid Petroleum Gas (LPG, Autogas) is usually available in the major centres, but is much harder to find once you get off the major highways. Prices vary from place to place. Once away from the major cities, prices can soar. Distance between fill-ups can be long in the outback and in some remote areas deliveries can be haphazard. Ring ahead if you want to be sure.

Outback Motoring

Serious Outback travel requires much research and planning. Among other things, you will need to find out the best time to go, the availability of drinking water, services and facilities, the likely condition of the roads and whether or not your vehicle will be suitable. Lonely Planet's Outback Australia guide is packed with essential information and is an excellent travelling companion.

Anybody who sets out to see the country in reasonable detail will have to expect some dirt-roads. If you seriously want to explore, you'd better plan on having a 4WD and a winch. A few useful spare parts, such as fan belts and radiator hoses should be carried if you're travelling in remote areas where garages are few and far between. There are a few tracks where your vehicle will need a long-range fuel tank, but on many others you'll be able to scrape by on your vehicle's standard tank with say, one or two 20 litre jerry cans.

The bitumen (asphalt, tar) on some outback roads is only wide enough for one vehicle. It's common to move the left half of the vehicle off the edge and expect the oncoming vehicle to do the same. Make sure you move well out if the way for an oncoming truck or road train. If an oncoming vehicle throws up so much dust that you can't see the road ahead, slow down (and turn on the headlights) or stop. Don't pass in dust clouds.

Carry sufficient water to get you through to the next supply point and still have plenty in reserve for emergencies. If you're planning a trip, allow 4 to 5 litres of drinking water per person, per day.

Kangaroos are common hazards on country roads; sheep and cattle too in the outback. A collision is likely to kill an animal and seriously damage your vehicle. Kangaroos are most active around dawn and dusk and they often travel in groups. If you see one hopping across the road in front of you, slow right down - its friends may be just behind it. To be safe, avoid driving between the hours of 5 pm and 8 pm on outback roads.

You should always let a responsible person know the details of your proposed activities so that the police will know where to look for you. Leave a map, showing where you're going, how you're getting there and how long you expect to take. Always check in as arranged, otherwise you may spark unnecessary and costly search and rescue operations – in which case, you'll be expected to pay the costs. Always stay with your vehicle if you break down – it's easier to spot a car than a human from the air.

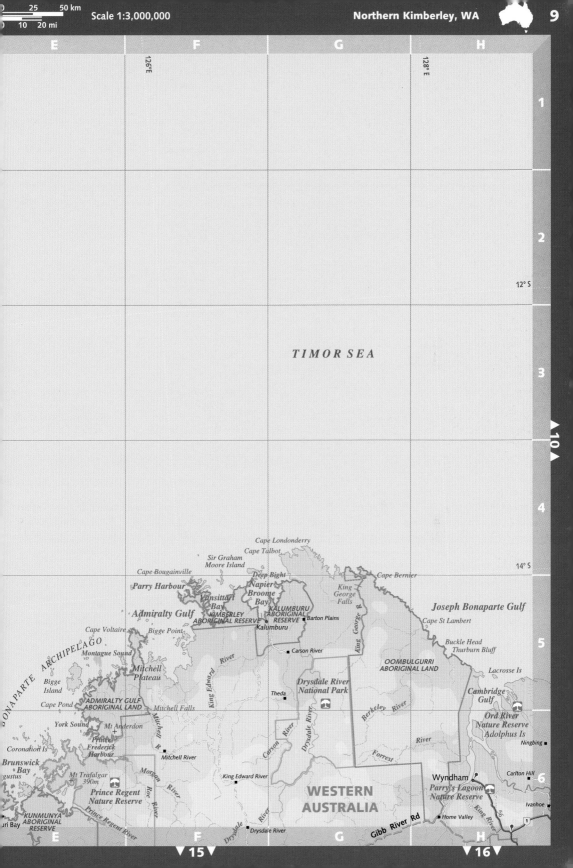

25   50 km

10   20 mi

126°E

128° E

1

2

12° S

TIMOR SEA

3

▲10▲

4

Cape Londonderry

Cape Talbot

Sir Graham
Moore Island

14° S

Cape Bougainville

Deep Bight

Cape Bernier

Parry Harbour

Napier
Broome
Bay

King
George
Falls

Joseph Bonaparte Gulf

*Vansittart
Bay*

KALUMBURU
ABORIGINAL
RESERVE

Admiralty Gulf

KIMBERLEY
ABORIGINAL RESERVE

■ Barton Plains

Cape St Lambert

Cape Voltaire

Bigge Point

Kalumburu ●

Buckle Head
Thurburn Bluff

5

Montague Sound

King
George
R

■ Carson River

OOMBULGURRI
ABORIGINAL LAND

BONAPARTE ARCHIPELAGO

*Mitchell
Plateau*

Lacrosse Is

*Bigge
Island*

*Drysdale River
National Park*

*Cambridge
Gulf*

Cape Pond

King Edward River

Theda ■

Berkeley River

*Ord River
Nature Reserve*

Adolphus Is

*ADMIRALTY GULF
ABORIGINAL LAND*

Mitchell Falls

Ningbing ■

York Sound

Mt Anderdon
+

Mitchell
R.

Mitchell River

Carson River

Drysdale River

River

Carlton Hill ■

Coronation Is

*Prince
Frederick
Harbour*

Forrest

Wyndham ■

Ivanhoe ■

*Brunswick
Bay*

Mt Trafalgar
390m

Morgan

Roe

River

*Parry's Lagoon
Nature Reserve*

gustus

*Prince Regent
Nature Reserve*

King
River

56

**WESTERN
AUSTRALIA**

King Edward River

Prince Regent River

DryAdle

River

Drysdale River

Gibb River Rd

■ Home Valley

1

ri Bay

*KUNMUNYA
ABORIGINAL
RESERVE*

6

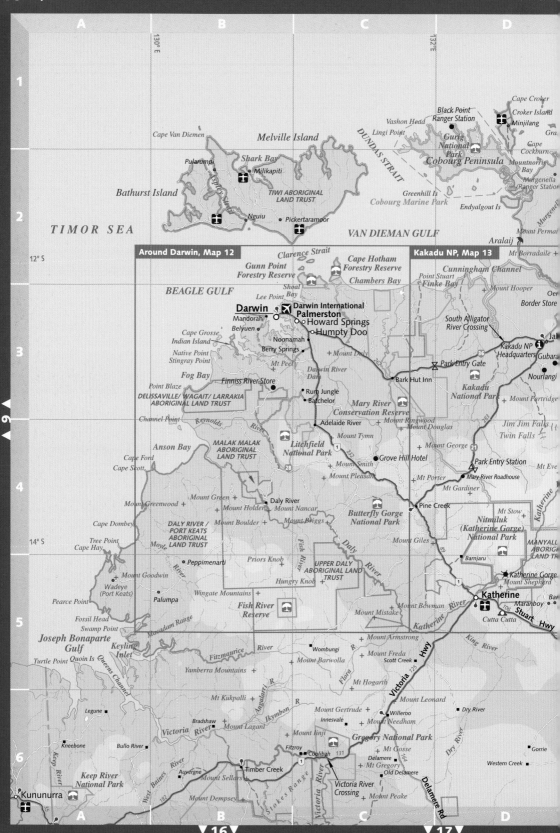

A | B | C | D

1

2

3

4

5

6

TIMOR SEA

Cape Van Diemen

Melville Island

Shark Bay
Pularumpi
• Milikapiti

Bathurst Island

Nguiu •
• Pickertaramoor

TIWI ABORIGINAL
LAND TRUST

DUNDAS STRAIT

Vashon Head
Lingi Point

Black Point
Ranger Station

Cape Croker
Croker Island
Minjilang

Gurig
National
Park
Cobourg Peninsula

*Cape
Cockburn*

Mountnorris
Bay

Margenella
(Ranger
Station)

Greenhill Is

Cobourg Marine Park

Endyalgout Is

Mount Permai

VAN DIEMAN GULF

Aralaij

Mt Borradaile

12° S

Around Darwin, Map 12

Clarence Strait

Cape Hotham
Forestry Reserve
Chambers Bay

Kakadu NP, Map 13

Cunningham Channel

Point Stuart
Finke Bay

Mount Hooper

BEAGLE GULF

*Gunn Point
Forestry Reserve*

Shoal
Bay

Lee Point

Darwin
Mandorah
Belyuen •

Darwin International
Palmerston
Howard Springs
Humpty Doo

Noonamah •
Berry Springs •

*Cape Grosse
Indian Island*
*Native Point
Stingray Point*

Fog Bay

Finniss River Store

Point Blaze

**DELISSAVILLE/ WAGAIT/ LARRAKIA
ABORIGINAL LAND TRUST**

Channel Point

Anson Bay

MALAK MALAK
ABORIGINAL
LAND TRUST

Reynolds River

Mt Peel

Darwin River
Dam

+ Mount Daly

Rum Jungle
Batchelor •

Adelaide River

Mary River
Conservation Reserve

Mount Tymn

Litchfield
National Park

Grove Hill Hotel

+ Mount Smith

+ Mount Pleasant

Cape Ford
Cape Scott

Mount Green +
• Mount Holden
Daly River •
Mount Nancar

Mount Boulder +

Mount Briggs +

Butterfly Gorge
National Park

Mt Porter +

Mount Giles +

Mount Ringwood +
Mount Douglas +

Mount George +

+ Mount Partridge

Park Entry Gate

Kakadu NP
Headquarters
Gubara

Nourlangi

Kakadu
National Park

Jim Jim Falls
Twin Falls

Mt Eve

Katherine

MANYALL
ABORIG
LAND T

Park Entry Station
Mary River Roadhouse

Mt Gardiner +

Pine Creek •

Nitmiluk
(Katherine Gorge)
National Park

Mt Stow +

Barnjaru •

Katherine Gorge
+ Mount Shepherd

14° S

Tree Point
Cape Hay

Cape Dombey

DALY RIVER /
PORT KEATS
ABORIGINAL
LAND TRUST

Mount Greenwood +

Peppimenarti •

Mowle River

Priors Knob +

UPPER DALY
ABORIGINAL
LAND TRUST

Fish River

Daly River

Hungry Knob +

Mount Goodwin +

Wadeye
(Port Keats)

Pearce Point

Fossil Head
Swamp Point

Joseph Bonaparte
Gulf

Keyling
Inlet

Palumpa •

Wingate Mountains +

Fish River
Reserve

Mosadam Range

Turtle Point Quoin Is
Queens Channel

Fitzmaurice River

Yamberra Mountains +

Legune •

Victoria River

Kneebone •

Keep River
National Park

Bullo River •

West Baines River

Auvergne •

Mount Sellars +

Mount Dempsey +

Kununurra

Keep River

Bradshaw •

Mt Kukpalli +

Mount Lagani +

Mount jinji +

Angururri R

Ikymbon R

Coolibah

Fitzroy

Timber Creek •

Stokes Range

Victoria River

Wombungi •

Mount Barwolla +

Flora River

Mt Hogarth +

Mount Gertrude +

Innesvale •

Mount Needham +

Gregory National Park

Mt Gosse +

Delamere •
Mt Gregory +
Old Delamere •

Mount Armstrong +

Mount Freda +
Scott Creek •

Mount Leonard +

Willeroo •

Victoria River
Crossing

+ Mount Peake

King River

Mary River
Conservation Reserve

Cutta Cutta

Maranboy •

Stuart Hwy

Victoria Hwy

Dry River

Gorrie •

Western Creek •

Delamere Rd

Dry River

A | B | C | D

▼ 16 ▼

▼ 17 ▼

0   25   50 km
0   10   20 mi

ARAFURA SEA

1

den Point
North Goulburn Is
South Goulburn Is

urari
Bay

2

Arrla
Bay
Braithwaite Point
Junction
Bay
Hawksbury Point

n Rock

River

Goomadeer
Nimbuwah
Nabarlek

ncer Range

Goomadeer

Mount Howship

ast Alligator River

Liverpool

Mount Gilruh

Manu River

River

Cadell River

Blyth

River

Goyder River

ARNHEM LAND

**NORTHERN
TERRITORY**

Parsons Range

Boucaut Bay
Maningrida
Milingimbi
Yabooma Is
Cape Stewart
False Point
Mooroongga Is
Warnga Point
Point Bristow
Howard Is
Banyan Is
**Castlereagh
Bay**
Ramingining

Arafura Swamp

Elcho Is
Galiwinku
**Buckingham
Bay**

Drysdale Is

Cotton Is
Astell Is
Inglis Is

Gapuwiyak

Flinders Peninsula

Mitchell Range

Frederick Hills

24

Pera Channel

Brown Strait

Maloy Road

WESSEL ISLANDS

Marchinbar Is

Guluwuru Is

Cape Wilberforce
12° S

Mount Bonner
Bremer Is

Nhulunbuy
Yirrkala
Cape
Arnhem
Dhupuma

Port
Bradshaw
Binanangoi Point

**Arnhem
Bay**

Gove Peninsula

Mount Alexander
Garrthalala
Point Alexander

Caledon River

Mount Caledon
Cape Grey
Bald Point

Wanyanmera Point

Wardarlea Bay

3

Bulman
Mount Marumba

Walken River

Rose River

Coast Range

Cape Shield
Isle Woodah
Nicol Is

**Blue Mud
Bay**

Burney Is
Cape Barrow
Bickerton Is

Winchelsea Is

4

Mountain Valley
Mainoru

Wilton River

Phelp River

WICK ABORIGINAL
LAND TRUST
swick

24

Mount Mott

Mount Furner
Mount Chrisp

Downers Range

Bennet
Bay
Connexion Is
Angurugu

Milyakburra
Alyangula
Umbakumba
14° S
Ilyungmadja
Point

**GROOTE
EYLANDT**

Cape Beatrice

Moroak
Roper Bar
Roper Hwy
Roper Valley
20
Mount Harriet

ataranka

Roper

Marwok Creek

Urapunga
Ngukurr
Roper River
Mount Eclipse
St Vidgeon
Mount Roper

Rantyirrity Point
South Point
Numbulwar
Nyinpinti Point
Edward Is
Warrakunta Point
Port Roper
Limmen Bight
Maria Is
MARRA ABORIGINAL LAND TRUST

**GULF OF
CARPENTARIA**

5

**Elsey
ational Park**

Larrimah

Cattle Creek

Strangways River

Maryfield

15A

Hodgson River

**HODGSON DOWNS
ABORIGINAL LAND**

Hodgson Downs

Nutwood Downs

Hodgson River

**ALAWA ABORIGINAL
LAND TRUST**

Arnold River

Cox River

Limmen Bight River

Nathan River

Lorella

Towns River

Beatrice Is
Mount Young

**Limmen Bight River
Fishing Camp**

Bing Bong

**NARWINBI ABORIGINAL
LAND TRUST**

Borroloola

West Is

North Is

Batten Ck

**SIR EDWARD
PELLEW GROUP**

Barranyi NP

South
West Is
Centre
Island
Port
McArthur

Vanderlin Is

Manangoora
16° S

6

134° E
136° E

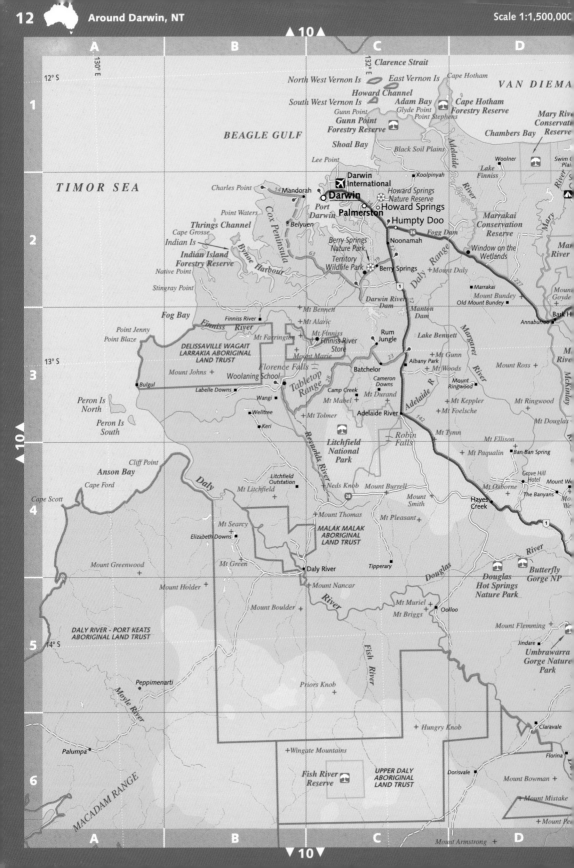

10 20 km
5 10 mi

▲ 10 ▲   ▲ 11 ▲

GULF

Field Island
Point Farewell
Tor Rock
Mt Borradaile
Goomadeer
134° E
136° E
12° S

Cunningham Channel

Middle Beach
Finke Bay
Point Stuart
Point Stuart
Coastal Reserve
Mt Hooper
Oenpelli
Nimbuwah
Nabarlek
Spencer Range

1

Swim Creek
Rainforest
Reserve
Four Mile
Hole
Munmarlary
Ubirr
Meri
Border Store
Mount Howship
Goomadeer River

Two Mile Hole
Mamukala
Wetlands
Mudginberri
Jabiluka

Wildman River
4WD Only
Kakadu Holiday
Village

East Alligator River

Liverpool River

2

Arnhem Hwy
Jabiru
Ranger
Park Entry
Gate
Kakadu National Park
Headquarters & Bowali
Information Centre
Mt Brockman

36
Red Lily
Billabong
Muirella Park
Gubara
Koongarra

Alligator
Billabong
Cooinda
Nourlangie
14° S

Mardugal
Jim Jim Billabong
Mount Basedow

Black Jungle
Spring
Jim Jim Creek
Table Top
Mount Gilruth

ARNHEM LAND

3

209
Mount Partridge

**KAKADU
NATIONAL
PARK**

Mary River
Maguk
Jim Jim
(Jim Jim Falls
Twin Falls

Mount Masson
Goodparla
Mount George
Mary River
21
Gunlom (Waterfall Creek)

▲ 11 ▲

Mount Saunders
Bukbukluk
Mount Callanan
Gimbat
Mount Evelyn

4

Mount Porter
Mount Daniels
Park Entry Gate
Ikoymarrwa
Pul Pul
Big Sunday

Esmeralda Farm
Mary River
Roadhouse
South Alligator

Mount Gardiner
Katherine River

Glen McLachlan
Pine Creek
Mount Stow

Stuart Hwy
Bonrook
River
Mount Ebsworth
Mount Lambell
16° S

Mount Giles
Black Mountain
Mount David
Mountain Valley

5

Fergusson
Edith River
Mount Todd
Barnjaru
**Nitmiluk (Katherine Gorge)
National Park**
Mount Harvey
Mount Felix

**MANUALLALUK
ABORIGINAL
LAND TRUST**

Edith Falls
Katherine
Gorge
Manyallaluk
24
Marwok Creek

Katherine Gorge
Visitor Centre
Mount Shepherd
**BESWICK ABORIGINAL
LAND TRUST**

Manbulloo
Katherine
Maranboy
Barunga

6

Victoria Hwy
King River
Cutta Cutta
106
Beswick
Mt Mott

▼ 10 ▼   ▼ 11 ▼

E   F   G   H

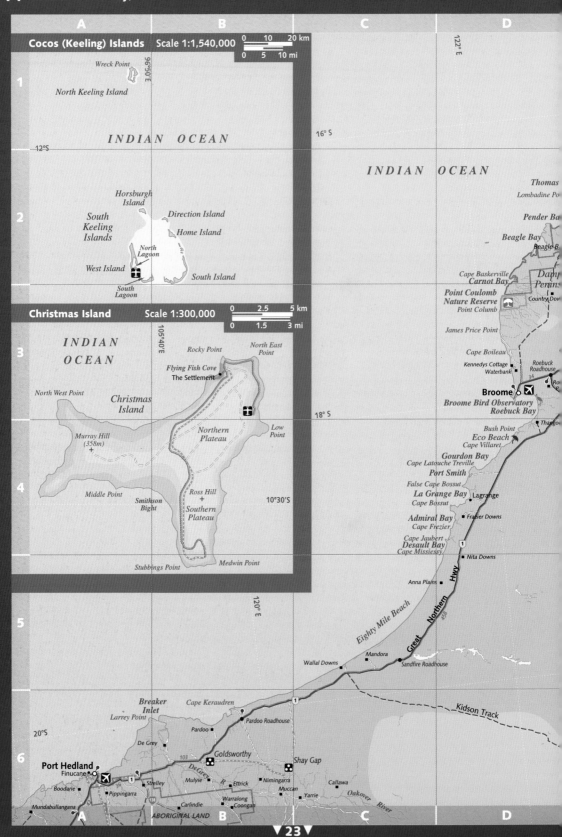

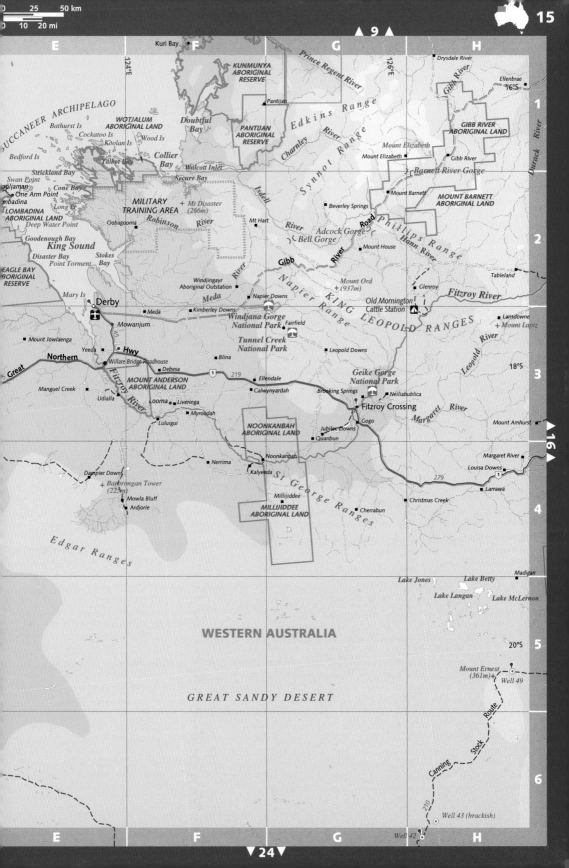

25 50 km
10 20 mi

Kuri Bay

124°E

126°E

Drysdale River

Ellenbrae

16°S

KUNMUNYA ABORIGINAL RESERVE

Prince Regent River

Edkins Range

Gibb River

GIBB RIVER ABORIGINAL LAND

Pantijan

1

PANTIJAN ABORIGINAL RESERVE

WOTJALUM ABORIGINAL LAND

Doubtful Bay

Charnley River

Synnot Range

Mount Elizabeth

Mount Elizabeth

Gibb River

Barnett River Gorge

Durack River

BUCCANEER ARCHIPELAGO

Bathurst Is

Cockatoo Is

Koolan Is

Wood Is

Collier Bay

Talbot Bay

Walcott Inlet

Secure Bay

Isdell

Mount Barnett

MOUNT BARNETT ABORIGINAL LAND

Bedford Is

Strickland Bay

Swan Point

poljaman

One Arm Point

mbadina

LOMBADINA ABORIGINAL LAND

Deep Water Point

Cone Bay

Long G.

MILITARY TRAINING AREA

+ Mt Disaster (266m)

Mt Hart

Adcock Gorge

Bell Gorge

Mount House

Phillips Range

Hann River

2

Oobagooma

Robinson

River

Mt Hart

Beverley Springs

EAGLE BAY ABORIGINAL RESERVE

Goodenough Bay

King Sound

Disaster Bay

Point Torment

Stokes Bay

Meda

River

Gibb

River

Road

K I N G

Mount Ord
+ (937m)

Glenroy

Tableland

Fitzroy River

Mary Is

Derby

Meda

Napier Downs

Windjana Gorge National Park

Windjingayr Aboriginal Outstation

Napier Downs

L E O P O L D   R A N G E S

Old Mornington Cattle Station

Lansdowne

+ Mount Laptz

Mowanjum

Fairfield

Tunnel Creek National Park

Leopold River

18°S

Hwy

Yeeda

Mount Jowlaenga

Leopold Downs

Geike Gorge National Park

Northern

Willare Bridge Roadhouse

Debesa

Blina

Great

Fitzroy River

MOUNT ANDERSON ABORIGINAL LAND

1   219

Ellendale

Brooking Springs

Fitzroy Crossing

Neiliabublica

Margaret

River

3

Manguel Creek

Udialla

Looma

Liveringa

Calwynyardah

Gogo

Mount Amhurst

Myroodah

NOONKANBAH ABORIGINAL LAND

Jubilee Downs

Luluigui

Quanbun

Margaret River

16

Louisa Downs

Dampier Downs

Nerrima

Noonkanbah

St   George   Ranges

279

1

+ Barbrongan Tower (225m)

Kalyeeda

Larrawa

Mowla Bluff

Millijiddee

Cherrabun

Christmas Creek

4

Ardjorie

MILLIJIDDEE ABORIGINAL LAND

Edgar   Ranges

Lake Jones

Lake Betty

Madigan

Lake Langan

Lake McLernon

WESTERN AUSTRALIA

20°S

5

Mount Ernest (361m) +

Well 49

GREAT   SANDY   DESERT

Route

Stock

6

Canning

210

Well 43 (brackish)

Well 42

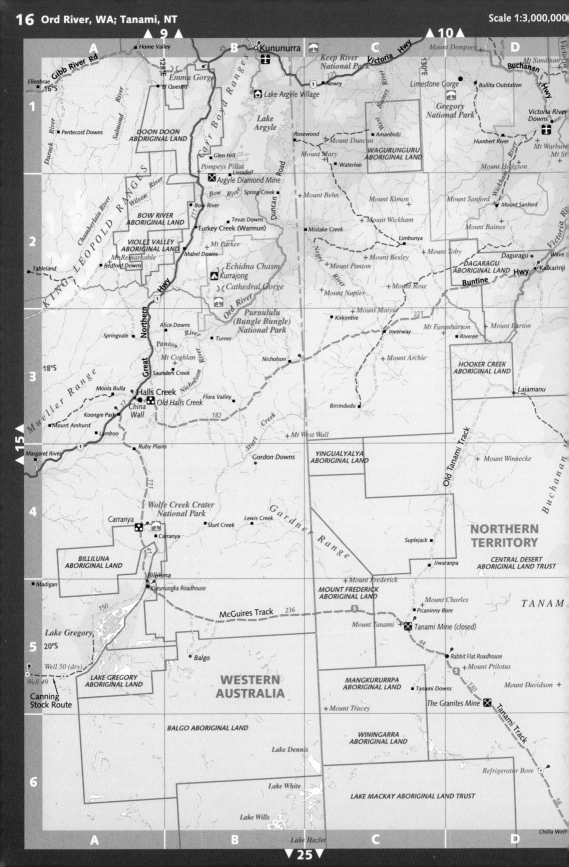

A ▲ 9 ▲ **B** **C** ▲ 10 ▲ **D**

Gibb River Rd

Home Valley

Kununurra

Keep River National Park

Victoria Hwy

Mount Dempsey

Mt Sandman

Buchanan Hwy

Mt St

Ellenbrae
16°S
Emma Gorge
Newry
Limestone Gorge
Bullita Outstation
Mt Warburt

Pentecost Downs
El Questro
Lake Argyle Village
Rosewood
Gregory National Park

Durack River
Salmond River

Glen Hill
Mount Duncan
Amanbidji
Victoria River Downs

DOON DOON ABORIGINAL LAND

Lake Argyle

Mount Mary
Waterloo
WAGURUNGURU ABORIGINAL LAND
Humbert River

1

Carr Boyd Ranges

Chamberlain River
Wilson River

Pompeys Pillar
Lissadell
Argyle Diamond Mine

Mount Behn
Mount Kimon
Mount Sanford
Mount Sanford

BOW RIVER ABORIGINAL LAND

Bow River
Spring Creek
Mount Wickham
Mount Baines

KING LEOPOLD RANGES

Tableland

VIOLET VALLEY ABORIGINAL LAND

Turkey Creek (Warmun)
Texas Downs
Mistake Creek
Limbunya
Mount Besley
Mount Toby
Daguragu
Kalkarinji

Mt Parker

Mt Remarkable
Bedford Downs
Mabel Downs

Echidna Chasm
Kurrajong
Cathedral Gorge

Mount Panton
Mount Napier
Mount Rose
DAGARAGU ABORIGINAL LAND
Hwy
Buntine
Wave

2

Northern Hwy

Ord River

Purnululu (Bungle Bungle) National Park

Mount Maiyu
Kirkimbie
Mt Farquharson
Mount Barton

Springvale
Alice Downs
Turner
Inverway
Riveren

Panton River

Mt Coghlan
Nicholson
Mount Archie
HOOKER CREEK ABORIGINAL LAND

3
18°S

Mueller Range

Saunders Creek
Birrindudu
Lajamanu

Moola Bulla
Halls Creek
Old Halls Creek
Flora Valley

China Wall

Koongie Park
Mount Amhurst
Limboo
182
Mt West Wall

YINGUALYALYA ABORIGINAL LAND
Old Tanami Track
Mount Winnecke
Buchanan

Margaret River
Ruby Plains
Gordon Downs

4

Wolfe Creek Crater National Park
Carranya
Lewis Creek
Gardner Range
NORTHERN TERRITORY

Carranya
Sturt Creek
Suplejack
Jiwaranpa
CENTRAL DESERT ABORIGINAL LAND TRUST

BILLILUNA ABORIGINAL LAND
Mount Frederick
MOUNT FREDERICK ABORIGINAL LAND
Mount Charles
Picaninny Bore
T A N A M

Madigan
Billiluna
Kururrungka Roadhouse
McGuires Track
236
Mount Tanami
Tanami Mine (closed)

5

Lake Gregory
20°S
Balgo
Rabbit Flat Roadhouse
Mount Ptilotus
Mount Davidson

Well 50 (dry)
LAKE GREGORY ABORIGINAL LAND
MANGKURURRPA ABORIGINAL LAND
Tanami Downs
Tanami Track

Well 49
Canning Stock Route
WESTERN AUSTRALIA
The Granites Mine

BALGO ABORIGINAL LAND
WININGARRA ABORIGINAL LAND
Mount Tracey

Lake Dennis

6

Lake White
LAKE MACKAY ABORIGINAL LAND TRUST
Refrigerator Bore

Lake Wills
Chilla Well

Lake Hazlet

A **B** ▼ 25 ▼ **C** **D**

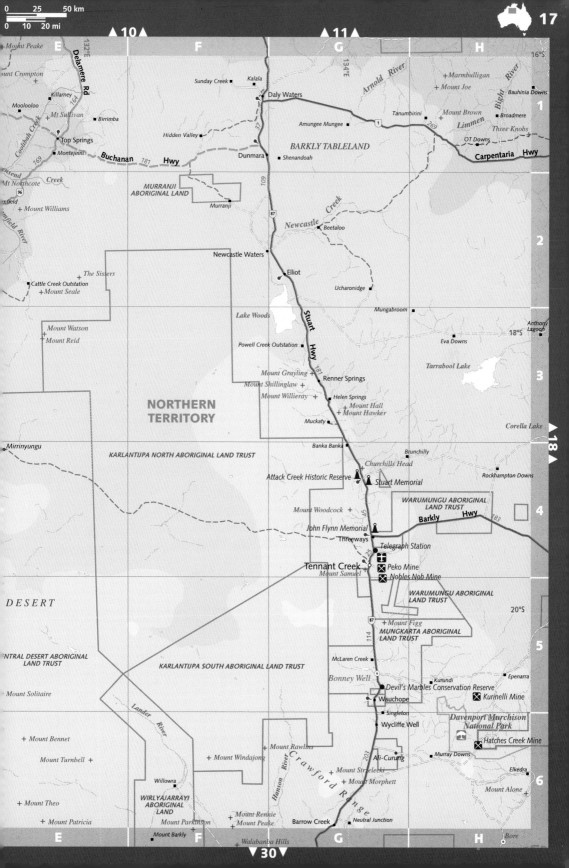

▲ 11 ▲

16°S

Pelican Spit

Borroloola
✝ + Mt Feathertop
Manangoora
NARWINBI
ABORIGINAL LAND
TRUST
Greenbank

GULF   OF

136°E
Bauhinia Downs
Billengarrah
Seven Emu

138°E

1

Three Knobs
Spring Creek
Pungalina

WELLESLEY ISLANDS
ABORIGINAL LAND

Mornington Is

McArthur River
Cape Crawford
Robinson River
Calvert
River

Gununa
Denham Is
🕏
Sydn

Balbirini

GARAWA ABORIGINAL
LAND TRUST

1

Pains Is
Andrew Island
Bayley Is
Bentinck Is

Mallapunyah

2

Wollogorang
Westmoreland

James   *Creek*

Swee

Kiana
Calvert Hills
Hell's Gate Roadhouse

Lagoon Creek
Settlement Creek
Cliffdale Creek

2

Wallhallow

Benmara

Nicholson   *River*

Corinda
Doomadgee
🕏

Escott
Burketown
Albert R

18°S

Anthony Lagoon

WAANYI / GARAWA
ABORIGINAL LAND

Almora

3

NORTHERN
TERRITORY

Lawn Hill
National Park

+ Mount Steiglitz
+ Mount Caroline
Lawn Hill

Planet Downs

Lawn Hill Creek

Gregory Downs
Hotel

▲ 17 ▲

Tablelands   Hwy
376

Corella Lake
Brunette Downs

Mittiebah
Connells Lagoon
Conservation Reserve
Mount Drummond

Old Herbert Vale
Riversleigh

Gregory River

Na

+ Mount Morgan
Alexandria

Gallipoli

Smiths Range

4

Lake Sylvester

Alroy Downs

+ *Mount Lamb*

Norfolk

Herbert Vale

McShanassy   *River*

Thorntonia
Undilla

Mt Oxide Mine
Mt Oxide +

Mount Gordon M
⚔
Gunpowder   *River*
Gunpowde

11

Georgina   *River*

4

Barkly
Homestead
(Roadhouse)
66
Barkly   Hwy

Wunura Store
260

Ranken   *River*

Camooweal
Split Rock

Waggaboonya Range

Lake Juliu

5

WAKAYA ABORIGINAL
LAND TRUST

Soudan
Avon Downs

Camooweal
Caves
National Park
Don

Kelvertoft
66

Lake
Moond

20°S

James   *River*

Old Wooroona
Buckley   *River*

Barkly Downs
Old May Downs

Parroo Range

5

ANURRETE ABORIGINAL
LAND TRUST

Georgina   River

Austral Downs
Wooroona

Mingera   *Creek*

Templeton

Mount Isa
🛬

River

Mount Michael
Arcadia
Bullecourt

The Three Sisters

Sandover Hwy
Alpururulam
Lake Nash

Lake Nash

Mount Woodhouse
+

Black Mounta

6

Elkedra
+ *Mount Alone*
Elkedra   River

Annitowa

Georgina

Sheila
Oban

155
33

Bushy Park +

Juenbe
Plum Mounta
Stanbroke

OORATIPPRA ABORIGINAL
LAND TRUST

Headingly
Warwick Downs

Urandangi

Moonah Ck

6

▼ 31 ▼

0   25   50 km
0 10 20 mi

CARPENTARA

E | **F** | **G** | **H**

140° E

142° E

Bingnoonganee Island

Bountiful Islands

Nassau *River*

Alice River

Kimba

Koolatah

Palmer River

King Junction
Strathleven

16° S

1

Inkerman

Dunbar

Drumduff

Galbraith

Mitchell River

Burke Developmental Rd

Highbury

Gamboola

Staaten R

Clark   Creek

Wyaaba Ck

Staaten   River

Staaten River
National Park

Lynd River

Point Burrowes
Point Austin

Delta Downs

Crooked Ck

Vanrook

Vanrook Ck

Smithburn River

Pelican Creek

Red River

Map 54

Bulimba

Blackdown

2

Fitzmaurice Point

Lotus Vale

Double Lagoon

Stirling

Miranda Downs

Torwood

Karumba

Maggieville

Glencoe

Bulleringa
National Park

ngaroo Point

Gore Point

Mutton Hole

Normanton

Minnies

Abingdon Downs

Einasleigh River

Van Lee

Bulleringa

Graynald

Carron River

Strathmore

Eden Vale

Dagworth

18° S

3

Wernadinga

231 Nardoo–Burketown

Flinders River

Gulf Developmental Rd

Wallabadah

Croydon

307

Inorunie

Gilbert River

Mount Darcy

O'Briens Creek
Gemfields

Eveleigh

Leichhardt Falls

Alexandra

Mount Victoria

Poverty Knob

Bang Bang

Warren Vale

Norman River

Wondoola

Vena Park

Alehvale

Georgetown

149

Mount Surcom

20

Augustus Downs

108

Sixty

Templeton

Langdon

Forsayth

Einasleigh

Talawanta

145

Burke Developmental Rd

River

Cloncurry River

River

Iffley

Yappar River

Clara River

Esmeralda

Spinifex Mountain

Prospect

Mount Clark

Perpendicular Peak

North Head

Glenora

Mount Misery

Cobbold Gorge

Kidston Goldmine

4

Lorraine

Myola

Forest Creek

Taldora

Fog Creek

Gilberton

Agate Creek Gemfields

Werrington

Kamilaroi

Burke & Wills
Roadhouse

Wurung

Canobie

Arizona

Dugald R

Mount Fort Bowen

Numil Downs

Victoria Vale

Bellfield

QUEENSLAND

Dobbyn

Alcala

Illistrin

Monstraven

Mount Brown

Euroka Springs

Millungera

Strathpark

Chudleigh Park

Coolullah

Donaldson

Spoonbill

Saxby River

Mouni Norman

Middle Park

ajabbi

Mount Cuthbert

83

Corella River

Julia Creek

Flinders River

Saxby Downs

Elmore

Solway Downs

Mount Norman

Gregory Range

5

Quamby

Cudgelgomena Ck

Bylong

Stawell   River

20° S

Mount Remarkable

Cloncurry River

Mount Margaret

Mount Marathon

Wills Developmental Rd

Gilliat River

Nelia Ponds

Dutton River

Bald Hill

Mount Moffatt

83

Cloncurry

Fort Roger

134

Gilliat

Julia Creek

Nelia

Flinders

Maxwelton

261

Richmond

Charlotte Plains

Rosebud

Landsborough (Matilda)

Williams River

Maxwelton

Hughenden

6

Mitakoodi

Mount Philp

Mount Norna

Malbom

McKinlay River

Marathon

Alick Creek

Richmond Hwy

183

Devoncourt

Kuridala

Fullarton River

McKinlay

341 Hwy

Stamford

Kennedy Developmental Road

hess

The Brothers

E Selwyn | **F** 66 | Beaudesert | **G** | **H**

▲ 21 ▲

▼ 32 ▼

▲ 20 ▼

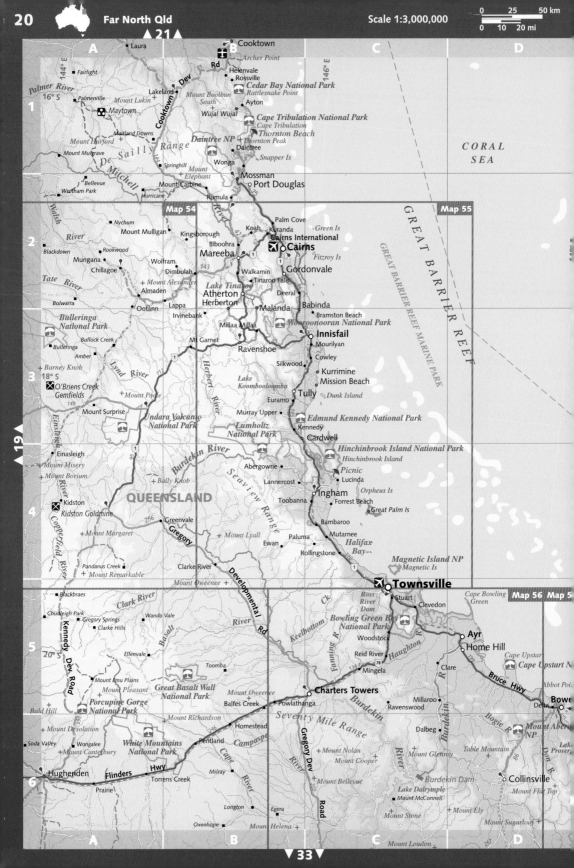

▲ **21** ▲

▲ **19** ▲

▼ **33** ▼

0   25   50 km
0   10   20 mi

TORRES STRAIT

Moa Is
Warral Is
Mokanab Is
Hammond Is
Wednesday Is
Thursday Is
Horn Is
Prince of Wales Is
Bampfield Head
Punsand Bay
Resort
Little Adolphus Is
Mount Adolphus Is
Cape York
Pajinka Wilderness Lodge
Endeavour Str
Seisia
Lockerbie
Bamaga
Van Spoult Head
Injinoo
Crab Is
Jardine
Turtle Head Is
Sharp Point
Furze Point
Vrilya Point
Left Hill
Ussher Point
Jardine River
National Park
Orford Bay
Orford Ness
Indian Head
Falls & Twin Falls
Puddingpan Hill
False Orford Ness
Cridland Hill
ABORIGINAL
LAND
Hunter Point
Heathlands
Reserve
Messum Hill
Heathlands
Ranger Station
Red Cliffs
Shelburne Bay
Port Musgrave
Cullen Point
Mapoon
Double
Point
Round Point
Conical Hill
Cape Grenville
Bramwell
Bertiehaugh
Olive
Ck
Bolt Head
Temple Bay
Mosquito Point
Fair Cape
**GULF OF
CARPENTARIA**
Duyfken Point
Landfall Point
Stones Crossing
Weipa
Portland Roads
Iron Range NP
Chilli Beach
Cape Griffith
Napranum
Batavia Downs
Mount Tozer
Lockhart River
Weymouth Bay
**Albatross
Bay**
Cape Direction
Boyd Point
ABORIGINAL
LAND
Pera Head
Merluna
Mount Carter
Round Point
False Pera
Head
Jacks Knob
Bobardt Point
Worbody Point
Aurukun
Eve Peak
Voaden Point
Table Mountain
Archer
Friendly Point
**Mungkan Kandju
National Park**
Archer River Roadhouse
Ben Lomond
Cape Sidmouth
Rokeby
Birthday Mountain
Campbell Point
Round Mountain
Merapah
ABORIGINAL
LAND
**Mungkan Kandju
National Park**
Colmer Point
Cape
Keerweer
Coen
Silver Plains
Claremont Point
Kendall
River
Evanson Point
**Flinders Group
National Park**
14° S
QUEENSLAND
Flinders Is
Twin Peaks
North Bay Point
Ebagoola
Yarraden
**Princess
Charlotte
Bay**
Barrow Point
Cape Melville National Park
Pollappa
Holroyd
River
Strathburn
Mt Ryan
Lilyvale
Marina Plains
Wakooka
Cape Bowen
Red Point
Murdoch Point
**Lizard
Island NP**
Old Strathgordon
New Bamboo
Lizard Is
Edward
River
Violet Vale
Musgrave
**Lakefield
National Park**
Lookout Point
New Strathgordon
Glen Garland
Kalpowar
Lakefield
Mt Stuckey (Numbargulme)
Kowanyama
Strathmay
Strathaven
Dixie
New Dixie
Mount Jack
**Starcke
National Park**
Mitchell River
**Mitchell and Alice Rivers
National Park**
Kalinga
Koolburra Mountain
Koolburra
Laura
Battle Camp
Hopevale
Nob Point
Rutland Plains
Eight Mile River
Fairview
Normanby
Endeavour
Cooktown
ormpuraaw
Kimba
Pinnacles
Laura
Mount McCormack
Archer Point
Nassau
River
Koolatah
Fairlight
Helenvale

142° E   144° E

12° S

**CORAL
SEA**

GREAT BARRIER REEF MARINE PARK

Peninsula Developmental Rd
McIlwraith Range
St William Thompson Range
Richardson Range
Dulhunty
Ducie R.
Wenlock
River
Mission
River
Embley River
Watson River
Archer River
Coleman River
Mitchell River
Alice River
Crosbie River
Stewart R.
Morehead R.
Hann R.
Kennedy R.
Normanby R.
Laura R.
Jack R.
Normanby R.

E   F   G   H

0 25 50 km
0 10 20 mi

▲ 14 ▲

E | **F** | **G** | **H**

Pippingarra
dabadullangana
Carlindi
Warralong
Muccan
ABORIGINAL LAND
Wallareenya
Lalla Rookh
Tabba Tabba
Shaw
1
Marble Bar
Turner
Yule River
Talga River
Warrawagine
120° E
145
122° E
Lake Waukarlycarly

Ilina
Kangan
River
Coongan River
Corunna Downs
Gregory Range

Yandeyarra
Hillside
Throssel Range

YANDEYARRA ABORIGINAL LAND
White Springs
Nullagine
22° S
2

Mungaroona Range Nature Reserve
Davis River
Oakover River
Oakover River

Hooley
Peak Hester
Mulga Downs
Bonney Downs
138
Noreena Downs
288
Rudall River National Park

Chichester Range
Hamersley Gorge
Wittenoom
27
32
Fortescue River
Balfour Downs
Tallawana Track

Oxers Lookout
Auski Roadhouse
Dales Gorge
Marillana
Roy Hill
Billinnooka
3
Mount Bruce (1235m)
Fortescue Falls
121
Ethel Creek
Walgun
Marandoo
Mindy
Jigalong
om Price
Karijini (Hamersley Range) National Park
Juna Downs
Robertson Range
Mount McHarry (1251m)
Great Northern Hwy
Mount Newman (1057m)
Newman
Shovelanna Hill

Hamersley Range
adio Hill
Ophthalmia Range
Prairie Downs
JIGALONG ABORIGINAL LAND
24

River
Turee Creek
24° S
Angelo
Deadman Hill
LITTLE SANDY DESERT
Well 14 (dry)
4
ount Boggola
Bulloo Downs
Weelarrana
WESTERN AUSTRALIA
Lake Wilderness
Well 13 (dry)
Ashburton
Mount Vermon
Well 12 (dry)
Lake Aerodrome
Ashburton River
Lofty Range
Yanneri Lake
Terminal Lake
White Lake
Mount Vernon
Tangadee
Well 11 (salty)
Well 10

Teano Range
Collier Range National Park
Lake Sunshine
Well 9 (Weld Springs)
Route
aldburg Range
Woodlands
Mulgul
Collier Range
Kumarina Roadhouse
Ten Mile Lake
Lake Kerrylyn
Well 8
5
Mount Egerton
Mingah Springs
Mount Methwin
Well 7
Glenayle
Three Rivers
141
Well 6 (Pierre Springs)
Milgun
Stock
Mount Clere
Gascoyne River
Well 5
Granite Peak
Earaheedy
Mount Labouchere
Neds Creek
Lake Nabberu
Well 4A
Granite Peak (402m)
Robinson Range
Bryah
Noonyereena Hill
Lake Gregory
Well 4 (salty)
Lake Teague
26° S
Canning
Peak Hill
Doolgunna
Mount Patterson
Well 3 (unreliable)
Trillbar
Yarlarweelor
Mount Fraser
Wongawal
Mount Padbury
Murchison River
New Springs
Cunyu
Well 2A
Lorna Glen
6
t Gould Lockup
Mount Gould
Mooloogool
Diamond Well
Well 2
Moorarie
Karalundi
Paroo
Yandil
Jundee
Millrose
Yelma
Mount Hale
Mount Hale
Lake Violet

E | **F** | **G** | **H**

▼ 37 ▼

▲ 15 ▲

	A	B	C	D

1

124° E

Well 43 (brackish)

Well 42

126° E

Well 41

Tobin Lake

Well 40

Percival Lakes

Well 39

76

713

Well 38 (not drinkable)

Canning Stock Route

2

22° S

Lake Dora

Well 37 (Liberal Well)

Well 36

Bungabinni Native Well

Lake Auld

Well 34 (dry)

Well 35

39

Well 33

Lake Blanche

Well 32

Well 30 (dry)

Emergency Telephone

34

Gary Junction

Well 29 (dry)

Well 31

488

Rudall River National Park

Lake George

Tabletop

Well 28 (dry)

255

Jupiter W

Lake Winifred

Well 27 (fair)

Lake Winifred

Well 26

Tallawana Track

Georgia Bore (good water)

Well 25 (dry)

GIBSON DESERT

135

Well 24 (dry)

Well 22 (dry)

36

Well 23 (not drinkable)

Windy Corner Rd

Tropic of Capricorn

Well 21 (poor)

3

Well 20 (dry)

178

Crossing can be boggy

205

Windy Corner

Well 19 (dry)

Lake Disappointment

Well 18 (dry)

Gary

Well 17 (Killagurra Springs)

Biella Spring

Durba Springs

Lake Cobb

Well 16 (not drinkable)

24° S

Hwy

McPhersons Pillar

Canning Stock Route

Well 15 (dry)

4

Well 14 (dry)

LITTLE SANDY DESERT

Lake Blair

Well 13 (dry)

195

Lake Newell

Well 12 (dry)

Lake Hancock

Gibson Desert Nature Reserve

Lake Jones

Charles Knob

Lake Keene

Lake Hoar

Mount Everard

Lake Bremner

122

MUNGILLI ABORIGINAL LAND

239

5

Glenayle

Lake Burnside

Gunbarrel Hwy

Gunbarrel Hwy

82

Lake Buchanan

Lake Breaden

Mount Samu

Coonabildie Range

SOUTHERN CENTRAL RESERVE ABORIGINAL LAND

Carnegie

Linke Lakes

Herbert Wash

TJIRRKARLI ABORIGINAL LAND

350

26° S

Lake Bedford

Lake Gillen

Great Central Rd

Wongawal

Lake Carnegie

Baker Lak

6

Windidda

225

WINDIDDA ABORIGINAL LAND

Prenti Downs

Yelma

▲ 23 ▲

23 ▲

	A	B	C	D

▼ 38 ▼

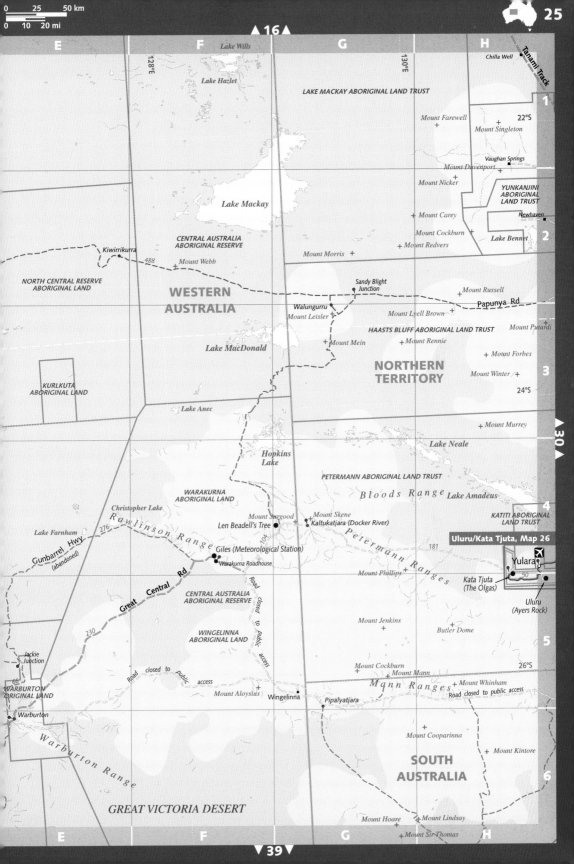

0   25   50 km
0 10 20 mi

E   F   G   H

Lake Wills

128°E

130°E

Chilla Well

Tanami Track

LAKE MACKAY ABORIGINAL LAND TRUST

Lake Hazlet

Mount Farewell

22°S

Mount Singleton

1

Vaughan Springs

Mount Davenport

Lake Mackay

Mount Nicker

YUNKANJINI
ABORIGINAL
LAND TRUST

CENTRAL AUSTRALIA
ABORIGINAL RESERVE

Mount Carey

Newhaven

Mount Cockburn

Lake Bennet

2

Mount Redvers

NORTH CENTRAL RESERVE
ABORIGINAL LAND

Kiwirrikurra

Mount Morris

488

Mount Webb

Sandy Blight
Junction

Mount Russell

WESTERN
AUSTRALIA

Walungurru

Papunya Rd

Mount Leisler

Mount Lyell Brown

Mount Putardi

HAASTS BLUFF ABORIGINAL LAND TRUST

Mount Mein

Mount Rennie

Lake MacDonald

NORTHERN
TERRITORY

Mount Forbes

3

KURLKUTA
ABORIGINAL
LAND

Mount Winter

24°S

Lake Anec

Mount Murrey

▲ 30 ▲

Lake Neale

Hopkins
Lake

PETERMANN ABORIGINAL LAND TRUST

Bloods Range   Lake Amadeus

WARAKURNA
ABORIGINAL LAND

Christopher Lake

KATITI ABORIGINAL
LAND TRUST

4

Rawlinson Range

Lake Farnham

276

Mount Sargood

Mount Skene

Uluru/Kata Tjuta, Map 26

Len Beadell's Tree

Kaltukatjara (Docker River)

Yulara

Gunbarrel Hwy
(abandoned)

Giles (Meteorological Station)

Petermann Ranges

50

181

Kata Tjuta
(The Olgas)

Great Central Rd

Warakurna Roadhouse

Mount Phillips

Uluru
(Ayers Rock)

230

CENTRAL AUSTRALIA
ABORIGINAL RESERVE

Road closed to public access

Mount Jenkins

Butler Dome

5

Jackie
Junction

WINGELINNA
ABORIGINAL LAND

Mount Cockburn

26°S

WARBURTON
ORIGINAL LAND

Road closed to public access

Mount Mann

Mann Ranges

Mount Whinham

Warburton

Mount Aloysius

Wingelinna

Pipalyatjara

Road closed to public access

Warburton Range

Mount Cooparinna

Mount Kintore

SOUTH
AUSTRALIA

6

GREAT VICTORIA DESERT

Mount Hoare

Mount Lindsay

E   F   G   H

Mount Sir Thomas

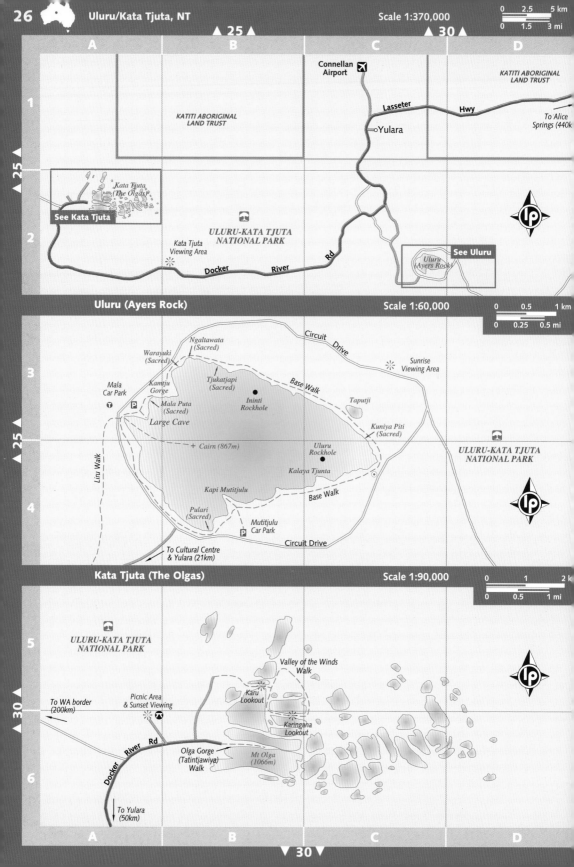

Uluru/Kata Tjuta, NT

▲ 25 ▲   **▲ 30 ▲**

Connellan Airport

KATITI ABORIGINAL LAND TRUST

KATITI ABORIGINAL LAND TRUST

Lasseter   Hwy

Yulara

To Alice Springs (440k

See Kata Tjuta

Kata Tjuta (The Olgas)

Kata Tjuta Viewing Area

ULURU-KATA TJUTA NATIONAL PARK

Docker   River   Rd

Uluru (Ayers Rock)

See Uluru

Uluru (Ayers Rock)   Scale 1:60,000

0   0.5   1 km
0   0.25   0.5 mi

Circuit   Drive

Ngaltawata (Sacred)

Warayuki (Sacred)

Sunrise Viewing Area

Kamtju Gorge

Tjukatjapi (Sacred)

Base Walk

Mala Car Park

Mala Puta (Sacred)

Large Cave

Ininti Rockhole

Taputji

Kuniya Piti (Sacred)

Liru Walk

+ Cairn (867m)

Uluru Rockhole

ULURU-KATA TJUTA NATIONAL PARK

Kalaya Tjunta

Kapi Mutitjulu

Base Walk

Pulari (Sacred)

Mutitjulu Car Park

Circuit Drive

To Cultural Centre & Yulara (21km)

Kata Tjuta (The Olgas)   Scale 1:90,000

0   1   2 k
0   0.5   1 mi

ULURU-KATA TJUTA NATIONAL PARK

Valley of the Winds Walk

Karu Lookout

To WA border (200km)

Picnic Area & Sunset Viewing

Karingana Lookout

Docker   River   Rd

Olga Gorge (Tatintjawiya) Walk

Mt Olga (1066m)

To Yulara (50km)

▼ 30 ▼

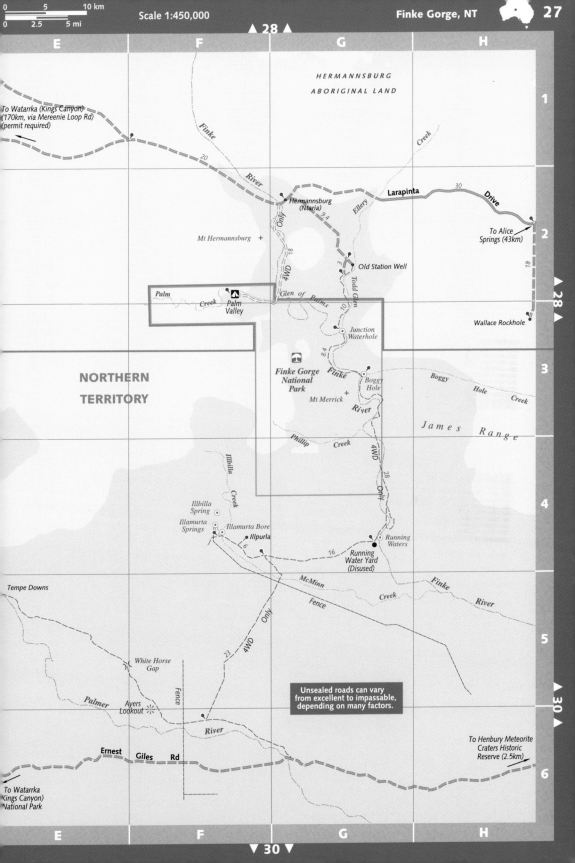

0   5   10 km
0   2.5   5 mi

▲ 28 ▲

HERMANNSBURG
ABORIGINAL LAND

To Watarrka (Kings Canyon)
(170km, via Mereenie Loop Rd)
(permit required)

Finke

River

20

Hermannsburg
(Ntaria)

Ellery

Creek

Larapinta   30   Drive

9.4

Mt Hermannsburg +

To Alice
Springs (43km)

18

4WD Only

3

Old Station Well

18

Todd Glen

Palm
Creek

Palm
Valley

Glen of Palms

▲ 28 ▲

Wallace Rockhole

10

Junction
Waterhole

8.4

NORTHERN

TERRITORY

Finke Gorge
National Park

Finke

Boggy
Hole

Boggy   Hole   Creek

+ Mt Merrick

River

James   Range

Phillip   Creek

4WD Only

28

Illbilla
Creek

Illbilla
Spring ⊙

Illamurta
Springs

Illamurta Bore

Running
Waters

Illpurla

6

16

Running
Water Yard
(Disused)

McMinn   Creek   Finke   River

Fence

Tempe Downs

23

4WD Only

White Horse
Gap

Fence

Palmer

Ayers
Lookout

River

▲ 30 ▲

Unsealed roads can vary
from excellent to impassable,
depending on many factors.

Ernest   Giles   Rd

To Henbury Meteorite
Craters Historic
Reserve (2.5km)

To Watarrka
(Kings Canyon)
National Park

▼ 30 ▼

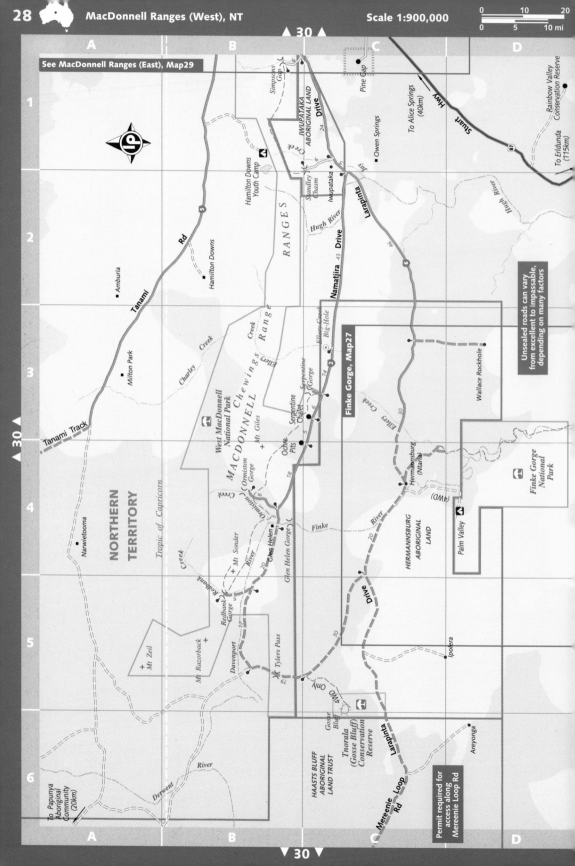

See MacDonnell Ranges (East), Map29

NORTHERN TERRITORY

Tropic of Capricorn

RANGES

Chewings Range

MACDONNELL

West MacDonnell National Park

IWUPATAKA ABORIGINAL LAND

Namatjira Drive

Larapinta Drive

Finke Gorge, Map27

Finke Gorge National Park

HERMANNSBURG ABORIGINAL LAND

HAASTS BLUFF ABORIGINAL LAND TRUST

Tnorala (Gosse Bluff) Conservation Reserve

Mereenie Loop Rd

Larapinta Drive

Stuart Hwy

Simpsons Gap
Pine Gap
Owen Springs
To Alice Springs (40km)
To Erldunda (115km)
Rainbow Valley Conservation Reserve

Hamilton Downs Youth Camp
Hamilton Downs
Amburla
Milton Park
Narwietooma
Mt Zeil
Mt Razorback
Davenport
Tylers Pass
Mt Sonder
Glen Helen
Glen Helen Gorge
Ormiston Gorge
Mt Giles
Ochre Pits
Serpentine Gorge
Serpentine Chalet
Ellery Creek Big-Hole
Standley Chasm
Iwupataka
Hermannsburg (Ntaria)
Palm Valley (4WD)
Wallace Rockhole
Ipolera
Areyonga
Gosse Bluff
Only 4WD

Tanami Rd
Tanami Track
Charley Creek
Ellery Creek
Hugh River
Hugh River
Finke River
Ellery Creek
Redbank Creek
Redbank Gorge
Derwent River
Finke River

To Papunya Aboriginal Community (20km)

Unsealed roads can vary from excellent to impassable, depending on many factors

Permit required for access along Mereenie Loop Rd

24
6
43
46
6
30
30
14
2
6
5
18
8
3
20
77
79
20
30
4
5

30

10   20 km
5   10 mi

▲ 31 ▲

E   F   G   H

Indiana

To Ringwood

1

Unsealed roads can vary
from excellent to impassable,
depending on many factors

Ruby Gap
Nature Park

River

Ruby
Gap

Hale

2

NORTHERN
TERRITORY

Florence   Creek

Arltunga
Historical
Reserve

(4WD 36 Only)

Atnarpa

Claraville

Goat Camp Creek

Giles

Creek

▲ 30 ▲

11

EAST

Mt Riddock

Ambalindum

Arltunga Hotel &
Bush Resort

Arltunga
Historic Goldfield

12

3

Cattlewater   Pass

4WD
Only   56

Hale

River   31

Ross River

82

8   (4WD 14 Only)

Ross   River

Todd River

Todd River

SANTA TERESA
ABORIGINAL
LAND TRUST

To Old Andado

RANGES

34

Ongeva   Creek

The
Garden

Tropic of Capricorn

Trephina
Gorge

4

Creek

Gerntree
Caravan Park

Waite

Harts   Range

23

MACDONNELL

Trephina Creek

Trephina Gorge
Nature Park

4

N'Dhala Gorge
Nature Park

Beef   Rd

To Erldunda
(150km)

Gilen   Creek

(4WD
Only)

Pinnacles
Bore

Benstead

Corroboree
Rock

Hwy

Corroboree Rock
Conservation
Reserve

Ringwood

Todd

Muller   Creek

40

49

Mile

River

Creek

Jessie   Creek

Emily & Jessie Gaps
Nature Park   28

Undoolya

Amoonguna

Ewaninga
Rock Carvings

5

Fifteen

Burt   Creek

Yambah   19

Stuart   Hwy   29

Sandy

H
opus

27

Tanami   Rd

West MacDonnell
National Park

Alice
Springs

20

Simpsons Gap   2

16

IWUPATAKA
ABORIGINAL
LAND

Pine Gap

6

See MacDonnells Ranges (West), Map28

E   F   G   H

▼ 28 ▼

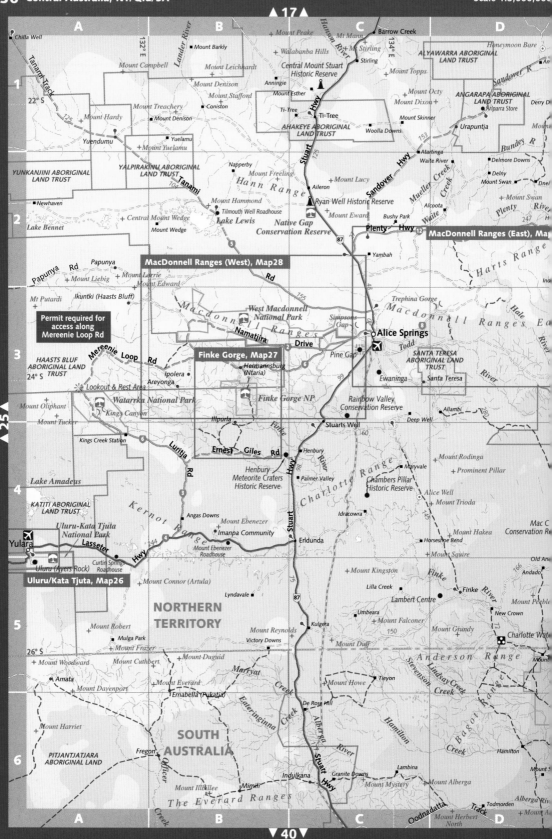

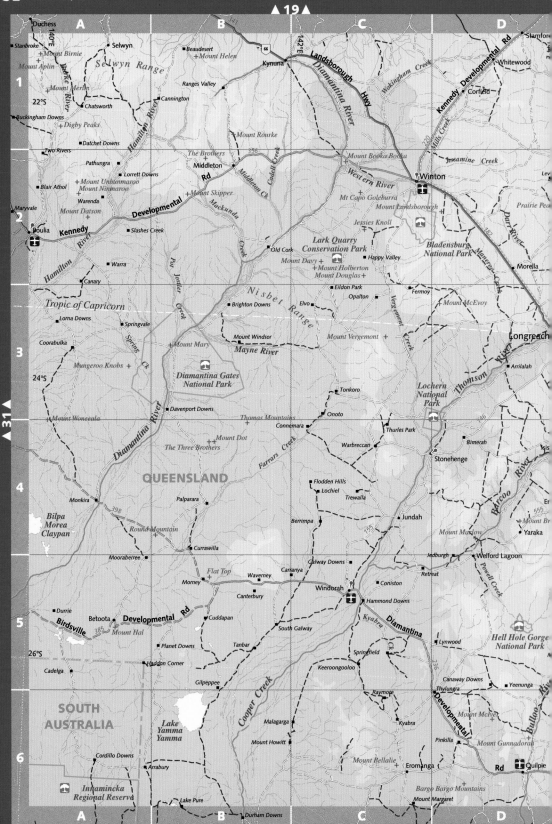

Scale 1:3,000,000

0   25   50
0   10   20 mi

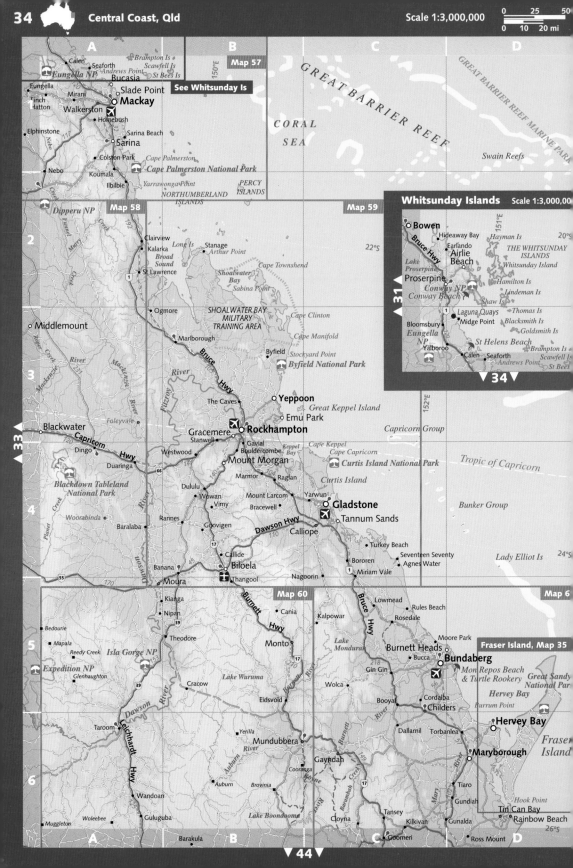

A

Calen
Seaforth
Andrews Point
Brampton Is
Scawfell Is
St Bees Is
Bucasia

B

Map 57

See Whitsunday Is

150°E

Eungella NP
Eungella
Mirani
Finch
Hatton
Walkerston
Mackay
Slade Point
Homebush
Elphinstone
Sarina Beach
Sarina
Colston Park
Nebo
Koumala
Ilbilbie
Yarrawonga Point
Cape Palmerston
Cape Palmerston National Park
NORTHUMBERLAND
ISLANDS
PERCY
ISLANDS

1

C

GREAT BARRIER REEF

CORAL
SEA

Swain Reefs

GREAT BARRIER REEF MARINE PARK

D

Dipperu NP Map 58

Map 59

Clairview
Kalarka
Long Is
Stanage
Arthur Point
Broad
Sound
St Lawrence
Ogmore
Shoalwater
Bay
Cape Townshend
Sabina Point
22°S

530°E

Whitsunday Islands Scale 1:3,000,00

Bowen
Hideaway Bay
Hayman Is
20°S
Earlando
Bruce Hwy
Airlie
Beach
Whitsunday Island
Lake
Proserpine
Proserpine
Hamilton Is
Conway NP
Lindeman Is
Conway Beach
Shaw Is
Bloomsbury
Laguna Quays
Thomas Is
Midge Point
Blacksmith Is
Eungella
NP
Yalboroo
St Helens Beach
Goldsmith Is
Calen Seaforth
Brampton Is
Scawfell Is
Andrews Point
St Bees
THE WHITSUNDAY
ISLANDS

▼ **34** ▼

31

Middlemount

SHOALWATER BAY
MILITARY
TRAINING AREA
Marlborough
Cape Clinton
Cape Manifold
Byfield
Stockyard Point
Byfield National Park

Bruce
Hwy
River
Fitzroy
Mackenzie
River
River

The Caves
Yeppoon
Great Keppel Island
Emu Park

Blackwater
Capricorn
Dingo
Duaringa
Hwy
Gracemere
Stanwell
Rockhampton
Gavial
Bouldercombe
Mount Morgan
Westwood
Keppel
Bay
Cape Keppel
Cape Capricorn
Curtis Island National Park
Capricorn Group
Tropic of Capricorn

Blackdown Tableland
National Park
Woorabinda
Dululu
Marmor
Raglan
Curtis Island
Bunker Group

33

4

Baralaba
Wowan
Vimy
Mount Larcom
Bracewell
Yarwun
Gladstone
Tannum Sands

Rannes
Goovigen
Dawson Hwy
Calliope
Lady Elliot Is
24°S

Banana
Callide
Biloela
Thangool
Turkey Beach
Seventeen Seventy
Agnes Water
Bororen
Miriam Vale
Nagoorin

Moura

Map 60

Map 6

Kianga
Nipan
Theodore
Burnett
Hwy
Cania
Kalpowar
Lowmead
Rules Beach
Rosedale
Bruce
Hwy

5

Bedourie
Mapala
Reedy Creek
Isla Gorge NP
Cracow
Monto
Lake Waruma
Lake
Monduran
Gin Gin
Wolca
Moore Park
Bucca
Bundaberg
Mon Repos Beach
& Turtle Rookery
Fraser Island, Map 35
Great Sandy
National Par
Hervey Bay

Expedition NP
Glenhaughton
Dawson
Eidsvold
Booyal
Cordalba
Childers
Burrum Point
Hervey Bay

Taroom
Leichhardt
Yerilla
Mundubbera
Auburn
River
Gayndah
Dallarnil
Torbanlea
Maryborough
Fraser
Island

6

Wandoan
Auburn
Brovinia
Lake Boondooma
Tiaro
Gundiah
Hook Point
Woleebee
Cooranga
Tansey
Kilkivan
Gunalda
Tin Can Bay
Muggleton
Cloyna
Goomeri
Ross Mount
Rainbow Beach
Barakula

A   **B**   **C**   **D**

0 5 10 km
0 2.5 5 mi

▲ 61 ▲

E   F   G   H

153°E

1

Sandy Cape

Lake
Marong

Manann
Beach

Panama

Rooney Point

Calarga
Lagoon

Lake
Wanhar

Ngkala Rocks

Marloo
Bay

Lake
Carree

H E R V E Y   B A Y

Lake
Minker

Platypus
Bay

2

Marloo

Orchid
Beach

Waddy Point

Wathumba

Middle Rocks

26°S

Indian Head

**The western beach is
dangerous for driving
due to soft sand and
swampy areas**

Triangle Cliff

**No swimming: sharks
and undertow**

GREAT SANDY
NATIONAL PARK

Yathon Cliffs

Lake
Guarann

Corroboree
Beach

Arch Cliff

Bimjella Hill
(174m)

Lake
Bowarrady

3

Coongul Point

Bowarrady
(244m)

Dundubara

Moon Point

FRASER
ISLAND

The Cathedrals

Cathedral Beach

The Pinnacles

**The eastern beach is good
for driving at low tide but
look out for landing aircraft**

Maheno

Vernon Point

Blackfellow
Point

Yidney
scrub

**Hervey
Bay**

Urangan

Big
Woody
Island

Maheno
Beach

S O U T H

Mangrove
Point

Lake
Garawongera

Happy Valley

Yidney Rocks Cabins

Rainbow Gorge

4

Kingfisher Bay
Resort & Village

Leading
Hill (184m)

Poyungan Valley

P A C I F I C

Susan

River

River
Heads

Poyungan Rocks

Wanggoolba

Lake
McKenzie

Lake Wabby

O C E A N

Mary

Central Station

Ungowa

Lake Jennings

Turkey
Island

Lake
Birrabeen

Eurong

To Maryborough
(3km)

Boomanjin
Hill (211m)

Lake
Boomanjin

Boorlye
Point

Maaroom

Yankee
Jack Lake

Dilli Village

5

Garry's Anchorage

Boonooroo

Stewart
Island

Figtree
Lake

Tuan

Poona

QUEENSLAND

The Bluff
(64m)

6

Tin Can
Bay

Hook Point

Inskip Point

WIDE BAY
MILITARY RESERVE

E   F   G   H

Naturaliste Channel
Cape
Inscription

Cape Peron North

Shark Bay Marine Park

François Péron NP

Big Lagoon

Denham
Sound

Monkey Mia

Denham

Peron

L'Haridon
Bight

Dirk
Hartog
Island

Dirk Hartog

Useless Loop

Steep Point

Nanga

Carrarang

Tamala

Henri
Freycinet
Harbour

Hamelin
Pool

Overlander Roadhouse

Hamelin

Meedo

Wooramel

Gladstone

Yaringa

Carbla

Old Woodleigh

Coburn

Billabong Roadhouse

Meadow

Woodleigh

Talisker

Yalardy

Ballythunna

Gilroyd

Wooramel River

Byro

Milly Milly

Beringarra

Nookawarra

Manfred

Curbur

Mount Narryer

Muggon

Murchison Settlement
Roadhouse
Meeberrie

Woolgorong

Mount Murchison

Scrubby Run

Boolardy

Nicholson Ran

Woolleen

Mount Barloweerie

Twin Peaks

Billabalong

Mount Luke

Murgoo

Mount Wittenoo

Booltharda Hill

Jingen

Toolonga Nature Reserve

Zuytdorp Nature Reserve

Zuytdorp Nature Reserve

Nerren Nerren

New Forest

Yallalong

Coolcalalaya

Lake Nerramyne

Woolgorong

Pinegrove

Bullardoo

Narloo

Yuin

Tallering Peak

Dividing Range

Kalbarri
National Park

Gantheaume Bay

The Loop

Murchison House

Jakes Corner

Kalbarri

Z-Bend Gorge

Mary Springs

Hawks Head Lookout

Carlton Lea

Binnu

Hutt

Yuna

Naraling

Greenough River

Tallering

Gabyon

Carlaminda

Yalgoo

No

245

123

Port Gregory

Lynton Convict Ruins

Northampton

Horrocks

Nabawa

Mullewa

Pindar

Barnong

Wilroy

North Island

Wallabi Group

Geelvink Channel

HOUTMAN ABLROLHOS ISLANDS

Easter Group

Pelsaert Island

Nanson

Geraldton

Point Moore

Narngulu

Eradu

Wongoondy

Tenindewa

96

116

Canna

Gutha

Mellenbye

Walkaway

Greenough

INDIAN

OCEAN

112°E

Koolanooka Springs

Morawa

Weelhan
Lake

Perenjor

Dongara

Port Denison

Irwin

Mount Lefroy

Three Springs

Map

Arrowsmith River

Carnamah

Latham

Yarra
Yarra
Lakes

Coorow

Bun

Illawong

Eneabba

Coolimba

Leeman

Green Head

Dynamite Bay

Jurien Bay

Jurien

Lesueur NP

Mount Lesueur

Drovers Cave NP

Badgingarra

Marchagee

Gunyidi

Watheroo NP

Watheroo

M

Brand Hwy

235

116

Badgingarra National Park

Cervantes

Nambung National Park

Grey

Cataby Roadhouse

Wedge Is

Moora

Dandaragan

Bindi Bind

Walebi

Piawa

Yene

New Norcia

Mogu

Lancelin

Ledge Point

Moore River
NP

Wannamal

Gingin

Bir

Moore River

99

60

95

Seabird

Guilderton

Two Rocks

Muchea

Mora

26°S

28°S

30°S

114°E

116°E

232

47

355

96

123

116

235

116

99

60

95

Yelma
WINDIDDA ABORIGINAL LAND
122°E
Lake Wells
124°E
Tjukayirla Roadhouse
Great Central Rd
255
126°E
Lake Throssel
176
Mount Maiden (590m)
Peegull Waterhole & Caves
Yeo Lake
Banjawarn
Bandya
Cosmo Newbery
COSMO NEWBERY ABORIGINAL LAND
Yamarna
Yeo Lake Nature Reserve
320
Neale Junction
Neale Junction Nature Reserve
86
POINT SALVATION ABORIGINAL LAND
Erlistoun
Nambi
White Cliffs
Laverton Downs
Rason Lake
Mount Windarra
Laverton
Gidgi Lakes
Mertondale
124
Mount Weld
Merolia
Hope Campbell Lake
GLENORN ABORIGINAL LAND
Red Knob Outstation
Leonora-Gwalia
Minara
Lake Carey
Plumridge Lakes
Melita
Glenorn
Plumridge Lakes Nature Reserve
Lake Reaside
Yundamindra
Mount Remarkable
Kookynie
Lake Reaside
Mount Celia
Lake Minigwal
Niagara Dam
Yerilla
37
Jeedamya
Mendleyarri
30
Lake Marmion
Menangina
Edjudina
Goongarrie National Park
Lake Rebecca
Pinjin
Connie Sue Hwy
Queen Victoria Spring Nature Reserve
Cindalbie
Yindi
Premier Downs
Mount Vetters
273
Broad Arrow
Lake Yindarlgooda
Gudarra
CUNDEELEE ABORIGINAL LAND
Black Flag Lake
Perkolilli
Lake Yindana
Kanandah
Kinclaven
White Flag Lake
Kalgoorlie-Boulder
Lake Roe
Gunnadorrah
TRANS-AUSTRALIAN RAILWAY
Hannan Lake
Avoca Downs
Coonana
Rawlinna
Mungari
Cowarna Downs
375
Coolgardie
Mount Monger
COONANA ABORIGINAL LAND
Lake Boonderoo
Woolibar
Kambalda
Madoonia Downs
Coolgardie-Esperance Hwy
Lake Lefroy
165
Mandilla
Widgiemooltha
Lake Cowan
66
Caiguna
Fraser Range
Newman's Rocks
Timberlana
Norseman
191
Wyralinu Hill
Eyre Hwy
Noondoonia
183
Dundas Nature Reserve
Balladonia
Woorlba
Balladonia

A   B   C   D
1 2 3 4 5 6

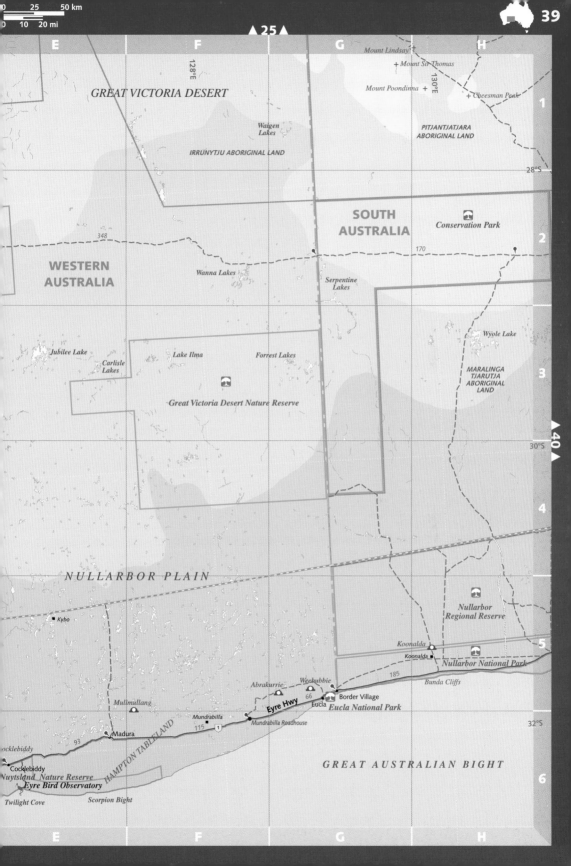

▲ **30** ▲

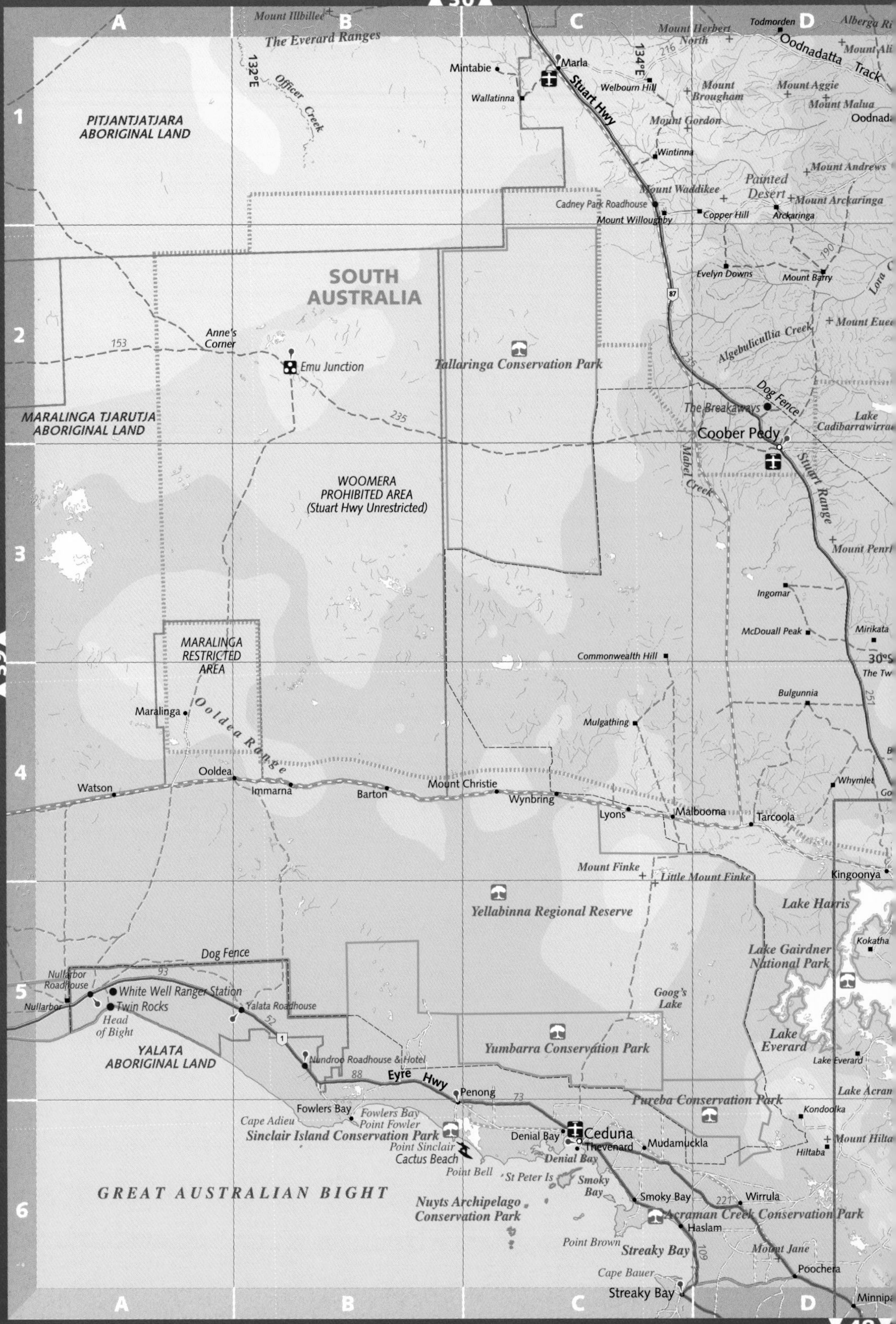

| A | B | C | D |

Mount Illbillee

The Everard Ranges

Mount Herbert North

Todmorden

Alberga Ri

Oodnadatta Track

Mount Ali

PITJANTJATJARA ABORIGINAL LAND

Mintabie

Marla

Welbourn Hill

Mount Brougham

Mount Aggie

Mount Malua

Officer Creek

Wallatinna

Stuart Hwy

Mount Gordon

Oodnada

1

132°E

134°E

216

Wintinna

Mount Andrews

Mount Waddikee

Painted Desert

Mount Arckaringa

Cadney Park Roadhouse

Copper Hill

Arckaringa

Mount Willoughby

Lora C

SOUTH AUSTRALIA

Evelyn Downs

Mount Barry

190

87

2

Anne's Corner

153

Emu Junction

Tallaringa Conservation Park

Mount Euee

Algebuticullia Creek

Dog Fence

Lake Cadibarrawirrae

MARALINGA TJARUTJA ABORIGINAL LAND

235

The Breakaways

Coober Pedy

Mabel Creek

WOOMERA PROHIBITED AREA (Stuart Hwy Unrestricted)

Stuart Range

Mount Penri

3

MARALINGA RESTRICTED AREA

Ingomar

▲ **39** ▲

Maralinga

Ooldea Range

Commonwealth Hill

McDouall Peak

Mirikata

30°S

The Tw

Bulgunnia

Mulgathing

251

Watson

Ooldea

Immarna

Barton

Mount Christie

Wynbring

Lyons

Malbooma

Tarcoola

Whymlet

Go

4

Kingoonya

Mount Finke

Little Mount Finke

Lake Harris

Yellabinna Regional Reserve

Lake Gairdner National Park

Kokatha

Nullarbor Roadhouse

Dog Fence

93

White Well Ranger Station

Goog's Lake

Lake Everard

Lake Everard

5

Nullarbor

Twin Rocks

Head of Bight

Yalata Roadhouse

52

Yumbarra Conservation Park

Lake Acran

YALATA ABORIGINAL LAND

1

Nundroo Roadhouse & Hotel

Pureba Conservation Park

Kondoolka

Mount Hilta

Fowlers Bay

88

Eyre Hwy

Penong

73

Kokatha

Mount Jane

Cape Adieu

Fowlers Bay

Point Fowler

Sinclair Island Conservation Park

Point Sinclair

Cactus Beach

Denial Bay

Ceduna

Thevenard

Mudamuckla

Hiltaba

Point Bell

Denial Bay

6

GREAT AUSTRALIAN BIGHT

Nuyts Archipelago Conservation Park

St Peter Is

Smoky Bay

Smoky Bay

Acraman Creek Conservation Park

Wirrula

221

Point Brown

Streaky Bay

Haslam

109

Cape Bauer

Poochera

Streaky Bay

Minnip

| A | B | C | D |

▼ **48** ▼

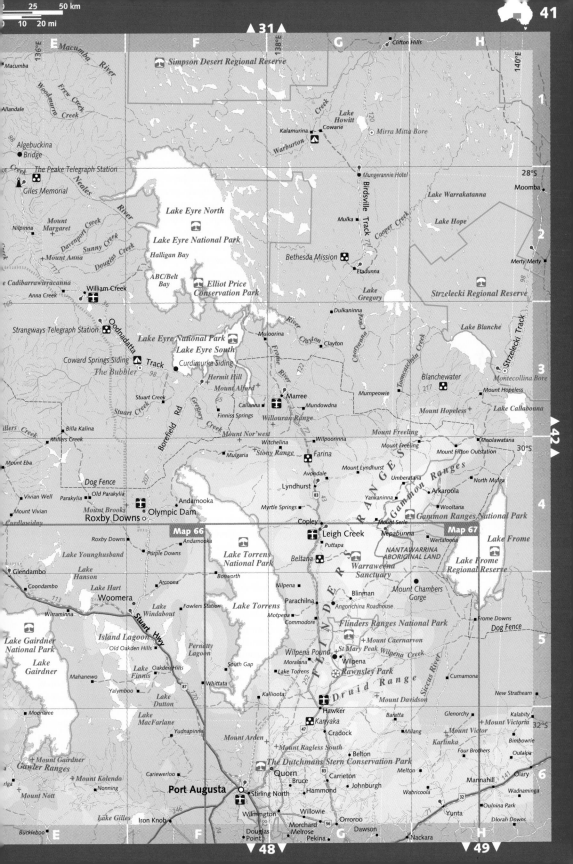

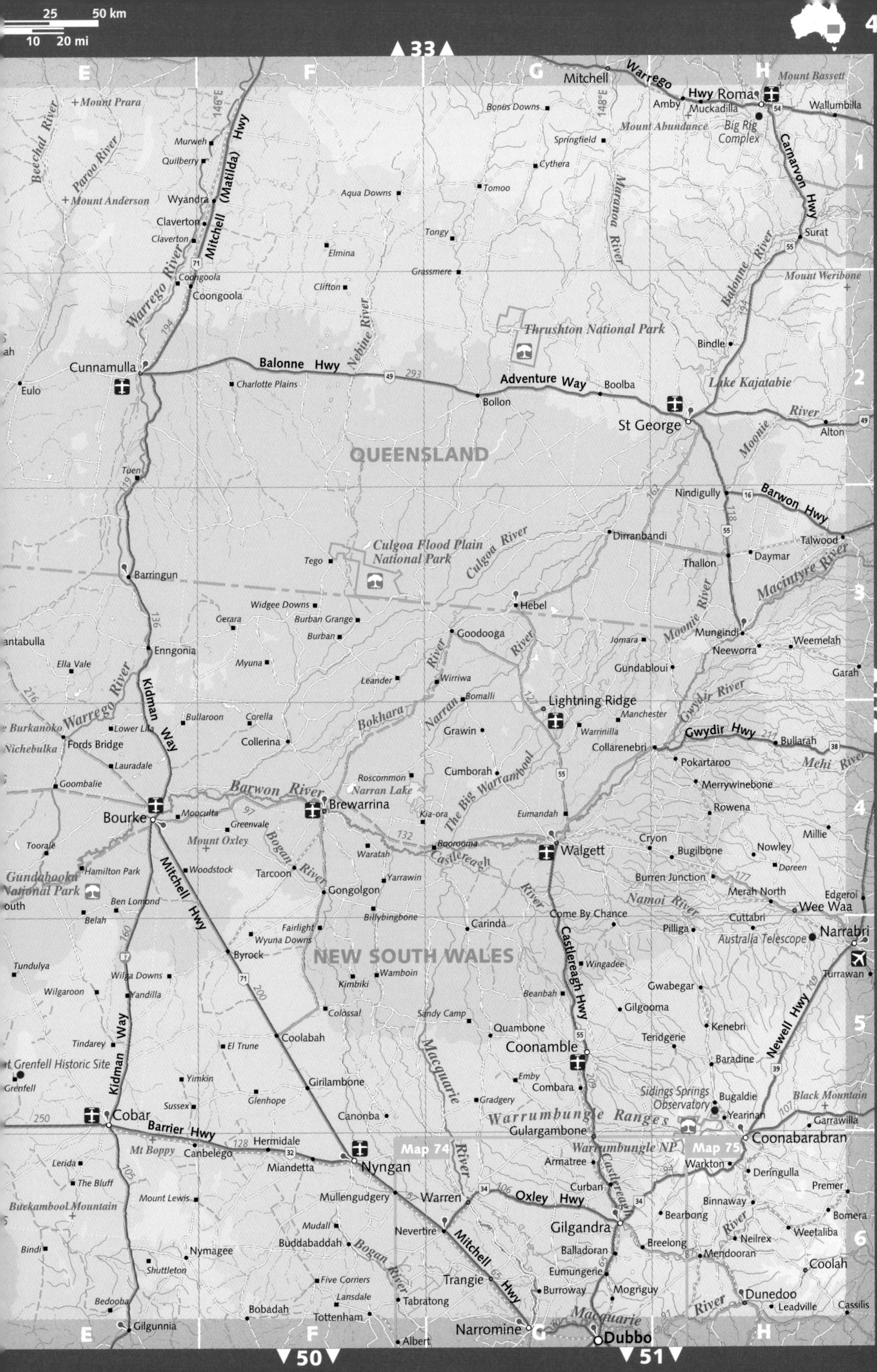

25   50 km
10   20 mi

QUEENSLAND

NEW SOUTH WALES

Mount Bassett
Mitchell
Warrego
Hwy Roma
Amby
Muckadilla
Wallumbilla
Bonus Downs
Mount Abundance
Big Rig Complex
Springfield
Cythera
Mount Prara
Beechal River
Murweh
Paroo River
Quilberry
Tomoo
Aqua Downs
Surat
Mount Anderson
Wyandra
Claverton
Claverton
Elmina
Tongy
Mount Weribone
Coongoola
Clifton
Grassmere
Coongoola
Thrushton National Park
Bindle
Cunnamulla
Balonne Hwy
Charlotte Plains
Adventure Way
Boolba
Lake Kajatabie
Eulo
Bollon
St George
Alton
Moonie River
Nindigully
Barwon Hwy
Talwood
Tuen
Culgoa Flood Plain National Park
Culgoa River
Dirranbandi
Daymar
Tego
Thallon
Macintyre River
Barringun
Widgee Downs
Hebel
Mungindi
Weemelah
Gerara
Burban Grange
Goodooga
Jomara
Neeworra
Garah
Enngonia
Burban
Leander
Wirriwa
Gundabloui
Ella Vale
Myuna
Bomalli
Lightning Ridge
Manchester
Burkandoo
Bullaroon
Corella
Grawin
Warrinilla
Gwydir Hwy
Bullarah
Nichebulka
Fords Bridge
Lower Lila
Collerina
Cumborah
Collarenebri
Pokartaroo
Mehi River
Lauradale
Roscommon
The Big Warrambool
Merrywinebone
Goombalie
Narran Lake
Kia-ora
Eumandah
Rowena
Toorale
Mooculta
Brewarrina
Booroona
Millie
Bourke
Greenvale
Waratah
Cryon
Bugilbone
Nowley
Doreen
Mount Oxley
Walgett
Burren Junction
Woodstock
Tarcoon
Yarrawin
Come By Chance
Merah North
Edgeroi
Gundabooka National Park
Hamilton Park
Gongolgon
Carinda
Namoi River
Cuttabri
Wee Waa
Ben Lomond
Belah
Billybingbone
Pilliga
Australia Telescope
Narrabri
Fairlight
Wamboin
Wingadee
Tundulya
Wyuna Downs
Beanbah
Gwabegar
Gilgooma
Turrawan
Wilga Downs
Byrock
Kimbiki
Colossal
Quambone
Teridgerie
Kenebri
Wilgaroon
Yandilla
Sandy Camp
Coonamble
Baradine
Tindarey
El Trune
Coolabah
Combara
Bugaldie
Black Mountain
Grenfell Historic Site
Yimkin
Girilambone
Emby
Gradgery
Sidings Springs Observatory
Yearinan
Garrawilla
Grenfell
Sussex
Glenhope
Canonba
Warrumbungle Ranges
Gulargambone
Warrumbungle NP
Coonabarabran
Cobar
Barrier Hwy
Hermidale
Gulargambone
Armatree
Warkton
Deriguulla
Lerida
Mt Boppy
Canbelego
Miandetta
Nyngan
Oxley Hwy
Curban
Binnaway
Premer
The Bluff
Map 74
Warren
Gilgandra
Bearbong
Bomera
Buckambool Mountain
Mount Lewis
Mullengudgerie
Nevertire
Balladoran
Breelong
Mendooran
Weetaliba
Bindi
Mudall
Buddabaddah
Eumungerie
Mogriguy
Neilrex
Coolah
Nymagee
Five Corriers
Trangie
Burroway
Dunedoo
Shuttleton
Lansdale
Tabratong
Leadville
Cassilis
Bedooba
Bobadah
Tottenham
Narromine
Dubbo
Gilgunnia
Albert
Macquarie River

Map 75
Mitchell (Matilda) Hwy
Carnarvon Hwy
Kidman Way
Mitchell Hwy
Newell Hwy
Castlereagh Hwy
Warrego River
Bogan River
Castlereagh River
Barwon River
Bokhara River
Narran River
Gwydir River
Moonie River
Balonne River
Nebine River
Maranoa River
Paroo River

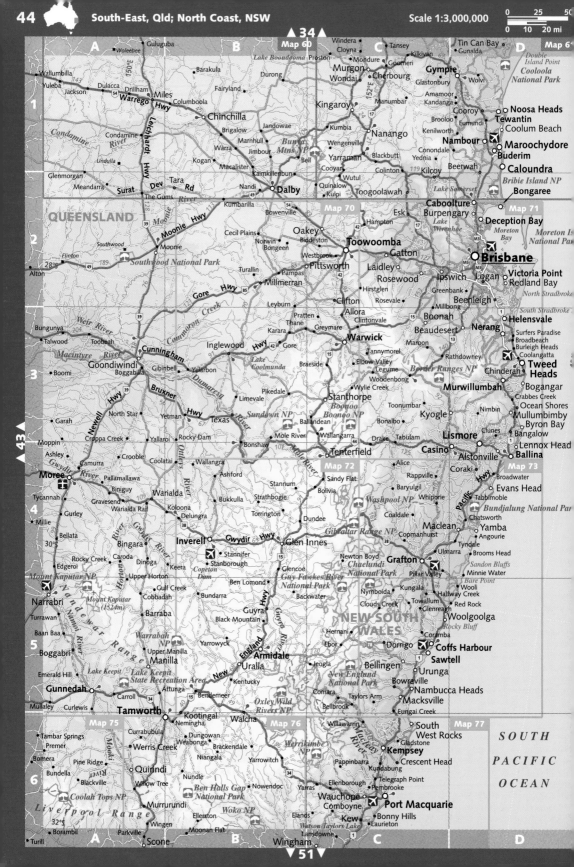

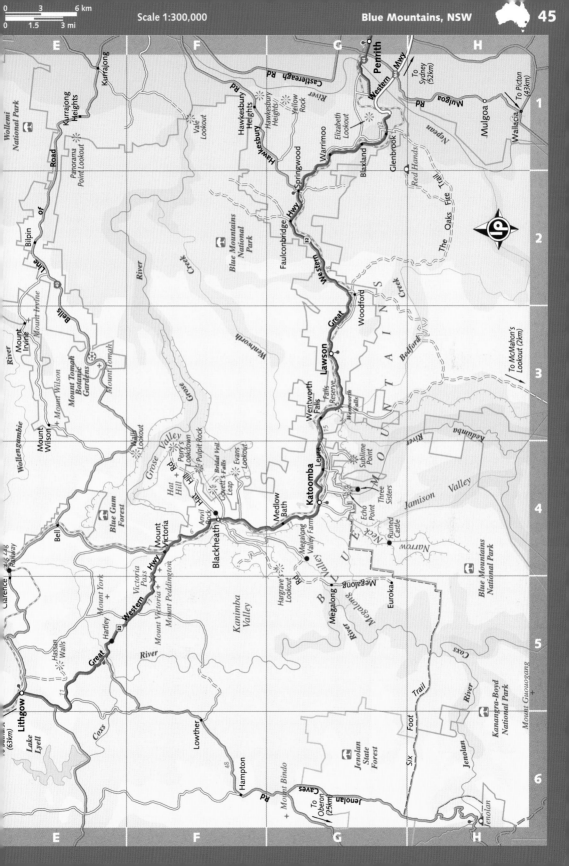

0 3 6 km
1.5
0 3 mi

E   F   G   H

Wollemi National Park

Kurrajong
Kurrajong Heights
Panorama Point Lookout
Bilpin
Bells Line of Road
Mount Irvine
Mount Irvine
River
Mount Wilson
Mount Tomah Botanic Gardens
Mount Tomah
Mount Wilson
Wollangambe

Vale Lookout
Hawkesbury Heights
Hawkesbury Heights
Hawkesbury Rd
Hawkesbury Heights
Yellow Rock
Springwood
Warrimoo
Elizabeth Lookout
Blaxland
Glenbrook
Red Hands
The Oaks Fire Trail

Penrith
To Sydney (52km)
Western Mwy
Mulgoa Rd
Nepean River
Castlereagh Rd
To Picton (43km)
Mulgoa
Wallacia

Faulconbridge
Blue Mountains National Park
Creek
Wentworth
Grose River
Western
Great
Woodford
Bedford
The Oaks Fire Trail

Lawson
Hwy
Lawson Reserve
Wentworth Falls
Wentworth Falls
Falls
15
Leura
Katoomba
Sublime Point
Echo Point
Three Sisters
Ruined Castle
Narrow Neck
Jamison Valley
Nedimba River
To McMahon's Lookout (2km)

Grose Valley
Perry's Lookdown
Pulpit Rock
Bridal Veil
Govett's Leap
Evans Lookout
Walls Lookout
Hat Hill Rd
Hat Hill
Anvil Rock
Blue Gum Forest
Bell
Mount Victoria
Blackheath
Medlow Bath
Megalong Valley Farm
Megalong Rd
Hargrave's Lookout
Megalong
Euroka
Blue Mountains National Park

Clarence
Zig Zag Railway
Mount York
Hartley
Great Western Hwy
Victoria Pass
Mount Victoria
Mount Peddington
Kanimba Valley
River
Coxs
Megalong River
Megalong
Six Foot Trail
Coxs River
Mount Guouogang

Lithgow
To ... (63km)
Lake Lyell
Coxs
Lowther
Hampton
Mount Bindo
Jenolan Caves
Jenolan Rd
To Oberon (25km)
Mount Bindo
Jenolan State Forest
Kanangra-Boyd National Park
Jenolan
Jenolan

E   F   G   H

1
2
3
4
5
6

▲ 36 ▲ | Map 62 | ▲ 37 ▲ | Map 63

A | **B** | **C** | **D**

Muntadgin

Row 1

Yanchep
Muchea
Cunderdin
Youndegin
Bruce Rock
King Rock
The Humps

Tamala Park
Lexia
Wooroloo
Northam
York
Shackleton
Narembeen
South Kumminin
Hyden
Wave Rock
Lake Carm

Sorrento
Parkerville
Balkuling
Dangin
Corrigin
Lake Hurlstone
Holt R

See Rottnest Is
Perth
Cottlesloe
Perth International
Kalamunda
Karragullen
Beverley
Bulyee
Bullaring
Kondinin

Rottnest Is
Jandakot
Armadale
Westdale
Brookton

Fremantle
Garden Is

Rockingham
Becher Point
Serpentine
Albany Hwy
Map 64
Yealering
Kulin
Jilakin Rock
SE Hyden
Map

Row 2

Mandurah
Peel Inlet
Wandering
Wickepin
Jitarning
Lake Camm

Dawesville
Pinjarra
Boddington
Cuballing
Harrismith
Newdegate

Lake Clifton
Coolup
Narrogin
Tarin Rock
Lake Grace
Lake Lockhart

Preston Beach
Waroona
Williams
Highbury
Kukerin
Pingrup

INDIAN OCEAN
Lake Preston
Myalup
Harvey
Wagin
Dumbleyung
Nyabing

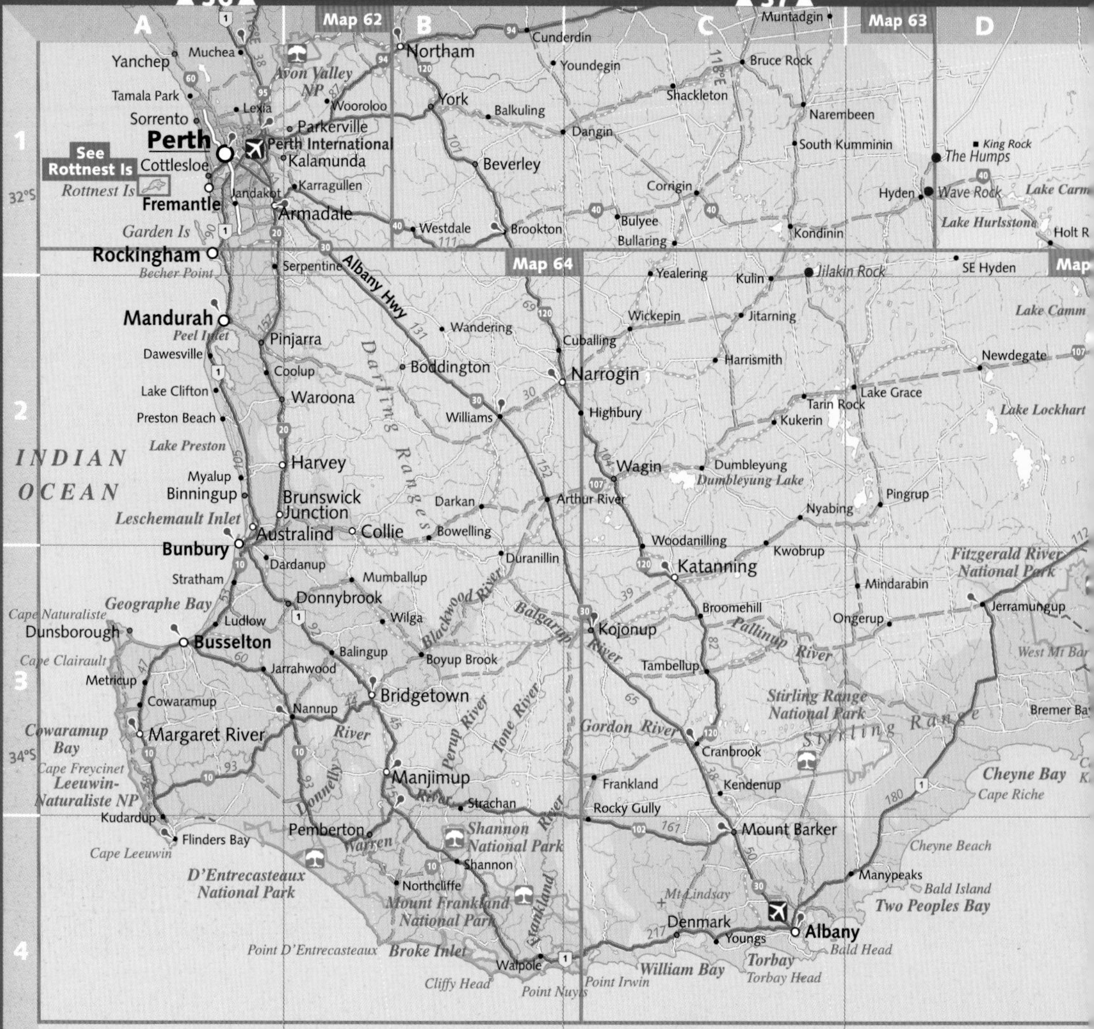

Binningup
Darkan
Arthur River
Dumbleyung Lake

Leschemault Inlet
Brunswick Junction
Bowelling
Woodanilling
Kwobrup

Bunbury
Australind
Collie
Duranillin
Katanning
Mindarabin
Jerramungup

Dardanup
Mumballup
Broomehill
Fitzgerald River National Park

Row 3

Stratham
Geographe Bay
Donnybrook
Wilga
Balgarup River
Kojonup
Tambellup
Pallinup River
West Mt

Cape Naturaliste
Dunsborough
Ludlow
Blackwood River
Bremer Ba

Cape Clairault
Busselton
Balingup
Boyup Brook
Tone River
Gordon River
Cranbrook
Stirling Range National Park
Stirling Range
Cheyne Bay
Cape Ki

Metricup
Jarrahwood
Bridgetown
Frankland
Kendenup
Cape Riche

Cowaramup
Nannup
River
Cheyne Beach

Cowaramup Bay
Margaret River
Manjimup
Strachan
Rocky Gully
Mount Barker
Bald Island

Cape Freycinet
Warren River
Manypeaks
Two Peoples Bay

Leeuwin-Naturaliste NP
Kudardup
Pemberton
Shannon National Park
Mt Lindsay
Bald Head

Row 4

Flinders Bay
D'Entrecasteaux National Park
Northcliffe
Shannon
Mount Frankland National Park
Denmark
Youngs
Albany
Torbay

Cape Leeuwin
Broke Inlet
Walpole
William Bay
Torbay Head

Point D'Entrecasteaux
Cliffy Head
Point Nuyts
Point Irwin

---

0 | 1 | 2 km
0 | 0.5 | 1 mi

36°S

Rottnest Island inset

INDIAN OCEAN

Parakeet Bay
Fay's Bay

Little Armstrong Bay
North Point
Geordie Bay
Longreach Bay
To Hillary's Boat Harbour

Thomson Bay
To Perth

ROTTNEST ISLAND
Bare Hill
Lake Baghdad
Herschel Lake
Thomson Bay
Phillip Point

32°S
Stark Bay
Wadjemup Hill
Serpentine Lake
Government House Lake

Marjorie Bay
Rocky Bay
Narrow
'Quokka Stop'
Oliver's Hill
Gun Emplacement
Lookout Hill
Bickley Bay

Eagle Bay
Conical Hill
Neck
Nancy Cove
Porpoise Bay

West End
Cape Vlamingh
Wilson Bay
Strickland Bay
Mary Cove
Salmon Bay
Salmon Point
Parkers Point

Jeannie's Lookout

A | **B** | **C** | **D**

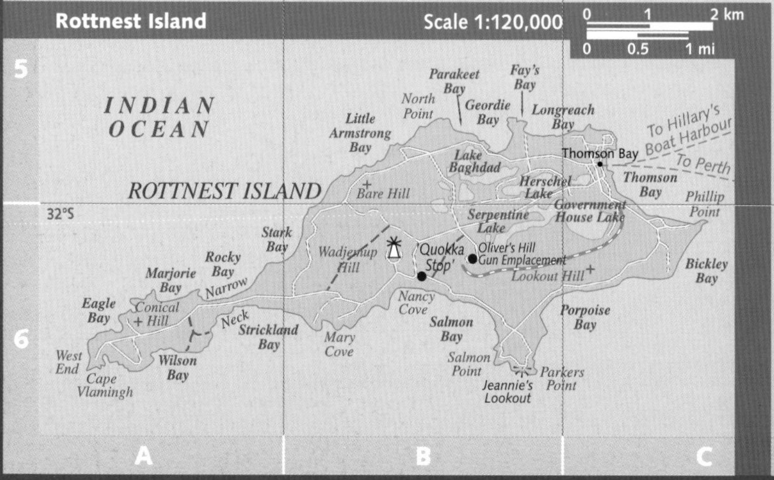

25   50 km
10   20 mi

120°E 32°S

E   **F**   **G**   **H**

Norseman

Southern Hills

Dundas Nature Reserve

Balladonia

Noondoonia   Woorlba

Balladonia

Dundas Rocks

Lake Dundas

Nanambinia

Booanya

1

Lake Hope

See Baxter Cliffs

Peak Charles National Park

Frank Hann National Park

Peak Charles
Peak Eleanora

Salmon Gums

Nuytsland Nature Reserve

Great Australian Bight

King

Grass Patch

Russell Range

+ Mt Ragged

Mount Madden

Cascade

Scaddan

Young River

Oldfield River

Glensoe

Israelite Bay

Eastern Group

2

Cape Arid National Park

Point Malcolm

Daw Is

34°S

ills

Coomalbidgup

Gibson

Condingup

Ravensthorpe

186

Munglinup

Gorey

Dalyup

Esperance

Wharton

Desmond

Jerdacuttup

Duke of Orleans Bay

+ Mt Arid
Cape Arid

Sandy Bight

River

Stokes Inlet NP

Shoal Cape

Cape Le Grand NP

Cape Le Grande

Rossiter Bay

Middle Is

ARCHIPELAGO OF THE RECHERCHE

Southern Ocean East Drive

Starvation Boat Harbour

West Group

Mondrain Is

Salisbury Is

3

Hopetoun

Woolbernup Hill

int Charles

nt Ann

r Cove

4

SOUTHERN   OCEAN

36°S

5

Baxter Cliffs   Scale 1:3,000,000

▲ 38 ▲

Nullarbor Plain

Point Dover

Baxter Cliffs

▲ 47 ▲

Nuytsland Nature Reserve

Point Culver

Great Australian Bight

6

E   **F**   **G**   **H**

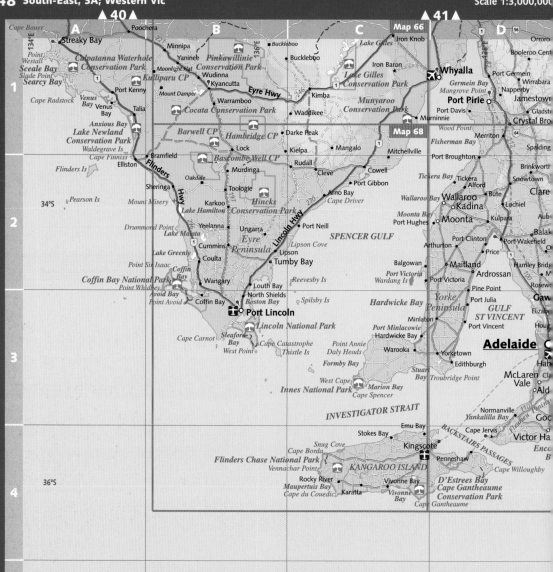

▲ 40 ▲ ▲ 41 ▲

Map 66

Map 68

A B C D

Cape Bauer
Poochera
Streaky Bay
Minnipa
Point Westall
Scale Bay
Slade Point
Calpatanna Waterhole Conservation Park
Yaninee
Pinkawillinie Conservation Park
Buckleboo
Lake Gilles
Iron Knob
Searcy Bay
Kulliparu CP
Wudinna
Buckleboo
Iron Baron
Whyalla
Port Kenny
Kyancutta
Eyre Hwy
Lake Gilles Conservation Park
Germein Bay
Cape Radstock
Mount Damper
Kimba
Munyaroo Conservation Park
Port Pirie
Venus Bay
Talia
Warramboo
Napperby
Jamestown
Venus Bay
Cocata Conservation Park
Waddikee
Murninnie
Port Davis
Crystal Bro
Anxious Bay
Barwell CP
Darke Peak
Wood Point
Merriton
Lake Newland Conservation Park
Hambridge CP
Kielpa
Mitchellville
Port Broughton
Spalding
Waldegrave Is
Lock
Cleve
Cowell
Brinkworth
Cape Finniss
Bramfield
Bascombe Well CP
Rudall
Tickera Bay
Tickera
Snowtown
Flinders Is
Elliston
Murdinga
Cleve
Port Gibbon
Wallaroo Bay
Alford
Bute
Clare
Oakdale
Sheringa
Toologie
Arno Bay
Moonta Bay
Wallaroo
Lochiel
34°S
Pearson Is
Mount Misery
Hincks Conservation Park
Cape Driver
Port Hughes
Kadina
Kulpara
Balak
Drummond Point
Karkoo
Lake Hamilton
Yeelanna
Ungarra
Port Neill
Moonta
Lake Malata
Cummins
Eyre Peninsula
Lipson Cove
Arthurton
Port Clinton
Price
Port Wakefield
Lake Greenly
Coulta
Lipson
SPENCER GULF
Balgowan
Maitland
Hamley Brid
Point Sir Isaac
Tumby Bay
Port Victoria
Ardrossan
Coffin Bay
Wangary
Reevesby Is
Wardang Is
Port Victoria
Pine Point
Rosew
Coffin Bay National Park
Louth Bay
Pt Whidbey
Avoid Bay
North Shields
Spilsby Is
Hardwicke Bay
Yorke Peninsula
Port Julia
Gaw
Point Avoid
Coffin Bay
Boston Bay
Port Minlacowie
Minlaton
Port Vincent
Elizabe
Port Lincoln
Hardwicke Bay
Houg
Lincoln National Park
Warooka
Yorketown
Adelaide
Cape Carnot
Sleaford Bay
Cape Catastrophe
Point Annie
Daly Heads
Edithburgh
McLaren Vale
Cla
West Point
Thistle Is
Formby Bay
Stuart Bay
Troubridge Point
Ald
West Cape
Innes National Park
Marion Bay
Normanville
Yankalilla Bay
Goo
Cape Spencer
INVESTIGATOR STRAIT
Cape Jervis
Victor Ha
Emu Bay
Enco
Stokes Bay
Kingscote
BACKSTAIRS PASSAGE
B
Snug Cove
Cape Borda
Flinders Chase National Park
Pennershaw
Vennachar Point
KANGAROO ISLAND
Cape Willoughby
Rocky River
Vivonne Bay
D'Estrees Bay
36°S
Maupertuis Bay
Cape du Couedic
Karatta
Vivonne Bay
Cape Gantheaume Conservation Park
Cape Gantheaume

SOUTHERN OCEAN

38°S

A B C D

25 50 km
10 20 mi

▲ 41 ▲ ▲ 42 ▲

E 32 **Map 67** **F** **G** **H**

Dlorah Downs

Cavindilla Lake Ashmont

Dawson Paratoo Manunda Lake Tandou River Rinchega Kaleentha Loop Boola Boolka
Nackara Lilydale National Park Gum Lake
Oodla Wirra Quondong Vale Oakvale Coombah Williba Sayers Lake
eterborough Roadhouse Popiltah Darnick
Sturt Vale Oakbank Lake Karoola Karpa Kora

1

Terowie Morgan Vale Twin Lakes Popiltah Travellers Bulgamurra C Lake
Whyte-Yarcowie Pine Valley Lake Lake Mulirulu
Collinsville **Danggali** **Scotia** Yelta Lake Manilla Pan Ban Lake
Conservation Park **Sanctuary** Nearie Lake Pooncarie

Hallett Koomooloo Canopus SILVER CITY HWY Tapio Garnpung
Mount Bryan Canegrass Hypurna Trelega Lake Leaghur Lake Gol Gol
Burra Grassville **SOUTH** Bunneringee Top Hut Lake Mungo **Mungo**

2

nson **AUSTRALIA** Warrakoo Huntingfield Lake Mungo **National Park**
ell Flat Warranangee Burtundy Lake Arumpo Chibnalwood
ack Springs Robertstown **Murray River** Lake Victoria Tapio Lakes Iona Langleydale
arrabel Bower **(Bulyong Island) NP** Cal Lal Wamberra Turlee 34°S Bidura
Eudunda Morgan **Booinook** **MURRAY** Wentworth Fletcher Lake Mallee Cliffs
Kapunda **Conservation Park** Kingston OM Lake Merbein Irymple **National Park** Prungle
Truro Waikerie Cooltong Victoria Warranangee Mildura Tin Tin Lake
Nuriootpa Blanchetown Barmera **Renmark** Sturt Hwy Cullulleraine Red Cliffs Penarie
Tanunda Moorook Berri Morkalla Mildura Pitarpunga
yndoch Maggea Wunkar **Murray River** Meringur Werrimull Carwarp Nangiloc Robinvale Lake
illiamstown Mantung Pata **(Katarapko) NP** Loxton Rocket Lake Nowingi **Hattah-Kulkyne NP** Robinvale
brook Swan Reach Veitch Happy Valley Balranald

3

Mount Torrens Nildottie Mercunda Paruna Hattah Boundary Bend
Mannum Copeville Wanbi Alawoona **Murray-Sunset National Park** Koolnong
Springton Purnong Halidon Mount Crozier Annuello Kyalite
oodside Perponda Sandalwood Berrook Bolton Tooleybuc
unt Barker **Billiat CP** Karte Mount Jess Ouyen Manangatang Wood Wood Nyah
Murray Bridge **Peebinga CP** Mount Jess Mittyack Chinkapook Tyntynder
stow **Karte CP** Walpeup Chillingollah Homestead
rathalbyn Tailem Bend Pinnaroo Mallee Hwy Boinka Nandaly Swan Hill

50

Wellington Mallee Hwy Murrayville Big Billy Bore Patchewollock Turriff Ultima **Map 85**
Narrung Lameroo **Scorpion Springs** Mt Observatory **Map 83** Kerang
Yumali **Conservation Park** Lascelles Lalbert Quambatook
Meningie Mount Timothy **Wyperfeld National Park** Yaapeet Hopetoun Culgoa 36°S

4

Kiki Coonalpyn Mount Timothy **Map 82** **VICTORIA** Rainbow Nullawil Dumosa Boort
Culburra Tintinara **Ngarkat Conservation Park** Lake Albacutya Beulah Birchip Wycheproof
Coorong Dukes Hwy Lake Jeparit Watchem Charlton
National Park Keith Hindmarsh Broughton **A79** Wedderburn
Salt Creek Bordertown Warracknabeal Litchfield Borung
Mundulla Nhill Sheep Hills Donald Calder
Kaniva Western Hwy Borung Minyip St Arnaud

5

Kingston SE Padthaway Dimboola Murtoa Bealiba Moliagul
Lacepede Bay Frances **Little Desert NP** Pimpinio Rupanyup North Marnoo Dunolly
Cape Jaffa Keppoch Minimay Natimuk Wimmera **Map 84** Natte Yallock
Reedy Creek Binnum **Horsham** Maryborough
Avenue Kybybolite Wonwondah North Avoca Elmhurst
Cape Thomas Lucindale Langkoop Douglas Glenorchy Newstead
Guichen Bay Crower Naracoorte Poolaijelo Stawell Campbelltown
Cape Dombey Robe Greenways Edenhope Harrow Halls Gap Ararat
Cape Rabelais Clay Wells Bool Chetwynd Balmoral **Grampians**
Coonawarra Lagoon Dergholm **National Park** **Map 91** **Map 92**
Cape Martin Penola Nangwarry **Map 90** Cavendish Maroona Beaufort Creswick
Rivoli Bay Beachport Tarpeena Casterton Coleraine Willaura
Cape Buffon Southend Glencoe Henty Wannon Dunkeld Lake Bolac Skipton **Ballarat**

6

Millicent Merino Hamilton Buninyong
Canunda National Park Tantanoola **Mount Gambier** Branxholme Penshurst
Lake Bonney Kongorong Dartmoor Caramut
Carpenter Rocks Allendale East Lyons Macarthur Lismore Meredith
Cape Northumberland Nelson Cressy
Port MacDonnell **Discovery Bay** Heywood Mortlake Inverleigh
Heathmere Woolsthorpe Camperdown

E **F** ▼ 52 ▼ **G** **H**

NEW SOUTH WALES

Darling River

Princes Hwy

25   50 km

10   20 mi

Map 74 E   F   G   H

Dunedoo   Cassilis   Wingen   Bobin
Borambil   Parkville   Hunter River   Laurieton
Birriwa   Turill   Merriwa   Buhnan   Manning River   Wingham   Moorland
Laheys Creek   Wappinguy   Scone   Gloucester   Gloucester   Taree   Crowdy Head
Dubbo   Ulan   Gungal   Aberdeen   Stratford   Wards River   Nabiac   Old Bar   32°S
Geurie   Spicers Creek   Cooyal   Bylong   Muswellbrook   Salisbury   Bandon Grove   Tuncurry
Wellington   Gulgong   Baerami   Denman   Lake Liddell   St Clair   Stroud   Markwell   Forster
Yeoval   Mudgee   Lue   Breakfast Creek   Singleton   Dungog   Bulahdelah   Elizabeth Beach
Cumnock   Lake Burrendong   Windeyer   Rylstone   Bulga   Branxton   Clarence Town   Seal Rocks
Larras Lee   Stuart Town   Olinda   Wollemi NP   Maitland   Raymond Terrace   Nelson Bay
Molong   Kerrs Creek   Sallys Flat   Ilford   Clandulla   Glen Alice   Cessnock   Kurri Kurri
Manildra   Mullion Creek   Sofala   Capertee   Wollombi   Newcastle   Charlestown
Map 79   Cudal   Orange   Peel   Cullen Bullen   Yengo National Park   Swansea
Cargo   Bathurst   Wallerawang   Colo Heights   Wyong   Budgewoi   Map 81
Canowindra   Blayney   Capertee River   Gosford   Toukley   The Entrance
Walli   Mandurama   Lithgow   Map 45   Richmond   Terrigal   2
Cowra   Rockley   Blackheath   Woy Woy   Patonga
Neville   Oberon   Penrith   Hornsby
Trunkey Creek   Katoomba   Springwood   Parramatta
Wyangala   Tuena   Burraga   Lawson   Blue Mountains NP   Liverpool   SYDNEY
Godfreys Creek   Limerick   Kanangra-Boyd National Park   Oakdale   Camden
Frogmore   Binda   Thirlmere   Waterfall
Gunnary   Bargo   Picton   Helensburgh   3
Borowa   Crookwell   Bannister   Mittagong   Stanwell Park   34°S
Bungendore   Tarlo   Bowral   Thirroul
Yass   Goulburn   Moss Vale   Wollongong
Hume Hwy   Bundanoon   Shellharbour
Collector   Marulan   Kiama
Murrumbateman   Bungonia   Gerringong
Bomaderry   Shoalhaven Heads
Map 88   Lake Bathurst   Nowra
Canberra   Tarago   Map 89
Queanbeyan   St Georges Basin   Huskisson   4
Hoskinstown   Braidwood   Sanctuary Point
Royalla   Rossi   Sussex Inlet
Captains Flat   Morton NP   Cudmirrah
Michelago   Araluen   Ulladulla
Kain   Burrill Lake
Bawley Point
Batemans Bay   TASMAN
Bredbo   Mogo   Malua Bay   SEA
Numeralla   Deua National Park   Mossy Point
Cooma   Bergalia   Moruya   5
Wadbilliga National Park   Bodalla   Tuross Head   36°S
Cobargo   Eurobodalla
Central Tilba   Narooma
Bermagui
Bemboka   Brogo
Bega   154°E
Bombala   Candelo   Tathra   6
Map 95
Wyndham   Pambula
South East Forests National Park   Pericoe   Eden
Kiah
Narrabarba
Wonboyn
Genoa
Cape Howe
Mallacoota
Croajingolong National Park

E   F   G   H

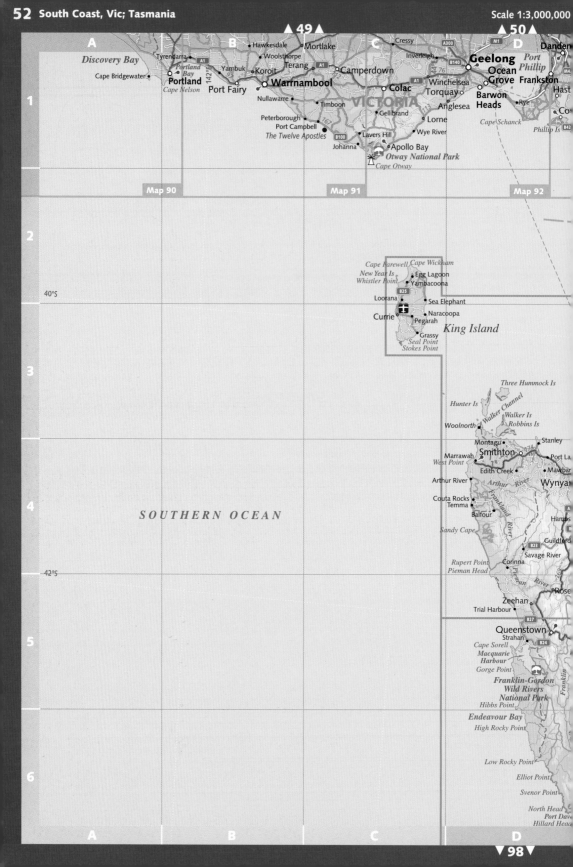

▲ 49 ▲   ▲ 50 ▲

A   **B**   **C**   **D**

Discovery Bay

Hawkesdale
Mortlake   Cressy

Tyrendarra   Woolsthorpe   Inverleigh
Portland   Yambuk   Terang   Camperdown   **Geelong**
Cape Bridgewater   *Bay*   Koroit   **Ocean**   *Port*
Portland   *Port Fairy*   Colac   Winchelsea   **Grove** *Phillip* **Frankston**
          Nullawarre   Torquay   **Barwon**   Hast
          Timboon   Gellibrand   Anglesea   **Heads**
          Peterborough   Lorne   Rye
          Port Campbell   Wye River   *Cape Schanck*
          The Twelve Apostles   Lavers Hill   *Phillip Is*
          Johanna   Apollo Bay
          Otway National Park
          Cape Otway

1

VICTORIA

Map 90   Map 91   Map 92

2

Cape Farewell *Cape Wickham*
New Year Is   Egg Lagoon
Whistler Point   Yambacoona

40°S   Loorana   Sea Elephant
          Naracoopa
Currie   Pegarah   *King Island*
          Grassy
          Seal Point
          Stokes Point

3

          Three Hummock Is

          Hunter Is   *Walker Is*
          Robbins Is
          Woolnorth

          Montagu   Stanley
          Marrawah   **Smithton**   Port La
SOUTHERN OCEAN   *West Point*   Edith Creek   Mawbar
          Arthur River   **Wynya**
          Couta Rocks   *Arthur   River*
          Temma
          Balfour   Hamps

          Sandy Cape   Savage River   Guildford

4   Corinna
          Rupert Point   Rose
          Pieman Head

42°S   Zeehan
          Trial Harbour
          Queenstown
          Strahan
          Cape Sorell
5   *Macquarie*
          Harbour
          Gorge Point   *Franklin-Gordon*
          Wild Rivers
          National Park
          Hibbs Point

          Endeavour Bay
          High Rocky Point

6   *Low Rocky Point*

          Elliot Point

          Svenor Point

          North Head
          Port Dav
          Hillard Hea

A   **B**   **C**   **D**

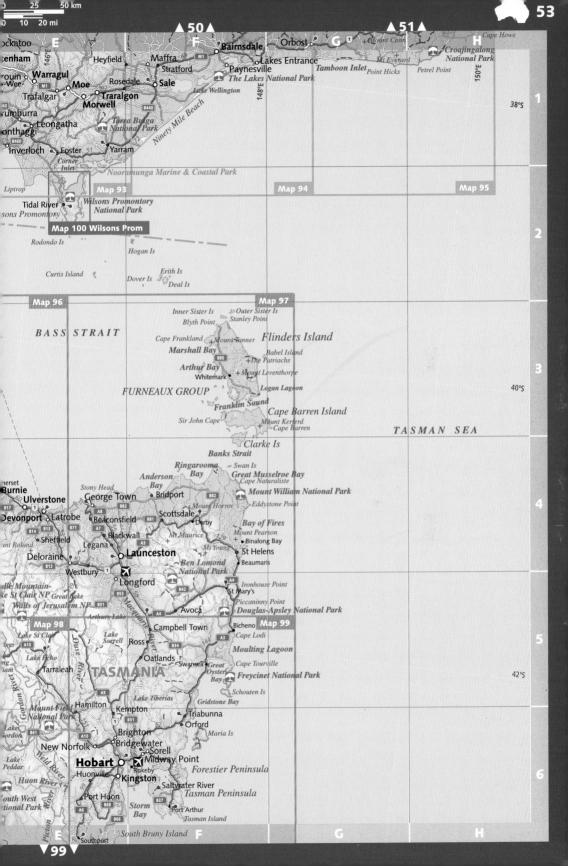

A ▲ 19 ▲ B C ▲ 20 ▲ D

143°E

1

17°S

Staaten River National Park

Bulimba

Lynd River

Walsh River

Blackdown

Nychum

Mount Mulligan

Kingsborough

Thornborough

Rookwood

Mungana

Chillagoe

Mount Angus

Wolfram

Dimb

2

Pelican Creek

Einasleigh River

Torwood

Chillagoe-Mungana National Park

Mount Alexander

143

Almaden

Burke Developmental Rd

Petford

Lappa

Mount Beauty

Crystal Brook

Bolwarra

Tate River

Ootann

Abingdon Downs

Bulleringa National Park

Bulleringa

Bullock Creek

Barwidgi

Mt Garne

Mount Cardwell

Amber

144°E

145°E

3

18°S

Eden Vale

Van Lee

Dagworth

Barney Knob

O'Briens Creek Gemfields

Cabana

Tallaroo Hot Springs

Byrimine

Mount Poole

Lynd River

112

19 ▲

Mount Darcy

Mount Turner

Gulf Developmental Rd

Georgetown

The Sisters

Eveleigh

Tallaroo

Brooklands

Mount Surprise

149

Mount Surprise

Forty Mile Scrub National Park

Minnamoolka

Yaramulla

Boomerang

Meadowbank

Mount Lang

4

Mount Sircom

Lawnvale

Mount Talbot

Forsayth

Einasleigh River

Einasleigh

Mount Redcap

Newcastle Range

Undara Volcanic National Park

Mount McMaster

1

96

Glendhu

Kinrara

Craigs Pocket

Mount Clark

Perpendicular Peak

Cobbold Gorge

Mount Helpman

Beverly Hills

The Oaks

Mount Borium

Spring Creek

Carpentaria Downs

Bally Knob

Kennedy Hwy

Burdekin River

5

19°S

North Head

South Head

Robin Hood

Mount Jordan

Kidston

Kidston Goldmine

Wyandotte

Lucky Downs

Agate Creek Gemfields

Mount Esk

47

114

Greenvale

Mount Margaret

Gilberton

Copperfield River

6

Bellfield

Gregory Range

Werrington

Pandanus Creek

Mount Remarkable

Clark River

Strathpark

Oak Valley

Blackbraes

A B C D

0 10 20 km
0 5 10 mi

E · F · G · H

Yule Point
Hockley
Oak Beach
Mount Molloy
Trinity
Bay
Ellis
Palm Cove
Clifton Beach
Trinity
Kuranda
- *Green Island*
Cape Grafton
Stratford
Grafton Passage
Fitzroy Island
Barron Gorge National Park
Cairns
Cairns International
Yarrabah
Woree
White Rock
Edmonton
Mareeba
Grey Peaks National Park
Bell Peak North
Gordonvale
Aloomba
Tinaroo Falls
Little Mulgrave
Walkamin
Palmer Point
Carbeen
Russell River National Park
Kairi
Frankland Islands
Tolga
Lake Tinaroo
Mt Massie
Deeral
Atherton
Bellenden Ker
Yungaburra
Peeramon
Wooroonooran NP
Babinda Boulders
Herberton
Malanda
Babinda
Mt Hypipamee NP
Mt Bartle Frere
Miriwinni
Josephine
Bramston Beach
Falls
Cooper Point
Tarzali
Minbun
Daradgee
Ella Bay National Park
Millaa Millaa
Eubenangee Swamp National Park
Kaban
Millaa Millaa
Lookout
Flying Fish Point
Tumoulin
Wangan
Innisfail
Ravenshoe
Mourilyan
South Johnstone
Innot Hot Springs
Paronella
Park
Moresby
Millstream
Crawfords
Mena Creek
Double Point
National Park
Lookout
Cowley
Silkwood
Kurrimine
Mount Marquette
El Arish
Bingil Bay
Lake
Koombooloomba
Feluga
Mission Beach
Glen Ruth
Tully
South Mission Beach
Hewitt
Dunk Island
Mount Sharpless
Euramo
Dunk Island
Gleneagle
National Park
Murray Upper
Bilyana
Rockingham
Princess Hills
Dallachy
Bay
Edmund Kennedy National Park
Kennedy
Goold Island
Carruchan
Cape Richards
Lumholtz National Park
Cardwell
Cape Sandwich
Hinchinbrook Island
National Park
Blacksand
Abergowrie
Banksia
Hinchinbrook Island
Hillock Point
Wallaman Falls
Picnic
Lake Lucy
Lucinda
Lannercost
Macknade
Pelorus Is
Trebonne
Halifax
Cordelia
Orpheus Is
Orpheus Island National Park
Upper Stone
Taylors
Curacoa Is
Ingham
Fantome Is
Palm Passage
Toobanna
Toolakea
Forrest Beach
Great Palm Is
Camel Creek
+Mount Bentley
Halifax
PALM ISLANDS
Mount Lyall
Bay
Havannah Is
Magnetic Passage
Hidden Valley
Bambaroo
Mutarnee
Paluma Range National Park
Ewan
Paluma
Moongobulla
= Acheron Is
Mount Zero
Rollingstone
Herald Is
Rattlesnake Is
Taravale
Horseshoe Bay
Magnetic Is
Magnetic Island National Park
Pallarenda
Toolakea
Saunders
Picnic Bay
Cape Cleveland
Cleveland
Townsville
Bay
Mount Oweenee
Australian Institute of Marine Science

Geranium Passage

GREAT BARRIER REEF

CORAL
SEA

GREAT BARRIER REEF MARINE PARK

146°E · 147°E

17°S

18°S

19°S

GREAT DIVIDING RANGE

Seaview Range

Herbert River

PALUMA RANGE

Bruce Hwy

Star River

Captain Cook Hwy

Kennedy Hwy

Burke Dev Rd

A   B   C   D

▲ 55 ▲

Townsville

CORAL
SEA

Star River
Keelbottom Creek
146°E
Ross River Dam
Stuart
Nome
Clevedon
Cungulla
Australian Institute of Marine Science
Cape Bowling Green
Bowling Green Bay
Antil Plains
Bowling Green Bay National Park
Giru
Alva
Toonpan
Barringna
Majors Creek
86
Brandon
Ayr
Woodstock
Manton
Rita Island
Burdekin River
Fanning River
Haughton River
78
Home Hill
Reid River
Cardington
Woodhouse
Arkendeith
Inkerman
Upstart Bay
Cape Upstart
Cape Ups National
Arthur Peak
20°S
134
Mingela
Clare
Bruce Hwy
RM Point
Abbo Bay
Sellheim
Mount Dalrymple
Mount Louisa
Gumlu
Kyburra
Guthalungra
Nobbies Look
Flinders Hwy
Charters Towers
Broughton
Mount Benjonney
Millaroo
Strathalbyn
Strathbogie
Mount Abbot
Mt Aberdeen National Park
Mount Adr
Jara
Powlathanga
Seventy Mile Mountain
Ravenswood
Burdekin River
Dalbeg
Mount King
Bogie River
Mount Pleasant
Binbee
Balfes Creek
Mount Bohle
Cardigan
Seventy Mile Range
Mount Farrenden
Brittania
Mount Sunrise
GREAT
Mount Cooper
Mount Glenroy
Table Mountain
Mount Bella Vista
Monte Chr
Mount Windsor
Mount Trafalgar
Mount Redan
Mount Nolan
Mount Cooper
Old Glenroy
Scottville
Collinsville
Mount Visto
Wambiana
Slogan Downs
DIVIDING
Lake Dalrymple
Burdekin Dam
Campaspe River
Victoria Downs
Mount Bellevue
Mount McConnell
Mount Malakoff
Harvest Home
Lornsleigh
Mount McConnell
RANGE
Emu P.
21°S
Egera
Gregory Developmental Rd
202
Dandenong Park
Mount Stone
Ukalunda
Pyramid
Hidden Valley
Mount Ely
Conway
Mount Sugarlo
Mount Helena
Bungobine Peak
Mount Loudon
257
Mount Harry Marsh
Bungobine
Newlands Coal Mine
Whynot
Mount Carmel
Bulgonunna Peak
Mount Bingeringo
Mount Hope
Blackwood National Park
Mount Coolon
Sutter River
Glende
Ibis Creek
Gleneva
Belyando Crossing
Mount Manaman
Belyando River
Lake Elphinsto
Hyde Park
Rocky Mountain
Mistake Creek
22°S
Carmichael
Diamond Creek
Broadmeadow
Labona
Doongmabulla
Mount Gregory
Moranbah

1

2

3

4

5

6

▲ 20 ▲

▲ 33 ▲

A   B   C   D

▼ 33 ▼   ▼ 58 ▼

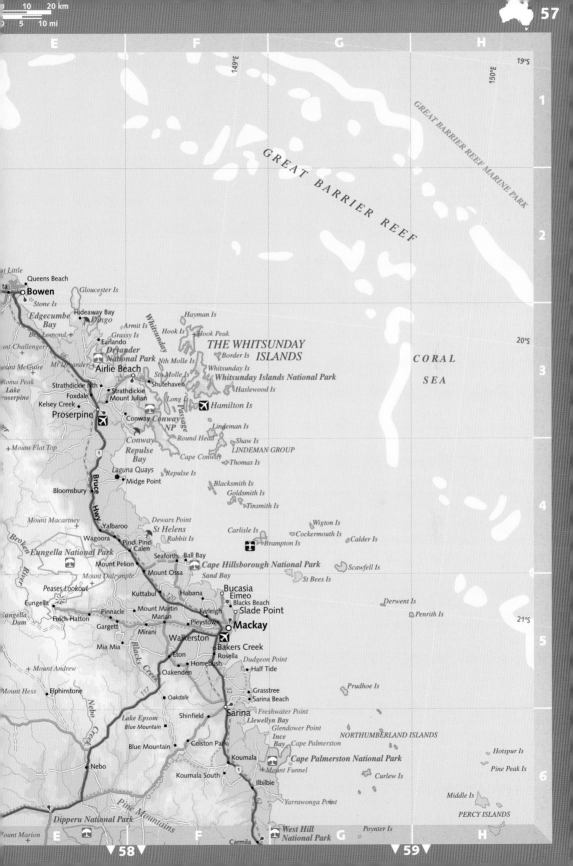

10   20 km
5   10 mi

GREAT BARRIER REEF MARINE PARK

19°S

1

2

GREAT BARRIER REEF

CORAL SEA

20°S

Queens Beach
Bowen
Gloucester Is
Stone Is
Edgecumbe Bay
Hideaway Bay
Dingo
Ben Lomond
Mt DIleander
Mount McGuire
ount Challenger
Roma Peak
Lake
oserpine

Armit Is
Grassy Is
Earlando
Dryander National Park
Airlie Beach
Strathdickie Nth
Foxdale
Kelsey Creek
Proserpine
Strathdickie
Mount Julian
Conway
Conway
NP

Whitsunday
Hook Is
Nth Molle Is
Sth Molle Is
Shutehaven
Long Is

Hayman Is
Hook Peak
Border Is
THE WHITSUNDAY ISLANDS
Whitsunday Is
Whitsunday Islands National Park
Haslewood Is
Hamilton Is
Lindeman Is

3

Mount Flat Top
Conway Repulse Bay
Laguna Quays
Midge Point
Bloomsbury

Round Head
Cape Conway
Shaw Is
LINDEMAN GROUP
Thomas Is
Repulse Is
Blacksmith Is
Goldsmith Is
Tinsmith Is

Mount Macartney
Yalbaroo
Wagoora
Eungella National Park
Mount Pelion
Pindi Pindi
Calen
Seaforth
Ball Bay
Mount Ossa

Dewars Point
St Helens
Rabbit Is
Carlisle Is
Cockermouth Is
Brampton Is
Wigton Is
Calder Is
Scawfell Is

4

Peases Lookout
Eungella
ungella Dam
Finch Hatton
Pinnacle
Gargett
Mirani
Mia Mia

Kuttabul
Habana
Mount Martin
Marian
Pleystowe
Mackay
Walkerston
Bakers Creek
Eton
Rosella
Homebush

Bucasia
Eimeo
Blacks Beach
Slade Point
Farleigh

Cape Hillsborough National Park
Sand Bay
St Bees Is
Derwent Is
Penrith Is

21°S

Mount Andrew
Mount Hess
Elphinstone
Oakden
Oakdale
Shinfield
Lake Epsom
Blue Mountain
Blue Mountain
Colston Park
Nebo
Koumala South

Dudgeon Point
Half Tide
Grasstree
Sarina Beach
Sarina
Freshwater Point
Llewellyn Bay
Glendower Point
Ince Bay
Cape Palmerston
Koumala
Ilbilbie
Mount Funnel
Cape Palmerston National Park

Prudhoe Is
NORTHUMBERLAND ISLANDS
Hotspur Is
Pine Peak Is
Curlew Is

5

6

Dipperu National Park
ount Marion
Carmila
West Hill National Park
Yarrawonga Point
Poynter Is
Middle Is
PERCY ISLANDS

E   F   G   H

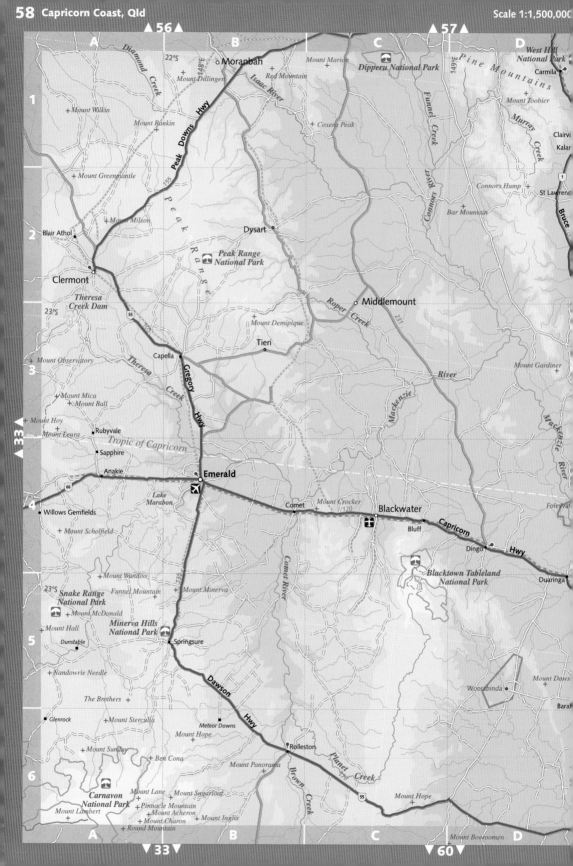

▲ 56 ▲   ▲ 57 ▲

A   B   C   D

22°S

Diamond Creek

○ Moranbah

Mount Dillingen

Mount Marion

Dipperu National Park

Pine Mountains

West Hill National Park

Carmila

Mount Wilkin

Mount Rankin

Red Mountain

Coxens Peak

Funnel Creek

Connors River

Mount Toobier

Murray Creek

Clairvi

Kalar

1

Peak Downs Hwy

Isaac River

Mount Greenmantle

55

Connors Hump

St Lawrenc

Bruce

2   Blair Athol

Mount Milson

Dysart

Peak Range National Park

Bar Mountain

Clermont

Theresa Creek Dam

23°S

55

Roper Creek

Middlemount

231

Mount Gardiner

3   Mount Observatory

Capella

Theresa Creek

Gregory Hwy

Mount Demipique

Tieri

River

Mackenzie

Mount Mica

Mount Ball

Mount Hoy

Mount Leura

Rubyvale

Tropic of Capricorn

Mackenzie River

▲ 33 ▲

Sapphire

Anakie

Emerald

4   66

Willows Gemfields

Lake Marabon

Comet

Mount Crocker

120

Blackwater

Capricorn Hwy

Dingo

Duaringa

Foleyva

Mount Scholfield

Bluff

Blacktown Tableland National Park

23°S

Mount Wandoo

135

Mount Minerva

Comet River

Mount Daws

Snake Range National Park

Funnel Mountain

Mount McDonald

Woorabinda

Barah

Mount Hall

Minerva Hills National Park

5   Dunstable

Springsure

Nandowrie Needle

Dawson Hwy

The Brothers

Glenrock

Mount Sterculla

Meteor Downs

Mount Hope

Planet Creek

Mount Hope

Mount Sunday

Ben Cona

Rolleston

Brown Creek

Mount Panorama

55

6   Carnavon National Park

Mount Lane

Mount Sugarloaf

Mount Lambert

Pinnacle Mountain

Mount Acheron

Mount Charon

Mount Inglis

Round Mountain

Mount Booroomen

A   B   C   D

A　58　B　59　C　D

149°E

Moura

Torsdale
Mt Scoria
Scoria
Thangool

Kroombit Tops
National Park

Burnett Hwy

151°E

55
166
Kianga

158

60

+ Mount Booroomen

Single Peak
Mount Nicholson +
+ Mount Aldis

Double Peak +

Nipan

39

Mount Shaw

Blue Mountain +

Cania
Coominglah

Cania Gorge
National Pa

172

Moonford

1

25°S
Bedourie

Theodore

Mount Margaret
+

Mon

Mapala
Ropers Peak +

Ghinghindah

Rawbelle River

17

+ The Battery

Reedy Creek

Isla Gorge
National Park

95

Camboon

Black Moun

2

Expedition
National Park

Leichhardt Hwy

Cracow

Lake Wuruma

Eidsvold

+ Surprise Mountain
+ Mount Weldon

Glenhaughton

Mount Moss
+

Dawson River

131

Burnett River

Auburn Range

Rockybar

Quaggy Mountain
+

Coonambula

37

33

Lynd Range

Taroom

Mundubbera

3

26°S

Dawson River

59

Eurombah Creek

170

Auburn River

Mount Narayen

Yerilla

Hawkwood

Auburn River
National Park
+ Mount Redhead

39

+ Mount Misery

Brovinia

104

+ Mount Organ

Wandoan

Mooyouee Peaks
Tobys Knob +
+

Auburn

4

+ Mount Combabula

Woleebee

Guluguba

Lake
Boond

Muggleton +

+ Chadford
Bendemere

Barakula

Durong

Wallumbilla

Yuleba

Dulacca West
Jackson

54

Thornborough

Dulacca

99

Drillham

Warrego Hwy

Miles

45

Columboola

Fairyland

Cooinda

43

5

114

33

Chinchilla

90

Jandowae

Cooranga North

27°S

Condamine River

Condamine

Brigalow

82

Warra

Marnhull

+ Cooranga

54

Bunya
Mountains

39

Kogan

124

Macalister

Jimbour

Bell

W

Surat
119

Glenmorgan

Undulla

91

Govana

Squaretop

Kaimkillenbun

Quin

6

+ Mount Weribone

Developmental

Meandarra

Tara

Nandi

Dalby

54

Rd

The Gums

70

Kumbarilla

49　44

83

45

A　44　B　C　70　D

10 20 km
5 10 mi

E   F   G   H

1

Many Peaks
Lowmead
Mt Fort William
Mount Molangul
owar   Mount Goondicum
Toonboro Mountain
Rules Beach
Gil Blas Point
Euleilah
Berajondo
Rosedale
Littabella National Park
Yandaran
Avondale
Moore Park
Bucca
Burnett Heads
Bargara
Bundaberg
Mon Repos Beach
& Turtle Rookery
Elliott Heads

CORAL
SEA

Fraser Island, Map 35

Sandy Cape

Rooney Point

Hervey
Bay

Waddy Point

25°S

Indian Head

2

River
Bullyard
Lake Monduran
Gin Gin
Boolboonda
Wolca
Mount Perry
Mount Perry
osslyn
Bandon
Binjour
Mount Steadman
Dallarnil
Mount Orsa
Booyal
Cordalba
Childers
Buxton
Kinkuna National Park
Woodgate
Woodgate National Park
Burrum Point
Burrum Heads
Burrum River National Park
Toogoom
Howard
Torbanlea
Hervey Bay
Mangrove
Point
North Head
Great Sandy
National Park
Fraser Island

3

Burnett River
Gayndah
Coalstoun
Lakes
Biggenden
Billygoan Mountain
Mt Walsh
National Park
Mount Benarige
Mary River
Bruce
Maryborough
Poona
National Park
Sandy Point
Hook Point

Mount Marcella
Mount Urah
Tiaro
Bauple
Gundiah
4

Barambah Creek
Windera
Tansey
Mount Atherton
Gunalda
Wide Bay Hwy
Kilkivan
Proston
Cloyna
Goomeri
Hivesville
Mondure
Goomeri
River
Upper Widgee
Widger Mountain
Glastonbury
Gympie
Wolvi
MILITARY
TRAINING
AREA
Tin Can Bay
Rainbow Beach
Double Island Point
Freshwater Camp
26°S

5

Murgon
Cherbourg
Wondai
Kingaroy
Taabinga
Tingoora
Haly Creek
Wooroolin
Memerambi
Kumbia
Wengenville
aidenwell
Burnett
Hwy
Lake Barambah
Mount Tewoo
Manumbar
Mt Kandanga
Imbil
Brooloo
Amamoor
Kandanga
Pinbarren
Boreen
Pomona
Cooroy
Eumundi
Belli Park
Yandina
Mapleton
Lake Cootharaba
Tewantin
Noosa Heads
Marcus
Peregian Beach
Coolum Beach
Yaroomba
Marcoola
SOUTH
PACIFIC
OCEAN

6

Nanango
Tarong
National
Park
Yarraman
South Nanango
Benarkin
Linville
Moore
Blackbutt
Colinton
Cooyar
Wutul
Highgrove
Djuan
Toogoolawah
Lagan
Kulpi
Haden
Crows Nest
Blackburn
Range
Jimma Range
Brisbane River
Brisbane Range
Mount Spencer
D'Aguilar Hwy
Kilcoy
Woodford
Lake Somerset
Somerset
Dam
Mount Mee
Caboonbah
Stanley River
Mt Beerwah
556m
Wamuran
Kenilworth
Conondale
National Park
Condondale
Yednia
Maleny
Landsborough
Glass House Mountains
Beerburrum
Summer Mountain
Montville
Woombye
Nambour
Bli Bli
Maroochydore
Mooloolaba
Buderim
Palmview
Beerwah
Caloundra
Bribie Island
Bribie Island National Park
Donnybrook
Bongaree
Bulwer
Cape Moreton
27°S

New
England
Hwy

E   F   G   H

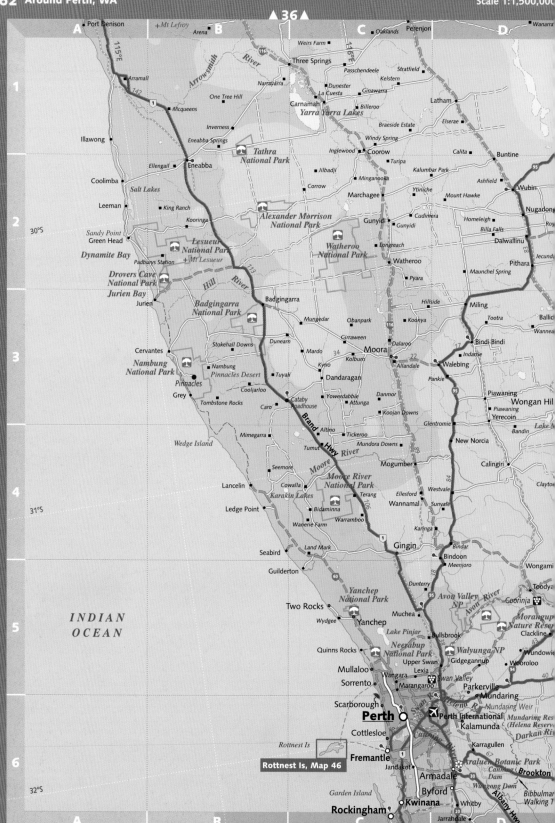

INDIAN
OCEAN

Port Denison
Mt Lefroy
Arena
Oaklands
Perenjori
Wanarra

Arrowsmith River
Weirs Farm
Three Springs
Passchendaele
Stratfield
Arramall
Narrayarra
Dunester
Kelstern
La Cuesta
Ginawarra
Latham
Elserae
Mcqueens
One Tree Hill
Carnamah
Billeroo
Yarra Yarra Lakes
Braeside Estate
Illawong
Inverness
Windy Spring
Eneabba Springs
Inglewood
Coorow
Calita
Buntine
Ellengail
Eneabba
Tathra National Park
Turipa
Nugadong
Coolimba
Jilbadji
Kalumbar Park
Ashfield
Wubin
Corrow
Minganooka
Ytiniche
Mount Hawke
King Ranch
Marchagee
Homeleigh
Billa Falls
Leeman
Kooringa
Alexander Morrison National Park
Gunyidi
Cudimera
Dalwallinu
Sandy Point
Salt Lakes
Gunyidi
Jecunda
Green Head
Lesueur National Park
Longreach
Pithara
Dynamite Bay
Mt Lesueur
Watheroo National Park
Watheroo
Maunchel Spring
Padburys Station
Pyara
Hill River
Drovers Cave National Park
Badgingarra
Hillside
Miling
Ballic
Jurien Bay
Badgingarra National Park
Mungedar
Obanpark
Koonya
Wannea
Jurien
Girraween
Dalaroo
Koonya
Bindi-Bindi
Stokehall Downs
Dunearn
Moora
Tootra
Cervantes
Mardo
Kolburn
Allandale
Walebing
Indarie
Nambung National Park
Nambung Pinnacles Desert
Tuyali
Kyno
Dandaragan
Pankie
Piawaning
Pinnacles
Cooljarloo
Yowerdabbie
Attunga
Danmor
Wongan Hil
Grey
Caro
Cataby Roadhouse
Koojan Downs
Piawaning
Yerecoin
Tombstone Rocks
Altino
Tickeroo
Glentromie
Bandin
Lake
Mimegarra
Tumut
Mundora Downs
Wedge Island
Seemore
Moore River
Mogumber
Calingiri
Clayto
Lancelin
Cowalla
Moore River National Park
Ellesford
Westvale
Karakin Lakes
Terang
Wannamal
Sunvale
Ledge Point
Bidaminna
Warramboo
Karinga
Wanerie Farm
Land Mark
Gingin
Bindar
Wongami
Seabird
Bindoon
Guilderton
Meenjoro
Toodya
Dunterry
Avon Valley
Avon River
Coorinja
Yanchep National Park
NP
Morangup Nature Reser
Two Rocks
Muchea
Clackline
Wydgee
Yanchep
Lake Pinjar
Bullsbrook
Walyunga NP
Wundowie
Quinns Rocks
Neerabup National Park
Upper Swan
Gidgegannup
Wooroloo
Mullaloo
Lexia
Wangara
Swan Valley
Sorrento
Marangaroo
Parkerville
Scarborough
Perth International
Mundaring
Perth
Kalamunda
Mundaring Weir
Mundaring Res (Helena Reservo
Cottlesloe
Darkan Ri
Karragullen
Fremantle
Jandakot
Araluen Botanic Park
Brookton
Rottnest Is
Canning Dam
Rottnest Is, Map 46
Armadale
Waingong Dam
Bibbulmar
Garden Island
Byford
Whitby
Bibbulmar
Walking
Rockingham
Kwinana
Albany Hwy
Jarrahdale
Serpentine

30°S
31°S
32°S
115°E

A   B   △ 62 △   C   △ 63 △   D

115°E

Garden Island   Whitby   Jalna   Brookton

Rockingham   Jarrahdale   Serpentine National Park   Kulyaling

Becher Point   Serpentine   Serpentine Dam   Moorumb

Stake Hill   Keysbrook   Albany   Pingelly

Secret Harbour   Bencullen   Karping

Madora   North Dandalup   Culford   Popanyinning

San Remo   Ravenswood   Wandering   Yornaning

Mandurah   Lake Banksiadale   Cuballing

Peel Inlet   Pinjarra   Hotham Valley   Bannister Downs   Dwarda

Kensington   Tourist Railway   Congelin   Dryandra
Woodland

Dawesville   Dwellingup   Murray River   Narrogin

Yalgorup National Park   Coolup   Boddington   Ranford   Ellerslie   Dumberning

Lake Clifton   Quforty   Waroona   Matlock   Geeralying
High

Lake Clifton   Charla Downs   Hamel   Williams

Preston Beach   Wagerup   Quindanning   Josbury

INDIAN   Old   Lake Preston   Darkan   Dardadine

OCEAN   Coast   Stirling Dam   Stenwood   Hillman

33°S   Rd   Harvey   Bibbulman   Arthur River   Arthur

Myalup   Wokalup   Walking Track   Gibbs Siding   Maybrook   Kylie

Binningup   Benger   Beaufor

Leschenault Inlet   Brunswick   Worsley   Collie   James Crossing   Duranillin   Beaufat

Leschenault   Junction   Burekup   Buckingham   Bowelling   Cordering Farm

Australind   Muja   Talia   Cardiff   Tarwilli

Eaton   Waterloo   Wellington Dam   Glenorchy

Bunbury   Dardanup   Wellington Mill   Cloverdale

Gelorup   Mumballup   Woodlands   Kamballan   Balga

Stratham   Oakland   River

Geographe Bay   Capel   Donnybrook   Newlands   Wilga   River

Cape Naturaliste   Eagle Bay   Ludlow   Yorana   Grimwade   Beninup   Blackwood   Dinninup   Narlingup   Mura

Sugarloaf Rock   Mt Duckworth   Greenwood   Kirup   Boyup Brook   Kulikup

Dunsborough   Busselton   Mullalyup   Balingup   Henty Vale   Jingali

Yallingup   Yoongarillup   Greenbushes   Mayanup   Allambe

Northern Margaret River   Carbunup River   Vasse   Jarrahwood   Hester   153   Holloway

Cape Clairault   Jindong   Walsall   Quongop   Bridgetown   Dorset Down

Leeuwin-Naturaliste   Metricup   Bibilup   Avondale   Mooringa

National Park   Woodlands   Cowaramup   Margaret River   Nannup   Bibbulman   Tone   River

Gracetown   Osmington   Walking Track   Perip

Margaret River   Darradup   Palgarrup   Kanangra   Lyndhurs

Cowaramup Bay   southern Margaret River   Blackwood   River   Manjimup   Unicup   Brae

Prevelly Park   Witchcliffe   Lake   Marranup   Lake Muir

Gnarabup   Forest Grove   River   Nyamup   Padgee   Byenup La

34°S   Lake Cave   Brockman   Vasse   Strachan   Shannon National Park

Cape Freycinet   Hwy   Donnelly   South   Shannon Lodge

Leeuwin-Naturaliste   Karridale Estate   Scott   Beedelup   Western   Shannon   Mount Frankland

National Park   Hamelin Bay   National Park   National Park   Hwy   National Park

Hamelin Bay   Kudardup   Milyeannup   Pemberton   Northcliffe   Mt Frankland

Cosy Corner   Jewel Cave   Lake Jasper   Warren   (422m)

Augusta   Black Point   Warren NP   Gardner River   Walpole-Nornalup   Deep River

Cape Leeuwin   Flinders Bay   D'Entrecasteaux National Park   National Park   Tree Top

SOUTHERN OCEAN   Point D'Entrecasteaux   Windy Harbour   Valley   Walpole   Nornn

35°S   A   B   Broke Reefs   C   Broke Inlet   Point Nuyts   D

Cliffy Head   Chatham Is

Bibbulman Walking Track

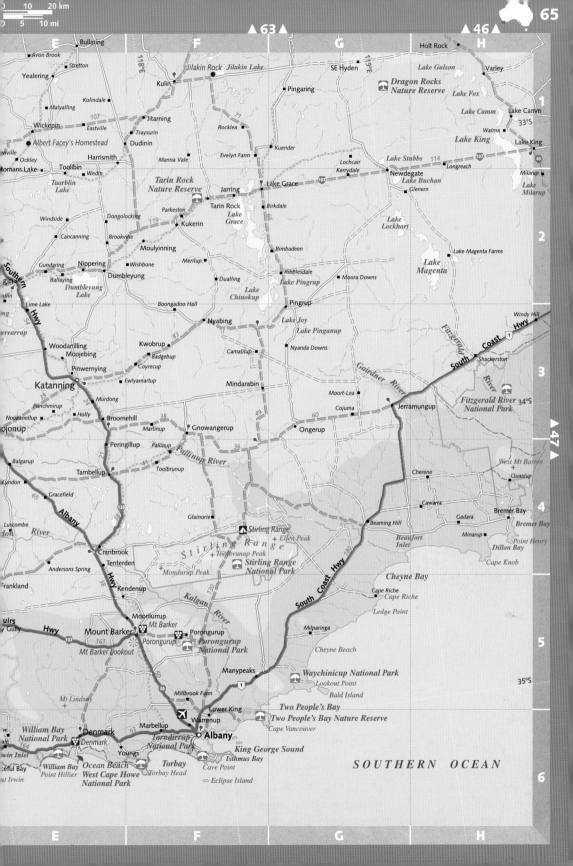

▲ **40** ▲   ▲ **41** ▲

A   **B**   **C**   **D**

Roxby Downs ○

135°E

1

Mount Eba +

87

Lake Curdlawidny

Gosses

WOOMERA PROHIBITED AREA
(Stuart Highway Unrestricted)

Roxby Downs

Purple Downs

Andamook

136°E

North Well

Lake
Younghusband

Lake
Hanson

Arcoona

137°E

Kingoonya

Glendambo

31°S

Coondambo

Lake Hart

Woomera

Fowlers Station

▲ **40** ▲

2

Lake
Harris

113

Lake
Hart

Pimba

Lake Windabout

Yeltacowi

Kokatha

Wirraminna

Island Lagoon

Stuart Hwy

Mount Gunson +

Pernatty

Lake Everard
National Park

Lake Gairdner
National Park

Old Oakden Hills

Pernatty
Lagoon

Lake Everard

Lake Gairdner

Oakden Hills

170

3

Lake Everard

Mahanewo

Lake Finnis

87

Whit

Yalymboo

Lake
Dutton

32°S

Moonaree

Lake
MacFarlane

Lake
Acraman

Mount Hiltaba +
Hiltaba

Mount St Mungo +

Yudnapinna

4

Mount Gairdner +

Gawler Ranges

Cariewerloo

Yardea

Kolendo
Mount Kolendo +

Thurlga

Nonning

Wartaka

Iller

Mount Nott +

Siam

Myall Creek

▲ **48** ▲

5

Uno

Lake
Gilles

Corunna

42

Iron Knob

Minnipa

Pinkawillinie
Conservation Park

Buckleboo

Mt Why

50

Yaninee

Mount Wudinna +

86

53

33°S

Buckleboo

Lake Gilles
Conservation Park

Iron Baron

1

Moonlight Flat

Wudinna

Mount Damper

Kyancutta

92

Koongawa

Kimba

Eyre Hwy

1

108

6

Warramboo

Cocata
Conservation Park

56

Hambridge
Conservation Park

Waddikee

Carappee Hill
Conservation Park

Erainia

Sheoak Hill
Conservation Park

Munyaroo
Conservation Park

Murnini

Gum Flat

A

B

Darke Peak

C

D

0 10 20 km
0 5 10 mi

E · F · G · H

▲ 41 ▲

Copley
Leigh Creek
Mountain Of Light
Aroona Dam
Aroona Sanctuary
Puttapa
Mount Serle
Angepena
Nepabunna
Manners Well
Mount McKinlay
Balcanoona
Italowie Gorge
Wertaloona
Gammon Ranges National Park

Lake Torrens National Park
Beltana
Beltana
Warraweena Sanctuary
NANTAWARRINA ABORIGINAL LAND
Nantawarrina
Pinda Springs
Mulga View
Lake Frome
Lake Frome Regional Reserve

1

Bosworth

FLINDERS RANGES

Narrina

31°S

Lake Torrens
Nilpena
Oratunga
Parachilna Gorge
Parachilna
Angorichina Roadhouse
Blinman
South Blinman
Point Well
Wirrealpa
Mount Chambers Gorge

2

Motpena
Commodore
Flinders Ranges National Park
Oraparinna
Mount Caernarvon

Frome Downs

Brachina Gorge
Bunyeroo Gorge
Martins Well
Erudina
Wilpena Creek

St Mary Peak
Wilpena Pound
Wilpena
Moralana
Lake Torrens
Arkaroo Rock
Rawnsley Park
Sacred Canyon
Willippa
Siccus River
Curnamona

3

South Gap
Cotabena
Arkaba
Wonoka
Glenlyle
Warcowie
Mount Davidson
Druid Range

Glenorchy

Wallerberdina
Kallioota
Hawker
Yourambulla
Holowilena
Bibliando
Baratta
Mount Victoria

32°S

Warrakimbo
Kanyaka
Willow Waters
Mattawarrangala
Milang
Mount Victor
Koonamore
Mount Victor
Plumbago

Yadlamalka
Cradock
Yednalue
Bagalowie
Four Brothers
Morialpa
Bonnie Brae

4

Mount Arden
Partacoona
Mount Ragless South
Belton
Melton
Wabricoola

The Dutchmans Stern Conservation Park
Quorn
Pichi Richi
Olive Grove
Bruce
Carrieton
Minburra
Meadow Downs
Yalpara
Teetulpa
Yunta
Oulnina Park

5

Port Augusta
Stirling North
Mount Brown (970m)
Hammond
Johnburgh
McCoys Well
Paratoo
Tiverton

Winninowie Conservation Park
Wilmington
Willowie
Morchard
Orroroo
Dawson
Nackara
Hill Grange
Manunda

Mount Remarkable National Park
Alligator Gorge
Mount Remarkable (963m)
Melrose
Pekina
Black Rock
Oodla Wirra
Pitcairn
Lilydale

Douglas Point
Conservation Park
Backy Point
Fitzgerald Bay
False Bay
Fullerville
Booleroo Centre
Yatina
Peterborough
Yongala
Porcupine Range

33°S

Whyalla
Lowly Point
Port Germein
Germein Bay
Germein Gorge
Murray Town
Tarcowie
Terowie
Pandappa

6

Spencer Gulf
Mangrove Point
Telowie Gorge Conservation Park
Napperby
Wirrabara
Stone Hut
Appila
Laura
Mannanarie
Caltowie
Jamestown
Pandappa CP
Whyte-Yarcowie
Pine Creek
Bendigo
Faraway Hill
Braemar

Port Pirie
Jarrold Point
Port Davis
Warnertown
Gladstone
Georgetown
Crystal Brook
Terowie
Mallett
Ketchowla
Collinsville
Woolamba
Kia-Ora

E · F · G · H

▲ 49 ▲

▲ 66 ▲

▲ 48 ▲

A

Gum Flat

Bramfield

Barwell
Conservation Park

Bascombe Well
Conservation Park

Flinders Hwy

Sheringa

Oakdale

Mount Misery

Lake
Hamilton

34°S

EYRE

Mount Hope
Drummond Point

Mount Drummond

Lake
Malata

Yeelanna

Lake Greenly

Greenly

Mount Greenly

Coulta

Point Sir Isaac

Gallipoli

Coffin Bay
Farm

Mount Dutton

Wangary

Coffin Bay
Peninsula

**Coffin Bay
National Park**

Avoid Bay

Kellidie Bay CP

Coffin Bay

Point Avoid

Whalers Way

Sleaford
Bay

Cape Carnot
Liguanea Is

Cape Wiles

35°S

**SOUTHERN
OCEAN**

36°S

B

Hambridge
Conservation
Park

Lock

Murdinga

Toologie

Karkoo

72

120

Hincks Conservation Park

105

1

Cummins

Mount Dutton

Warilla

Louth Bay

North Shields
Boston Bay
Boston Is

Port Lincoln

**Lincoln
National Park**

Taylor Is

Grindal Is

West Point
Williams Is

Cape
Catastrophe

C

Carappee Hill
Conservation Park

Darke Peak

Kielpa

Rudall CP

Rudall

Cleve

Arno Bay

Arno Bay
Cape Driver

Port Neill
Cape Hardy

Lincoln Hwy

Lipson Cove

Lipson

Tumby Bay

Tumby Bay
Cape Euler

109

47

Louth Is

Point Bolingbroke

Reevesby Is

Roxby Is

Spilsby Is

Thistle Is

Sheoak Hill
Conservation Park

Mangalo

Yeldulknie CP

Middlecamp Hills
Conservation Park

35

6

Elbow Hill

Port Gibbon

Spencer Gulf

Cape Elizabe

**POINT PEARCE
ABORIGINAL LAND**

Corny Point

Point Annie

Daly Heads

Point Margaret
Formby Bay

Royston Head

Pondalowie Bay

Wreck of the Ethel

D

Munninie

Munyaroo
Conservation Park

Mount Geharty

Mitchellville

Cowell
Franklin Harbour

**Franklin Harbour
Conservation Park**

Balgow

Port Victo

Wardang Is

Port Ric
Hardwicke
Barkers Ro

Bluff Beau
Port Minlacowi
Hardwicke Bay

Warooka

**Warrenben
Conservation Park**

Sturt

**Inney
National Park**

Foul Bay

Marion
Bay

Point Yorke
Hillock Point

Cape Spencer

Investigator Strai

Cape
Cassini

Cape
Dutton

Stokes Bay

Emu

Snelling

Western River Cove

Snug Cove
Cape Torrens

Cape Borda

Western River CP

Cape Torrens CP

Parndana CP

Parndana

95

86

Ma
La

Vennachar Point
West Bay

**Flinders Chase
National Park**

KANGAROO ISLAND

Rocky River

Karatta

Vivonne Bay

Seal Bay C

Cape Bedout

Maupertuis Bay

Cape du Couedic

Cape
Bouquer

**Kelly Hill Caves
Conservation Park**

Vivonne
Bay CP

Vivonne Bay

Gantheaum

Cap
Ganthea

135°E

136°E

137°E

100

1

2

3

4

5

6

A **B** **C** **D**

10   20 km
5   10 mi

E   F   G   H

Wood Point
Fisherman Bay
Crystal Brook
138°E
Georgetown
Merriton
Narridy
Gulnare
Mallett
Woolamba
Collinsville
Kia-Ora
Fords Lagoon
1
Port Broughton
Redhill
Spalding
Hallett
Mount Bryan
139°E
Glenora
Murkaby
Woolgangi
Koomooloo
Old Koomooloo
Mundoora
Brinkworth
Yacka
Mount Bryan
Kungara
Tickera Bay
Snowtown
Booborowie
Burra
Grassville
Tickera
Barunga Gap
Clare
Hanson
Redcliffe
Balah
Alford
Bute
Blyth
Farrell Flat
Black Springs
Samson Well
140°E
Wallaroo
Lochiel
83
Clare Valley
Conservation Park
Watervale
Robertstown
Morgan
Cadell
34°S
Kadina
Kulpara
Hoyleton
Auburn
Manoora
Point Pass
2
Moonta Bay
Clinton CP
Bowmans
Halbury
Rhynie
Marrabel
Bower
Mount Mary
Waikerie
Moonta
Port Wakefield
Balaklava
Saddleworth
Hamilton
Sutherlands
Arthurton
Port Clinton
Owen
Alma
Tarlee
Eudunda
Brookefield
Conservation Park
Blanchetown
Ardrossan
Price
Avon
Pinery
Hamley Bridge
Kapunda
Dutton
Truro
Sturt Hwy
YORKE PENINSULA
Windsor
Mallala
Wasleys
Freeling
Stockwell
Greenock
Nuriootpa
Angaston
Keyneton
Swan Reach
Bakara CP
3
Pine Point
Parham
Dublin
Roseworthy
Barossa Valley
Tanunda
Swan Reach CP
Port Alfred
Black Point
Lower Light
Two Wells
Gawler
Lyndoch
Eden Valley
Sedan
Marne Valley CP
Greenways
Bakara
Mercunda
Port Julia
Angle Vale
Adelaide Plains
Williamstown
Springton
Cambrai
Nildottie
Galga
Minlaton
GULF ST VINCENT
Elizabeth
Kersbrook
Mount Pleasant
49
Port Vincent
Gumeracha
Birdwood
Purnong
Copeville
Houghton
Mount Torrens
Oyster Bay
Port Adelaide
Norton Summit
Lobethal
Mannum
Lowan CP
4
Stansbury
Wool Bay
Adelaide
Adelaide International
Uraidla
Woodside
Balhannah
35°S
Coobowie
Edithburgh
Holdfast Bay
Glenelg
Stirling
Hahndorf
Mount Barker
Perponda
Sultana Point
Belair National Park
Echunga
Monarto
Monarto
Mypolonga
Karoonda
Troubridge Point
Reynella
Clarendon
Wistow
SE Fwy
Murray Bridge
Swanport
Kangarilla
Seaford
McLaren Vale
Macclesfield
Woodchester
Ferries McDonald CP
McLaren Vale
Meadows
Aldinga
Willunga
Strathalbyn
Tailem Bend
5
Aldinga Bay
Mount Compass
Langhorne Creek
Wellington
Carrickalinga
Myponga
Finniss
Milang
Lake Alexandrina
Normanville
Kyeema CP
Spring-Mount CP
Clayton
Yankalilla Bay
Cox's Scrub CP
Narrung
Yumali
Rapid Bay
Inman Valley
Goolwa
Hindmarsh Is
Kiki
Point Marsden
Rapid Bay
Port Elliot
Delamere
Cape Jervis
Victor Harbor
Murray Mouth
Lake Albert
Map 82
Carcuma CP
Cape Jervis
Encounter Bay
Deep Creek
Conservation Park
Newland Head
Conservation Park
Meningie
Coonalpyn
Kingscote
Nepean Bay
Penneshaw
Cuttlefish Bay
Cape Coutts
Antechamber Bay
Cape St Albans
BACKSTAIRS PASSAGE
Younghusband Peninsula
The Coorong
Mount Boothby
Conservation Park
Dukes Hwy
American River
Point Reynolds
Dudley CP
Moncrief Bay
Cape Willoughby
Culburra
Mount Boothby
Tintinara
6
D'Estrees Bay
Cape Hart
Cape Hart CP
Princes Hwy
Point Tinline
Coorong National Park
36°S
Cape Linois
Messent
Conservation Park
Salt Creek
Martins Washpool

▲ 60 ▲ ▲ 61 ▲

A **B** **C** **D**

Moonie River
Kumbarilla
44
151°
49
Moonie Hwy
69
DARLING

1

DOWNS

Tipton

Warrego Hwy
Bowenville
54
Kulpi
Haden
Jondaryan
Sabine
Acland
Goombunge
Jondaryan Woolshed Complex
Mount Maria
85
Oakey
Boodua
Yalangur
Caba

Cecil Plains
Norwin
Bongeen
Aubigny
Kingsthorpe
Highfields
Gowrie
Biddeston
Wellcamp
Mount Tyson
North Branch
Toowoomba
With

2

Weir River
Condamine River
Southbrook
Westbrook
Wyreema

Yarranlea
Brookstead
Cambooya
Turallin
Pampas
85
Pittsworth

QUEENSLAND
Yandilla
Felton East
Greenmount

28°S
Millmerran
Tummaville
Nobby
84
Pilton

Gore Hwy
85
Back Plains
Spring C

3

121
Commoron Creek
70
Mount Emlyn
Ellangowan
Clifton

Mount Domville
Leyburn
Pratten
Allora
Kital

Hendon
Goom

Thanes Creek
Cunningham
Clinto

Mount Bodumba
Thane
Greymare
Freesto

Karara
111
Lake Leslie

4

▲ 44 ▲
Gore
Cement Mills
Warwick
Mount Burrabaranga

Inglewood
Cunningham Hwy
42
15

Whetstone
Lake Coolmunda
Braeside
Elbow Valley

97
Macintyre Creek
Dalveen

Yelarbon
Pozieres
Cottonvale
Gibinbell
Mount Ballaganang
Thulimbah
Dumaresq
Amiens
The Summit
Wylie Cr

Pikedale
Applethorpe

5

Beebo
Liston
Limevale
Stanthorpe
Amosfield

River
Severnlea
Macintyre
Granite Belt
New England Hwy
Yetman
Bruxner Hwy
67
Texas
Pike Creek
Ballandean
Boonoo Boo
National P
Silverspur
Sundown National Park
Severn River
Girraween National Park
Bald Rock
National P

NEW SOUTH WALES
Lake Glenlyon
Boonoo Boonoo
Sandy

Rocky Dam
Wallangarra
29°S
Bonshaw
Mole River
Mole River
Sunnyside
Cataract River
Black Swar

6

Limestone Caves
44
79

102
Tenterfield
Coolatai
A **B** **C** **D**
Bungulla

▼ 72 ▼

0 10 20 km
0 5 10 mi

Brisbane

QUEENSLAND

NEW SOUTH WALES

Crows Nest Falls National Park
Lake Cressbrook
Lake Perseverance
Ravensbourne National Park
Perseverance
Mount Perseverance
Mount Halton
Esk
Brisbane Valley Hwy
Mount Esk
Lake Wivenhoe
Somerset Dam
Caboonbah
Mount Mee
Wamuran
Toorbul
Woorim
Skirmish Point
Bulwer
Cowan Cowan
Mt Tempest
Moreton Island National Park
Caboolture
Bongaree
Beachmere
Burpengary
Deception Bay
Scarborough Point
Tangalooma Resort
Moreton Island
Dayboro
Narangba
Redcliffe
Margate
Brighton
Moreton Bay
Mud Island
Maiala National Park
Mt Glorious
Brisbane Forest Park
Petrie
Lawnton
Sandgate
Albany Creek
Samford
Mount Nebo
Australian Woolshed
Mt Coot-Tha
Wynnum
Manly
Wooloongabba
Darling Point
Wellington Point
Fisherman Islands
St Helena Island National Park
Amity Point
Kooringal
Moreton Island
Peel Island
Oyster Point
Cleveland
Point Lookout
Dunwich
Blue Lake National Park
Victoria Point
Redland Bay
Macleay Island
Russell Island
North Stradbroke Island
Eden Island
SOUTH PACIFIC OCEAN
South Stradbroke Island
Gold Coast
Surfers Paradise
Broadbeach
Burleigh Heads
Coolangatta
Tweed Heads
Banora Point
Chinderah
Kingscliff
Cudgen
Tumbulgum
Murwillumbah
Bogangar
Hastings Point
Pottsville
Mooball
Crabbes Creek
Wooyung
New Brighton
Ocean Shores
Brunswick Heads
Mullumbimby
Tyagarah
Cape Byron
Byron Bay
Broken Head
Bangalow
Newrybar
Lennox Head
Knockrow
Ballina
Empire Vale
Alstonville
Wollongbar
Lismore
McKees Hill
Casino
Bruxner Hwy
Tatham
Coombell
Leeville
Mallanganee
Tabulam
Drake
Mount Richmond
Alice
Pretty Gully
Bonalbo
Old Bonalbo
Mummulgum
Fairy Hill
Bentley
Richmond Range National Park
Kyogle
Ettrick
Cedar Point
Georgica
The Channon
Dunoon
Clunes
Bexhill
Nimbin
Cawongla
Whian Whian State Forest
Mount Nardi (800m)
Billinudgel
Nightcap National Park
The Cape
Wiangaree
Toonumbar
The Risk
Lynchs Creek
Kunghur
Uki
Cudgera Creek
Burringbar
Mount Warning National Park
Mount Warning (1157m)
Oxley River
Tweed River
Chillingham
Tyalgum
Old Grevillia
Grevillia
Rukenvale
Mount Lion
Loadstone
Cougal
Urbenville
Tooloom National Park
Border Ranges National Park
Toonumbar National Park
Woodenbong
Lower Acacia Creek
Legume
Killarney
Tannymorel
Emu Vale
Yangan
Upper Freestone
ryvale
Cunningham Gap
Cunninghams Gap
Spicers Peak
Main Range National Park
Mount Asplenium
Maroon Dam
Maroon
Mount Alford
Boonah
Aratula
Lake Moogerah
Bromelton
Beaudesert
Josephville
Laravale
Kerry
Kooralbyn
Rathdowney
Palen Creek
Innisplain
Mount Alexander
Mount Barney National Park
Mount Barney
Lamington National Park
Mount Waningara
Binna Burra
Hillview
Springbrook National Park
Springbrook
Upper Tallebudgera
Currumbin
Tugun
Palm Beach
Tallebudgera
Neranwood
Mudgeeraba
Numinbah Valley
Beechmont
Advancetown Lake
Advancetown
Gilston
Nerang
Pacific Hwy
Mount Tamborine
Maudsland
Moondarewa
Southport
Eagle Heights
Oxenford
North Tamborine
Tamborine Mountain
Sanctuary Cove
Coomera
Wongawallan
Tamborine
Woodhill
Gleneagle
Jimboomba
Lindesay Hwy
Logan River
Ormeau
Pimpama
Jacobs Well
Yatala
Logan Village
Maclean
Buccan
Stapylton
Beenleigh
Loganholme
Waterford
Greenbank
Browns Plains
Slacks Creek
Logan
Goodna
Churchill
Purga
Ipswich
Rosewood
Calvert
Marburg
Walloon
Laidley
Forest Hill
Hatton Vale
Gatton
Grantham
Ma Ma Creek
Upper Tenthill
Mount Whitestone
Mount Sylvia
Helidon
Hampton
Murphys Creek
Junction View
Mount Haldon
Mount Lowe
Mount Mistake
Main Range National Park
Mount Castle
Mount Cordeaux
Thornton
Mount Bean Brummell
Townson
Warrill View
Rosevale
Fassifern
Kalbar
Harrisville
Millbong
Peak Crossing
Flinders Peak
Warrill Creek
Mistake Mountains
Lowood
Tarampa
Glenore Grove
Brightview
Minden
Glamorgan Vale
Ferrnvale
Coominya
Buaraba Creek
Mount Tarampa
Clarendon
Bryden
Dundas
Alma Park Zoo
Brisbane International
Lone Pine Koala Sanctuary
Capalaba
Mount Richmond

GREAT DIVIDING RANGE

27°S
28°S
29°S

▲ 70 ▲

A B C D

1

Coolatai
Wallangra
Limestone
Ashford
Bukkulla
Severn
Beardy
River
River
Tenterfield
Bungulla
Mole
Bluff Rock
River
Sandy Flat
Bolivia
Mount Bajimba
Stannum
Hwy
England
Strathbogie
Emmaville
Torrington
Deepwater
New
Washpo
National

2

Delungra
Gwydir
Hwy
Kings Plains
National Park
Sapphire
Inverell
Wellingrove
Dundee
Glen Elgin
Timbarra
Gibraltar R
National

Brodies Plains
38
65
Matheson
Glen Innes
Red Range
Mann River
Copeton Dam
Gilgai
Elsmore
Furracabad
Stonehenge
Stannifer
RANGE
Copeton State
Recreation Area
30° S
Stanborough
Tingha
Glencoe

3

Newton Boyd
Guy Fawkes Riv
National Park
97
Ben Lomond
DIVIDING
Wandsworth
15
Backwater
Bundarra
Llangothlin
Guy
Guyra
Fawkes
Mt Hylar

4

Gwydir
River
Guyra River
Black Mountain
Mount Duval
Hernani
Yarrowyck
Cathedral Rock
National Park
Ebor Falls
170
Ebor
Warrabah
National Park
Namoi
GREAT

5

Armidale
Wollomombi
New Engla
National Pa
Rocky River
Hwy
Dangarsleigh
Hillgrove
Wollomombi Falls
Uralla
Jeogla
Watsons Creek
Gostwyck
Dangars Falls
River
New
England
Kentucky
Macleay

6

Moonbi
Range
15
Bendemeer
Wollun
Lower Creek
Comara
31° S
Oxley
Woolbrook
49
Hwy
Baynes Mountain
Bellbrook
Kootingal
34
Walcha
Oxley Wild Rivers
National Park
Nemingha

A B C D

Moona Plains

▲ 44 ▲

10 20 km
5 10 mi

E   F   G   H

Tatham

Coombell

Alice

Wyan

Rappville

Coraki

Ballina

Empire Vale

Wardell

Broadwater

29°S

Broadwater National Park

River

Baryulgil

New Italy

Evans Head

Snapper Point

Camira Creek

Whiporie

Tabbimoble

1

Clarence

Mt Marsh

Fortis Creek
National Park

Bundjalung National Park

Fine Flower

Coaldale

Lawrence Road

Chatsworth

Woody Head

2

Cangai

Maclean

Iluka

Palmers Island

Jackadgery

Lawrence

Harwood

Yamba

Copmanhurst

Brushgrove

Angourie

Ramornie

Eatonsville

Cowper

Tyndale

Shelley Beach Head

mboida
nal Park

Gwydir

Hwy

Ulmarra

Buccarumbi

Chambigne

OBX Creek

Grafton

Tucabia

Brooms Head

3

Clouds Creek

Nymboida

Coutts Crossing

Pillar Valley

Sandon Bluffs

Creek

Dundurrabin

Tyringham

Nymboida
River

Minnie Water

Yuraygir National Park

Bare Point

Wooli

Chaelundi
National Park

Nymboi Binderay
National Park

Halfway Creek

Kungala

Corindi

Red Rock

SOUTH

PACIFIC

154°E

Dunggir
tional Park

Towallum

Glenreagh

Nana Glen

Lowanna
Ulong

Lower Bucca

Arrawarra

Mullaway

Woolgoolga

Emerald Beach

Rocky Bluff

OCEAN

30°S

4

Clarence

River

Orara

River

Pacific

Hwy

stobrick

Megan

Coramba

Korora

Macauley's Headland

Dorrigo
National Park

The

Waterfall

Dorrigo

Gleniffer

Boambee

Coffs Harbour

5

Darkwood

Bellinger

River

Way

Bellingen

Bonville

Sawtell

Bundageree Head

Mylestom

Hungry Head

Urunga

Missabotti

Wenonah Head

Valla

Valla Beach

Bowraville

Tewinga

Nambucca Heads

Nambucca Heads

Macksville

6

Warrell Creek

Scotts Head

Taylors Arm

Stuarts Point

Eungai Creek

Stuarts Point

illawarrin

E   F   G   H

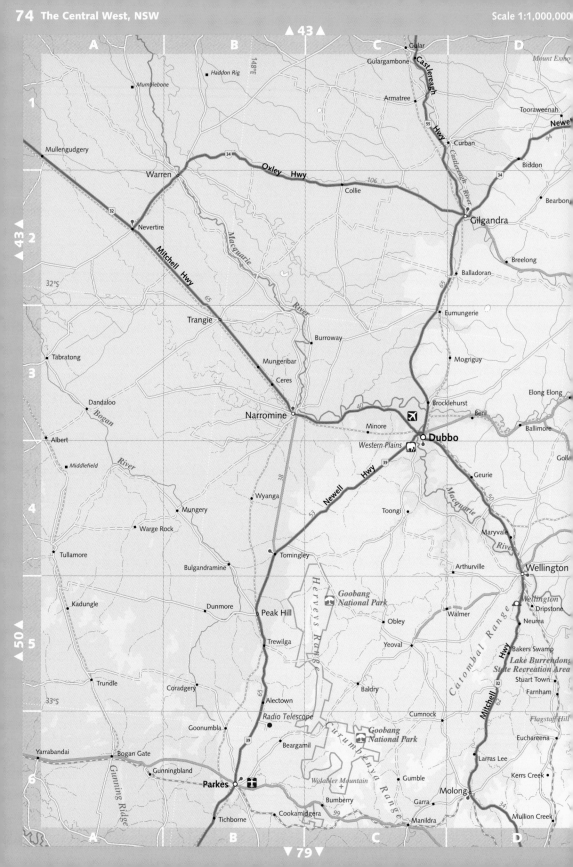

▲ 43 ▲

A   B   C   D

Gular
Gulargambone
Castlereagh
Armatree
Mumblebone
Haddon Rig
Tooraweenah
Newe
Curban
55
148°E
Mullengudgery
34
Oxley Hwy
106
Biddon
Warren
Collie
94
Castlereagh River
Bearbon
32
Hwy
Gilgandra
34
Nevertire
Mitchell Hwy
Macquarie
Breelong
32°S
Balladoran
65
65
Trangie
Eumungerie
River
Burroway
Mogriguy
Tabratong
Mungeribar
Elong Elong
Dandaloo
Ceres
Brocklehurst
Bent
40
Narromine
Ballimore
Bogan
Minore
Golle
Albert
Dubbo
River
Western Plains
Middlefield
Geurie
39
Macquarie
50
38
Newell   Hwy
Toongi
Maryvale
Wyanga
River
Mungery
53
Wellington
Warge Rock
Arthurville
Wellington
Tullamore
Tomingley
Dripstone
Bulgandramine
Catombal Range
Neurea
Kadungle
Herveys Range
Goobang
National Park
Walmer
Bakers Swamp
Dunmore
Peak Hill
Obley
Lake Burrendong
State Recreation Area
Stuart Town
Trewilga
Yeoval
32
Farnham
Trundle
59
Baldry
Mitchell
Coradgery
Alectown
Cumnock
Flagstaff Ra
33°S
Radio Telescope
Curumbenya Range
Hwy
64
Eucharena
Goonumbla
Goobang
National Park
Gumble
Kerrs Creek
39
Beargamil
Yarrabandai
Bogan Gate
Larras Lee
Gunningbland
Wolabler Mountain
Molong
Parkes
Bumberry
Garra
34
Gunning Ridge
Tichborne
Cookamidgera
99
Manildra
Mullion Creek

▼ 79 ▼

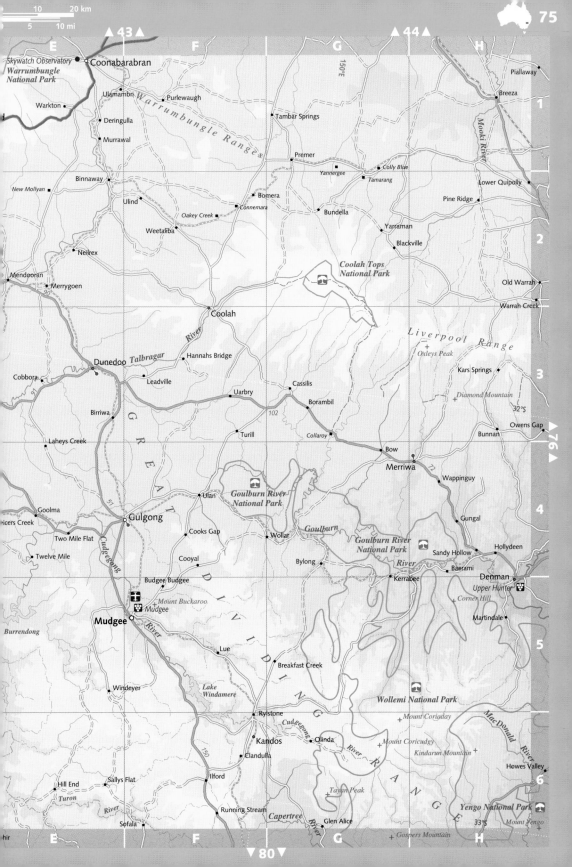

10   20 km
5   10 mi

▲ 43 ▲   ▲ 44 ▲

E   **F**   **G**   **H**

Skywatch Observatory
*Warrumbungle
National Park*   • Coonabarabran   Piallaway •
                                                                        Breeza •   **1**
        • Ulamambn   • Purlewaugh   *Mooki River*
• Warkton   • Tambar Springs

        • Deringulla   • Premer   Lower Quipolly •
                                          Yannergee •   • Colly Blue
        • Murrawal   Tamarang •
New Mollyan •   • Binnaway   • Pine Ridge
                              • Bomera   **2**
            • Ulind   *Oakey Creek* • • Connemara   • Yarraman
                                          • Bundella   • Blackville
            • Weetaliba
                                                                    Old Warrah •
    • Neilrex   **Coolah Tops**
• Mendooran   **National Park**   Warrah Creek •
        • Merrygoen   *Liverpool   Range*
                                                            +
                    • Coolah   *Oxleys Peak*   **3**
                                                                        Kars Springs •
    • Dunedoo *Talbragar* • Hannahs Bridge   *Diamond Mountain*
Cobbora •   • Leadville   +   32°S
                                                                            Owens Gap ▼
    • Birriwa   River   • Uarbry • Cassilis   Bunnan •
                                      102   • Borambil
• Laheys Creek   • Turill   *Collaroy*
                                                            • Bow   **4**
                                                          Merriwa •
                                                                • Wappinguy
            • Ulan   **Goulburn River**   72
• Goolma   **National Park**
                                                                • Gungal
cers Creek • Gulgong • Cooks Gap   • Wollar   *Goulburn*
    • Two Mile Flat   **Goulburn River**   Hollydeen •
• Twelve Mile   • Cooyal   **National Park**
                                      • Bylong   *River*   Sandy Hollow •
                • Budgee Budgee   • Baerami
        ✛   *Mount Buckaroo*   • Kerrabee   **Denman** •   **5**
        ✛ • Mudgee   *Upper Hunter*
Mudgee   + *Corner Hill*
Burrendong   Martindale •
                • Lue
        River
                    • Breakfast Creek
                                                        Wollemi National Park
        • Windeyer   *Lake
                    Windamere*   + *Mount Corioday*
                                                                        MacDonald River
                • Rylstone   *Cudgegong*   + *Mount Coricudgy*
        • Kandos • Olinda   *Kindarun Mountain*   Howes Valley •   **6**
            • Clandulla   *River*
    Hill End • Sallys Flat   • Ilford
Turon   *Tayan Peak*   Yengo National Park
        River   33°S   Mount Yengo
    • Sofala   • Running Stream *Capertree* • Glen Alice   +
                                                  Gospers Mountain

▼ 80 ▼

▲ 44 ▲
▲ 72 ▲

A   B   C   D

Kootingal
Piallaway
Tamworth
Nemingha
Wareel
Duri
Currabubula
Dungowan
Weabonga
Walcha
Moona Plains
Oxley Hwy
Tia River
Apsley River
152°E
Kangaroo
Brackendale
Niangala
Werris Creek
Woolomin
1

Lower Quipolly
Bowling Alley Point
Yarrowitch
34
Myrtle Sca
Quirindi
Nundle
Mount Seaview
2

Willow Tree
Old Warrah
Warrah Creek
Ardglen
Murrurundi
Temple Court
Blandford
Ben Halls Gap National Park
GREAT DIVIDING RANGE
Woko National Park
Manning River
Tibbuc
Knorrit Flat
Apple Tree F
3
Burning Mountain Nature Reserve
Ellerston
Wingen
Moonan Flat
Parkville
Rookhurst
Mount George
Owens Gap
32°S
Gundy
Belltrees
Bundook
Kim
Mount Moobi
Scone
Hunter River
Barrington Tops National Park
Rawdon Vale
Barrington
Gloucester
Belbora
Krambar
4
Aberdeen
Rouchel Brook
Mount Scrumlo
Cockcrow Mountain
Gloucester River
Copeland
Mount Royal
Stratford
Bells Mountain
Craven
Buny
Muswellbrook
Williams River
Chichester River
Salisbury
Eccleston
Wards River
Weismantels
Lake Liddell
Upper Hunter
Liddell
St Clair
Lostock
Halton
Bandon Grove
Bendolba
Upper Myall
Coolongo
Wootto
5
Ravensworth
Mount Olive
Paterson River
Central Mountain
Stroud Road
Markwell
Rosenthal
Jerrys Plains
Camberwell
Gresford
East Gresford
Dungog
Stroud
New England Hwy
Singleton
Glendon Brook
Trevallyn
Booral
Bulahdelah
Warkworth
Mount Thorley
Hunter River
Clarence Town
Williams River
Limeburners Creek
Pacific Hwy
Myall I National
Bulga
Branxton
Greta
Paterson
Karuah
Port Stephens
Tea Gardens
Hunter Valley
North Rothbury
Lochinvar
Hinton
Medowie
Soldiers Point
Hawks Nest
Broke
Morpeth
Tilligerry
Shoal Bay
Howes Valley
Maitland
Nelson Bay
6
Lower Hunter
Neath
Raymond Terrace
Anna Bay
Fingal Bay
Paynes Crossing
Bellbird
Cessnock
Kurri Kurri
Hexham
Tomaree National Park
Yengo National Park
Millfield
Abernethy
Minmi
Mount Yengo
Paxton
Ellalong
Mulbring
33°S
Wollombi

▼ 81 ▼

A   B   C   D

10 20 km
5 10 mi

▲72▲   ▲73▲

E

Oxley Wild Rivers
National Park

Willawarrin   Eungai Creek

153°E

Arakoon State Recreation Area
South West Rocks   Trial Bay Gaol
Jerseyville   Smoky Cape
Kinchela
Smithtown
✈ Fredrickton   Gladstone
Korogoro Point
● Kempsey   Hat Head

Werrikimbe
National Park   Hat Head National Park   **1**

31°S

Pappinbarra
Wilson   Kundabung   Crescent Head
River   Telegraph Point   Crescent Head

Hastings River   Delicate Nobby   **2**
Big Hill Point
Yarras   Ellenborough Falls   Point Plomer
Ellenborough Long Flat
Beechwood   Pembrooke
34   Billabong   Port Macquarie
Wauchope   Koala Park
Byabarra   Hastings Valley
Tacking Point
Comboyne   Lake
Innes   Lake Cathie   **3**
Elands   Queens   Lake Cathie
Kendall   Lake   Bonny Hills
Kew   Grants Head
Bobin   Laurieton   North Haven
Dunbogan
Johns River   Watson Taylors Lake
Lansdowne   Diamond Head
Moorland
Coopernook   Crowdy Bay National Park

Wingham   Crowdy Head
● Taree   Harrington
ll Creek Purfleet
Tinonee
Farquhar Inlet   **4**
Rainbow Flat   Old Bar
biac   Diamond Beach
Red Head
Hallidays Point
Nine Mile Beach
Tuncurry   Forster
Cape Hawke
Green Point   Booti Booti National Park
Wallis
ific Palms Lake
Elizabeth Beach   **5**
Boomerang Beach
Blueys Beach
Bungwahl
Seal Rocks

32°S

SOUTH
PACIFIC
OCEAN   **6**

F   **G**   **H**

Norfolk Island   Scale 1:100,000

0   1   2 km
0 0.5   1 mi

167°56'E

Point Vincent
Duncombe   Captain Cook
Bay   Memorial   SOUTH
Anson   Bird Rock   PACIFIC
Point   OCEAN
Anson
Bay   Mt Bates
(321m)   Cascade
Mt Pitt   Norfolk Island   Bay
(320m)   National Park
Puppy's   Cascade   Steels
Point   Botanic Gardens   Bridge   Point
Broken   Creek
Cascade Rd   Cascade
Mission Rd
St Barnabas Chapel   Burnt Pine   Norfolk Island
Watermill   Middlegate   Stockyard Rd
Headstone   Creek   Point
Point   Blackbourne
Rocky   Ball Bay
Point   Kingston   Collins Head
Sydney   Cemetery
Bay   Emily Cemetery Bay
Point Ross   Bay Golf Course
Point
Hunter

29°04'S

Nepean
Island

▲50▲

A B C D

Mern Merrigal

Lake Brewster

Burgooney

Tullibigeal

Bogandillon Swamp

1

146°E

147°E

Mount Bygalorie

Weja

Bena

Nerang Cowal

Naradhan

Gubatta

Kikoira

Thulloo

Ungarie

96

Lake Cowal

Newell H

Rankins Springs

2

Erigolia

Mid Western Hwy

Weethalle

Yalgogrin

144

24

West Wyalong

39

Marsden

24

37

Wyalong

34°S

Buddigower

Cocoparra National Park

Mount Brogden

Alleena

Belarwi

49

Barmedman

Morang

Murrumbidgee

Beelbangera

Binya

3

Yenda

Bilbul

82

Barellan

Moombooldool

Kamarah

79

Mirrool

Ariah Park

85

Reefton

Gidginbung

Griffith

Narrandera Range

Ardlethan

Quandary

94

Brobenah Hills

Colinroobie

48

Temora

4

Whitton

88

Wamoon

Mount Misery

39

Spring

Leeton

Yanco

99

Mimosa

Sebastopol

Sturt Hwy

20

Narrandera

Grong Grong

Junee Reef

5

Cuddell

Matong

82

Newell Hwy

Corobimilla

Ganmain

Coolamon

Marrar

Old Junee

Illabo

Morundah

144

Murrumbidgee River

Junee

Sandigo

75

35°S

39

Kywong

Galore

Currawarna

Millwood

Downside

Harefield

Eurongil

Widgiewa

Birrego

20

Sturt Hwy

Boree Creek

Galore Scenic Reserve

Collingullie

24

Wagga Wagga

Wantabadgery

6

Lake Urana

Lake Cullivel

Yuluma

Gumly Gumly

Forest Hill

Kapooka

Alfred Town

Cullivel

Lockhart

Milbrulong

31

Uranquinty

A B C D

▼87▼

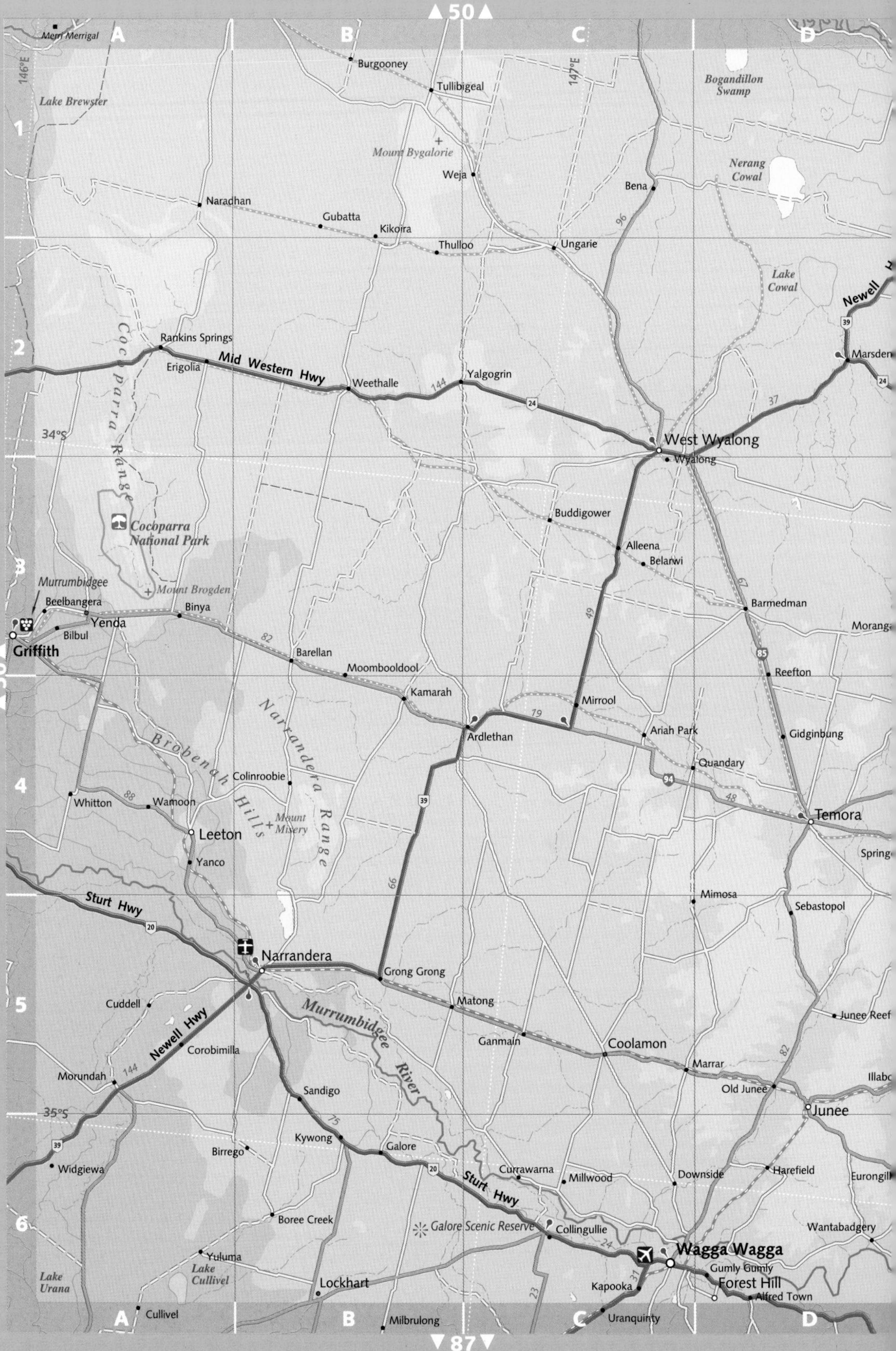

10   20 km
5   10 mi

E   F   G   H

Map place names and features:

Tichborne
Cookamidgera
Manildra
Mullion Creek
Ophir

Bedgerebong
Daroobalgie
House Of Lords Mountain
Cudal
Cheesemans Creek
Borenore
Nashdale
Orange Wineries
Orange
Newell Hwy
148°E
39
Forbes
Toogong
Mount Canobolas (1395m)
Lucknow
Byng
Shadforth

Grawlin
Eugowra
Mt Taylor
Mt Nangar
Nangar National Park
Cargo
Columbine Mountain
Forest Reefs
Beneree
Millthorpe

Bundaburrah
Garema
Tallabung Mountain
Lachlan
Canowindra
Blayney
Carcoar

Wirrinya
Gooloogong
Soldiers Mountain
Walli
Mt Macquarie
Mandurama
Neville

Ooma Creek
Warraderry
Billimari
Lyndhurst
Garland
Hobbys Yards

Pullabooka
River
Woodstock

Caragabal
Bogolong
Conimbla National Park
Yambira Mountain
Cowra
Holmwood
Pine Mountain

Berendebba
Grenfell
Mid Western Hwy
Cowra
Trunkey Creek

Weddin Mountains National Park
Black Spring Mountain
Broula
Bumbaldry
Noonbinna
Darbys Falls Observatory
Darbys Falls
Wyangala Waters State Recreation Area
Lake Wyangala
Abercrombie

Quandialla
Weddin Mountain Range
Bimbi
Greenethorpe
Wattamondara
Morongla Creek
Wyangala
34°S

Bribbaree
Mount Crowther
Koorawatha
Mount Darling
Tuena

Thuddungra
Wirrimah
Crowther
Bigga
Blanket Flat

Monteagle
Bendick Murrell
Godfreys Creek

Grogan
Milvale
Tubbul
Taylors Flat
Frogmore
Crookwell River
Binda

Young
Murringo
Gunnary
Rugby
Narrawa

Stockinbingal
Wombat
Kingsvale
Boorowa

Nubba
Wallendbeen
Rye Park
Bevendale
Wheeo
Grabben Gullen
Biala

Baulkora Hill
Murrumburrah
Harden
Cunningar
Galong
Kangiara
Pudman Creek
Gurrundah

Cootamundra
Bethungra Mountain
Beggan Beggan
McMahons Reef
Mount Bobbara
Binalong
Tangmangaroo
Lachlan River

Brawlin
Bethungra
Mount Ulandra
Muttama
Muttama Hill
Illalong Creek
Dalton

Goondah
Bowning
Coolalie
Jerrawa
Gunning
Breadalbane

The Sisters
Wambidgee
Jugiong
Hume Hwy
31
Bookham
Yass
Yass River
Mount Dixon

Coolac
Pettit
The Dog on the Tuckerbox
Burrinjuck State Recreation Area
Murrumbateman
Bellmount Forest
Collector
Currawang
35°S

Nangus
Gundagai
Kangaroo Mountain
Burrinjuck
Burrinjuck Dam
Murrumbateman
Gundaroo

Adjungbilly

E   F   G   H

▲ 80 ▼

1 2 3 4 5 6

▲ 75 ▲

33°S

A | B | C | D

Running Stream

Sofala

Ophir

Glen Alice

Gospers Mountain

150°E

Turon River

Capertee

Wollemi National Park

69

1

The Brothers Mountain

Ben Bullen

Glen Davis

Capertee River

Colo River

Byng

Peel

Macquarie River

Cullen Bullen

86

Dunkeld

Portland

Lidsdale

Colo Heigh

32

Bathurst

Great

Western

Hwy

Wallerawang

Colo River

2

Blayney

Perthville

Georges Plains

Locksley

Mount Lambie

Rydal

Lithgow

Mount Wilson

Bilpin

Blue Mountains, Map 45

Newbridge

Moorilda

Mount Evernden

Mount Tarana

32

Hartley

Mt Tomah Botanic Gardens

40

Freemans Reach

Wilbe

Ben Chifley Dam

Coxs River

Mt Victoria

69

Richmond

Hobbys Yards

Charlton

Hampton

Blackheath

Bridal Veil Falls

Blue Mountains National Park

Windsor

Rockley

Mount Bindo

Oberon

Blue Mountains National Park

Springwood

32

Penrith

3

Trunkey Creek

Lake Oberon

Katoomba

34°S

Abercrombie

Edith

Jenolan State Forest

Lawson

55

Nepean River

National

Burraga

Black Springs

Jenolan

Blue Mountains

M4 Western Mw

Tuena

Abercrombie River

Shooters Hill

Mount Guouogang

Mulgoa

44

Porters Retreat

Wallacia

▲ 79 ▲

Peelwood

Abercrombie River National Park

Mount Werong

Kanangra-Boyd National Park

Liverpoo

Lake Burragorang

Luddenham

4

Limerick

Black Bett Mountain

Mount Colong

Blue Mountains National Park

Cobbitty

Fullerton

Blue Mountains National Park

Oakdale

The Oaks

Camden

Campbellto

M5

Thalaba

Camden

Menangle

Western

Binda

Golspie

Richlands

Nattai National Park

Thirlmere Lakes National Park

Picton

South

Appin

Heathcote National Park

Helensbu

Wombeyan

Couridjah

Thirlmere

Laggan

Mount Wanganderry

Buxton

Tahmoor

Wilton

89

Stanwell P

5

Crookwell

McAllister

Mount McAlister

Bargo

Myrtleville

Wollongong

Kiala

Chatsbury

Hilltop

Yanderra

31

Colo Vale

Yerrinbool

88

Thirro

Bulli

Bannister

Woodhouselee

Tarlo River National Park

Southern

Port Kemb

Gurrundah

Mount Wayo

Tarlo

Mittagong

Mount Lindsey

Berkeley

Kingsdale

Bowral

Lake Illawarra

Kenmore

Hume Hwy

Exeter

Moss Vale

Macquarie Pass National Park

Albion Park

Shellharbour

Goulburn

Marulan

Penrose

Robertson

50

Bass Point

6

Breadalbane

Yarra

Mount Towrang

Towrang

Wingello

Bundanoon

Fitzroy Falls

Budderoo National Park

Jamberoo

Kiama

31

Tirrannaville

Tallong

Budderoo National Park

Princes

Kiama

23

Komungla

Bungonia

Kangaroo Valley

Berry

Gerroa

Gerringong

Collector

Black Head

35°S

Currawang

Morton National Park

Cambewarra

Seven Mile Beach National Park

Bomaderry

Shoalhaven Heads

A | Lake Bathurst | B | C | **Nowra** | Comerong Is | D

▼ 89 ▼

▲ 76 ▲

10   20 km
5   10 mi

E   **F**   **G**   **H**

Paxton
Ellalong
Wollombi
Mulbring
Minmi

151°E
152°E

Mt Yengo
Port Hunter
○ **Newcastle**

Yengo
National Park

Freemans Waterholes
Charlestown
Warners Bay

Mount Warrawolong

Koolang
Astronomical
Observatory
Awaba
Toronto
Belmont

33°S

Bucketty
Coorandong
Morisset
Wangi Wangi
111

Kulnura
Swansea

Lake
Macquarie
Nords Wharf

Jilliby
Wyee
Catherine Hill Bay

St Albans
☐ **Munmorah State Recreation Area**

Peats Ridge
Wyong
Budgewoi

Wisemans Ferry
Tuggerah
Toukley

Dharug
National Park
Tuggerah
Lake
Norah Head

Mount Olive
Ourimbah
The Entrance

Marramarra NP
Cowan
○ Gosford
☐ **Wyrrabalong National Park**

Glenorie
Terrigal
Avoca

Galston
○ Woy Woy
☐ **Bouddi National Park**

Brisbane Waters
National Park
Pearl Beach

Patonga
Broken Bay

Barrenjoey Head
Palm Beach

Hornsby ○
Ku-Ring-Gai Chase
National Park

Frenchs
Forest
Mona Vale

Long Reef Point
Dee Why

Parramatta
Manly
☐ **Sydney Harbour National Park**

Ryde
Port Jackson

○ SYDNEY
Bondi

Bankstown
Coogee

Kingsford Smith International

Botany
Bay
La Perouse

☐ **Botany Bay National Park**

34°S

hcote
Bate Bay

Cronulla

Royal
National Park

Garie

Lord Howe Island   Scale 1:125,000

0   1   2 km
0   0.5   1 mi

159°05'E

Admiralty
Islands

31°30'S

Sugarloaf
Soldiers Cap
Passage

Fishy
Point
Kims
Malabar Hill
(210m)

Mt Eliza
(150m)
Neds Beach

North
Head
North
Bay
Searles Point

Hunter
Bay
Clear Place
Point

Lagoon
Beach

Blackburn
Island
Transit Hill
(120m)

Blinky Beach

Blinkenthorpe
Bay
Mutton Bird
Island

Prince William
Henry Bay
Mutton Bird
Point

Lovers
Bay
Intermediate
Hill (258m)
Rocky Run
Boat Harbour

Salmon Beach

**SOUTH
PACIFIC
OCEAN**

Mt Lidgbird
+ (777m)
East
Point

George Bay

Little Island
Red
Point

Lord Howe Island
The
Saddle

31°35'S

Mt Gower
+ (875m)

TASMAN SEA

King
Point

**SOUTH
PACIFIC
OCEAN**

E   **F**   **G**   **H**

▲ 49 ▲

A   **B**   **C**   **D**

Map 69

Kiki

140°E

141°E

Carcuma
Conservation Park

Mount Timothy

Mount Timothy

Mount Timothy

Scorpion Springs
Conservation Park

Coonalpyn

1

Big Desert
Wilderness Pa

Ngarkat
Conservation Park

Mount Boothby
Conservation Park

Culburra

Mount Boothby

Emu Springs

Tintinara

Mount Shaugh

Mount Shaugh
Conservation Park

◄ 49 ►
◄ 49 ►

38

36°S

2

Messent
Conservation Park

**SOUTH
AUSTRALIA**

Mount Rescue

Mount Rescue
Conservation Park

Keith

VICTORIA

Salt Creek

Martins Washpool

Coorong
National
Park

Martins Washpool
Conservation Park

Dukes Hwy

46

Telopea D

Younghusband Peninsula

83

Mount Monster

Mount Monster
Conservation Park

Dinyarrak

Wolseley

80

Lillimur

3

Gum Lagoon
Conservation Park

8

Bordertown

Serviceton

Kani

Princes Hwy

Mundulla

113

Jip Jip
Conservation Park

Desert Camp
Conservation Park

4

**SOUTHERN
OCEAN**

Padthaway
Region

Padthaway
Conservation Park

Little Desert
National Park

Padthaway

Bangham
Conservation Park

Keppoch

Frances

Minima

108

Kingston SE

Mount Scott
Conservation Park

Fairview
Conservation Park

Binnum

Lacepede Bay

Butchers Gap
Conservation Park

Kybybolite

Cape Jaffa

Reedy Creek

37°S

Avenue

Lucindale

Naracoorte

Hynam

Apsley

5

1

67

54

Cape Thomas

Naracoorte Caves
Conservation Park

Guichen Bay

Cape Dombey

Crower

Eden

Robe

Big Heath
Conservation Park

Bool
Lagoon

Bool Lagoon
Game Reserve &
Hacks Lagoon
Conservation Park

Langkoop

Little Dip
Conservation Park

Lake
Eliza

Greenways

Poolaijelo

Lake
St Clair

Bailey's Ro

6

Cape Rabelais

Clay Wells

36

63

Coonawarra

C211

Coonawarra

Lake
George

Penola

Dergh

Beachport

A   **B**   **C**   **D**

▼ 90 ▼

0 10 20 km
0 5 10 mi

Big Billy Bore

Wyperfeld National Park

Big Desert

Mount Mattingley

142°E

Turriff

Sea Lake

Moonlight Tank

Lascelles

Sumraysia Hwy

Woomelang

Lake Albacutya

Yaapeet

Hopetoun

Curyo

Wagon Flat

Broken Bucket Tank

Broken Bucket Camp

Rainbow

C227

C243

Beulah

Western Stream

Birchip

36°5

Wimmera

C245

B200

Brim

Netherby

Jeparit

Watchem

Broughton

Yanac

Tarranyurk

Lake Buloke

Lorquon

Antwerp

Borung Hwy

Warracknabeal

C234

B220

Litchfield

Boyeo

Miram

Diapur

Nhill

Salisbury

A8

Kiata

Gerang Gerung

38

40

Sheep Hills

Western Hwy

Winiam

Pink Lake

Donald

85

Little Desert Lodge

Dimboola

Wail

Garup

Minyip

Richardson River

142°E

Little Desert National Park

Little Desert

Wimmera River

36

Pimpinio

Rich Avon

Rupanyup North

Banyena

Goroke

Gymbowen

Lake Wynwyn

Mitre Lake

Mitre

Mt Arapiles

Dooen

Murtoa

B240

Rupanyup

Wimmera Hwy

Marnoo

Horsham

The Grampians (Gariwerd), Map 84

Wallaloo

Natimuk

Wimmera Hwy

Vectis South

Haven

Pine Lake

Lubeck

C235

C235

Kanya

C240

Noradjuha

Wonwondah North

Mackenzie River

Mt Zero

Mount Stapylton

Laharum

Dadswells Bridge

Glenorchy

Campbells Bridge

Clear Lake

98

Wimmera River

37°S

Wombelano

Toolondo Reservoir

Mount Talbot

A200

Henty Hwy

The Black Range

Mount Difficult Range

Lake Lonsdale

Deep Lead

Mount Dryden

Stawell

Concongella

Douglas

White Lake

Byron Mount

Mt Gar (Mount Difficult) (810m)

Zumsteins

Lake Wartook

McKenzie Falls

Mount Victory

Bugara

Halls Gap

Lake Fyans

Bunjils Shelter

Great Western

Kadnook

Harrow

Glenelg River

Mount Bepcha

THE GRAMPIANS

Rocklands Reservoir

Buandik Mount Thackeray

Lake Bellfield

Mount Didjun Cassel

Pomonal

Grampians National Park

Grampians

Jallukar

Ararat

B180

Chetwynd

C206

Balmoral

C216

Moyston

Mount Arnot

A8

Vasey

The Chimney Pots

Mooralla

207

90

91

The Grampians (Gariwerd), Vic

Scale 1:500,000

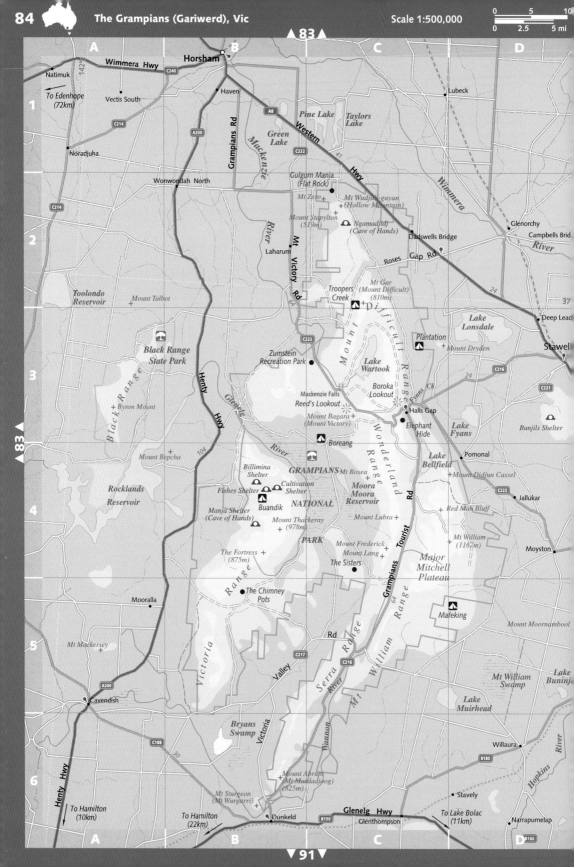

A

Wimmera Hwy
Natimuk
To Edenhope (72km)
Vectis South
Noradjuha
C214
C214
A200
Grampians Rd
Wonwondah North
Haven
Horsham
A8
Western Hwy
Pine Lake
Green Lake
Taylors Lake
Lubeck
Glenorchy
Campbells Brid
River
Mackenzie River
Mt Victory Rd
Laharum
Gulgurn Manja (Flat Rock)
Mt Zero
Mount Stapylton (519m)
Mt Wudjub-guyun (Hollow Mountain)
Ngamadjidj (Cave of Hands)
Dadswells Bridge
Roses Gap Rd
Wimmera
Toolondo Reservoir
Mount Talbot
Black Range State Park
Byron Mount
Mount Bepcha
Mt Gar (Mount Difficult) (810m)
Troopers Creek
Mount Difficult Range
Zumstein Recreation Park
Lake Wartook
Plantation
Mount Dryden
Lake Lonsdale
Deep Lead
Stawell
C222
Henty Hwy
Glenelg River
Mackenzie Falls
Reed's Lookout
Mount Bagara (Mount Victory)
Boreang
Boroka Lookout
Fyans Ck
Halls Gap
Elephant Hide
Lake Fyans
Bunjils Shelter
C216
C221
Rocklands Reservoir
Billimina Shelter
Fishes Shelter
Cultivation Shelter
Buandik
Manja Shelter (Cave of Hands)
GRAMPIANS
NATIONAL
PARK
Mt Rosea
Moora Moora Reservoir
Mount Thackeray (978m)
Mount Lubra
Red Man Bluff
Lake Bellfield
Mount Didjun Cassel
Pomonal
Jallukar
Moyston
Mt William (1167m)
Grampians Tourist Rd
Wonderland Range
C222
Mooralla
The Fortress (875m)
The Chimney Pots
Victoria Range
Mount Frederick
Mount Lang
The Sisters
Major Mitchell Plateau
Mafeking
Mount Moornambool
Mt Mackersey
A200
Cavendish
Serra Range
Victoria Valley Rd
C217
C216
Mt William Range
Wannon River
Mt William Swamp
Lake Buninj
Lake Muirhead
Bryans Swamp
C188
Mount Abrupt (Mt Mudadjoog) (825m)
Mt Sturgeon (Mt Wurgarri)
Willaura
B180
Hopkins River
Henty Hwy
To Hamilton (10km)
To Hamilton (22km)
Dunkeld
B150
Glenelg Hwy
Glenthompson
To Lake Bolac (11km)
Stavely
Narrapumelap
B160

A   **B**   **C**   **D**

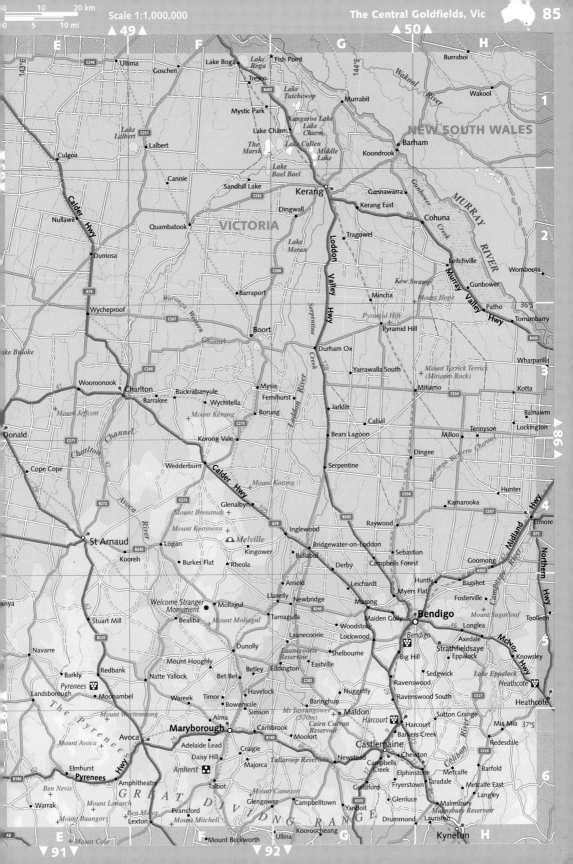

10   20 km
0   5
10 mi

▲ 49 ▲   ▲ 50 ▲

E   **F**   **G**   **H**

1
C246
Ultima   Goschen   Lake Boga   Lake Boga   Fish Point
Lake Tutchewop   Burraboi
B400   Wakool
Mystic Park   Tresco
Lake Charm   Kangaroo Lake   Murrabit
Lake Lalbert Lake Charm   Lake Charm
C51   The Marsh   Lake Cullen Middle Lake   NEW SOUTH WALES
Lalbert   Koondrook   Barham
Culgoa   Cannie   Lake Bael Bael
Sandhill Lake   Gannawarra
Calder Hwy   C262   Kerang   Kerang East   Cohuna
Nullawil   Dingwall
Quambatook   VICTORIA   Tragowel   Murray River
A79   Barraport   Lake Meran Mincha   Leitchville
Dumosa   Loddon Valley Hwy   Gunbower   Womboota
Wycheproof   C266   Pyramid Hill Kow Swamp   Patho   36°S
C267   Boort   Mount Hope   Torrumbarry
Lake Buloke   Durham Ox   Yarrawalla South   B400
Wooroonook   Channel   Mount Terrick Terrick   Wharparilla
C266   Charlton   Mysia   (Mitiamo Rock)   Kotta
Donald   Barrakee   Fernihurst Jarklin   Mitiamo   Bamawm
Mount Jeffcott Buckrabanyule Wychitella Calivil   Lockington
C271   Mount Kerang Borung   Milloo   Tennyson
Charlton Channel C273   Korong Vale Bears Lagoon   Dingee
Cope Cope   Wedderburn   Calder Hwy   Serpentine Yorinbga Western Channel
B272   Mount Korong   Hunter
Avoca River   C273   Glenalbyn   Inglewood   B260   Kamarooka
St Arnaud   Mount Brenanah   Raywood   C337
B240   Mount Kooyoora Melville   Bridgewater-on-Loddon   Goornong   Elmore
Logan   Kingower   Bullabul   Sebastian   A300   375
Kooreh   Burkes Flat   Rheola   Derby   Campbells Forest Huntly Bagshot
Navarre   Arnold   Leichardt   Marong   Myers Flat Fosterville
Stuart Mill   Llanelly   Newbridge   Maiden Gully Bendigo   Toolleen
Welcome Stranger Moliagul   B240   Woodstock   Mount Sugarloaf Longlea
Monument   Mount Moliagul Tarnagulla   Lockwood   Bendigo   Axedale Knowsley
Barkly   Bealiba   Laanecoorie Shelbourne Big Hill   Strathfieldsaye Lake Eppalock
Redbank   Dunolly   Luanecoorie Eastville   Eppalock   Heathcote
Pyrenees   Mount Hooghly Reservoir   Nuggetty   Ravenswood C327
Landsborough Natte Yallock Betley   Eddington   Ravenswood South
Moonambel   Timor   Havelock   Baringhup   Sutton Grange
Wareek   Simson   Mt Tarrangower Maldon Harcourt   Mia Mia 37°S
The Pyrenees Alma   Carisbrook   (570m)   Harcourt Barkers Creek Redesdale
Mount Avoca   Maryborough Adelaide Lead Craigie   Cairn Curran Chewton C326
Avoca   Daisy Hill   Moolort   Reservoir   Castlemaine Barfold
Elmhurst   Amherst   Majorca   Newstead   Campbells Creek Metcalfe
Pyrenees   Talbot   Glengower   Campbelltown Guildford Elphinstone Metcalfe East
Ben Nevis   Evansford   Mount Cameron Yandoit   Glenluce   Fryerstown Langley
Warrak   Lexton   Kooroocheang Drummond   Malmsbury Reservoir Malmsbury
Mount Buangor Mount Mitchell Ullina   GREAT DIVIDING RANGE Lauriston
A8   Mount Cole   Mount Beckworth   Kyneton

▼ 91 ▼   ▼ 92 ▼

E   **F**   **G**   **H**

▲ 50 ▲

A B C D

NEW SOUTH WALES

VICTORIA

145°E | 145°E

1

Conargo
Dahwilly
Jerilderie
Lake

Mayrung
Logie Brae

Deniliquin

Riverina Hwy
Cobb Hwy
Blighty
58

Finley
Berrigan
Oak
Re

2

Mathoura
Savernake

MURRAY RIVER
Womboota
Barmah State Forest
Lake Moira
103
Tocumwal
Warragoon

Koonoomoo
Strathmerton
Barooga
Cobram
Cobram
Murray Valley Hwy
Burramine
Mulwala
Lake Mulwala

3

Wharparilla
Moama
Kanyapella
Barmah
Barmah East
Narioka
Barwo
Nathalia
Waaia
Picola
B400
Katunga
Numurkah
Katamatite
Yarrawonga
B400
Bundalong

Echuca
Murray Valley Hwy
Koyuga
Kotupna
Goulburn River
Kaarimba
Wunghnu
Invergordon North
Youanmite
Telford
Boomahnoomoonah
Wilby

Bamawm
B75
Tongala
Wyuna
Wyuna East
St Germains
Bunbartha
C363
Katandra West
Yabba North
Tungamah
C373

Nanneella
Kyvalley
Undera
Tallygaroopna
Katandra
Lake Rowan
Mount Killawarra

4

Fairy Dell
Kyabram
Lancaster
Congupna
Yabba South
St James
Mount

Rochester
Timmering
Willowdene
Gillieston
Mooroopna North
Lemnos
Cosgrove
Dookie
Devenish
Thoona
Mount War

Girgarre
Merrigum
Ardmona
Shepparton
Mount Major
C371
Gooram bat
Mount Meg
Mount

Midland Hwy
Byrneside
75
Mooroopna
Midland Hwy
A300
60
Glenrowan

Corop
Stanhope
Girgarre East
Tatura
Hendersyde
Kialla
Caniambo
Upotipotpon
Glenrow

Elmore
Lake Cooper
Carag Carag
Harston
Toolamba West
Toolamba
Koonda
Lake Mokoan

Mount Burramboot
C356
Dhurringile
Tamleugh North
Winton
Greta V

Colbinabbin
Mathiesons
C347
Arcadia
Tamleugh West
Benalla
Baddaginnie
Greta S

5

Colbinabbin West
C145
Rushworth
Murchison
Murchison East
Moglonemby
Lurg
Lurg Up

Northern Hwy
Waranga Basin
Whroo Historic Reserve
Violet Town
Mount Pleasant
Kilfeera

Mount Camel
Reedy Lake
Wahring
M31
Warrenbayne
Mount Beller
Tatong

Mount Camel
Goulburn Weir
Goulburn Weir
Euroa
Boho South
Swanpool
Myrr

Mount Block
Nagambie
Lake Nagambie
Longwood
Strathbogie
Midland Hwy
B300
Drum Ti

6

Mount Ida
Graytown
C344
A39
Nagambie
Mitchellstown
Hume Fwy
Gooram
Strathbogie Ranges
Mount Strathbogie
Tallangallook
Tolmie

Heathcote
Costerfield
Avenel
Ruffy
Mount Wombat
Maroondah Hwy
Merton
Bonnie Doon
Mount Battery

Tooborac
C384
PUCKAPUNYAL MILITARY AREA
Mount Bernard
Mount Alexina
Mangalore
Northwood
Mount Puckapunyal
Puckapunyal
Strathbogie
Maindample
Lake Eildon
Mansfield
Merrijig

Pyalong
B75
Northern Hwy
Tallarook
Seymour
Goulburn Valley Hwy
Highlands
Mount Stewart
Yarck
Mount Concord
Lake Eildon National Park

Moranding
Mount William
Broadford
Tyaak
Trawool
Yea
B340
Molesworth
Alexandra

A B C D

▼ 92 ▼ | ▼ 93 ▼

◄ 85 ◄

10 20 km
5 10 mi

E F G H

Lake Cullivel
Lockhart
Kapooka
Alfred Town
Milbrulong
Uranquinty
Forest Hill
Cullivel
The Rock
Nature Reserve
French Park
Tootool
Ladysmith
Pleasant Hills
The Rock Hill
The Rock
Tarcutta
Yerong Creek
Urangeline East
Mangoplah
Oberne
Munyabla
Burrandana
Kilgowla
Mountain
Henty
Kyeamba
Rand
Cookardinia
Humula
Daysdale
Bulgandry
Walbundrie
Culcairn
Morven
Little Billabong
Carabost
Coreen
Hume Hwy
Lowesdale
Walla Walla
Holbrook
Lankeys Creek
Buraja
Brocklesby
Gerogery
Woomargama
Mount Narra Narra
Balldale
Burrumbuttock
Mullengandra
Corowa
Howlong
Jindera
Bowna
Dora Dora
Jingellic
Wahgunyah
Rutherglen
Mount Ophir
Table Top
Talmalmo
Ournie
Valley
Olympic Hwy
Ettamogah
Wildlife
Sanctuary
Wagra Mountain
Thologolong
Walwa
Rutherglen
Hwy
Lake Hume
MURRAY RIVER
Barnawartha
Albury
Talgarno
Wymah
Burrowye
Mount Lawson
Pine Mountain
Burrowa-Pine Mountain
National Park
Chiltern
Wodonga
Mitta Junction
Granya
Mount Burrowa
(1278m)
Cudgewa North
Tintaldra
Springhurst
Chiltern-Box Ironbark
National Park
Bandiana
Ebden
Bethanga
Cudgewa Falls
Eldorado
Baranduda
Mount
Granya
Bullioh
Koetong
Towong
Woorragee
Staghorn Flat
Old Tallangatta
Mount Bullioh
Shelley
Cudgewa
Corryong
Tangambalanga
Tallangatta
Tallangatta East
Berringama
Yackandandah
Kiewa
Allans Flat
Colac Colac
Mount Sugarloaf
Beechworth
Osbornes Flat
Sandy Creek
Mitta Mitta River
Lucyvale
Mount Cudgewa
Stanley
Kergunyah
Mount Unicorn
Mount
Big Ben
Kergunyah South
Mount St John
Wangaratta
Tarrawingee
Milawa
Everton
Mount Stanley
Mudgeegonga
Dederang
Eskdale
Bucheen Creek
Gentle Annie
Mount Boebuck
Markwood
Whorouly
Kiewa Valley Hwy
Mount Tawonga
Mitta Mitta
Mount Benambra
Bobinawarrah
Whorouly South
Merriang
Myrtleford
Kiewa River
Mount Elmo
Dartmouth
Mount Sassafras
Claremont
Carboor
Ovens
Mount Yorke
Dartmouth Reservoir
Alpine National Park
Edi
Ovens River
Eurobin
Mount Emu
King Valley
Mount Porepunkah
Tawonga
Omeo Hwy
Mount Martin
Mount Buffalo
National Park
Porepunkah
Mount Cooper
Whitfield
Lake Buffalo
Mt Buffalo
Bright
Tawonga South
Mount Bogong
(1986m)
Trail
Cheshunt
Mount Emu
Wandiligong
Freeburgh
Mount Beauty
Black Range
Mount Buffalo
(1723m)
Mount Arthur
Mount Pleasant
Ebenezer Mount
Bogong
Mount Nalse
Mount Wills
Australian Alps Walking
Mount View
Mount Mary
Falls Creek
(1780m)
Falls
Creek
Falls Creek
Glen Wills
Mount Fraser
Mount McIver
Mount Angus
Harrietville
Rocky Valley
Reservoir
Glen Valley
Mount Heatherton
(1922m)
Mount Hotham
(1868m)
Mitta Mitta River
Mount Type
GREAT DIVIDING RANGE
Mt Hotham
Dinner Plain
Anglers Rest
Benambra
Lake Omeo
Mount Tambo
Mount Cobbler
Barry Mountains
Bingo Munjie North
Hinnomunjie
Mount Pendergast
Mount Bullen
Alpine Village
Mount Tabletop

▲ 79 ▲

A   B   C   D

Hume Hwy
Tumblong
Tumbarumba
Adjungbilly
Wee Jasper
Mount Hartwood
Gundaroo
Mount Spring
Mount Horeb
Brungle
Mount Wee Jasper
Brindabella National Park
Sutton
Federal Hwy
Bywong
Tabletop Mountain
Adelong
Bondo
Lake Burley Griffin
Canberra
Fairbairn
Bungendore
Oberne
Tumut
Wondalga
Bowering Reservoir
Cotter River
Bendora Dam
Queanbeyan
Batlow
Bogong Mountain
Mount Franklin
Gibraltar Falls
Hoskinstown
Mount Molon
Kunama
Talbingo
Dubbo Hill
Mount Gingera
Namadgi National Park
Royalla
NEW SOUTH WALES
Laurel Hill
Bago Range
Talbingo Reservoir
Yarrangobilly
Mount Morgan
Bimberi Peak 4910m
Orroral
Captains Flat
Tumbarumba
Granite Mountain
Yarrangobilly
Kosciuszko National Park
Tantangara Reservoir
AUSTRALIAN CAPITAL TERRITORY
Tinderry Peak
Michelago
Tooma
Mount Selwyn (1492m)
Mount Selwyn
Kiandra
Yaouk Peak
Mt Clear
Tumanmang Mountain
Tintaldra
Cabramurra
Jagumba Mountain
Far Bald Mountain
Anglers Reach
Shannons Flat
Jerangle
Bald Mour
Towong
Australian Alps Walking Trail
Adaminaby
Old Adaminaby
Bredbo
Corryong
Lake Eucumbene
Snowy Mountains Hwy
Peak View
Khancoban
Wesley Mountain
Eucumbene
Frying Pan Creek
Bunyan
Numeralla
Mount Unicorn
Buckenderra
Cooma
Numeralla Mountain (1237m)
Gentle Annie
Mount Townsend
Guthega (1630m)
Smiggin Holes (1680m)
Lake Jindabyne
Berridale
Rock Flat
Wadbilli National
Mount Boebuck
Charlotte Pass (1780m)
Perisher Village
Perisher Blue
East Jindabyne
Jindabyne
Mount Kosciuszko (2228m)
Charlotte Pass
Bullocks Flat
Thredbo
Thredbo (1370m)
Thredbo Village
Dalgety
Nimmitabel
SNOWY MOUNTAINS
Ingebyrah
Maffra
Pigeon Boy Mountain (1400m)
The Pilot
Mulligans Mountain
Merriangaah Peak
Bembo
Pinch Mountain
Jimenbuen
Bungarby
Bull Mountain
VICTORIA
Black Jack Mountain
Suggan Buggan
Tingaringy
Round Hill
Bibbenluke
Cathcart
Tamawangalo Mountain
Mount Taylor
Bombala

Murray River, Murrumbidgee River, Snowy River, Monaro Hwy, Monaro Range, Great Dividing Range, Kybeyan Range, Bombala River

◄ 87 ◄

10   20 km
5   10 mi

▲ 80 ▲

150°E

151°E

Currawang

Lake Bathurst
Lake Bathurst
The Morass
Windellama
Tarago
Sandy Point
Boro
52
Nerriga
Sassafras

Morton
National Park
Mount Tianjara

Charleyong

Kings Hwy

Shoalhaven River

Bomaderry
Nowra
Coolangatta
Greenwell Point
Penguin Head
Culburra Beach
Klimpton
Callala Bay
Tomerong
Huskisson
Currarong
Beecroft Head
Beecroft Peninsula
35°S
Vincentia
Jervis
Bay
St Georges Basin
Sanctuary Point
St Georges
Basin
Sussex Inlet
Jervis Bay
Jervis Bay
(ACT)
Cudmirrah
Booderee National Park
St Georges Head

Hill Top
Conjola
Fishermans Paradise
Yatteyattah
Bendalong & Manyana
Lake Conjola
Milton
Ulladulla
Warden Head
Burrill Lake

Mongarlowe

Pigeon House Mountain
Currockbilly Mountain

Clyde River

Princes Hwy

Termeil

Braidwood

Bawley Point

Mount Budawang

Ballalaba
Majors Creek

Badawang
National Park

Merry
Murramarang National Park
Durras Lake

Togganoggera
Araluen

Oranmeir

Deua River

Gundillion

Nelligen
Cullendulla
Durras
Long Beach

Batemans Bay

Murramarang Coast

Wyanbene Caves Mountain

Deua National Park

Batemans Bay

Mogo
Malua Bay
Tomakin
Mossy Point
Broulee

Moruya
Moruya Heads
Eurobodalla National Park
Congo
Bergalia
Meringo
Mullimburra Point
Coila Lake
Bingie Bingie Point
Tuross Head

TASMAN SEA

Bodalla
Tuross Lake
Potato Point

Nerrigundah

Tuross River

Eurobodalla
Eurobodalla National Park
Dalmeny

Belowra Mountain

Peak Alone

Narooma

Montague
Island
36°S

Central Tilba
Eurobodalla National Park
Tilba Tilba

Princes Hwy
Cobargo
68
Wallaga Lake National Park

Murrabrine Mountain
Quaama
Bermagui
Bermagui South

Brogo River

Brogo

Mumbulla Mountain
Armonds Bay
Goalen Head

Biamanga
National Park

Doctor George
Mountain
Tanja
Bega
Mimosa Rocks National Park
Nelson Lagoon
Tathra
Tathra Head

Bournda
National Park
Wolumla

Turingal Head

E   F   G   H

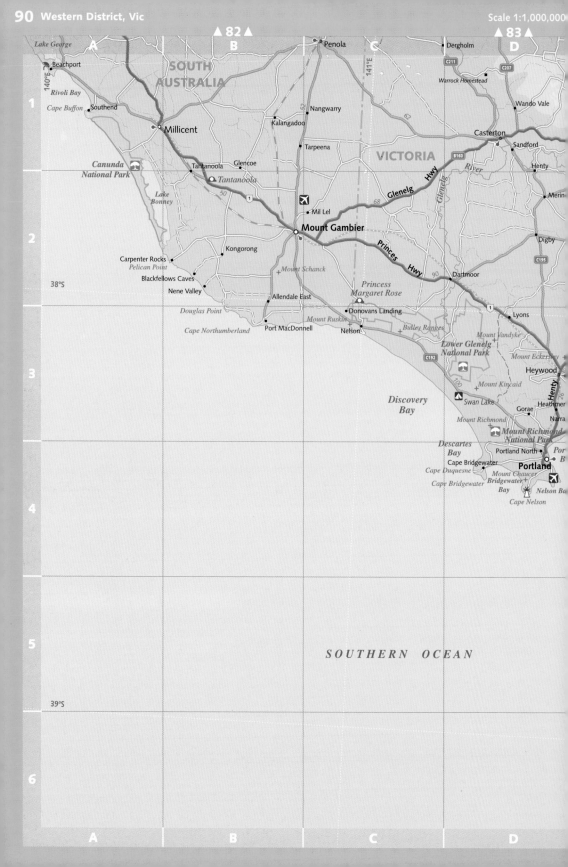

△ 82 △   △ 83 △

Lake George

SOUTH AUSTRALIA

Penola

Dergholm

C211

Warrock Homestead

C207

• Beachport

140°E

Rivoli Bay

Cape Buffon   • Southend

Wando Vale

1

Nangwarry

Kalangadoo

Casterton

Sandford

Millicent

Tarpeena

VICTORIA

B160

Henty

Canunda National Park

Tantanoola   • Glencoe

Glenelg Hwy

River

Lake Bonney

50

Tantanoola

Merin

1

68

Glenelg

Mil Lel

Glenelg

Digby

Mount Gambier

2

C195

Kongorong

Princes

38°S

Carpenter Rocks

Pelican Point

Mount Schanck

Hwy

90

Dartmoor

Blackfellows Caves

Princess Margaret Rose

1

Lyons

Nene Valley

Allendale East

Donovans Landing

Mount Ruskin

Bulley Ranges

Mount Vandyke

Douglas Point

Nelson

Lower Glenelg National Park

Cape Northumberland   Port MacDonnell

C192

Heywood

3

Mount Kincaid

Henty

Swan Lake

26

Discovery Bay

Heathmer

Mount Richmond

Gorae

Narra

Mount Richmond National Park

Descartes Bay

Portland North

Por B

Cape Bridgewater

Portland

Cape Duquesne

Mount Chaucer

Bridgewater Bay

Cape Bridgewater

Nelson Ba

4

Cape Nelson

5

SOUTHERN   OCEAN

39°S

6

A   B   C   D

10 20 km
5 10 mi

▲ 83 ▲ ▲ 85 ▲

The Grampians (Gariwerd), Map 84

Mooralla
The Chimney Pots
Mount Nelson
Marum Marum
Grampians NP
Mount Moornambool
Mt William Swamp
Moyston
Ararat
Mount Cole
Mount Buangor
Buangor
Raglan
Western Hwy
Mount Challicum
Beaufort

Mount Dundas
Mt Mackersey
Cavendish
Maroona
Rossbridge
Tatyoon
Yalla-Y-Poora
Mount Weejort

Meraine
Mahoneys Swamp
Mount Abrupt
Dunkeld
Glenthompson
Glenelg
Willaura
Narrapumelap
Mininera
Mount Widderin

River
Wannon
Strathkellar
Warrayure
Wickliffe
Hwy
Westmere
Streatham
Skipton

Yulecart
Hamilton
Lake Linlithgow
Lake Bolac
Mount Widderin
Mount Widderin

Tarrington
Croxton East
Woodhouse
Nareeb
Lake Hamilton
Mount Vite Vite

Branxholme
Buckley Swamp
Penshurst
Chatsworth
Lake Terrinallum

Wallacedale
Byaduk
Mount Napier
(443m)
Mount Rouse
Woorndoo
Derrinallum
Lismore

Condah
Byaduk
Hamilton
Caramut
Hexham
Mount Shadwell
Darlington
Mount Elephant
(393m)

Weerangourt
Ripponhurst
Minhamite
Lake Gnarpurt

Macarthur
Mt Eccles
(179m)
Mount Eccles National Park
Broadwater
Hawkesdale
Mortlake
Lake Colongulak
Lake Corangamite

Bessiebelle
Willatook
Hopkins Hwy
Ellerslie
Camperdown
Tyrendarra
Orford
Warrong
Woolsthorpe
Ballangeich
The Sisters
Noorat
Mount Noorat
Boorcan
Weerite

Tyrendarra East
St Helens
Tower Hill State Game Reserve
Winslow
Framlingham
Terang
Hwy
Lake Bullen Merri
Nalangil

Codrington
Kirkstall
Koroit
Grassmere
Mailer Flat
Purnim
Princes
Garvoc
Dixie
Cobrico
Cobden
Bostock Creek
Pomborneit
Stoneyford

Yambuk
Crossley
Killarney
Illowa
Bushfield
Wangoom
Panmure
Floating Islands Reserve
Swan Marsh

Aringa
Rosebrook
Dennington
Port Fairy
Warrnambool
Allansford
Naringal
Ralph Illidge Sanctuary
Irrewillipe

Lady Julia
Percy Island
Lady Bay
Mepunga West
Nullawarre
Scotts Creek
Timboon
Simpson

Buttress Point
The Cove
Nirranda

Bay of Islands
Peterborough
Port Campbell
Carlisle River
London Bridge
Loch Ard Gorge
Port Campbell National Park
Chaple Vale
Wyelangta

The Twelve Apostles
Gibson Steps
Princetown
Point Ronald
Lavers Hill
Yuulong
Johanna

Pebble Point
Moonlight Head
Glenaire
Cape Otway

38°S
39°S

▲ 92 ▲

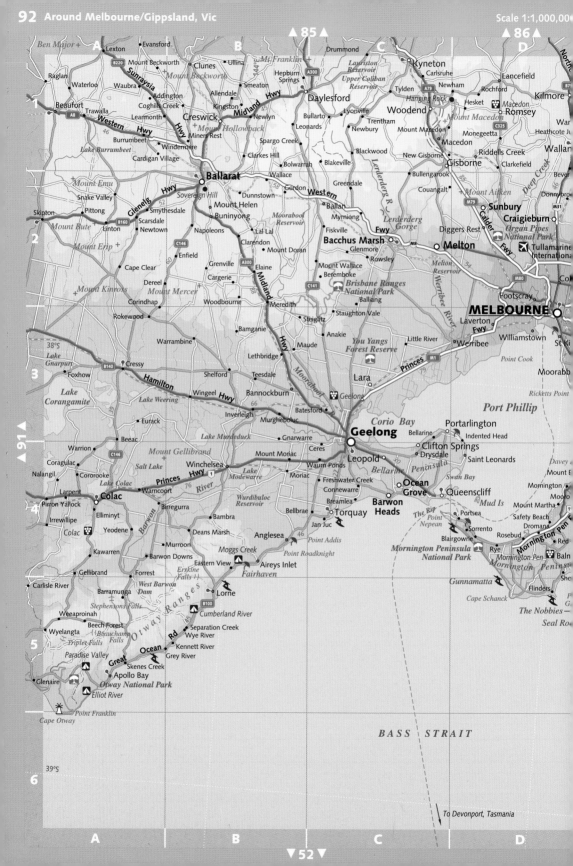

10 20 km
5 10 mi

E   F   G   H

Mount Concord
Molesworth
Goulburn Valley Hwy
Bradford
Tyaak
Strath Creek
Reedy Creek
Yea
Alexandra
Acheron
Thornton
Eildon
Lake Eildon
Goughs Bay
Howqua
Merrijig
Mirimbah
Mount Stirling (1747m)
Mount Buller
Mount Buller (1805m)
Mount Buller Alpine Village
Mount Howitt
Mount Lovick
Snowy Range

Flowerdale
Acheron
Taggerty
Rubicon
Lake Eildon National Park
Jamieson
Mount Darling
Howqua River

Mount Disappointment
Glenburn
Mount Despair
Buxton
Mount Torbreck
Kevington
Alpine National Park
Mt Reynard

Whittlesea
Kinglake National Park
Kinglake
St Andrews
Hurstbridge
Eltham
Yarra Glen
Coldstream
Toolangi
Narbethong
Marysville
Steavensons Falls
Lake Mountain (1433m)
Mount Terrible
Mount Duffy
Gaffneys Creek
A1 Mine Settlement
Woods Point
Matlock
Mount Selma
Licola
Macalister River
Great Dividing Range
Australian Alps

Healesville
Healesville Wildlife Sanctuary
Mt Donna Buang (1250m)
McMahons Creek
Yarra Ranges National Park
Upper Yarra Reservoir
Mount Gregory
Mount Easton
Aberfeldy
Mount Useful
Ben Cruachan

Doncaster
Maroondah Hwy
Lilydale
Woori Yallock
Seville
Millgrove
Warburton
Yarra Junction
Gladysdale
Powelltown
Mount Horsfall
Tanjil Bren
Mount Baw Baw (1564m)
Lake Thomson
Beardmore

Mt Dandenong (633m)
Dandenong Ranges National Park
Silvan Res
Hoddles Creek
Monbulk
Vesper
Icy Creek
Noojee
Mt Baw Baw Alpine Village
Mount Erica
Aberfeldy River
Walhalla
Glenmaggie

Belgrave
Churchill National Park
Emerald
Cockatoo
Gembrook
Mt Beenak
Spion Kopje
Nayook
Neerim
Baw Baw National Park
Walhalla Goldfields Railway
Rawson
Erica
Seaton

Dandenong
Beaconsfield Upper
Cardinia Reservoir
Berwick
Pakenham Upper
Maryknoll
Jindivick
Neerim South
Tarago Reservoir
Tyers Junction
Mount Tanjil
Dawson
Heyfield
Cowwarr
Thomson River

Carrum Downs
Cranbourne
Pakenham
Nar Nar Goon
Labertouche
Tynong
Garfield
Bunyip
Longwarry
Tarago
Rokeby
Buln Buln
Blue Rock Lake
Moondarra
Willow Grove
Toongabbie
Glengarry
Rosedale

Frankston
Baxter
Pearcedale
Somerville
Tyabb
Hastings
Crib Point
Stony Point
Koo-Wee-Rup
Tooradin
Bunyip River
Cora Lynn
Bayles
Yannathan
Caldermeade
Lang Lang
Modella
Ripplebrook
Lardner
Athlone
Ellinbank
Drouin
Warragul
Darnum
Yarragon
Moe
Newborough
Yallourn North
Tyers
Latrobe River
Yallourn Open Cut
Trafalgar
Morwell Open Cut
Morwell
Traralgon
Traralgon South
Willung
Gormandale
Flynn
Princes Hwy

Western Port
French Island National Park
French Island
Nyora
Poowong East
Poowong
Strzelecki
Seaview
Topiram
Mt Worth
Allambee
Coalville
Narracan
Thorpdale
Childers
Yinnar
Churchill
Koornalla
Hazelwood Pondage

Cowes
Phillip Island
Coronet Bay
Corinella
Grantville
Kernot
Glen Forbes
Woodleigh
Loch
Jeetho
Bena
Krowera
Ranceby
Mt Eccles
Wooreen
Allambee South
Mirboo North
Boolarra
Budgeree
Balook
Morwell National Park
Toms Cap
Carrajung

Newhaven
San Remo
Kilcunda
Dalyston
Bass
Woolamai
Kongwak
Leongatha
Leongatha South
Ruby
Coal Creek Historic Park
Mirboo
Boolarra South
Tarra-Bulga National Park
Hiawatha
Wonwron
Woodside North
Napier
Woodside
Hyland Hwy
Hotham Ranges

Cape Woolamai
Powlett River
Outtrim
Koonwarra
Dumbalk North
Wonyip
Staceys Bridge
Yarram
Alberton West
Balloong
Tarraville

Wonthaggi
Inverloch
Cape Paterson
Bunurong Marine Park
Venus Bay
Anderson Inlet
Meeniyan
Dollar
Buffalo
Foster
Toora
Port Franklin
Welshpool
Port Welshpool
Hedley
Manns Beach
Port Albert

Tarwin Lower
Tarwin River
Fish Creek
Gippsland Hwy
Barry Beach
Corner Inlet
Sunday Island
Nooramunga Marine & Coastal Park

Mount Liptrap
Sandy Point
Walkerville
Waratah Bay
Cape Liptrap
Yanakie
Wilsons Promontory Marine Park
Snake Island

Wilsons Promontory National Park, Map 100

Mount Roundback
Wilsons Promontory National Park

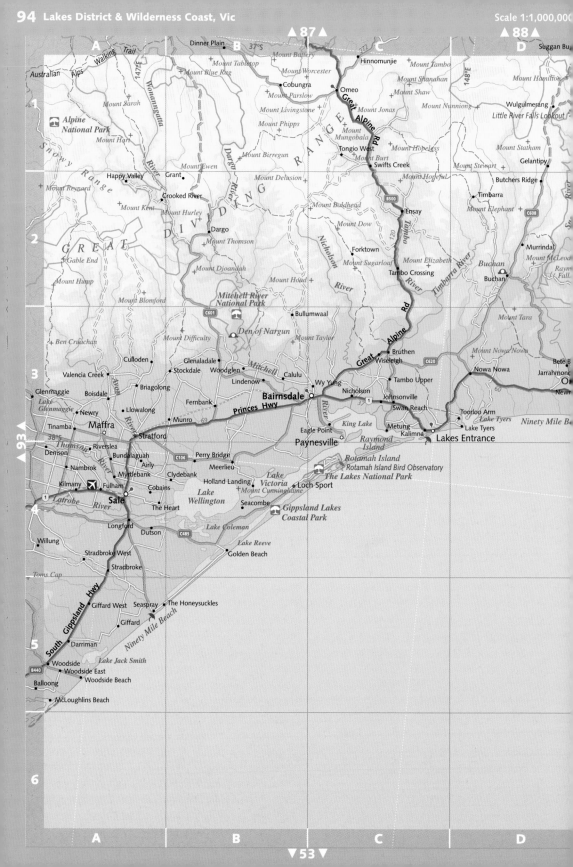

10   20 km
5   10 mi

E   F   G   H

Tingaringy •
+ Round Hill
Cathcart
Wolumla

NEW SOUTH WALES
Bombala
Wolumla Peak
Wyndham   Merimbula Lake
Tura Beach
Merimbula

Mount Taylor +
Rocky Hall
Pambula
Pambula Beach
1

MacKillop's Bridge
Delegate River •
Coolangubra Mountain
Burragate
Nethercote
Haycock Point
37°S

+ Mount Deddick
Delegate
Mount Delegate
Craigie
Mila
South East Forests National Park
Towamba
Eden
Mewstone Rock

nowy River ational Park
+ Mount Bowen
Bendoc
Bonang
Mount Tennyson
Wog Wog Mountain
Pericoe
Kiah
Ben Boyd National Park
Twofold Bay

Brown Mountain
Errinundra National Park
Mount Coopracambra
Wog Wog River
Narrabarba
Wonboyn
Wog
Mount Imlay
Mount Imlay National Park
Mount Imlay
Ben Boyd National Park
2

Mount Jersey
Goongerah
Errinundra
Chandlers Creek
Coopracambra National Park
Mount Denmarsh
Wallagaraugh
Mount Poole
Wonboyn Lake
Mount Victoria
Disaster Bay

Mount Ellery (1291m)
Combienbar
Mount Kaye
Genoa River
Narrabarba
Nadgee Nature Reserve
Black Head

Mount Murrungowar
VICTORIA
Cann River
Genoa
Gipsy Point
Mount Carlyle
Cape Howe

t Buck
Murrungower
Lind National Park
Princes Hwy
Mount Cann
Tuross River
Wingan River
Mallacoota Inlet
Lake Barracoota
Bastion Point
3

Lake Curlip
Corringle
Cabbage Tree Creek
Swan Lake
Lake Furnell
Tamboon
Alfred National Park
Mount Everard
Wingan Inlet
Croajingolong National Park
Little Rame Point
Mallacoota
Gabo Island

arlo
Bemm River
Pearl Point
Sydenham Inlet
Tamboon Inlet
Point Hicks
Wingan Inlet
Sandpatch Point
Petrel Point

4

38°S

TASMAN SEA

5

6

A **52** B C **53** D

BASS STRAIT

See King Island

40°S

145°E

144°E

King Island inset

Cape Wickham
Cape Farewell
Disappointment Bay
Phoques Bay
New Year Is
Egg Lagoon
Yambacoona
Whistler Point
Lavinia Nature Reserve
Lavinia Point
BASS STRAIT
Reekara
B25
SOUTHERN OCEAN
Loorana
KING ISLAND
Cowper Point
Sea Elephant
Currie
30
Sea Elephant Bay
Naracoopa
Fraser Bluff
Pegarah
40°S
Lymwood
Yarra Creek
Cataraqui Point
Mt Stanley
Bold Head
Grassy
Grassy Harbour
Calcified Forest
Seal Point
Stokes Point

King Island
Same scale as main map

146°E

Cape North West
Cape Keraudren
Cape Rochon
Three Hummock Island
Cape Adamson
Wallaby Point
Hope Channel
Walker Channel
Hunter Island
Hunter Passage
Trefoil Island
Cape Buache
Walker Island
Cape Grim
Woolnorth Point
Boullanger Bay
Robbins Island
Woolnorth
Kangaroo Island
Flat Topped Bluff
Private Road
Robbins
Cape Elie
Passage
North Point
Mount Cameron West
West Montagu
Perkins Island
Stanley
Marrawah
Montagu
Perkins Bay
The Nut
Mella
Smithton
Wiltshire
West Point
Marrawah
Christmas Hills
Forest
Black River
Redpa
Togari
Irishtown
Sth Forest
Port Latta
Brittons
Swamp
Merigha
Hellyer
Detention River
Bluff Hill Point
Edith Creek
Alcomie
Mawbanna
Sisters
41°S
Nabageena
Myalla
Sisters Creek
Boat Harbour
Arthur River
Roger River
Trowutta
Milabena
Lapoinya
Flowerdale
Sundown Point
Arthur River
Meunna
Calder
Somerset
Wynyard
Couta Rocks
Milkshake Hills Forest Reserve
Preolenna
Kelliater
Mooreville
Wivenhoe
Burnie
Temma
Lake Chisholm Forest Reserve
Yolla
Stowport
Sulphur Creek
Balfour
West Takone
Takone
Ridgley
Cuprona
Penguin
Mount Balfour
Mount Frankland
Henrietta
Natone
Gawler
Ulverstone
Highclere
Riana
Forth
Turners Beach
Mount Bertha
Tewkesbury
Upper Natone
Abbotsham
Don
Devonport
Mount Hazelton
Hellyer Gorge State Reserve
Oonah
Hampshire
South Riana
Sprent
Spreyton
Arthur Pieman Protected Area
Parrawe
B18
Preston
Central Castra
Melrose
Latrobe
Sandy Cape
A10
Heka
Warringa
Lower Barrington
Mount Norfolk
St Valentines Peak (1106m)
Gunns Plains
Upr Castra
Barrington
Railton
Mount Vero
Guildford
Loongana
Nietta
Wilmot
Lake Burrington
Sheffield
Waratah
Talbots Lagoon
Black Bluff (1339m)
Roland
Kimberley
Rupert Point
Savage River
Luina
River
Mount Pearse
Lake Gairdner
Gowrie Park
Staverton
Claude Road
Mount Meredith
Lake Lea
Mount Cattley
Moina
Lower Beulah
Mount Donaldson
Donaldson
Mount Ramsay
Lake Cethana
Lorinna
Mersey
King Solomon
Pieman Head
Corinna
Mount Livingstone
Mount Remus
Daisy Dell
Liena
Mayberry
Mole Creek
Reece Dam
Mackintosh
Lake Rosebery
Cradle Valley
Marakoopa
Caveside
Granville Harbour
Lake Pieman
Bastyan Dam
Lake Mackintosh
Lake Dove
Cradle Mountain (1545m)
King Parangana
Devil's Gullet
SOUTHERN OCEAN
Renison Bell
Rosebery
Tullah
Granite Tor
Lake Will
Fisher Bluff
Lake Mackenzie
Williamsford
Murchison Dam
Cradle Mountain-Lake St Clair National Park
Blue Peaks
Clummer Bluff
Lake Rowallan
Mount Heemskirk
Mt Read
Montezuma Falls
Mt Murchison (1275m)
Meander
Mount Agnew
Zeehan
Mt Pelion West
Mount Jerusalem (1458m)
Trial Harbour
Mt Zeehan
B27
Mount Ossa (1617m)
Walls of Jerusalem National Park
Lake Myrtle
Eldon Bluff

A B C D

0 10 20 km
0 5 10 mi

53

E F G H

147°E 148°E

1

Craggy Island Inner Sister Island Outer Sister Island
Stanley Point Holloway Point
Blyth Point Palana
Mount Killiecrankie
Killiecrankie
Cape Frankland Mount Tanner
Bun Beetons Point **FLINDERS ISLAND**

Marshall Bay
Lughrata Memana Babel Island
Emita The Patriachs
40°S Furneaux Lookout
Prime Seal Is Sellers Lagoon
Arthur Bay Walkers Lookout
Long Point Mount Leventhorpe
Parrys Bay Whitemark Cameron Inlet
The Dutchman
East Kangaroo Is Ranga
Big Green Is Logan Lagoon
Loccota Strzelecki Peaks
Mt Chappell Is Pot Boil Point
Strzelecki NP Lady Barron
Goose Is Great Dog Island
Badger Is Vansittart Island

2

B A S S S T R A I T

F U R N E A U X

Franklin Sound
Long Is Cape Barren Island
Sir John Cape Mount Munro
Cape Barren Island
Mount Kerferd
Cape
Preservation Is Barren
Armstrong Channel Cone Point
Foam Point Passage Is
Forsyth Is
Clarke Island Moriarty Point

3

G R O U P

Banks Strait

Cape Portland Swan Island

Waterhouse Island
Waterhouse
Croppies Point Point **Great Musselroe Bay**
Ringarooma
East Sandy Point **Bay** Poole
West Sandy Point Tomahawk Cape Naturaliste
Five Stony Head **Anderson Bay** Bowlers Picnic Rocks
Mile **Noland Bay** Big Lagoon Mt William Boulder Point
Low Bluff Lulworth Weymouth Waterhouse Boobyalla **Mount William**
Head Beechford Bellingham **Bridport** Lake **National Park**
Greens Low Gladstone Eddystone Point
Beach Head George Town Pipers River North Forester Mt Cameron 41°S
Kelso Lefroy Pipers Brook Scottsdale South Ansons Bay
Pipers River Jetsonville Mount
Beauty The Glen Golconda Lietinna Cameron Pioneer
Point Tunnel **Scottsdale** Herrick **Bay of Fires**
Bangor Nabowla Tulendeena Derby
Holwell Karoola Lilydale Branxholm Weldborough
Winkleigh Turners Marsh Tonganah Legerwood Lottah Mount Pearson
Glengarry Underwood Sth Springfield Ringarooma Goulds Country Binalong Bay
Bridgenorth Patersonia Targa Talawa Pyengana St Helens Point
Birralee Rosevale Nunamara Saint Diddleum Plains Alberton St Columba Falls Priory St Helens
Reedy Selbourne Legana Patricks Mount Young Parnella
Marsh River Ben Nevis Mount Saddleback **Evercreech** Parkside
Westbury Hadspen **Launceston** Burns Creek Upper Esk **Forest Reserve** Beaumaris
Osmaston Hagley Cataract Gorge Upper Scamander
Quamby Glenore White Hills Mathinna Scamander
Brook Cluan **Perth** Upper Carr Villa Ski Resort Mt Nicholas Falmouth
Golden Valley Bishopsbourne **Longford** Blessington Legges Tor Cornwall Four Mile Creek **TASMAN**
Liffey Bracknell Clarendon **Ben Lomond** Ironhouse Point
Liffey Falls Cressy Nile **National Park** St Marys **SEA**
Blackwood Creek Deddington Mangana Gray
Poatina Epping Forest Storeys Creek Fingal Chain of Lagoons
Mount Blackwood Rossarden **Douglas Apsley** Piccaninny Point
Cramps Cleveland Ormley **National Park**
Conara Avoca St Pauls River Long Point
St Pauls Dome Mt St John Maclean Bay

4

5

6

E F G H

E | F | G | H

Cramps
Little Lake
B51
Arthurs Lake
Barren Tier
Steppes
addamana
Lagoon of Islands
Millers Bluff
Mount Penny West
Woods Lake

Epping Forest
Cleveland
Conara
Esk **Main Rd**
5th Esk River
Avoca
A4
St Pauls Dome
St Pauls River
Royal George
Mount Henry
Mt St John
Snow Hill

Douglas-Apsley National Park
Maclean Bay
Bicheno
Cape Lodi
Butlers Point

Campbell Town

Mt Augusta
Ross
Lake Leake
Lake Leake
Hobgoblin
Rawlinna Hill
Swansea
Cranbrook
B34

42°S

Interlaken
Lake Sorell
Mount Franklin
Tunbridge
Woodbury
Antill Ponds
Old Mans Head
Table Mountain (1095m)
Woods Quoin
Oatlands
Vincents Hill
York Plains
Pawtella
Nala
Andover
Lemont
Parattah
Mount Seymour
Stonehenge
Baden
Whitefoord
Tooms Lake

Moulting Lagoon
Mount Peter
Mount Paul
Swanwick
Coles Bay
Swansea
Waterloo Pt
Great Oyster Bay
Cape Tourville
Mount Dove
Cape Forestier
Spiky Bridge
Mount Freycinet
A3
Freycinet National Park
Cape Degerando
Schouten Passage
Schouten Is
Cape Sonnerat

Bothwell
Green Hill
Mount Anstey
A5
Mount Reid
Jericho
Apsley
1
Stonor
Mount Clark
Melton Mowbray
Rhyndaston
Lake Tiberia
Kempton
Eldon
Colebrook
Mt Bains
Hollow Tree
Pelham
Elderslie
Eldon
Levendale
Woodsdale
Mount Hobbs
Bluestone Tier
Triabunna

Little Swanport
Little Swanport
Little Swanport
Point Bailly
Gridstone Bay
Mount Murray
Cape Bougainville
Cape Boullanger
Louisville
Darlington
Mount Maria (709m)
Maria Island National Park
MARIA ISLAND
Cape Maurouard

Dysart
Broadmarsh
B10
Gretna
Derwent River
Bagdad
Mangalore
Mt Dromedary
Pontville
Campania
Rekuna
Prosser River
Orford
Shelly Beach
Spring Beach
Buckland
Three Thumbs
Rheban
Sandspit River Reserve

Hayes
B62
Magra
Dromedary
Boyer
Bridgewater
Brighton
Granton
Old Beach
Richmond
Orielton
Pawleena
Penna
Nugent
Kellevie
Cape Peron
Mercury Passage

New Norfolk
Lachlan
Collinsvale
Risdon Vale
Cambridge
A10
Sorell
Midway Point
Lewisham
Bream Creek
Copping
Marion Bay
Cape Paul Lamanon

Glenfern

Hobart
A3
26
Hobart
Dodges Ferry
Carlton
Primrose Sands
Dunalley
Cape Fredrick Hendrick

Mt Wellington
Fern Tree
Rokeby
Lauderdale
Mount Forestier
High Yellow Bluff

Mt Misery
Mountain River
Neika
Cremorne
Frederick Henry Bay
Forestier Peninsula
Murdunna
Cape Surville

Crabtree
Grove
Taroona
Kingston
Ranelagh
Lucaston
Sandfly
Clifton Beach
Norfolk Bay
Eaglehawk Neck
Waterfall Bay

Huon
lips Hill
Huonville
Pelverata
Blackmans Bay
Howden
South Arm
Saltwater River
Premaydena
Taranna
Tasman Peninsula

Franklin
Snug
Margate
Tinderbox
Coningham
Koonya
Nubeena
Fortescue Bay

Cradoc
B33
Grey Mtn
Oyster Cove
Barnes Bay
Wedge Bay
Oakwood

Huon
Geeveston
Kettering
Woodbridge
NORTH BRUNY ISLAND
Highcroft
Port Arthur
Remarkable
A6
Waterloo
Lymington
Flowerpot
Garden Is
Stormlea
Fortescue Bay

devie
Police Point
Surveyors Bay
Dover
Verona Sands
Simpsons Bay
B66
Cape Queen Elizabeth
Stormlea
Munro Bight
Cape Pillar

Port
Esperance
D'Entrecasteaux Channel
Alonnah
Lunawanna
Adventure Bay
Partridge Is
Cookville
Cape Raoul
Mount Raoul
Maingon Bay
Tasman Is

Southport
Labillardiere State Reserve
Mangana Point
SOUTH BRUNY ISLAND
Mt Barren
Mount Bruny
South Bruny Island National Park
Tasman Head
Cape Bruny
Eliza Point
B68

TASMAN SEA

43°S

149°E

147°E
148°E

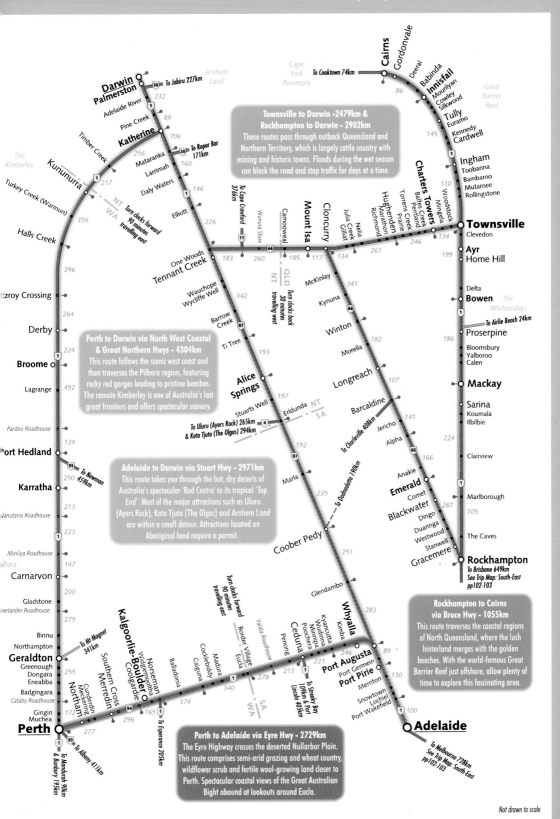

Darwin
Palmerston

To Jabiru 227km

Arnhem Land

Cape York Peninsula

Cairns
Gordonvale
Deeral
Babinda
Innisfail
Mourilyan
Cowley
Silkwood

To Cooktown 74km

86

Great Barrier Reef

Adelaide River
232

Pine Creek
89

Katherine
106

To Roper Bar 171km
20

Mataranka
256

Larrimah
160

Daly Waters
146

Elliott
226

Timber Creek

Kununurra
217

NT / WA
Turn clocks forward 90 minutes travelling east

Turkey Creek (Warmun)
356

Halls Creek
296

zroy Crossing
264

Derby
224

Broome
492

Lagrange

To Cape Crawford 376km

Wunara Store

Camooweal
11
183
260
66
185
117
134

Mount Isa

One Woods
Tennant Creek

Wauchope
Wycliffe Well
342

Barrow Creek
87

Ti Tree
193

Alice Springs
197

QLD / NT
Turn clocks back 30 minutes travelling west

McKinlay

Kynuna
66
341

Winton
182

Morella

Longreach
107

Barcaldine
141

Jericho

Alpha
224
66
166

Anakie

Tully
Euramo
Kennedy
Cardwell
145

Ingham
Toobanna
Bambaroo
Mutarnee
Rollingstone
110

Woodstock
Mingela
Charters Towers
Nelia
Julia Creek
Gilliat
261

Cloncurry

Baltes Creek
Pentland
Torrens Creek
Prairie
Hughenden
Marathon
Richmond
246
134

Townsville
Clevedon

Ayr
Home Hill
199

Delta

Bowen
The Whitsundays

To Airlie Beach 24km
186

Proserpine
Bloomsbury
Yalboroo
Calen

Mackay

Sarina
Koumala
Ilbilbie

Clairview

Perth to Darwin via North West Coastal & Great Northern Hwys - 4304km
This route follows the scenic west coast and then traverses the Pilbara region, featuring rocky red gorges leading to pristine beaches. The remote Kimberley is one of Australia's last great frontiers and offers spectacular scenery.

Townsville to Darwin -2479km & Rockhampton to Darwin -2902km
These routes pass through outback Queensland and Northern Territory, which is largely cattle country with mining and historic towns. Floods during the wet season can block the road and stop traffic for days at a time.

Pardoo Roadhouse
139

ort Hedland
95
To Newman 459km
250

Karratha
213

lanutarra Roadhouse
223

Minilya Roadhouse
lbara
147

Carnarvon
200

Gladstone
erlander Roadhouse
279

To Uluru (Ayers Rock) 265km & Kata Tjuta (The Olgas) 294km
Stuarts Well
Erldunda
4
192
NT / SA

Marla
235

Adelaide to Darwin via Stuart Hwy - 2971km
This route takes you through the hot, dry deserts of Australia's spectacular 'Red Centre' to its tropical 'Top End'. Most of the major attractions such as Uluru (Ayers Rock), Kata Tjuta (The Olgas) and Arnhem Land are within a small detour. Attractions located on Aboriginal land require a permit.

87

To Oodnadatta 190km
To Charleville 408km

Coober Pedy
251

Emerald
Comet
Blackwater
261

Dingo
Duaringa
Westwood
Stanwell

Gracemere

Marlborough
105

The Caves

Rockhampton
To Brisbane 649km
See Trip Map: South-East pp102-103

Rockhampton to Cairns via Bruce Hwy - 1055km
This route traverses the coastal regions of North Queensland, where the lush hinterland merges with the golden beaches. With the world-famous Great Barrier Reef just offshore, allow plenty of time to explore this fascinating area.

Binnu
Northampton
Geraldton
To Mt Magnet 341km
255
Greenough
Dongara
Eneabba
Badgingarra
Cataby Roadhouse

Gingin
Muchea
172

Perth
30
To Albany 411km
To Mandurah 90km & Bunbury 195km

Kalgoorlie-Boulder
Southern Cross
Merredin
Northam
Cunderdin
Meckering

Wongan
Wialki
Bullfinch
Coolgardie
Norseman

Balladonia
374

Border Village
Eucla
278
340

Yalata Roadhouse

Madura
Cocklebiddy
Caiguna

Ceduna
Penong
227

Kyancutta
Wudinna
Minnipa
Poochera

Kimba

Whyalla
283

Iron Knob

Glendambo

94
165
To Esperance 205km
277
296

SA / WA

Port Augusta
246
Port Germein
Port Pirie
213
1
Merriton

To Streaky Bay 109km & Port Lincoln 403km

Snowtown
Lochiel
Port Wakefield
130

Adelaide
100
To Melbourne 728km
See Trip Map: South-East pp102-103

Perth to Adelaide via Eyre Hwy - 2729km
The Eyre Highway crosses the deserted Nullarbor Plain. This route comprises semi-arid grazing and wheat country, wildflower scrub and fertile wool-growing land closer to Perth. Spectacular coastal views of the Great Australian Bight abound at lookouts around Eucla.

Border Village
Turn clocks forward 90 minutes travelling east

Not drawn to scale

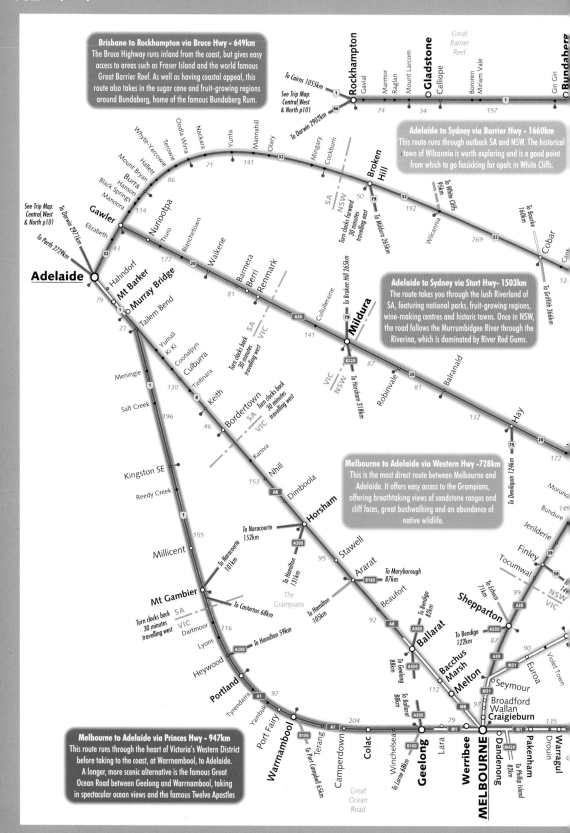

Brisbane to Rockhampton via Bruce Hwy - 649km
The Bruce Highway runs inland from the coast, but gives easy access to areas such as Fraser Island and the world famous Great Barrier Reef. As well as having coastal appeal, this route also takes in the sugar cane and fruit-growing regions around Bundaberg, home of the famous Bundaberg Rum.

Adelaide to Sydney via Barrier Hwy - 1660km
This route runs through outback SA and NSW. The historical town of Wilcannia is worth exploring and is a good point from which to go fossicking for opals in White Cliffs.

Adelaide to Sydney via Sturt Hwy- 1503km
The route takes you through the lush Riverland of SA, featuring national parks, fruit-growing regions, wine-making centres and historic towns. Once in NSW, the road follows the Murrumbidgee River through the Riverina, which is dominated by River Red Gums.

Melbourne to Adelaide via Western Hwy -728km
This is the most direct route between Melbourne and Adelaide. It offers easy access to the Grampians, offering breathtaking views of sandstone ranges and cliff faces, great bushwalking and an abundance of native wildlife.

Melbourne to Adelaide via Princes Hwy - 947km
This route runs through the heart of Victoria's Western District before taking to the coast, at Warrnambool, to Adelaide.
A longer, more scenic alternative is the famous Great Ocean Road between Geelong and Warrnambool, taking in spectacular ocean views and the famous Twelve Apostles

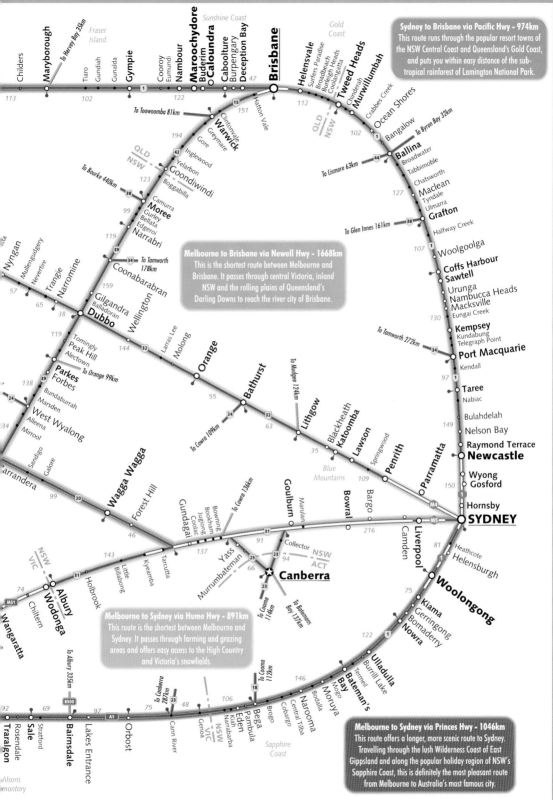

Sydney to Brisbane via Pacific Hwy - 974km
This route runs through the popular resort towns of the NSW Central Coast and Queensland's Gold Coast, and puts you within easy distance of the sub-tropical rainforest of Lamington National Park.

Melbourne to Brisbane via Newell Hwy - 1668km
This is the shortest route between Melbourne and Brisbane. It passes through central Victoria, inland NSW and the rolling plains of Queensland's Darling Downs to reach the river city of Brisbane.

Melbourne to Sydney via Hume Hwy - 891km
This route is the shortest between Melbourne and Sydney. It passes through farming and grazing areas and offers easy access to the High Country and Victoria's snowfields.

Melbourne to Sydney via Princes Hwy - 1046km
This route offers a longer, more scenic route to Sydney. Travelling through the lush Wilderness Coast of East Gippsland and along the popular holiday region of NSW's Sapphire Coast, this is definitely the most pleasant route from Melbourne to Australia's most famous city.

Not drawn to scale

ROUTES

Tollway
Autoroute à péage
gebührenpflichtige Autobahn
Autopista

Freeway
Autoroute
Autobahn
Autovía

Freeway underground
Autoroute souterraine
Autobahn untertunnelt
Autopista Subterránea

Primary Road
Route Principale
Fernstraße
Carretera Principal

Secondary Road
Route Secondaire
Nebenstraße
Carretera Secundaria

Street; Lane
Rue; Allée
Straße; Gasse
Calle; Paseo

On/Off Ramp
Entrées/sorties d' autoroute
Straßenauf
Entrada/Salida

Ramp underground
Entree/sortie souterraine
untertunnelte Straßenauf
Entrada/Salida Subterránea

Unsealed Roads
Route non bitumée
unversiegelte Straße
Carretera sin Asfaltar

Pedestrian Mall
Zone construite
Fußgängerzone
Zona Peatonal

Steps
Escalier
Stufen
Escaleras

Path
Sentier pédestre
Pfad
Sendero

Footbridge
Passerelle
Fußgängerbrücke
Puente Peatonal

One Way Street
Sens unique
Einbahnstraße
Calle de Sentido Único

TRANSPORTATION

Railway; Rail Station
Voie de chemin de fer; Gare Ferroviaire
Eisenbahn; Bahnhof
Ferrocarril; Estació de Ferrocarril

Railway underground
Voie de chemin de fer souterraine
Eisenbahn untertunnelt
Ferrocarril subterránea

Metro
Métro
U-Bahn
Metro

Tram
Tramway
Staßenbahn
Tram

Light Rail
Tramway
S-Bahn
Ferrocarril Ligero

Light Rail underground
Tramway souterrain
S-Bahn untertunnelt
Ferrocarril Ligero Subterráneo

Monorail
Monorail
Magentschwebebahn
Monorrail

Ferry; Ferry Terminal
Route de ferry; Terminal du ferry
Fährroute; Fähranlegestelle
Transbordador; Estación Marítima

AREA FEATURES

Major Building
Bâtiment
Hauptgebäude
Edificio Importante

Hotel; Theatre
Hôtel; Thèâtre
Hotel; Theater
Hotel; Teatro

Park; Campus
Parc; Campus
Park; Campus
Parque; Campus

Shops; Market
Magasins; Marché
Geschäfte; Markt
Tiendas; Mercado

SYMBOLS

Bus Station
Station de bus
Bushaltestelle
Estación de Autobuses

Cinema
Cinéma
Kino
Cine

Golf Course
Terrain de Golf
Golfplatz
Campo de Golf

Information Centre
Centre d'information
Informationszentrum
Centro de Información

Museum
Musée
Museum
Museo

Point of Interest
Curiosités
Sehenswerter Ort
Punto de Interés

Post Office
Bureau de Poste
Postamt
Correos y Telégrafos

Church, Cathedral
Église; Cathédrale
Kirche, Dom
Iglesia, Catedral

Embassy, Consulate
Ambassade, Consulat
Botschaft, Konsulat
Embajada, Consulado

Hospital
Hôpital
Krankenhaus
Hospital

Monument
Monument
Denkmal
Monumento

Parking Area
Parking
Parkplatz
Aparcamiento

Police Station
Police
Polizeirevier
Comisaría

Swimming Pool
Piscine
Schwimmbad
Piscina

250 500 m
250 500 yd

E F G H

Canberra Nature Park

Cooyong St
Drill Hall
Kingsley St
Rudd St
Alinga St
East Row
Northbourne Ave
Petrie Plaza
See Enlargement

Donaldson St
Chapman St
Batman St
Olim's Canberra
Ainslie Ave

University Ave
Fellows Oval
Clunies Ross St
Daley Rd
University Ave
Eliery Cres
Childers St
Allsopp St
University Ave
Clark St
Marcus Clarke St
Hobart
West Row
Civic
Vernon Circle

Gorman House Community Arts Centre
Kogarah La
Glebe Park
Ballumbir St
Allambee St
Gooreen St
Coranderrk St
Corranderrk St
Limestone Ave
Treloar Cres
Australian War Memorial

Daley Rd
Ward Rd
Fellows Rd
Garran Rd
Eggleston Rd
East Rd
Liversidge
South Oval
ScreenSound Australia
Australian Academy of Science
Canberra Centre
Canberra Museum & Gallery
Bunda St
Akuna St
Reid Park

Acton
AUSTRALIAN NATIONAL UNIVERSITY
University House
Rivett Rd
Balmain Cr
Lennox Crossing
City Hill
Canberra Theatre Centre
Goethe Institute
Allara
London Circuit
Electric Shadows Cinema & Bookshop
Casino
National Convention Centre
Durrawan St
Currong St
Euree St
Geelong Gardens
Elimatta St
Reid
Ryrie St
Blamey St

Parkes Way
Lennox
Lawson
Cres
West Basin
Acton Park Ferry Terminal & Boat Hire
Mr Spokes Bike Hire
Edinburgh Ave
Commonwealth Park
Barrine Dr
Regatta Pl
Olympic Swimming Pool
Nerang Pool
Amaroo St
Booroondara St
Constitution Ave
Parkes Way
Chowne St
Rankin St
Creswell St
Patey St
Anzac Pde
Anzac Park West
East
Savige St
Campbell
Carsia St

Springbank Island
Acton Peninsula
Hospital Point
National Museum of Australia
National Capital Exhibition
Barrine Dr
Captain Cook Memorial Water Jet
Regatta Point
Central Basin
Church of St John the Baptist; St John's Schoolhouse Museum
Blundell's Cottage
Feakes St
Getting Cres
Jacka St
Blamye St
Borella St
Russell Dr

Attunga Point
Albert Hall
Flynn Pl
Commonwealth Avenue Bridge
National Library of Australia
West
Parkes Place
LAKE BURLEY GRIFFIN
National Carillon
Wendouree Dr
Kings Park
To Australian-American Memorial

Lotus Bay
Lennox Gardens
Kaye St
Kaye Pl
Dr
Langton Cres
King
Parkes Pl
Edward
Enid Lyons St
Questacon (National Science & Technology Centre)
High Court
East
National Gallery of Australia
Aspen Island
Kings Ave
Grevillea Park
To Australian-American Memorial

Alexandrina Dr
Stirling Park
Forster Cres
Coronation Dr
UK High Commission
NZ High Commission
Canadian High Commission
PNG High Commission
King George Tce
Parkes
Tce
Parkes Pl
Bowen
Administration Pl
Kings Avenue Bridge
Kings Way
To Airport (8km)

Malaysian High Commission
Indonesia
Perth Ave
France
Arkana
Ireland
Germany
Turrana St
Wonna St
USA
Moonah Pl
Indian High Commission
State Circle
Capital Circle
Queen Victoria Tce
Old Parliament House
Kings Ave
Barton
Bligh St
Blackall Pl
Broughton St
Blackall St
Macquarie St
Bowen Dr
East Basin
Bowen Park
Mundaring Dr

Yarralumla
Thailand
Adelaide Ave
The Lodge
Parliament Dr
Capital Hill
Parliament House
Circle
York Park
Circuit
Brisbane Ave
Blackall St
Darling St
Bourke St
Macquarie St
Young St
West Park
East Park
Gosse St
LP
Kingston
Wentworth Ave

Royal Australian Mint (5km),
Mt Stromlo Observatory (14km),
Cotter Dam (18km)
Somers Cres
Forrest
National Sydney Ave
New South
Gipps St
Fitzroy St
Wales Cres
Telopea Park
Telopea
Curry Cres
Giles
Manuka Swimming Pool
Canberra Ave
Serbian Orthodox
Franklin St
Tench St
Jardine St
Hovitt St
Kingston Shopping Centre
Kennedy St
To Canberra Railway Museum (200m)

Travellers' Medical & Vaccination Centre
Jolimont Centre & Canberra Visitors' Centre
Government Info Shop
0 200 m
0 200 yd
Griffin Centre
Café Cactus
Greater Union
Cinema Centre & Gilbert's Bookshop
Smith's Alternative Bookshop
Alinga St
West Row
Northbourne Ave
Mort St
East Row
GPO
Women's Information & Referral Centre
Civic Bus Interchange
Petrie Plaza City Market
Hobart Pl

For more detail around Canberra, refer to Map 88

125 250 m
125 250 yd

Grid reference E F G H / 1 2 3 4 5 6

Hughes St
Orwell St
Regent's Court
Earl St
Roslyn St
Kings Cross Rd
Ward Ave
To Double Bay (2km)
Barcom Ave
Glenview St
Liverpool
Paddington
Glenmore
Oxford St
To Bondi Beach (5.5km)
Moore
Park
Road

Victoria
Kellett St
Bayswater Rd
Kings Cross
Craigend
Nimrod St
Surrey St
Womerah
West St
Campbell Ave
Hopewell St
Glenmore
Gipps St
Cascade St
Co-ee Aboriginal
Art Gallery
Victoria Barracks

Woolloomooloo
McElhone
Brougham
Kings Cross
Stables
Medusa
Kirketon Rd
Liverpool
Hardie St
St Vincent's
Barcom Ave
Academy
Twin
Verona
Napier St
Albion Ave
Church
Selwyn
Greens
Iris St
Josephson St
Anzac Pde

Dowling St
Judge St
Forbes St
William St
Farrell Ave
Tewkesbury Ave
Darley St
Darlinghurst
Old Darlinghurst Gaol
Darlinghurst Courthouse
South Dowling St
Sturt St
Taylor St
Sims St
Chisholm St
Hanram St
Hutchinson St
Nichols St
Marshall
Prospect St
Bennett St
Sydney Antique Centre

Harmer St
Charles St
Forbes St
Clapton Pl
Thomson St
Burton
Victoria
Oxford St
Flinders St
Bourke St
Short St
Hill St
Fitzroy St
Eastern Distributor

Eastern Distributor
Toll Booths (northbound only)
Chapel St
Palmer St
Foley St
Denham St
Taylor St

Sir John Young
Parking Station
Cathedral
Kennedy St
Crown St
Riley St
East Sydney
Liverpool
Sydney Gay & Lesbian Mardi Gras Parade route
Oxford St
Crown St
Albion St
Surry Hills
Fitzroy St
Richards Ave
Alexander Ave
Phelps
Rainford St

St Mary's Rd
Cook & Phillip Park
Australian Museum
NSW Police Headquarters
Sydney Francis Marriott
Hyde Park Plaza
Stanley St
Norman St
Poplar St
Pelican St
Goulburn St
Campbell St
Riley St
Goodchap St
Ann St
Little Albion St
Bellevue St
Belmore St
Norton St
Collins
Sunday Market
Arthur
Lacey St
Adelaide

St Mary's Cathedral
Archibald Memorial Fountain
College St
Whitlam
Commonwealth St
Brisbane St
Smith St
Commonwealth
Foster St
Little Albion St
Albion St
Albion
Foveaux
Sophia
Hercules
Kippax
Utter St
Gladstone St
Devonshire St

Sheraton on the Park
Great Synagogue
Hyde Park
Anzac Memorial
Pool of Reflection
Hyde Park
Museum
Travel Bookshop
Nithsdale St
Women & Girls Emergency Centre
Clarke St
Hunt
Reservoir
Mary
Cooper
Holt
Butt St
Brumby St

Centrepoint
Centennial City Centre
Park Plaza
Elizabeth
Castlereagh
Pitt
Castlereagh St
Clisdell St
Elizabeth
Rutland St
Buckingham St
Chalmers
Prince Alfred Park

State City
Sydney Hilton
The Galleries Victoria
Town Hall
Bathurst St
Wilmot St
Central St
Capitol Theatre
Hay St
Sydney Coach Terminal & Travellers Information Services
Central
Central SLR
Suburban Trains
Central Station

Queen Victoria Building (QVB)
St Andrew's Cathedral
Cinema Complex
World Square
Goulburn St
George St
Campbell St
Capitol Sq
SLR
Belmore Park
County Trains
Railway Square

YHA Membership & Travel Centre
Town Hall
Druitt St
Kent
Albion Pl
Liverpool St
Sussex St
Chinatown
Furama
Haymarket SLR
Haymarket
Barlow St
Rawson Pl
Pitt St
Thomas St
Lee St
To Sydney Airport (6.8km)

Cockle Bay Wharf
IMAX
Darling Harbour Visitors Centre
Darling Walk
Darling Harbour
Timbulong Park
Chin Exe Garden
Dixon St
Sydney Entertainment Centre
Market City
Her Majesty's
Kensington St

Market
Queen St
Day St
Darling
Harbour St
Harbourside
Quay
Ultimo
ABC Radio
To Sydney University (2.5km)

Cockle Bay
Harbourside
Pier St
Sydney Exhibition Centre
Haymarket SLR
Powerhouse Museum
Ultimo
Sydney Institute of Technology
Chippendale
Meagher St

Pyrmont
Novotel Sydney
Convention Sydney Convention SLR
Western Distributor
Harris
William Henry St
To Globe (1.5km)
Ultimo Rd
Wattle St
Broadway
Abercrombie St
Buckland
Myrtle St

Bunn St
Murray
Darling Dr
To ANZAC Bridge
Bulwara
Quarry St
Jones
MacArthur St
Maryann St
Small St
Pine St

125 250 m
125 250 yd

E **F** **G** **H**

Royal Exhibition Building
To IMAX Cinema (100m)
To Melbourne Museum (100m)

Rathdowne St
Nicholson St

Palmer St
Royal La
Marion La
Fitzroy
Australian Toy Museum
Napier St
George St
Gore St
Peel St

Gertrude St

Alma St

Carlton Gardens

Carlton

Royal Society

23,24,34 CityCircle

Princes St

St Vincent's

Fitzroy St

Brunswick St

Young St

Fitzroy Historic Precinct

Little Victoria St
Smith St
Mason St
Derby St
Oxford St

Victoria Pde

86,96

City Circle

Royal Australasian College of Surgeons

Natural Resources & Environment Information Centre

St Vincent's Private

11,112

END 30,34

32

END 12,31

23,24,27,29,42,47,48,109

Victoria Pde

Fire Services Museum of Victoria

Eye & Ear

Eades St
Dallas Brooks Hall

Freemasons Medical Centre

Albert St

Exploration La
Bennetts La
Little Lonsdale St
Telstra
Rockman's Regency
Jones La
Lumiere
Comedy
um of Chinese ustralian History
Her Majesty's
Punch La
Cohen Pl
Parliament
Smythe
Princess
Little Bourke St
Chinatown
Chinatown Gate
Crossley St
Liverpool St
Harwood Pl
Mellwraith
Coverlid La
Bien La
Market La
Hill of Content
Paramount Centre
Corrs La
A'Beckett La
Hoyts
Little Collins St
Gaslight
Meyers Pl
Melbourne
Ridgway Pl
Coates La East
Windsor

Albert St

Bourke St

Exhibition St

Russell St

Spring St

86,96

Parliament

Gisborne St

St Patrick's Cathedral

Cathedral Pl

Parliament Gardens

Parliament House

Parliament Pl

11,12,31,42,109,112

St Andrew's Pl

Park Hyatt
Tasma Terrace (National Trust)
Peter MacCallum Cancer Institute

Macarthur St

Lansdowne St

Dolphin Fountain

Fitzroy Gardens

Grey St
Freemasons
Mercy Hospital for Women
Gipps St

Little Collins St
Nauru House
Britain
Alfred Pl
St Michael's Uniting
Scots
Norway

Sunday Market

11,12,31,42,109,112

Old Treasury Building
Premiers Office

Treasury Theatre

State Government Offices

Treasury Pl

Model Tudor Village
Fairy Tree

Conservatory

Captain Cook's Cottage

Clarendon St

Hotham St

East Melbourne

George St

Collins St

Kino
Sofitel

Clarke Monument

Collins Place

Aboriginal Art Gallery of Australia

Burns Monument

JFK Memorial

Treasury Gardens

101 Collins
Grand Hyatt
Georges
Corporation La

Flinders La
Higson La
Oliver's La

Throssall La
Spark La

Lindrum

Flinders St

48,70,75 CityCircle

Rutledge La
Hosier La
Forum

Flinders St

Jacksons

Federation Square

Australian Centre For The Moving Image
Ian Potter Centre:
NGV Australian Art
Atrium
Cross Bar
Amphitheatre
Function Centre
Yarra Building
Stage Screen
Yarra Ferry Terminal

Batman Ave

Birrarung Marr

30

Wellington Pde

Wellington Pde South

48,75
Hilton on the Park

Jolimont

Maxwell La

Jolimont

Jolimont Rd
Jolimont La
Agnes St
Palmer St
Charles St
Sophie La
Jolimont Tce
Jolimont St

Australian Gallery of Sport & Olympic Museum

MCC Pavilion Library & Museum

Federation Bells

Speakers Corner

Yarra

Pde

Jeffries

Boatsheds
Sunday Market
Skate Park

Alexandra Gardens

Melbourne Park National Tennis Centre

70,76

Rod Laver Arena

Melbourne Cricket Ground

Brunton Ave

Alexandra Ave

Queen Victoria Gardens

National Gallery of Victoria (Closed for Renovation e-reopens 2003)

St Kilda Rd

Floral Clock

Kings Domain

To Government House (500m), Shrine of Remembrance (550m), & Observatory (600m)

Linlithgow Ave

The Tan

Yarra Bike Path

Alexandra Ave

Swan St Bridge

River

Batman Ave

To Royal Botanic Gardens (50m)

Sidney Myer Music Bowl

Swan St

To Monash Fwy (250m)

Old Scotch Oval

Vodafone Arena

Yarra Park

END 22

E **F** **G** **H**

| 0 | 125 | 250 m |
| 0 | 125 | 250 yd |

250   500 m
250   500 yd

E   F   G   H

Hackney

Botanic St   Westbury St   King William St   North Tce   Rundle St   Tce

Dequetteville

Hackney Rd

Wakefield Rd   East Tce   Victoria Park Racecourse

Bartels Rd

St John La   St John St   East Tce

1

National Wine Centre of Australia (under construction)

Plane Tree Dr   Rymill Park

Botanic Park   Botanic Garden   Botanic Gardens

Botanic

Harvey St   Tomsey St   South Tce   To Adelaide Hills (15km) & Hahndorf (29km)

Rundle Rd   Angas St   Vincent St   Marion St   Power St   Gilles St

Zoological Gardens   First   Royal Adelaide Gardens

University of South Australia

Frome Rd

Carrington St   Kate St   Halifax St

Corryton St   Hutt St   Hutt Rd

North Tce   Botanic   Tce   East

Ayers Historic House   Palace East End; IMAX   Tandanya Cultural Centre

Cairns St   Glen Osmond Rd

2

University of Adelaide   University of South Australia   Art Gallery of South Australia

Europa House   Bookshop   La Nova   Moger   Union St

Tucker St   Flinders St   Hume St   Hume La   McLaren St   Blackburn St   Himeji Gardens

Ngaparti Multimedia   Rundle St   Bent St   Grenfell St   Pirie St   Frome St

Dawkins Pl   Regent St N   Eden St   Charlotte St

Sudholz Pl   Cypress St   Bewes St   Harriet St   Disability Information Centre

Torrens   River

Migration Museum   Institute Building (The Bradman Collection)   State Library

South Australian Museum   National War Memorial

Angus & Robertson   York St   Hindmarsh Square

Ifould   Gunson St   Wakefield St   Pulteney St   Hurdle Square   Pulteney St   Unley Rd

3

University Oval   Pennington Gardens   Memorial Dr   Victoria Dr   Kintore Ave

Pioneer Womens Memorial Gardens   Parliament House   Old Parliament House   Government House

Dymocks   Rundle Mall   Charles   Gawler Pl   Myer   City Ave   Stephens Pl

Twin St   Arcade La   Hoyts   Hyde St   Roper St   Divett Pl   Chancery La

Wyatt St   Angas St   Princess St   Queen St   Stephens St   Hallett St   Halifax St   Gilles St   South Tce

RAA   St Francis Xavier Cathedral   Magistrate's Court   Moore St   Carrington St   St Helena St   To Belair National Park (12km)

Elder Park   Festival Centre   King William Rd

American Express Travel Services   Grenfell St   Town Hall   Old Treasury Building   Nelson St   Suffen St   Symonds Pl   Delhi St   South Tce

Traveller's Medical & Vaccination Centre   Exchange Pl   King William St   Supreme Court   Victoria Square   Glenelg Tram   King William St   Peacock Rd

Adelaide Oval   Creswell Gardens   North Adelaide

Adelaide Bridge

Radisson Playford   SA Visitor & Travel Centre   Stamford Plaza   Adelaide Casino   Hyatt Regency

Grosvenor   Edmund Wright House   Bentham St   GPO   Moralta St   Sir Samuel Way Building   Magistrate's Court   Mill St   Frew St   John St

4

Festival Dr   Adelaide Convention Centre

Holy Trinity   Imprints Booksellers   Rosina St   Victoria St   Leigh St   Currie St   Waymouth St

Bank St   Eliza St   Young St   Pitt St   Central   Bowen St   Moonta St   Field St   Thomas St   Compton St   Russell St   Owen St   Norman St   O'Halloran St   Hobsons St   Sturt St   Wright St   Veale Gardens

Chinatown   Hilton International   Central Market & Plaza   Whitmore Square   Gilbert St   Sir Lewis Cohen Ave

Novotel   Hindley St   Light Square   Firefly Express   Morphett St   Bartels St   Hamley St

Lion Arts Centre; Jam Factory   Fenn Pl   Clarendon St   Elizabeth St   Franklin St   Grote St   Gouger St   Wright St   Winifred St   Lundie Gardens

5

Aquatic Centre (1.6km)   Montefiore Park   Montefiore Dr   Victoria Bridge

Torrens   Memorial Dr

Rose St   Liverpool St   Philip St   Currie St   Gray St   Crowther St   Waymouth St   North Tce   West Tce   West Tce

Grattan St   St Mary's Convent   Selby St   Storr St   Byron Pl   Morney St   Marlborough St   Caxton St   Gray Ct   George Ct   Logan St   Little Gilbert St   Chatham St   Little Sturt St   Willcox St   Vinrace St   South Tce

Alfred St   O'Brien St   Goodwood Rd   Anzac Hwy

Bonython Park   To Port Adelaide (11km)

Old Adelaide Gaol   Gaol Rd   Railway Institute Oval

Port Rd   Glover Rd   To Henley Beach (9km)

Ellis Park   Sir Donald Bradman Dr   To Airport (5km)

Kingston Gardens

West Terrace Cemetery

Mile End Goods   Keswick Station (Interstate & Country Rail Terminal)   To Glenelg (9km) & the Fleurieu Peninsula

6

Mile End

E   F   G   H

Scale 1:10,000

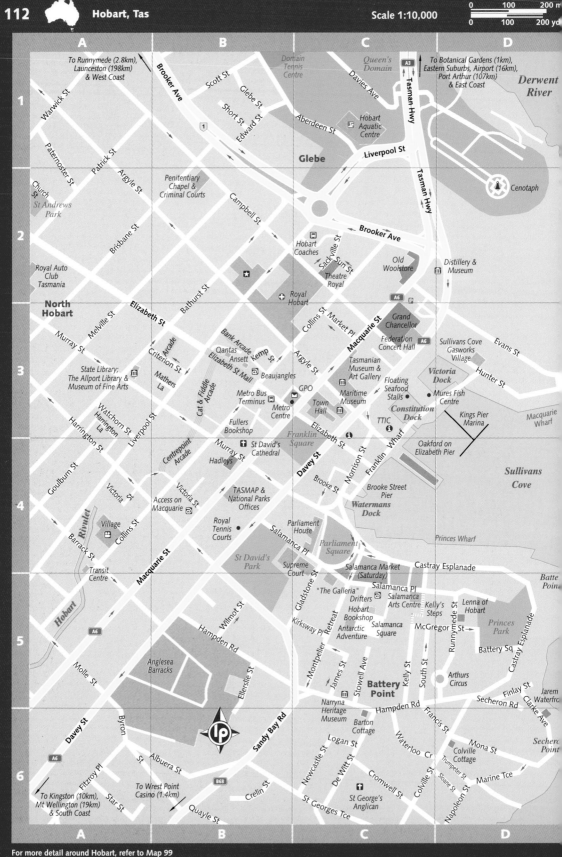

Scale 1:12,500

0   125   250 m
0   125   250 yd

A   B   C   D

1

To Mindil Beach (800m)
To Botanic Gardens (600m)
To Airport (9km)

Stuart Park

Malabar Ct
Marsina Ct
Morinda St
Smith St
Houston St
Barossa St
Mitchell St
Montoro Ct
Packard Pl
Packard St
Mauna Loa St
Manoora St
Dashwood Cr
Gardens Rd

Palmerston Park

Buffalo Ct
Woods St
Cashman St
Dashwood Pl
Finniss St
Mirambeena St
Burt St
Stuart Hwy

Dinah
Duke St
Beach Rd

2

Larrakeyah

Doctors
Gully Rd
Peary St
Harriet Pl
Daly St

Greek Orthodox

Smith St
McLachlan St
Shepherd St
Lindsay St
McMinn St
Harvey St
Barneson St

Brennan Dr

Aquascene

Doctors Gully

Marin

3

Bicentennial Park

Walking
Esplanade

Darwin Entertainment Centre

Carlton
McLachlan
Mitchell St
Briggs St
Mott Ct
AANT
Whitfield St
Cavenagh St
International Vaccination Clinic
Searcy St
Stott La
Woods St
GPO Plaza
Manton St
Gardiner St
Knuckey St
Foelsche St
Carey St
St

Tiger
Frances Bay Dr
Fishermi

4

Leichhardt Memorial

Lameroo Beach

Novotel Atrium
Peel St
Darwin City
Darwin Transit Centre
Saville
Internet Outpost
Lyons Cottage
Admiralty House

Global Gossip
Shadforth
Nuttall La Central
Arc
Pl
Knuckey St
Darwin Plaza
Tourism Top End
Galleria
West La
Rydges Plaza

Edmunds
Austin La
Spain Pl
Paspalis Centrepoint
Anthony Plaza
Bookworld
Commercial Bank

NT General Store
Didjworld Internet
American Express
Garuda
Litchfield St
Bennett St
Chinese Temple

Department of Primary Industry & Fisheries

Qantas
Harry Chan
McMinn St
Indonesia
Ave
Mavie St

5

Port Darwin

Herbert St
ANZAC Memorial

Bennett Park
Darwin Bus Depot
Old Town Hall
Brown's Mart
Church La

Parliament House
Telegraph Cable Monument
Government House
Hughes

Police Station & Old Courthouse
Supreme Court
Esplanade
Steps
Ave
Kitchener
Christ Church Cathedral
Survivors' Lookout
Dr
WWII Oil Storage Tunnels

Stokes Hill

Deckchair

Indo-Pacific Marine & Australian Pearling Exhibition

Wharf Precinct

Franc Bay

Darwin Harbour

6

Iron Ore Wharf

Fort Hill Wharf

Old Fort Hill Wharf

The Arcade

Stokes Hill Wharf

A   B   C   D

For more detail around Darwin, refer to Map 12

LONELY PLANET

MAPS & ATLASES

Lonely Planet's City Maps feature downtown and metropolitan maps as well as public transport routes and walking tours. The maps come with a complete index of streets and sights and are plastic coated for extra durability.

Road Atlases are an essential navigation tool for serious travellers. Cross-referenced with the guidebooks, they feature distance and climate charts and a comprehensive index.

Amsterdam City Map
ISBN 1 86450 081 6
US$5.95 • UK£3.99

Athens City Map
ISBN 1 74059 320 0
US$5.99 • UK£3.99

Bangkok City Map
ISBN 1 74059 101 1
US$5.99 • UK£3.99

Barcelona City Map
ISBN 1 86450 174 X
US$5.95 • UK£3.99

Beijing City Map
ISBN 1 86450 255 X
US$5.95 • UK£3.99

Berlin City Map
ISBN 1 86450 005 0
US$5.95 • UK£3.99

Boston City Map
ISBN 1 86450 175 8
US$5.95 • UK£3.99

Brisbane & Gold Coast City Map
ISBN 1 74059 434 7
US$5.99 • UK£3.99

Brussels City Map
ISBN 1 86450 256 8
US$5.95 • UK£3.99

Budapest City Map
ISBN 1 86450 077 8
US$5.95 • UK£3.99

Buenos Aires City Map
ISBN 1 86450 079 4
US$5.99 • UK£3.99

Cairo City Map
ISBN 1 86450 257 6
US$5.95 • UK£3.99

Cape Town City Map
ISBN 1 86450 076 X
US$5.95 • UK£3.99

Chicago City Map
ISBN1 86450 006 9
US$5.95 • UK£3.99

Dublin City Map
ISBN 1 86450 176 6
US$5.95 • UK£3.99

Edinburgh City Map
ISBN 1 74059 015 5
US$5.99 • UK£3.99

Florence City Map
ISBN 1 74059 321 9
US$5.99 • UK£3.99

Frankfurt City Map
ISBN 1 74059 016 3
US$5.99 • UK£3.99

Hong Kong City Map
ISBN 1 86450 007 7
US$5.95 • UK£3.99

Honolulu & Oahu City Map
ISBN 1 86450 290 8
US$5.99 • UK£3.99

Istanbul City Map
ISBN 1 86450 080 8
US$5.95 • UK£3.99

Jerusalem City Map
ISBN 1 86450 096 4
US$5.95 • UK£3.99

Kathmandu City Map
ISBN 1 74059 266 2
US$5.99 • UK£3.99

Las Vegas City Map
ISBN 1 74059 428 2
US$5.99 • UK£3.99

London City Map
ISBN 1 86450 008 5
US$5.95 • UK£3.99

Los Angeles City Map
ISBN 1 86450 258 4
US$5.95 • UK£3.99

Madrid City Map
ISBN 1 74059 322 7
US$5.99 • UK£3.99

Melbourne City Map
ISBN 1 86450 009 3
US$5.95 • UK£3.99

Miami City Map
ISBN 1 86450 177 4
US$5.95 • UK£3.99

New Orleans City Map
ISBN 1 74059 017 1
US$5.99 • UK£3.99

New York City Map
ISBN 1 74059 194 1
US$5.95 • UK£3.99

Paris City Map
ISBN 1 86450 011 5
US$5.95 • UK£3.99

Prague City Map
ISBN 1 86450 012 3
US$5.95 • UK£3.99

Rio de Janeiro City Map
ISBN 1 86450 013 1
US$5.95 • UK£3.99

Rome City Map
ISBN 1 86450 259 2
US$5.95 • UK£3.99

San Francisco City Map
ISBN 1 86450 014 X
US$5.95 • UK£3.99

Seattle City Map
ISBN 1 74059 323 5
US$5.99 • UK£3.99

Singapore City Map
ISBN1 1 86450 178 2
US$5.95 • UK£3.99

St Petersburg City Map
ISBN 1 86450 179 0
US$5.95 • UK£3.99

Sydney City Map
ISBN 1 86450 015 8
US$5.95 • UK£3.99

Toronto City Map
ISBN 1 74059 433 9
US$5.99 • UK£3.99

Vancouver City Map
ISBN 1 74059 018 X
US$5.99 • UK£3.99

Venice City Map
ISBN 1 74059 429 0
US$5.99 • UK£3.99

Washington D.C. City Map
ISBN 1 86450 078 6
US$5.95 • UK£3.99

Australia Road Atlas
ISBN 1 86450 065 4
US$14.99 • UK£8.99

Southern Africa Road Atlas
ISBN 1 86450 101 4
US$14.99 • UK£8.99

Thailand, Vietnam, Laos & Cambodia Road Atlas
ISBN 1 86450 102 2
US$14.99 • UK£8.99

India & Bangladesh Road Atlas
ISBN 1 86450 101 4
US$14.99 • UK£8.99

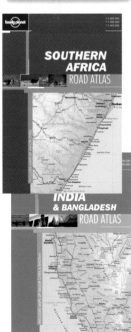

LONELY PLANET

You already know that Lonely Planet produces more than this one road atlas, but you might not be aware of the other products we have on this region. Here is a selection of titles that you may want to check out as well:

Australia
ISBN 1 74059 065 1
US$25.99 • UK£15.99

New South Wales
ISBN 0 86442 706 9
US$19.99 • UK£12.99

Northern Territory
ISBN 0 86442 791 3
US$16.95 • UK£10.99

Queensland
ISBN 0 86442 712 3
US$19.99 • UK£11.99

South Australia
ISBN 0 86442 716 6
US$16.95 • UK£10.99

Tasmania
ISBN 1 74059 230 1
US$17.99 • UK£11.99

Victoria
ISBN 1 74059 240 9
US$19.99 • UK£12.99

Western Australia
ISBN 0 86442 740 9
US$15.99 • UK£10.99

Islands of Australia's
Great Barrier Reef
ISBN 0 86442 563 5
US$14.95 • UK£8.99

Outback Australia
ISBN 1 86450 187 1
US$24.99 • UK£14.99

Melbourne
ISBN 1 74059 181 X
US$16.99 • UK£10.99

Sydney
ISBN 1 74059 062 7
US$16.99 • UK£10.99

Melbourne City Map
ISBN 1 86450 009 3
US$5.95 • UK£3.99

Sydney City Map
ISBN 1 86450 015 8
US$5.95 • UK£3.99

Australian phrasebook
ISBN 0 86442 576 7
US$5.95 • UK£3.99

Walking in Australia
ISBN 0 86442 669 0
US$21.99 • UK£13.99

Cycling Australia
ISBN 1 86450 166 9
US$21.99 • UK£13.99

Watching Wildlife Australia
ISBN 1 86450 032 8
US$19.99 • UK£12.99

Healthy Travel - Australia,
NZ & the Pacific
ISBN 1 86450 052 2
US$5.95 • UK£3.99

Aboriginal Australia &
the Torres Strait Islands
ISBN 1 86450 114 6
US$19.99 • UK£12.99

Sydney Condensed
ISBN 1 86450 200 2
US$11.99 • UK£5.99

Diving & Snorkeling
Australia's Great Barrier Reef
ISBN 0 86442 763 8
US$17.95 • UK£11.99

Diving & Snorkeling
Australia: Southeast
Coast & Tasmania
ISBN 1 55992 059 9
US$14.95 • UK£7.99

Sean & David's Long Drive
ISBN 0 86442 371 3
US$10.95 • UK£5.99

**Available wherever
books are sold**

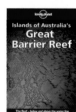

LONELY PLANET

GUIDES BY REGION

L onely Planet is known worldwide for publishing practical, reliable and no-nonsense travel information in our guides and on our Web site. The Lonely Planet list covers just about every accessible part of the world. Currently there are 15 series: travel guides, Shoestring guides, Condensed guides, Phrasebooks, Read This First, Healthy Travel, Walking guides, Cycling guides, Pisces Diving & Snorkeling guides, City Maps, Travel Atlases, Out to Eat, World Food, Journeys travel literature and Pictorials.

AFRICA Africa on a shoestring • Africa – the South • Arabic (Egyptian) phrasebook • Arabic (Moroccan) phrasebook • Cairo • Cape Town • Cape Town city map • Central Africa • East Africa • Egypt • Ethiopian (Amharic) phrasebook • The Gambia & Senegal • Healthy Travel Africa • Kenya • Malawi, Mozambique & Zambia • Morocco • North Africa • Read This First Africa • South Africa, Lesotho & Swaziland • Southern Africa road atlas • Swahili phrasebook • Tanzania, Zanzibar & Pemba • Trekking in East Africa • Tunisia • West Africa • Zimbabwe, Botswana & Namibia • Zimbabwe, Botswana & Namibia Travel Atlas • World Food Morocco

Travel Literature: The Rainbird: A Central African Journey • Songs to an African Sunset: A Zimbabwean Story • Mali Blues: Traveling to an African Beat

AUSTRALIA & THE PACIFIC Auckland • Australia • Australian phrasebook • Australian road atlas • Bushwalking in Australia • Bushwalking in Papua New Guinea • Cycling NZ • Fiji • Fijian phrasebook • Healthy Travel Australia, NZ and the Pacific • Islands of Australia's Great Barrier Reef • Melbourne • Melbourne city map • Micronesia • New Caledonia • New South Wales & the ACT • New Zealand • Northern Territory • Outback Australia • Out To Eat – Melbourne • Out to Eat – Sydney • Papua New Guinea • Pidgin phrasebook • Queensland • Rarotonga & the Cook Islands • Samoa • Solomon Islands • South Australia • South Pacific • South Pacific Languages phrasebook • Sydney • Sydney city map • Sydney Condensed • Tahiti & French Polynesia • Tasmania • Tonga • Tramping in New Zealand • Vanuatu • Victoria • Western Australia

Travel Literature: Islands in the Clouds • Kiwi Tracks: A New Zealand Journey • Sean & David's Long Drive

CENTRAL AMERICA & THE CARIBBEAN Bahamas, Turks & Caicos • Bermuda • Central America on a shoestring • Costa Rica • Costa Rica (Spanish) phrasebook • Cuba • Dominican Republic & Haiti • Eastern Caribbean • Guatemala, Belize & Yucatán: La Ruta Maya • Jamaica • Mexico • Mexico City • Panama • Puerto Rico • Read This First Central & South America • World Food Mexico

Travel Literature: Green Dreams: Travels in Central America

EUROPE Amsterdam • Amsterdam city map • Amsterdam Condensed • Andalucía • Austria • Baltic States phrasebook • Barcelona • Barcelona city map • Berlin • Berlin city map • Britain • British phrasebook • Brussels, Bruges & Antwerp • Budapest • Budapest city map • Canary Islands • Central Europe • Central Europe phrasebook • Corfu & Ionians • Corsica • Crete • Crete Condensed • Croatia • Cyprus • Czech & Slovak Republics • Denmark • Dublin • Dublin city map • Eastern Europe • Eastern Europe phrasebook • Edinburgh • Estonia, Latvia & Lithuania • Europe on a shoestring • Finland • Florence • France • French phrasebook • Georgia, Armenia & Azerbaijan • Germany • German phrasebook • Greece • Greek Islands • Greek phrasebook • Hungary • Iceland, Greenland & the Faroe Islands • Ireland • Italian phrasebook • Italy • Krakow • Lisbon • The Loire • London • London city map • London Condensed • Malta • Mediterranean Europe • Mediterranean Europe phrasebook • Moscow • Munich • Norway • Paris • Paris city map • Paris Condensed • Poland • Portugal • Portugese phrasebook • Prague • Prague city map • Provence & the Côte d'Azur • Read This First Europe • Romania & Moldova • Rome • Russia, Ukraine & Belarus • Russian phrasebook • Scandinavian & Baltic Europe • Scandinavian Europe phrasebook • Scotland • Slovenia • Spain • Spanish phrasebook • St Petersburg • St Petersburg city map • Sweden • Switzerland • Trekking in Spain • Tuscany • Ukrainian phrasebook • Venice • Vienna • Walking in Britain • Walking in France • Walking in Ireland • Walking in Italy • Walking in Spain • Walking in Switzerland • Western Europe • Western Europe phrasebook • World Food Ireland • World Food Italy • World Food Spain

Travel Literature: The Olive Grove: Travels in Greece

INDIAN SUBCONTINENT Bangladesh • Bengali phrasebook • Bhutan • Delhi • Goa • Hindi & Urdu phrasebook • India • Indian Himalaya • Karakoram Highway • Kerala • Mumbai (Bombay) • Nepal • Nepali phrasebook • Pakistan • Rajasthan • Read This First: Asia & India • South India • Sri Lanka • Sri Lanka phrasebook • Tibet • Tibetan phrasebook • Trekking in the Indian Himalaya • Trekking in the Karakoram & Hindukush • Trekking in the Nepal Himalaya

Travel Literature: • Hello Goodnight • In Rajasthan • Shopping for Buddhas • The Age Of Kali

LONELY PLANET

MAIL ORDER

Lonely Planet products are distributed worldwide. They are also available by mail order from Lonely Planet, so if you have difficulty finding a title please write to us. North and South American residents should write to 150 Linden St, Oakland CA 94607, USA; European and African residents should write to 10a Spring Place, London, NW5 3BH, UK; and residents of other countries to PO Box 617, Hawthorn, Victoria 3122, Australia.

ISLANDS OF THE INDIAN OCEAN Madagascar & Comoros • Maldives • Mauritius, Réunion & Seychelles

MIDDLE EAST & CENTRAL ASIA Bahrain, Kuwait & Qatar • Central Asia • Central Asia phrasebook • Dubai • Hebrew phrasebook • Iran • Israel & the Palestinian Territories • Istanbul • Istanbul City Map • Istanbul to Cairo on a shoestring • Jerusalem • Jerusalem City Map • Jordan • Lebanon • Middle East • Oman & the United Arab Emirates • Syria • Turkey • Turkish phrasebook • World Food Turkey • Yemen

Travel Literature: The Gates of Damascus • Kingdom of the Film Stars: Journey into Jordan • Black on Black: Iran Revisited

NORTH AMERICA Alaska • Backpacking in Alaska • Baja California • Boston • Boston city map • California & Nevada • California Condensed • Canada • Chicago • Chicago city map • Deep South • Florida • Hawaii • Honolulu • Las Vegas • Los Angeles • Miami • Miami city map • New England • New Orleans • New York City • New York city map • New York Condensed • New York, New Jersey & Pennsylvania • Oahu • Pacific Northwest USA • Puerto Rico • Rocky Mountain • San Francisco • San Francisco city map • Seattle • Southwest USA • Texas • USA • USA phrasebook • Vancouver • Washington, DC & the Capital Region • Washington DC city map

Travel Literature: Drive Thru America

NORTH-EAST ASIA Beijing • Cantonese phrasebook • China • Hong Kong • Hong Kong city map • Hong Kong, Macau & Guangzhou • Japan • Japanese phrasebook • Japanese audio pack • Korea • Korean phrasebook • Kyoto • Mandarin phrasebook • Mongolia • Mongolian phrasebook • Seoul • South-West China • Taiwan • Tokyo

Travel Literature: Lost Japan • In Xanadu

SOUTH AMERICA Argentina, Uruguay & Paraguay • Bolivia • Brazil • Brazilian phrasebook • Buenos Aires • Chile & Easter Island • Colombia • Ecuador & the Galapagos Islands • Healthy Travel Central & South America • Latin American Spanish phrasebook • Peru • Quechua phrasebook • Rio de Janeiro • Rio de Janeiro city map • South America on a shoestring • Trekking in the Patagonian Andes • Venezuela

Travel Literature: Full Circle: A South American Journey

SOUTH-EAST ASIA Bali & Lombok • Bangkok • Bangkok city map • Burmese phrasebook • Cambodia • Hanoi • Healthy Travel Asia & India • Hill Tribes phrasebook • Ho Chi Minh City • Indonesia • Indonesia's Eastern Islands • Indonesian phrasebook • Indonesian audio pack • Jakarta • Java • Laos • Lao phrasebook • Malay phrasebook • Malaysia, Singapore & Brunei • Myanmar (Burma) • Philippines • Pilipino (Tagalog) phrasebook • Read This First Asia & India • Singapore • Singapore city map • South-East Asia on a shoestring • South-East Asia phrasebook • Thailand • Thailand's Islands & Beaches • Thailand, Vietnam, Laos & Cambodia road atlas • Thai phrasebook • Thai audio pack • Vietnam • Vietnamese phrasebook • World Food Thailand • World Food Vietnam

ALSO AVAILABLE: Antarctica • The Arctic • Brief Encounters: Stories of Love, Sex & Travel • Chasing Rickshaws • Lonely Planet Unpacked • Not the Only Planet: Travel Stories from Science Fiction • Sacred India • Travel with Children • Traveller's Tales

State and Territory Abbreviations

ACT . . . . . .Australian Capital Territory
CI . . . . . . .Christmas Island
CKI . . . . .Cocos (Keeling) Islands

LHI . . . . . .Lord Howe Island
NI . . . . . . .Norfolk Island
NSW . . . . .New South Wales

NT . . . . . .Northern Territory
QLD . . . . .Queensland
SA . . . . . .South Australia

TAS . . . . . .Tasmania
VIC . . . . . .Victoria
WA . . . . . .Western Australia

A

A1 Mine Settlement **93** G2
Abbot Bay **56** D2
Abbot Point **20** D5
Abbotsham **96** D5
Abercrombie Caves **80** A3
Abercrombie River **80** A3
Abercrombie River National Park **80** A4
Aberdeen **76** A4
Aberfeldy **93** G2
Aberfeldy River Camp **93** H3
Abergowrie **55** F5
Abernethy **76** B6
Abingdon Downs **54** A2
Abrakurrie Cave **39** G5
Acacia Downs **42** B5
Acheron **93** F1
Acheron Island **55** G6
Ackland **71** D1
Acraman Creek Conservation Park **40** C6
Acton **97** E2
Adam Bay **12** C1
Adaminaby **88** C4
Adam Range **98** C2
Adamsfield **98** D3
Adavale **33** E5
Adcock Gorge **15** G2
Addington **92** A1
Adelaide **69** F4
Adelaide Gate **42** C3
Adelaide Lead **85** F6
Adelaide Plains Wineries **69** F3
Adelaide River **12** C3
Adelong **88** A1
Adelong Aboriginal Land **37** H4
Adjungbilly **79** F6
Admiral Bay **14** D4
Admiralty Gulf **9** F5
Admiralty Gulf Aboriginal Land **9** E5
Admiralty Islands **81** G4
Adolphus Island **9** H6
Advancetown **71** G4
Advancetown Lake **71** G4
Adventure Bay **99** E5
Agate Creek Gemfields **54** A5
Agnes Water **59** H6
Agnew **37** G2
Ahakeye Aboriginal Land Trust **30** B1
Aileron **30** C2
Aireys Inlet **92** B4
Airlie Beach **57** F3
Airly **94** A4
Alawa Aboriginal Land Trust **11** F6
Alawoona **49** F3
Albany **65** F6
Albany Creek **71** G1
Albany Highway **64** C1
Albany Park **12** C3
Albatross Bay **21** E3
Alberga River **30** D6
Albert **74** A3
Albert Facey Homestead **65** E1

Alberton **97** G5
Alberton West **93** H5
Albert River **18** D2
Albion Downs **37** G2
Albion Park **80** D5
Albury **87** F3
Alcala **19** E5
Alcomie **96** B4
Alcoota **30** D2
Aldinga **69** F5
Aldinga Bay **69** F5
Alectown **74** B5
Alehvale **19** G3
Alexander Morrison National Park **62** B2
Alexandra **93** F1
Alexandra River **19** E3
Alexandria **18** B4
Alford **69** E2
Alfred National Park **95** G3
Alfred Town **78** D6
Algebuckina Bridge **41** E1
Algebulicullia Creek **40** D2
Alice **73** E1
Alice Downs **16** B3
Alice River (QLD) **21** F6
Alice River (QLD) **33** F3
Alice Springs **30** C3
Alice Well **30** C4
Alick Creek **19** G6
Ali-Curung **17** G6
Allambee (SA) **64** D4
Allambee (VIC) **93** G4
Allambee South **93** G4
Allambi **30** D3
Allandale (SA) **41** E1
Allandale (WA) **62** C3
Allans Flat **87** F4
Allansford **91** F4
Alleena **78** C3
Allendale **92** B1
Allendale East **90** B2
Allendry **42** C4
Alligator Billabong **13** F2
Allora **70** D3
Alma (NSW) **50** A2
Alma (SA) **69** F3
Alma (VIC) **85** F6
Almaden **54** D2
Alma Lake **50** A2
Almora **18** D3
Alonnah **99** E5
Aloomba **55** F2
Alpha **33** F3
Alpha Creek **33** F3
Alpine National Park **50** C6
Alpurrulam **18** C6
Alroy Downs **18** A4
Alstonville **71** G6
Altino **62** C4
Alton **43** H2
Alton Downs **31** H6
Alva **56** D1
Alyangula **11** H4

Alyawarra Aboriginal Land Trust **30** C1
Amamoor **61** F5
Amanbidji **16** C1
Amaroo Thorn **63** G5
Amata **30** A5
Ambalindum **29** F3
Ambathala **33** E6
Amber **54** C3
Ambrose **59** F5
Amburla **28** A2
Amby **43** H1
American Beach **69** E6
American River **69** E6
Amherst **85** F6
Amiens **70** C5
Amity Point **71** H2
Ammaroo **30** D1
Amoonguna **29** G5
Amosfield **70** D5
Amphitheatre **85** E6
Amungee Mungee **17** G1
Amys Peak **59** F6
Anakie (QLD) **58** A4
Anakie (VIC) **92** C3
Andado **30** D5
Andamooka **41** F4
Andamooka Homestead **66** D1
Anderson Bay **97** F4
Anderson Inlet **93** F5
Anderson Range **30** C5
Anderson Rocks **63** H5
Andersons Spring **65** E4
Andover **99** F2
Andrew Island **18** D2
Andrews Point **34** A1
Angalarri River **10** B6
Angarapa Aboriginal Land Trust **30** D1
Angas Downs **30** B4
Angaston **69** G3
Angelo River **23** E4
Angepena **67** G1
Anglers Reach **88** B4
Anglers Rest **87** G6
Anglesea **92** B4
Angle Vale **69** F3
Angorichina Roadhouse **67** F2
Angourie **73** G2
Angurugu **11** H4
Ankuri **63** F6
Anna Bay **76** D6
Annaburroo **12** D3
Anna Creek **41** E2
Annandale **31** G5
Anna Plains **14** D5
Anningie **30** B1
Annitowa **18** B6
Annuello **49** H3
Anser Island **100** B6
Anson Bay (NI) **77** F4
Anson Bay (NT) **12** A4
Anson Point **77** F4
Ansons Bay **97** H4
Antechamber Bay **69** E6

Anthony Lagoon **18** A3
Antill Ponds **99** F2
Antil Plains **56** B1
Antwerp **83** F3
Anurrete Aboriginal Land Trust **18** A6
Anvil Rock **45** F4
Anxious Bay **48** A1
Apollo Bay **92** A5
Appila **67** F6
Appin **80** D4
Applethorpe **70** D5
Apple Tree Flat **76** D3
Apsley (TAS) **99** E2
Apsley (VIC) **82** D5
Apsley River **76** D1
Aqua Downs **43** F1
Arafura Sea **11** F1
Arafura Swamp **11** F3
Aralaij Beach **10** D2
Araluen **89** E3
Araluen Botanic Park **62** D6
Aramac **33** E2
Aramac Creek **33** E2
Arapunya **31** E1
Ararat **83** H6
Aratula **71** F3
Arcadia (QLD) **18** C6
Arcadia (VIC) **86** B4
Arch Cliff **35** F3
Archer Point **20** B1
Archer River **21** F4
Archer River Roadhouse **21** F4
Archipelago of the Recherche **47** H3
Arckaringa **40** D1
Arckaringa Creek **40** D1
Arcoona **66** D2
Ardglen **76** A3
Ardjorie **15** F4
Ardlethan **78** C4
Ardmona **86** B4
Ardmore **31** H1
Ardrossan **69** E3
Arena **62** B1
Areyonga **28** D7
Argadargada **31** F1
Argyle Diamond Mine **16** B2
Ariah Park **78** C4
Aringa **91** E4
Arizona **19** F4
Arkaba **67** F3
Arkaroola **41** H4
Arkendeith **56** C2
Arlparra Store **30** D1
Arltunga Historical Reserve **29** F3
Arltunga Historic Goldfield **29** F3
Arltunga Hotel & Bush Resort **29** F3
Armadale **62** D2
Armatree **74** C1
Armidale **44** B5
Armit Island **57** E3
Armonds Bay **89** E6
Armraynald **19** E3
Armstrong Channel **97** G3

Arnhem Bay **11** G3
Arnhem Highway **13** E2
Arnhem Land **11** F3
Arnhem Land Aboriginal Land Trust **13** H3
Arno Bay **68** C2
Arnold **85** G5
Arnold River **11** F6
Arrabury **32** A6
Arramall **62** A1
Arrawarra **73** F4
Arrilalah **32** D3
Arrla Bay **11** E2
Arrowsmith River **62** B1
Arthur Bay **97** G2
Arthur Peak **56** A2
Arthur Pieman Protected Area **96** A5
Arthur Point **34** B2
Arthur Range **98** C4
Arthur River (TAS) **96** A4
Arthur River (WA) **64** D2
Arthurs Lake **99** E1
Arthurs Seat **59** H6
Arthurton **69** E2
Arthurville **74** D4
Arundel **63** E4
Asbestos Range National Park **97** E5
Ashburton Downs **22** D4
Ashburton River **23** E4
Ashfield **62** D2
Ashford **72** A1
Ashley **44** A4
Ashmont **42** C6
Aspley Strait **10** B2
Astell Island **11** H2
Atartinga **30** C2
Atherton **55** E2
Athlone **93** F4
Atitjere **30** D2
Atley **37** F3
Atnarpa **29** G3
Atnetye Aboriginal Land **31** E3
Attack Creek Historic Reserve **17** G4
Attunga (QLD) **44** A5
Attunga (WA) **62** C3
Atula **31** E2
Aubigny **70** C2
Auburn (QLD) **60** C4
Auburn (SA) **69** F2
Auburn Range **60** C3
Auburn River **60** C3
Auburn River National Park **60** D3
Augathella **33** F5
Augusta **64** B5
Augustus Downs **19** E3
Augustus Island **9** E6
Aurari Bay **11** E2
Aurukun **21** E4
Auski Roadhouse **23** E2
Austral Downs **18** C5
Australian Alps Walking Trail **88** B4, **93** H2
Australian Institute of Marine Science **56** C1
Australian Woolshed **71** G2
Australia Telescope **43** H5
Australind **64** B3
Auvergne **10** B6
Avenel **86** B5
Avenue **82** B5
Avoca (TAS) **97** F6
Avoca (VIC) **85** F6
Avoca Downs **38** B5
Avoca River **85** E4
Avoid Bay **68** A3

Avon **69** F3
Avon Brook **65** E1
Avondale (QLD) **61** F1
Avondale (SA) **41** G4
Avondale (WA) **64** C4
Avon Downs **18** B5
Avon Farm **63** E5
Avonmore **33** G4
Avon River (VIC) **94** A3
Avon River (WA) **62** D5
Avon Valley National Park **62** D5
Awaba **81** F1
Axedale **85** H5
Ayers Lookout **27** E5
Ayers Rock (Uluru) **30** A5
Ayr **56** C1
Ayton **20** B1

B

Baan Baa **44** A5
Babakin **63** G5
Babel Island **97** H2
Babinda **55** F2
Babinda Boulders **55** F2
Bacchus Marsh **92** C2
Back Plains **70** D3
Backstairs Passages **69** E5
Backwater **72** C4
Backy Point **67** E5
Baddaginnie **86** C5
Baden **99** F2
Baden Park **42** D6
Badgebup **65** F3
Badger Island **97** G3
Badgingarra **62** B3
Badgingarra National Park **62** B3
Baerami **75** H4
Bagalowie **67** G4
Bagdad **99** F2
Bago Range **88** A2
Bagot Range **30** D6
Bagshot **85** H5
Bailey's Rocks **82** D6
Bairnsdale **94** C3
Bajool **59** F5
Bakara **69** H3
Bakara Conservation Park **69** H3
Baker Lake **24** D6
Bakers Creek **57** F5
Bakers Swamp **74** D5
Balah **69** H1
Balaklava **69** F2
Balbirini **18** A1
Balcanoona **67** H1
Bald Head **46** C4
Bald Hill **20** A5
Bald Island **65** G5
Bald Mountain **88** D4
Bald Point **11** H3
Bald Rock National Park **70** D6
Baldry **74** C5
Balfes Creek **20** B5
Balfour **96** B4
Balfour Downs **23** G3
Balgarup **65** E4
Balgarup River **64** D3
Balgo **16** B5
Balgo Aboriginal Land **16** B6
Balgowan **68** D3
Balhannah **69** G4
Balingup **64** C4

Balkuling **63** E5
Balladonia **47** H1
Balladoran **74** D2
Ballalaba **89** E2
Ballan **92** C2
Ballandean **70** D5
Ballandool River **43** G3
Ballangeich **91** G3
Ballara **42** A6
Ballarat **92** B2
Ballaying **65** E2
Ball Bay **77** H6
Balldale **87** E3
Balliang **92** C2
Ballidu **62** D3
Ballimore **74** D3
Ballina **71** H6
Balloong **93** H5
Bally Knob **54** D5
Ballythunna **36** C1
Balnagowan **59** F4
Balnarring **92** D4
Balmoral **83** F6
Balonne Highway **43** F2
Balonne River **43** B4
Balook **93** H5
Balranald **49** H3
Bamaga **21** F1
Bamawm **85** H3
Bambaroo **55** F5
Bambra **92** B4
Bamganie **92** B3
Bampfield Head **21** E1
Banana **59** E6
Ban Ban Spring **12** D4
Bancannia Lake **42** B5
Bandiana **87** F4
Bandin **62** D4
Bandon **61** E3
Bandon Grove **76** C5
Bandya **38** A2
Bangalow **71** H6
Bang Bang **19** E3
Bangham Conservation Park **82** D4
Bangor **97** E5
Banjawarn **37** H2
Banka Banka **17** G4
Banksia **59** E2
Banksia Beach **55** F4
Banks Strait **97** G3
Bankstown **81** E4
Bannister **80** A5
Bannister Downs **64** C1
Bannockburn **92** B3
Banora Point **71** H4
Banyan Island **11** G2
Banyans, The **12** D4
Banyena **83** H4
Baradine **43** H5
Barakula **60** C4
Baralaba **58** D5
Barambah Creek **61** E4
Baranduda **87** F4
Baratta **67** G4
Barbrongan Tower **15** E4
Barcaldine **33** E3
Barcaldine Downs **33** E3
Barclay **63** G6
Barcoo River **32** D4
Bare Hill (TAS) **98** D5
Bare Hill (WA) **46** B5
Barellan **78** B3

Bare Point **73** G3
Barfold **85** H6
Bargara **61** F2
Bargo **80** C5
Bargo Bargo Mountains **32** D6
Barham **85** G1
Baringhup **85** G5
Barker Lake **37** H6
Barkers Creek **85** G6
Barkers Rocks **68** D3
Bark Hut Inn **12** D3
Barkly **85** E5
Barkly Downs **18** C5
Barkly Highway **17** A4, **18** H4
Barkly Homestead (Roadhouse) **18** A4
Barkly Tableland **17** G1
Barlee Range **22** C4
Barlee Range Nature Reserve **22** C4
Barmah **86** A3
Barmah East **86** B3
Barmedman **78** D3
Barmera **49** F2
Bar Mountain **58** D2
Barnato **42** D6
Barnawartha **87** E3
Barnes Bay **99** E4
Barnett River Gorge **15** H2
Barney Knob **54** B3
Barneys Lake **50** A1
Barnjaru **13** E3
Barnong **36** D3
Barooga **86** C2
Barossa Valley Wineries **69** G3
Barraba **44** A5
Barrakee **85** F3
Barrambie **37** F2
Barramunga **92** A5
Barranyi National Park **11** H6
Barraport **85** F2
Barrenjoey Head **81** E3
Barren Tier **99** E1
Barrier Highway **42** C5
Barrier Range **42** B6
Barringna **56** B1
Barrington (NSW) **76** D4
Barrington (TAS) **96** D5
Barrington Peak **31** G3
Barrington Tops National Park **76** C4
Barringun **43** E3
Barron Gorge National Park **55** F1
Barron River **55** E1
Barrow Creek **17** G6
Barrow Island **22** B1
Barrow Point **21** H5
Barry Beach **93** G6
Barry Creek **100** C3
Barry Creek Campsite **100** C3
Barry Mountains **87** E6
Barton **105** G5
Barton Highway **88** D1
Barton Plains **9** G5
Barunga **13** G6
Barunga Gap **69** E2
Barwell Conservation Park **68** A1
Barwidgee **37** H1
Barwidgi **54** C3
Borwo **86** B3
Barwon Downs **92** A4
Barwon Heads **92** C4
Barwon Highway **43** H3
Barwon River (NSW) **43** F4
Barwon River (VIC) **92** A4

Baryulgil **73** E1
Basalt River **20** B5
Bascombe Well Conservation Park **68** A1
Bass **93** E5
Bass Highway (TAS) **96** A4, D5
Bass Highway (VIC) **93** F5
Bass Point **80** D6
Bass Strait **52** C2, **53** E3
Bastion Point **95** H3
Bastyan Dam **96** B6
Batavia Downs **21** F3
Batchelor **12** C3
Batemans Bay **89** F3
Batesford **92** C3
Bathurst **80** A2
Bathurst Harbour **98** C5
Bathurst Island (NT) **10** A2
Batlow **88** A2
Batten Creek **11** H6
Battery, The **60** A2
Battery Point **112** C5
Battle Camp **21** H6
Bauhinia Downs **18** A1
Bauloora Hill **79** E5
Bauple **61** F4
Baw Baw National Park **93** G3
Bawley Point **89** G3
Baxter **93** E4
Baxter Cliffs **47** H6
Bayles **93** F4
Bayley Island **18** D2
Baynes Mountain **72** C6
Bay of Fires **97** H5
Bay of Islands **91** G5
Beachmere **71** G1
Beachport **90** A1
Beacon **63** F2
Beaconsfield **97** E5
Beaconsfield Upper **93** E3
Beadon Point **22** B2
Beagle Bay **14** D2
Beagle Bay Aboriginal Reserve **15** E2
Beagle Gulf **12** B1
Bealiba **85** F5
Beaming Hill **65** G4
Beanbah **43** G5
Bearbong **74** D2
Beardmore **93** H3
Beardy River **72** B1
Beargamil **74** B6
Bears Lagoon **85** G3
Beatrice Island **11** G5
Beauchamp Falls **92** A5
Beaudesert **71** G3
Beauflat **64** D3
Beaufort **92** A1
Beaufort Inlet **65** G4
Beaufort River **64** D3
Beaumaris **97** H5
Beauty Point **97** E5
Becher Point **64** B1
Bedford Creek **45** H3
Bedford Downs **16** A2
Bedford Island **15** E1
Bedgerebong **79** E1
Bedooba **43** E6
Bedourie (QLD) **31** H4
Bedourie (QLD) **60** A1
Beeac **92** A3
Beebo **70** A5
Beebyn **37** E1
Beechal River **43** E1

Beechford **97** E4
Beech Forest **92** A5
Beechmont **71** G4
Beechwood **77** F2
Beechworth **87** E4
Beecroft Head **89** H1
Beecroft Peninsula **89** H1
Beedelup National Park **64** C5
Beelbangera **78** A3
Beenleigh **71** G3
Beerburrum **61** G6
Beerwah **61** G6
Beetaloo **17** G2
Bega **89** E6
Beggan Beggan **79** F5
Belah **43** E4
Belair National Park **69** F4
Belarabon **42** D6
Belarabon Range **42** D6
Belarwi **78** C3
Belbora **76** D4
Belele **37** E1
Belgrave **93** E3
Bell (QLD) **60** D6
Bell (NSW) **45** E4
Bellarine **92** C3
Bellarine Peninsula **92** C4
Bellata **44** A4
Bellbird **76** B6
Bellbrae **92** C4
Bellbrook **72** D6
Bellenden Ker **55** F2
Bellevue **20** A2
Bellfield **54** A6
Bell Gorge **15** G2
Bellingen **73** E5
Bellinger River **73** E5
Bellingham **97** F4
Belli Park **61** G5
Bellmount Forest **79** H6
Bell Peak North **55** F2
Bells Line of Road **45** E3
Bells Mountain **76** A4
Belltrees **76** B3
Belmont **81** F1
Belowra Mountain **89** E5
Beltana **67** F1
Belton **67** G4
Belyando Crossing **56** B5
Belyando River **56** B6
Belyuen **10** B3
Bemboka **88** D6
Bemm River **95** F2
Bena (NSW) **78** C1
Bena (VIC) **93** F5
Benalla **50** B5
Benambra **87** H6
Benaraby **59** G5
Benarkin **61** E6
Ben Boyd National Park **95** H1-2
Ben Bullen **80** C1
Ben Chifley Dam **80** B2
Ben Cona **58** A6
Ben Cruachan **94** A3
Bencubbin **63** F3
Bencullen **64** C1
Bendalong & Manyana **89** G2
Bendemeer **72** A6
Bendemere **60** A4
Bendick Murrell **79** F4
Bendigo (SA) **67** H6
Bendigo (VIC) **85** H5

Bendoc **95** F1
Bendolba **76** C5
Bendora Dam **88** C2
Beneree **79** H2
Benger **64** B2
Ben Halls Gap National Park **76** B2
Beni **74** D3
Benjinup **64** C3
Ben Lomond (NSW) **43** E4
Ben Lomond (NSW) **72** C3
Ben Lomond (QLD) **21** F4
Ben Lomond (QLD) **57** E3
Ben Lomond National Park **97** F6
Ben Major **85** E6
Benmara **18** B3
Bennet Bay **11** G4
Ben Nevis (TAS) **97** F5
Ben Nevis (VIC) **85** E6
Bennison Island **100** C2
Bens Knob **59** F5
Benstead Creek **29** F5
Bentinck Island **18** D2
Bentley **71** G6
Berajondo **61** F1
Berat **70** D3
Berawinnia Downs **42** C3
Beremboke **92** C2
Berendebba **79** E3
Bergalia **89** F4
Beringarra **36** D1
Berkeley **80** D5
Berkeley River **9** G5
Berkshire Valley Folk Museum **62** C3
Bermagui **89** E5
Bermagui South **89** E5
Bernier Island **22** A6
Berridale **88** C5
Berri **49** F2
Berrigan **86** D2
Berrima **80** C5
Berrimpa **32** C4
Berringama **87** H4
Berrook **49** F3
Berry **80** D6
Berry Springs **12** C2
Berry Springs Nature Park **12** C2
Bertiehaugh **21** F3
Berwick **93** E3
Bessiebelle **91** E3
Beswick **13** G6
Beswick Aboriginal Land Trust **13** G6
Bet Bet **85** F5
Bete Bolong **94** D3
Bethanga **87** F3
Bethungra **79** F5
Bethungra Mountain **79** E5
Betley **85** F5
Betoota **32** A5
Beulah **83** G2
Bevendale **79** H5
Beveridge **92** D1
Beverley **63** E6
Beverley Springs **15** G2
Beverly Hills **54** B5
Bexhill **71** G6
Biala **79** H5
Biamanga National Park **89** E6
Bibbenluke **88** C6
Bibbulman Walking Trail **62** D6, **64** C2
Bibilup **64** B4
Bibliando **67** G3
Biboohra **55** E1

Bicheno **99** G1
Bickerton Island **11** H4
Bickley Bay **46** C6
Bidaminna **62** C4
Biddeston **70** D2
Biddon **74** D1
Bidura **49** H2
Biella Spring **24** A3
Big Bell Mine **37** E2
Big Billy Bore Campsite **49** F4
Big Desert **83** E1
Big Desert Wilderness Park **82** D1
Bigga **79** H3
Bigge Island **9** E5
Biggenden **61** F3
Bigge Point **9** F5
Big Green Island **97** G2
Big Heath Conservation Park **82** C5
Big Hill **85** G5
Big Hill Point **77** F2
Big Jim Lake **98** D1
Big Lagoon Campsite **36** A1
Big Red (Sandhill) **31** H5
Big Sunday **13** F4
Big Warrambool, The **43** G4
Big Waterhouse Lake **97** F4
Big Woody Island **35** G4
Bijerkerno **42** B5
Bijiji Lake **42** B6
Bilbarin **63** G6
Bilbul **78** A3
Billabalong **36** D2
Billabong Roadhouse **36** B2
Billa Falls **62** D2
Billa Kalina **41** E3
Billengarrah **18** A1
Billericay **63** G6
Billeroo **62** C1
Billiat Conservation Park **49** F3
Billilla **42** C6
Billiluna **16** A5
Billiluna Aboriginal Land **16** A4
Billimari **79** G2
Billimina Shelter **84** B4
Billinnooka **23** G3
Billinudgel **71** H5
Billybingbone **43** F4
Billygoat Mountain **61** F3
Billys Creek **73** E4
Biloela **59** F6
Bilpa Morea Claypan **31** H4
Bilpin **45** E2
Bilyana **55** F4
Bimbadeen **65** G2
Bimberi Peak **88** C3
Bimbi **79** E3
Bimbijy **37** F4
Bimbowrie **41** H6
Bimerah **32** D4
Bimjella Hill **35** F3
Binalong Bay **97** H5
Binalong **79** H5
Binananngoi Point **11** H3
Binbee **56** D3
Binda **79** H4
Bindar **62** D4
Bindi **43** E6
Bindi Bindi **62** D3
Bindle **43** H2
Bindoon **62** D4
Bingara (NSW) **44** A4
Bingara (QLD) **42** D2

Bing Bong **11** H6
Bingie Bingie Point **89** F4
Bingil Bay **55** F3
Bingo Munjie North **87** G6
Biniguy **44** A4
Binjour **61** E3
Binna Burra **71** G4
Binnaway **75** E2
Binningup **64** B2
Binnu **36** C3
Binnum **82** D4
Binthalya **22** B5
Binya **78** A3
Birchip **83** H2
Bird Rock **77** G4
Birdsville **31** H5
Birdsville Developmental Road **32** A5
Birdsville Track **31** H6, 41G2
Birdwood **69** G4
Birkdale **65** F2
Birkhead **33** F4
Birralee **97** E5
Birrego **78** B6
Birregurra **92** A4
Birrimba **17** E1
Birrindudu **16** C3
Birriwa **75** E3
Birthday Mountain **21** F4
Bishopsbourne **97** E6
Bittern **93** E4
Black Bett Mountain **80** A4
Black Bluff **96** C5
Black Bobs **98** D2
Blackbraes **20** A5
Blackburn Island **81** G5
Blackbutt **61** E6
Blackbutt Range **61** E6
Blackdown **54** B1
Blackdown Tableland National Park **34** A4
Blackfellow Point **35** F4
Blackfellows Caves **90** B2
Black Flag **37** H5
Black Flag Lake **37** H5
Black Head (NSW) **80** D6
Black Head (NSW) **95** H3
Black Head (QLD) **59** G5
Blackheath **45** F4
Black Hill **37** G2
Black Jack Mountain **88** B6
Black Jungle Spring **13** E3
Blackmans Bay **99** E4
Black Mountain (NSW) **43** H5
Black Mountain (NSW) **72** B4
Black Mountain (NT) **13** E5
Black Mountain (QLD) **18** D6
Black Mountain (QLD) **59** E4
Black Mountain (QLD) **60** D2
Black Point (SA) **69** E3
Black Point (WA) **64** B5
Black Point Ranger Station **10** D1
Black Range (VIC) **84** A3
Black Range (VIC) **87** E5
Black Range State Park **84** A3
Black River **96** B3
Black Rock **67** F5
Blacksand Beach **55** F4
Blacks Beach **57** F5
Blacks Creek **57** F5
Blacksmith Island **57** F4
Black Soil Plains **12** C1
Black Spring Mountain **79** E3
Black Springs (NSW) **80** B3

Black Springs (SA) **69** G2
Black Swamp **70** D6
Blacktown **81** E3
Blacktown Tableland National Park **58** C4
Blackville **75** G2
Blackwall **97** E5
Blackwater **58** C4
Blackwater Creek **33** E5
Blackwood **92** C1
Blackwood Creek **97** E6
Blackwood National Park **56** B5
Blackwood River **64** B4, D4
Bladensburg National Park **32** C2
Blair Athol (QLD) **32** A2
Blairgowrie **92** D4
Blakeville **92** C1
Blanchetown **69** H3
Blanchewater **41** H3
Bland **79** E2
Blandford **76** A3
Blanket Flat **79** H4
Blantyre **42** C6
Blaxland **45** G1
Blayney **79** H2
Blessington **97** F6
Bli Bli **61** G5
Blighty **86** C1
Blina **15** F3
Blinkenthorpe Bay **81** H5
Blinky Beach **81** H5
Blinman **67** G2
Bloods Range **25** G4
Bloomsbury **57** E4
Blowering Reservoir **88** B2
Blue Gum Forest **45** E4
Blue Lake National Park **71** H2
Blue Mountain (QLD) **31** G2
Blue Mountain (QLD) **57** F6
Blue Mountain (QLD) **60** D1
Blue Mountains **80** C3
Blue Mountains National Park **80** C3-4
Blue Mud Bay **11** G4
Blue Peaks **96** D6
Blue Range **93** F1
Blue Rock Lake **93** G3
Bluestone Tier **99** F3
Blueys Beach **77** E5
Bluff **58** C4
Bluff, The (NSW) **43** E6
Bluff, The (QLD) **35** F6
Bluff Beach **68** D4
Bluff Hill Point **96** A4
Bluff Rock **72** D1
Blyth **69** F2
Blythe River **96** C5
Blyth Point **97** G1
Blyth River **11** F3
Boambee **73** F5
Boat Harbour **96** C4
Boat Harbour Beach **96** C4
Bobadah **43** F6
Bobardt Point **21** G4
Bobinawarrah **87** E5
Bobin **77** E3
Bobs Knobs **98** D5
Bodalla **89** F4
Boddington **64** C2
Bogandillon Swamp **78** D1
Bogangar **71** H5
Bogan Gate **74** A6
Bogan River **43** F6
Bogarella **33** G5

Boggabilla **44** A3
Boggabri **44** A5
Boggy Hole **27** G3
Boggy Hole Creek **27** H3
Bogie River **56** D3
Boglands **63** E5
Bogolong **79** E2
Bogong **87** G6
Bogong Mountain **88** B2
Bogong Mountain Range **88** B2
Boho South **86** C5
Boinka **49** G3
Boisdale **94** A3
Bokhara River **43** F4
Bold Head **92** D2
Bolivia **72** D1
Bollards Lagoon **42** A3
Bollon **43** G2
Bolt Head **21** F3
Bolton **49** H3
Bolwarra **54** C2
Bolwarrah **92** B1
Bomaderry **80** C6
Bomali **43** G3
Bombala **95** G1
Bombala River **88** D6
Bomera **75** F2
Bonalbo **71** E6
Bonang **95** E2
Bonaparte Archipelago **9** E6
Bon Bon **40** D4
Bondi Beach **81** E4
Bondo **88** B1
Bond Springs **30** C3
Bonegilla **87** F4
Bongaree **71** G1
Bongeen **70** C2
Bonney Downs **23** F2
Bonney Well **17** G5
Bonnie Brae **67** H4
Bonnie Doon **86** C6
Bonnie Rock **63** G2
Bonny Hills **77** F3
Bonrook **13** E5
Bonshaw **70** B6
Bonus Downs **43** G1
Bonville **73** F5
Booanya **47** H1
Booborowie **69** G1
Boobyalla **97** G4
Boodarie **14** A6
Booderee National Park **89** G2
Boodua **70** D1
Boogardie **37** E3
Booginook Conservation Park **49** F2
Bookham **79** F6
Boola Boolka **49** H1
Boolardy **36** D2
Boolarra **93** G5
Boolarra South **93** G5
Boolathana **22** A5
Boolba **43** G2
Boolboonda **61** E2
Boolcoomata **42** A6
Booleroo Centre **67** F5
Booligal **50** B2
Bool Lagoon **82** C5
Bool Lagoon Game Reserve **82** C5
Boologooro **22** B5
Booltharda Hill **36** D2
Boolygoo Range **37** G2
Boomahnoomoonah **86** D3

Boomanjin Hill **35** F5
Boomerang **54** D4
Boomerang Beach **77** E5
Boomi **44** A3
Boonah **71** F3
Boona Mountains **50** C1
Boondara **50** A1
Boondoon **33** E5
Boongadoo Hall **65** F3
Boonoo Boonoo **70** D6
Boonoo Boonoo National Park **70** D6
Boonooroo **35** E5
Boorabbin National Park **37** H6
Booral **76** D5
Boorara **42** D2
Boorcan **91** G3
Boorhaman **87** E4
Boorlye Point **35** F5
Boorooma **43** G4
Booroorban **50** A3
Boorowa **79** G4
Boort **85** F3
Booti Booti National Park **77** E5
Booyal **61** F2
Booylgoo Spring **37** G2
Borambil **75** G3
Border Downs **42** A4
Border Island **57** F3
Border Ranges National Park **71** F5
Border Store **13** G2
Bordertown **82** C3
Border Village **39** G5
Boree Creek **78** B6
Boreen **61** G5
Boree Plains **49** H2
Borefield Road **41** F4
Borenore Caves **79** H1
Borgden Point **11** E2
Boro **89** E1
Boroka Lookout **84** C3
Bororen **59** G6
Borroloola **18** A1
Borung **85** F3
Borung Highway **83** G3
Bostobrick **73** E4
Bostock Creek **91** H4
Boston Bay **48** B3
Boston Island **68** B3
Bosworth **67** E1
Botany Bay **81** E4
Botany Bay National Park **81** E4
Botherling **63** E4
Bothwell **99** E2
Boucaut Bay **11** F2
Bouddi National Park **81** F2
Bouldercombe **59** F4
Boulder Point **97** H4
Boulder Range **100** C6
Boulia **31** H2
Boullanger Bay **96** A3
Boundary Bend **49** H3
Bountiful Islands **19** E1
Bourke **43** E4
Bournda National Park **89** E6
Bow **75** G4
Bowalli **42** D1
Bowarrady **35** G3
Bowelling **64** C3
Bowen **57** E2
Bowen River **56** D4
Bowenvale **85** F5
Bowenville **70** C1

Bower **69** G2
Bowie **33** F1
Bowlers Lagoon **97** G4
Bowling Alley Point **76** B2
Bowling Green Bay **56** C1
Bowling Green Bay National Park **56** C1
Bowmans **69** F2
Bowna **87** G3
Bowning **79** G6
Bowral **80** C5
Bowraville **73** E6
Bow River **16** B2
Bow River Aboriginal Land **16** A2
Box Hill **93** E3
Box Tank **42** B6
Boyd Point **21** E3
Boyeo **83** E3
Boyer **99** E3
Boyne Island **59** G5
Boyne River **34** C4
Boyup Brook **64** C4
Bracewell **59** F5
Brackendale **76** C1
Bracknell **97** E6
Bradshaw **10** B6
Brady Swamp **84** C6
Braedawn **64** D5
Braemar **67** H6
Braeside **70** D4
Braeside Estate **62** C1
Braidwood **89** E2
Braithwaite Point **11** E2
Bramfield **48** B2
Brampton Island **57** F4
Bramston Beach **55** F2
Bramwell **21** F3
Brand Highway **62** C3
Brandon **56** C1
Bransby **42** B2
Branxholm **97** G5
Branxholme **91** E2
Branxton **76** B6
Brawlin **79** E5
Breadalbane (NSW) **80** A6
Breadalbane (QLD) **31** H3
Breaker Inlet **14** A6
Breakfast Creek **75** G5
Bream Creek **99** F3
Breamlea **92** C4
Bredbo **88** C4
Breelong **74** D2
Breeza **75** H1
Bremer Bay **65** H4
Bremer Island **11** H2
Breona **97** E6
Brewarrina **43** F4
Briagolong **94** A3
Bribbaree **79** E3
Bribie Island **61** G6
Bribie Island National Park **61** G6
Brick House **22** A6
Bridal Veil Falls **45** F4
Bridgenorth **97** E5
Bridgetown **64** C4
Bridgewater **99** E3
Bridgewater Bay **90** D4
Bridgewater-on-Loddon **85** G4
Bridport **97** F4
Brier Holme Head **98** B4
Brigalow **60** C5
Bright **87** F5
Brighton (QLD) **71** G1

Brighton (TAS) **99** E3
Brighton Downs **32** B3
Brightview **71** F2
Brim **83** G2
Brimpaen **84** B2
Brindabella National Park **88** C1
Brindabella Range **88** C2
Bringagee **50** B3
Brinkworth **69** F1
Brisbane **71** G2
Brisbane Forest Park **71** F1
Brisbane Range **61** F5
Brisbane Ranges National Park **92** C2
Brisbane River **61** F5, **71** G2
Brisbane Valley Highway **71** F1
Brisbane Water National Park **81** E2
Brittania **56** A3
Brittons Swamp **96** A4
Broad Arrow **38** A5
Broadbeach **71** H4
Broadford **93** E1
Broadmarsh **99** E3
Broadmeadow **56** D6
Broadmere **17** H1
Broadmount **59** F4
Broadribb River **95** E3
Broad Sound **59** E2
Broad Sound Channel **59** F1
Broadwater (NSW) **73** G1
Broadwater (VIC) **91** E3
Broadwater National Park **73** G1
Brobenah Hills **78** A4
Brocklehurst **74** C3
Brocklesby **87** F2
Brockman Highway **64** B5
Brodies Plains **72** B2
Brogo **89** E6
Brogo River **89** E5
Broke **76** A6
Broke Inlet **64** D6
Broken Bay **81** E3
Broken Bridge Creek **77** G5
Broken Bucket Camp **83** E2
Broken Bucket Tank **83** E2
Broken Hill **42** B6
Broken River (QLD) **57** E4
Broken River (VIC) **86** D5
Bromelton **71** G3
Bronte Park **98** D1
Brookefield Conservation Park **69** H3
Brooke Reefs **64** D6
Brooking Springs **15** G3
Brooklands **54** C4
Brookstead **70** C2
Brookton **63** E6
Brookton Highway **62** D6
Brookville **65** E2
Brooloo **61** F5
Broome **14** D3
Broome Bird Observatory **14** D3
Broome Head **59** F2
Broomehill **65** E3
Brooms Head **73** G3
Brothers, The **58** A5
Brothers Mountain, The **80** A1
Broughams Gate **42** A4
Broughton (QLD) **56** B2
Broughton (VIC) **83** E3
Broula **79** G3
Broulee **89** F4
Brovinia **60** D4
Brown Creek **58** C6

Brown Head **100** D5
Brown Mountain **95** E2
Browns Plains **71** G2
Brown Strait **11** G2
Bruce **67** F5
Bruce Highway **55** G6, **61** E1
Bruce Rock **63** G5
Brunchilly **17** G4
Brunette Downs **18** A3
Brungle **88** B1
Brunswick Bay **9** E6
Brunswick Heads **71** H5
Brunswick Junction **64** B3
Brushgrove **73** F2
Bruthen **94** C3
Bruxner Highway **70** A5, **71** F6
Bryah **23** F6
Bryans Swamp **84** B6
Bryden **71** F1
Buandik Campsite **84** B4
Buangor **91** H1
Buaraba Creek **71** E1
Bucasia **57** F5
Bucca **61** F2
Buccan **71** G3
Buccaneer Archipelago **15** E1
Buccarumbi **73** E3
Buchan **94** D2
Buchanan Highway **17** E1
Buchanan Hills **16** D4
Buchan Caves **94** D2
Bucheen Creek **87** G5
Buckambool Mountain **43** E6
Buckenderra **88** C4
Buckingham **64** C3
Buckingham Bay **11** G2
Buckingham Downs **31** H1
Buckland **99** F3
Buckland Plains **33** G4
Buckleboo **66** C5
Buckle Head **9** H5
Buckley River **18** C5
Buckley Swamp **91** E2
Buckrabanyule **85** F3
Budawang National Park **89** F2
Buddabaddah **43** F6
Budderoo National Park **80** D6
Buddigower **78** C3
Budderim **61** G6
Budgee Budgee **75** F5
Budgeree **93** G5
Budgewoi **81** F2
Buffalo **93** F5
Buffalo River **87** E6
Bugaldie **43** H5
Bugilbone **43** H4
Bukbukluk Lookout **13** E4
Bukkulla **72** A2
Bulahdelah **76** D5
Bulga **76** A5
Bulga Downs **37** G3
Bulgamurra **49** H1
Bulgandramine **74** B4
Bulgandry **87** E2
Bulgonunna Peak **56** C5
Bulgul **12** A3
Bulgunnia **40** D4
Bulimba **54** B1
Bullabul **85** G4
Bullara **22** A3
Bullarah **43** H4
Bullardoo **36** C3

Bullaring **63** G6
Bullaroon **43** E4
Bullarto **92** C1
Bullecourt **18** C6
Bullengarook **92** C2
Bulleringa **54** B3
Bulleringa National Park **54** B3
Bulley Ranges **90** C3
Bulli **80** D5
Bullioh **87** G4
Bullita Outstation **16** D1
Bull Mountain **88** D6
Bullock Creek **54** C3
Bullocks Flat Ski Field **88** B5
Bulloo Creek **42** A6
Bulloo Downs (QLD) **42** C2
Bulloo Downs (WA) **23** F4
Bulloo River **32** D6, **42** C2
Bullo River **10** A6
Bullsbrook **62** C5
Bullumwaal **94** B3
Bullyard **61** F2
Bulman **11** F4
Buln Buln **93** F4
Bulwer **71** H1
Bulyee **63** F6
Bumbaldry **79** F3
Bumberry **74** C6
Bunbartha **86** B3
Bun Beetons Point **97** G1
Bunbury **64** B3
Bundaberg **61** F2
Bundaburrah **79** E1
Bunda Cliffs **39** H5
Bundageree Head **73** F5
Bundalaguah **94** A4
Bundalong **86** D3
Bundanoon **80** C6
Bundarra **72** A4
Bundella **75** G2
Bundey River **30** D1
Bundjalung National Park **73** G2
Bundook **76** D4
Bundure **50** B4
Bungabinni Native Well **24** C2
Bungarby **88** C6
Bungendore **88** D1
Bungle Bungle (Purnululu) National Park **16** B3
Bungobine **56** C5
Bungobine Peak **56** C4
Bungonia **80** B6
Bungulla (QLD) **72** D1
Bungulla (WA) **63** F5
Bungunya **44** A3
Bungwahl **77** E5
Buninyong **92** B2
Bunjil's Shelter **84** D3
Bunker Gap **34** D4
Bunketch **63** E2
Bunnan **75** H3
Bunneringee **49** G2
Buntine **62** D2
Buntine Highway **16** D2
Bunurong Marine Park **93** F5
Bunyah **76** D4
Bunya Mountains National Park **60** D6
Bunyan **88** C4
Bunyip **93** F4
Bunyip River **93** E4
Buraja **87** E3
Burakin **63** E2

Burban **43** F3
Burban Grange **43** F3
Burdekin Dam **55** C3
Burdekin River **54** C3, **56** D5
Burekup **64** B3
Burgooney **78** B1
Burke & Wills Dig Tree **42** A1
Burke & Wills Roadhouse **19** E4
Burke Developmental Road **19** E5, **54** D2
Burke River **31** H2, **32** A1
Burkes Flat **85** F4
Burketown **18** D3
Burleigh Heads **71** H4
Burnamwood **42** D5
Burnerbinmah **37** E3
Burnett Heads **61** F2
Burnett Highway **59** E5, **61** E5
Burnett River **60** D2, **61** F2
Burney Island **11** H4
Burnie **96** C4
Burns Creek **97** F5
Burnt Pine **77** G5
Burpengary **71** G1
Burraboi **85** H1
Burracoppin **63** G4
Burra **69** G1
Burraga **80** A3
Burragate **95** G1
Burramine **86** D3
Burrandana **87** G1
Burran Rock **63** G4
Burrell Creek **77** E4
Burren Junction **43** H4
Burrill Lake **89** G2
Burringbar **71** H5
Burringurrah National Park **22** D5
Burrinjuck **79** F6
Burrinjuck Dam **79** F6
Burrinjuck State Recreation Area **79** G6
Burrowa-Pine Mountain National Park **87** H3
Burroway **74** C3
Burrowye **87** H3
Burrumbeet **92** A1
Burrumbuttock **87** F3
Burrum Heads **61** G2
Burrum Point **61** G2
Burrum River National Park **61** G3
Burta **42** A6
Burt Creek **29** E6
Burthong **50** C1
Burtundy **49** G2
Bush Bay **22** A6
Bushfield **91** F4
Bush Point **14** D4
Bushy Park (QLD) **18** D6
Bushy Park (SA) **30** C2
Bushy Park (TAS) **99** E3
Bussell Highway **64** A4
Busselton **64** B4
Butchers Gap Conservation Park **82** A5
Butchers Ridge **94** D2
Bute **69** E2
Butler Dome **25** H5
Butlers Gorge **98** D2
Butlers Point **99** H1
Butterfly Gorge National Park **12** D4
Buttress Point **91** G4
Buxton (NSW) **80** C4
Buxton (QLD) **61** G2
Buxton (VIC) **93** F1
Byabarra **77** E3
Byaduk **91** E2

Byaduk Caves **91** E2
Byenup Lagoon **64** D5
Byfield **59** F3
Byfield National Park **59** F3
Byford **62** D6
Bylong (NSW) **75** G4
Bylong (QLD) **19** G5
Bynoe Harbour **12** B2
Bynoe River **19** E2
Byrimine **54** C3
Byrneside **86** B4
Byrock **43** F5
Byro **36** D1
Byron Bay **71** H6
Byron Mount **83** F6
Bywong **88** D1

C

Cabana **54** B3
Cabarlah **70** D1
Cabbage Tree Creek **95** E3
Caboolture **71** G1
Caboonbah **71** F1
Cabramurra **88** B3
Cactus Beach **40** B6
Cadelga **32** A5
Cadell **69** H2
Cadell Creek **32** B2
Cadell River **11** F3
Cadney Homestead **40** C1
Cadoux **63** E3
Caiguna **38** D6
Cairn Curran Reservoir **85** F6
Cairns **55** F1
Caiwarro **42** D3
Calarga Lagoon **35** F1
Calcified Forest **96** C2
Calder **96** C4
Calder Freeway **92** D2
Calder Highway **85** F4
Calder Island **57** G4
Caldermeade **93** E4
Caledon Bay **11** H3
Calen **57** F4
Calingiri **62** D4
Calita **62** D1
Calivil **85** G3
Callagiddy **22** B6
Cal Lal **49** F2
Callala Bay **89** G1
Callanna **41** F3
Callawa **14** C6
Callawadda **83** H5
Callide **59** F6
Callide Dam **59** F6
Callindary **42** B4
Calliope **59** G5
Callytharra Springs **22** C6
Caloundra **61** G6
Calpatanna Waterhole Conservation Park **48** A1
Caltowie **67** F6
Calulu **94** B3
Calvert **71** F2
Calvert Hills **18** B2
Calvert River **18** B2
Calwynyardah **15** F3
Camalilup **65** F3
Camberwell **76** A5
Cambewarra **80** C6
Camboon **60** C2

Cambooya **70** D2
Cambrai **69** G3
Cambridge **99** F3
Cambridge Gulf **9** H5
Camden **80** D4
Camel Creek **55** E5
Cameron Corner **42** A3
Cameron Downs **12** C3
Cameron Inlet **97** H2
Camfield **17** E2
Camfield River **17** E2
Camira Creek **73** F1
Camoola **33** E2
Camooweal **18** C5
Camooweal Caves National Park **18** C5
Campania **99** F3
Campaspe River (QLD) **56** A3
Campaspe River (VIC) **85** H4
Campbell **105** H3
Campbell Point **21** G4
Campbells Bridge **85** D2
Campbells Creek **85** G6
Campbells Forest **85** G4
Campbelltown (NSW) **80** D4
Campbelltown (VIC) **85** G6
Campbell Town **99** F1
Camp Creek **12** C3
Camperdown **91** H4
Camurra **44** A4
Canal Creek **59** F3
Canary **32** A2
Canaway Downs **32** D5
Canbelego **43** E6
Canberra **88** D1
Cancanning **65** E2
Candelo **88** D6
Canegrass **49** E2
Cane River **22** B2
Cane River Homestead **22** C3
Cangai **73** E2
Cania **60** D1
Cania Gorge National Park **60** D1
Caniambo **86** C4
Canna **36** D4
Cannie **85** F2
Canning Dam **62** D6
Canning River **62** C6
Canning Stock Route **16** A5, **23** H5
Cannington **32** B1
Cann River **95** F3
Canobie **19** F4
Canonba **43** F5
Canopus **49** F1
Canowindra **79** G2
Canterbury **32** B5
Canunda National Park **90** A1
Canungra **71** G4
Capalaba **71** G2
Cape, The **71** F5
Cape Adamson **96** B2
Cape Adieu **40** B6
Cape Arid **47** G2
Cape Arid National Park **47** G2
Cape Arnhem **11** H3
Cape Banks **90** A1
Cape Barren **97** H3
Cape Barren Island **97** H3
Cape Barrow **11** G4
Cape Baskerville **14** D2
Cape Bauer **40** C6
Cape Beatrice **11** H5
Cape Bedout **68** C6

Cape Bernier **9** G5
Cape Boileau **14** D3
Cape Borda **68** C5
Cape Bossut **14** D4
Cape Bougainville **99** G3
Cape Boullanger (TAS) **99** G3
Cape Boullanger (WA) **22** A6
Cape Bouquer **68** D6
Cape Bowen **21** H5
Cape Bowling Green **56** C1
Cape Bridgewater **90** D4
Cape Bruny **99** E5
Cape Buache **96** A3
Cape Buffon **90** A1
Cape Byron **71** H6
Cape Capricorn **59** G4
Cape Carnot **68** B4
Cape Cassini **68** D5
Cape Catastrophe **68** B4
Cape Clairault **64** A4
Cape Clear **92** A2
Cape Cleveland **55** H6
Cape Clinton **59** G2
Cape Cockburn **10** D2
Cape Conran **95** E3
Cape Conway **57** F4
Cape Cossigny **22** D1
Cape Coutts **69** E6
Cape Couture **22** A6
Cape Crawford **18** A1
Cape Croker **10** D1
Cape Cuvier **22** A5
Cape Degerando **99** G2
Cape Direction **21** G3
Cape Dombey (SA) **82** A5
Cape Dombey (NT) **10** A4
Cape Driver **68** C2
Cape du Couedic **68** C6
Cape Duquesne **90** D4
Cape Dutton **68** D5
Cape Elie **96** B3
Cape Elizabeth **68** D2
Cape Euler **68** B3
Cape Farewell **96** C1
Cape Farquhar **22** A4
Cape Finniss **48** A2
Cape Ford **12** A4
Cape Forestier **99** H2
Cape Frankland **97** G1
Cape Fredrick Hendrick **99** G4
Cape Freycinet **64** A5
Cape Frezier **14** D4
Cape Gantheaume **68** D6
Cape Gantheaume Conservation Park **68** D6
Cape Grafton **55** F1
Cape Grenville **21** G2
Cape Grey **11** H3
Cape Griffith **21** G3
Cape Grim **96** A3
Cape Grosse **12** B2
Cape Hardy **68** C2
Cape Hart **69** E6
Cape Hart Conservation Park **69** E6
Cape Hawke **77** E5
Cape Hay **10** A4
Cape Hillsborough National Park **57** F4
Cape Hotham **12** C1
Cape Hotham Forestry Reserve **12** C1
Cape Howe **95** H3
Cape Inscription **36** A1
Cape Jaffa **82** A5
Cape Jaubert **14** D4

Cape Jervis **69** E5
Cape Keerweer **21** E4
Cape Keppel **59** G4
Cape Keraudren (TAS) **96** A2
Cape Keraudren (WA) **14** B6
Cape Knob **65** H4
Capel **64** B3
Cape Latouche Treville **14** D4
Cape Leeuwin **64** B5
Cape Le Grande **47** F3
Cape Le Grand National Park **47** G2
Cape Linois **69** E6
Cape Liptrap **93** F6
Capella **58** B3
Cape Lodi **99** H1
Cape Londonderry **9** G5
Cape Manifold **59** G3
Cape Martin **49** E6
Cape Maurouard **99** G3
Cape Melville National Park **21** H5
Cape Missiessy **14** D4
Cape Moreton **71** H1
Cape Naturaliste (TAS) **97** H4
Cape Naturaliste (WA) **64** A3
Cape Nelson **90** D4
Cape Northumberland **90** B3
Cape North West **96** A2
Cape Otway **92** A6
Cape Otway Lighthouse **92** A6
Cape Palmerston **57** G6
Cape Palmerston National Park **57** G6
Cape Paterson **93** E5
Cape Paul Lamanon **99** G4
Cape Peron **99** G3
Cape Peron North **22** A6
Cape Pillar **99** G5
Cape Pond **9** E5
Cape Portland **97** G4
Cape Preston **22** C1
Cape Queen Elizabeth **99** F5
Cape Rabelais **82** A6
Cape Radstock **48** A1
Cape Range National Park **22** A3
Cape Raoul **99** F5
Cape Richards **55** F4
Cape Riche **65** G5
Cape River **20** B6
Cape Rochon **96** B2
Cape Ronsard **22** A6
Capertee **80** B1
Capertree River **75** G6, **80** C1
Cape Sandwich **55** F4
Cape Schanck **92** D5
Cape Scott **12** A4
Cape Shield **11** H4
Cape Sidmouth **21** G4
Cape Sonnerat **99** G2
Cape Sorell **98** B1
Cape Spencer **68** D5
Cape St. Cricq **22** A6
Cape St Albans **69** E6
Cape Stewart **11** F2
Cape St Lambert **9** H5
Cape Surville **99** G4
Cape Talbot **9** G4
Cape Thomas **82** A5
Cape Torrens **68** C5
Cape Torrens Conservation Park **68** C5
Cape Tourville **99** H2
Cape Townshend **59** F2
Cape Tribulation **20** B1
Cape Tribulation National Park **20** B1

Cape Upstart **56** D2
Cape Upstart National Park **56** D2
Cape Vancouver **65** F6
Cape Van Diemen **10** B1
Cape Villaret **14** D4
Cape Vlamingh **46** A6
Cape Voltaire **9** E5
Cape Wellington **100** D5
Cape Wickham **96** C1
Cape Wilberforce **11** H2
Cape Wiles **68** B4
Cape Willoughby **69** E6
Cape Woolamai **93** E5
Cape York **21** F1
Capricorn Group **59** H5
Capricorn Highway **58** C4
Captain Cook Highway **55** F1
Captains Flat **88** D2
Carabost **87** H2
Caradoc **42** C4
Caragabal **79** E2
Carag Carag **86** A4
Caramut **91** F3
Carandotta **31** G1
Carappee Hill Conservation Park **68** C1
Carbeen **55** E2
Carbine **37** H5
Carbla **36** B1
Carboor **87** E5
Carbunup River **64** A4
Carcoar **79** H2
Carcuma Conservation Park **82** B1
Cardabia **22** A4
Cardiff **64** C3
Cardigan **56** B3
Cardigan Village **92** A1
Cardington **56** B2
Cardinia Reservoir **93** E3
Cardwell **55** F4
Carey Downs **22** C6
Cargerie **92** B2
Cargo **79** G1
Cariewerloo **66** D4
Carinda **43** G5
Carisbrook **85** F6
Carlaminda **36** D3
Carlindie **14** B6
Carlindi **23** F1
Carlisle Island **57** F4
Carlisle Lakes **39** E3
Carlisle River **91** H5
Carlo **31** G3
Carlsruhe **92** C1
Carlton (VIC) **109** E1
Carlton (TAS) **99** F4
Carlton Hill **9** H6
Carlton Lea **36** C3
Carmichael **56** A6
Carmila **58** D1
Carnamah **62** C1
Carnarvon **22** A6
Carnarvon Developmental Road **33** H5
Carnarvon Highway **43** H2
Carnavon National Park **58** A6
Carnegie **24** B5
Carnot Bay **14** D2
Caro **62** B3
Caroda **44** A4
Carpentaria Downs **54** C5
Carpentaria Highway **17** H1
Carpenter Rocks **90** B2
Carrabin **63** H4

Carrajung **93** H5
Carranya (QLD) **32** C5
Carranya (WA) **16** A4
Carrarang **36** A2
Carrathool **50** B3
Carr Boyd Ranges **16** B1
Carrickalinga **69** F5
Carrieton **67** F4
Carroll **44** A5
Carron River **19** F3
Carruchan **55** F4
Carrum **93** E3
Carrum Downs **93** E3
Carson River (WA) **9** G5
Carson River (WA) **9** G6
Carwarp **49** G3
Carwell **33** F4
Cascade (NI) **77** H5
Cascade (WA) **47** F2
Cashmere Downs **37** G3
Casino **F6**
Cassilis **75** G3
Casterton **90** D1
Castlemaine **85** G6
Castlereagh Bay **11** F2
Castlereagh Highway **74** C1
Castlereagh Road **45** G1
Castlereagh River **43** G4, **71** D1
Castle Rock **33** H5
Castlevale **33** G4
Cataby Roadhouse **62** B3
Catamaran **98** D5
Cataract Gorge **97** E5
Cataract River **70** D6
Cataraqui Point **96** C2
Cathcart **88** D6
Cathedral, The **100** D4
Cathedrals, The **35** G3
Cathedral Beach **35** G3
Cathedral Gorge **16** B2
Cathedral Range **93** F1
Cathedral Rock National Park **72** D5
Catherine Hill Bay **81** F1
Catombal Range **74** D5
Cattai National Park **80** D3
Cattle Creek **11** E6
Cattle Creek Outstation **17** E2
Cattlewater Pass Track **29** E3
Cavendish **84** A5
Cave Point **65** F6
Caves, The **59** F4
Caveside **96** D6
Cawarra **65** H4
Cawnalmurtee **42** C4
Cawndilla Lake **42** B6
Cawongla **71** G5
Cecil Plains **70** B1
Cedar Bay National Park **20** B1
Cedric Mountain **59** F5
Ceduna **40** C6
Cement Mills **70** C4
Cemetary Bay **77** H6
Central Australia Aboriginal Reserve **25** F2-5
Central Castra **90** D5
Central Desert Aboriginal Land Trust **16** D4
Central Mount Stuart Historic Reserve **30** C1
Central Mount Wedge **30** A2
Central Station **35** F5
Central Tilba **89** E5
Centre Island **11** H6
Ceres (NSW) **74** B3

Ceres (VIC) **92** C4
Cervantes **62** B3
Cessnock **76** B6
Chadford **60** A4
Chaelundi National Park **73** E4
Chain of Lagoons **97** H6
Challa **37** F3
Chamberlain River **16** A2
Chambers Bay **12** D1
Chambers Pillar Historic Reserve **30** C4
Chambigne **73** E3
Chandlers Creek **95** F2
Channel Point **10** B4
Channon, The **71** G6
Chaple Vale **91** H5
Charla Downs **64** B2
Charles Gardner Reserve **63** F5
Charles Knob **24** C5
Charles Point **12** B2
Charlestown **81** G1
Charleville **33** F6
Charley Creek **28** B3
Charleyong **89** E2
Charley Peak **59** F3
Charlotte Pass Ski Field **88** A5
Charlotte Plains (NSW) **43** F2
Charlotte Plains (QLD) **19** H6
Charlotte Range **30** C4
Charlotte Waters **30** D5
Charlton (NSW) **80** A2
Charlton (VIC) **85** E3
Charlton Channel **85** E4
Charnley River **15** G1
Charon Point **59** E2
Charters Towers **56** A2
Chatfield Point **98** C5
Chatham Island **64** D6
Chatsbury **80** B5
Chatsworth (NSW) **73** G2
Chatsworth (QLD) **32** A1
Chatsworth (VIC) **91** G2
Cheepie **33** E6
Cheesemans Creek **79** G1
Cheesman Peak **39** H1
Cherbourg **61** E5
Cherene **65** H4
Cherrabun **15** G4
Cheshire **33** F4
Cheshunt **87** E5
Chesterton **33** G5
Chesterton Range **33** G5
Chesterton Range National Park **33** G6
Chetwynd **83** E6
Chewings Range **28** B3
Chewton **85** G6
Cheyne Bay **65** G5
Cheyne Beach **65** G5
Chibnalwood Lakes **49** H2
Chichester Range **23** E2
Chichester River **76** C4
Childers (QLD) **61** F2
Childers (VIC) **93** G4
Chillagoe **54** C2
Chillagoe-Mungana National Park **54** C2
Chilla Well **55** H1
Chilli Beach **21** G3
Chillingham **71** G5
Chillingollah **49** H3
Chiltern **87** E3
Chiltern-Box Ironbark National Park **87** E3
Chimney Pots, The **84** B5
Chinaman Beach **100** C1

Chinamans Creek **100** C2
Chinamans Knob **100** C2
China Wall **16** A3
Chinchilla **60** C5
Chinderah **71** H4
Chinkapook **49** H3
Christmas Creek **15** G4
Christmas Hills **96** B3
Christmas Island **14** B4
Christopher Lake **25** E4
Chudleigh Park **20** A5
Churchill (QLD) **71** F2
Churchill (VIC) **93** G4
Churchill National Park **93** E3
Churchills Head **17** G4
Circuit Drive **26** C3
Citadel Island **100** A6
Civic **105** F1
Clackline **62** D5
Clairview **58** D1
C Lake **49** H1
Clandulla **75** F6
Clara River **19** F4
Claravale **12** D6
Claraville **29** F3
Clare (NSW) **50** A2
Clare (QLD) **56** C2
Clare (SA) **69** F2
Claremont **87** E5
Claremont Point **21** G5
Clarence **45** E5
Clarence River **71** E5, **73** E2
Clarence Strait **12** C1
Clarence Town **76** C5
Clarendon (QLD) **71** F2
Clarendon (SA) **69** F4
Clarendon (TAS) **97** F6
Clarendon (VIC) **92** B2
Clare Valley Wineries **69** F2
Clark Creek **19** G1
Clarkefield **92** D1
Clarke Hills **20** A5
Clarke Island **97** G3
Clarke River **55** E6
Clarkes Hill **92** B1
Clark River **20** A5
Claude Road **96** D5
Claverton (NSW) **43** F1
Clayton **69** G5
Clayton Homestead **41** G3
Clayton (WA) **62** D4
Clay Wells **82** B6
Clear Hill **98** D3
Clear Lake **83** F5
Clear Place Point **81** H4
Clear Range **88** C3
Clermont **58** A2
Cleve **68** C1
Clevedon **56** C1
Cleveland (QLD) **71** H2
Cleveland (TAS) **97** F6
Cleveland Bay **55** G6
Cliffdale Creek **18** D2
Cliff Point (NT) **12** A4
Cliff Point (QLD) **59** G3
Cliffy Head **64** D6
Clifton (QLD) **70** D3
Clifton (WA) **63** E3
Clifton Beach (QLD) **55** F1
Clifton Beach (TAS) **99** F4
Clifton Downs **42** C3
Clifton Hills **31** G6

Clifton Homestead **43** F2
Clifton Springs **92** C4
Clinton Conservation Park **69** E2
Clintonvale **70** D3
Cloncurry **19** E6
Cloncurry River **19** E4-5
Clouds Creek **73** E4
Cloverdale **64** C3
Clover Downs **37** H3
Cloyna **61** E4
Cluan **97** E6
Clummer Bluff **96** D6
Clunes (NSW) **71** G6
Clunes (VIC) **92** B1
Cluny **31** H4
Clydebank **94** B4
Clyde River **89** F2
Coal Creek Historic Park **93** F5
Coaldale **73** F2
Coal River **99** F3
Coalstoun Lakes **61** E3
Coalville **93** G4
Coast Range **11** G4
Cobains **94** A4
Cobar **43** E5
Cobargo **89** E5
Cobbadah **44** A5
Cobb Highway **42** C6, **50** A2
Cobbold Gorge **54** A5
Cobbora **75** E3
Cobden **91** H4
Cobham **42** B4
Cobourg Marine Park **10** C2
Cobourg Peninsula **10** D2
Cobra **22** D5
Cobram **86** C3
Cobrico **91** G4
Cobungra **94** B1
Coburg **92** D2
Coburn **36** B2
Cocata Conservation Park **66** A6
Cockatoo **93** E3
Cockatoo Island **15** E1
Cockburn **42** A6
Cockcrow Mountain **76** B4
Cockermouth Island **57** G4
Cockle Biddy **39** E6
Cocklebiddy Cave **39** E6
Cockle Creek **98** D5
Cocoparra National Park **78** A3
Cocoparra Range **78** A2
Codrington **91** E3
Coen **21** F5
Coen River **21** F4
Coffin Bay **68** A3
Coffin Bay National Park **68** A3
Coffin Bay Peninsula **68** A3
Coffs Harbour **73** F5
Coghills Creek **92** B1
Cogla Downs **37** F2
Cohuna **85** H2
Coila Lake **89** F4
Cojuma **65** G3
Colac **92** A4
Colac Colac **87** H4
Colbinabbin **86** A4
Colbinabbin West **86** A4
Coldstream **93** E2
Coleambally **50** B3
Colebrook **99** F3
Coleman River **21** E6
Coleraine **91** E1

Coles Bay **99** G2
Coliban River **85** H6
Colinroobie **78** B4
Colinton **61** F6
Collarenebri **43** H4
Collaroy **75** G3
Collector **79** H6
Collerina **43** F4
Collie (NSW) **74** C2
Collie (WA) **64** C3
Collier Bay **15** F1
Collier Range **23** F5
Collier Range National Park **23** F5
Collingullie **78** C6
Collins Head **77** H6
Collinsvale (TAS) **99** E3
Collinsville (QLD) **56** D3
Collinsville (SA) **67** G6
Colly Blue **75** G1
Colmer Point **21** E4
Colo Heights **80** D2
Colo River **80** D1
Colossal **43** F5
Colovale **63** F6
Colo Vale **80** C5
Colston Park **57** F6
Columbine Mountain **79** G1
Columboola **60** B5
Columb Point **14** D3
Comara **72** D6
Combara **43** G5
Combienbar **95** F2
Comboyne **77** E3
Come By Chance **43** G5
Comerong Island **80** D6
Comet **58** B4
Comet River **58** B4
Commodore **67** F2
Commonwealth Hill **40** C3
Commoron Creek **70** A3
Conara **97** F6
Conargo **86** B1
Concongella **83** H6
Condah **91** E2
Condamine **60** B5
Condamine River **60** A5, **70** B2
Condingup **47** G2
Condobolin **50** C1
Cone Bay **15** E2
Cone Point **77** H3
Congelin **64** D1
Congo **89** F4
Congupna **86** C4
Conimbla National Park **79** F2
Coningham **99** E4
Coniston (NT) **30** B1
Coniston (QLD) **32** C5
Conjola **89** G2
Connells Lagoon Conservation Reserve **18** A3
Connemara (NSW) **75** F2
Connemara (QLD) **32** C4
Connewarre **92** C4
Connexion Island **11** G4
Connie Sue Highway **38** D4
Connors Hump **58** D2
Connors River **58** C2
Connulpie **42** C3
Conoble Lake **50** B1

Conondale **61** F6
Conondale National Park **61** F6
Conservation Park **39** H2
Conway **57** E3
Conway Beach **57** F3
Conway Homestead **56** C4
Conway National Park **57** F3
Coober Pedy **40** D3
Coobowie **69** E4
Coodardy **37** E2
Cooinda (QLD) **60** D5
Cooinda (NT) **13** F3
Cookamidgera **74** B6
Cookardinia **87** G2
Cooks Gap **75** F4
Cooktown **21** H6
Cooktown Developmental Road **20** A1
Cookville **99** E5
Coogee **81** E4
Coolabah **43** F5
Coolac **79** E6
Cooladdi **33** E6
Coolah **75** F3
Coolah Tops National Park **75** G2
Coolalie **79** G6
Coolamon **78** C5
Coolamen **63** G3
Coolangatta **71** H4
Coolangubra Mountain **95** G1
Coolatai **72** A1
Coolcalalaya **36** C2
Coolgardie-Esperance Highway **38** A5
Coolgardie **37** H5
Coolibah **10** C6
Coolibah Creek **17** E1
Coolimba **62** A2
Cooljarloo **62** B3
Coolongolook **76** D5
Cooloola Section Great Sandy National Park **61** G4
Cooltong **49** F2
Coolullah **19** E5
Coolum Beach **61** G5
Coolup **64** B2
Cooma **88** C4
Coomalbidgup **47** F2
Coombah Roadhouse **49** G1
Coombell **73** F1
Coomera **71** H3
Coominglah **60** D1
Coominya **71** F1
Coonabarabran **75** E1
Coonabildie Range **24** A5
Coonama Aboriginal Land **38** B5
Coonamble **43** G5
Coonambula **60** D3
Coonana **38** B5
Coonana Aboriginal Land **38** B5
Coonawarra **82** C6
Coonawarra Wineries **82** C6
Coondambo **66** B2
Cooneel **59** E5
Coongan **14** B6
Coongan River **23** F1
Coongoola **43** E2
Coongul Point **35** F3
Cooper Creek **32** B6
Coopernook **77** E3
Cooper Point **55** F2
Coopracambra National Park **95** G2
Coorabulka **32** A3
Cooralya **22** B5

Cooranbong 81 F1
Cooranga 60 D6
Cooranga North 60 D5
Coordewandy (WA) 22 C6
Coorinja Winery 62 D5
Coorong, The 69 G6
Coorong National Park 69 G6
Coorow 62 C1
Cooroy 61 G5
Cooryanna Creek 41 G3
Cootamundra 79 E5
Cooyal 75 F4
Cooyar 61 E6
Cope Cope 85 E4
Copeland 76 C4
Copeton Dam 72 A3
Copeton State Recreation Area 72 A3
Copeville 69 H4
Copley 41 G4
Copmanhurst 73 E2
Copperfield River 54 B6
Copper Hill 40 D1
Copping 99 F4
Coradgery 74 B5
Coragulac 92 A4
Coraki 73 G1
Coral Bay 22 A4
Coral Sea 55 H3
Cora Lynn 93 F4
Coramba 73 F4
Cordalba 61 F2
Cordelia 55 F5
Cordering Farm 64 D3
Cordillo Downs 32 A6
Coreen 87 E2
Corella (NSW) 43 F4
Corella (SA) 42 A6
Corella Lake 18 A3
Corella River 19 E5
Corfield 32 D1
Corinda 18 C3
Corindhap 92 A3
Corindi 73 F4
Corinella 93 E4
Corinna 96 B6
Corinya 63 F6
Corio Bay 92 C3
Corner Cove 47 E3
Corner Hill 75 H5
Corner Inlet 100 B1
Corner Inlet Marine & Coastal Park 100 B2
Cornwall (QLD) 33 H6
Cornwall (TAS) 97 G6
Corobimilla 78 A5
Corona 42 B5
Coronation Island 9 E6
Coronet Bay 93 E5
Corop 86 A4
Cororooke 92 A4
Corowa 87 E3
Corrigin 63 G6
Corroboree Beach 35 G3
Corroboree Rock 30 C3
Corroboree Rock Conservation Reserve 29 G5
Corrow 62 C2
Corryong 87 H4
Corunna 66 D5
Corunna Downs 23 F1
Cosgrove 86 C4
Cosmo Newbery 38 B2
Cosmo Newbery Aboriginal Land 38 B2
Costerfield 86 A5

Cosy Corner 64 A5
Cotabena 67 F3
Cotter River 88 C2
Cotters Lake 100 B3
Cottlesloe 62 C6
Cottonbush Creek 31 H2
Cotton Island 11 H2
Cottonvale 70 D5
Couangalt 92 C2
Cougal 71 F5
Coulomb Point 14 D3
Coulomb Point Nature Reserve 14 D3
Coulta 68 A3
Country Downs 14 D3
Couridjah 80 C4
Couta Rocks 96 A4
Couti Uti 59 E2
Coutts Crossing 73 F3
Cove, The 91 G4
Cowalla 62 C4
Cowan 81 E3
Cowan Cowan 71 H1
Cowaramup 64 A4
Cowaramup Bay 64 A4
Cowarie 41 G1
Cowarna Downs 38 B5
Cowcowing 63 F3
Cowcowing Lakes 63 E3
Cowell 68 D1
Cowes 93 E5
Cowley 55 F3
Cowper 73 F3
Cowper Point 96 D1
Cowra 79 G3
Cowwarr 93 H4
Coxens Peak 58 C1
Cox Peninsula 12 B2
Cox River 11 F6
Coxs River 80 C2
Cox's Scrub Conservation Park 69 F5
Coyrecup 65 F3
Crabbes Creek 71 H5
Crab Island 21 E1
Crabtree 99 E4
Cracow 60 C2
Cradle Mountain 96 C6
Cradle Mountain- Lake St Clair National Park
   96 C6
Cradle Valley 96 C6
Cradoc 99 E4
Cradock 67 F4
Craggy Island 97 G1
Craigie (NSW) 95 F1
Craigie (VIC) 85 F6
Craigieburn 92 D2
Craigs Pocket 54 D5
Cramps 97 E6
Cranbourne 93 E3
Cranbrook (TAS) 99 G1
Cranbrook (WA) 65 E4
Crater Lakes National Park 55 E2
Craven 76 D4
Crawford Range 17 G6
Crawfords Lookout 55 F3
Credo 37 H5
Cremorne 99 F4
Crescent Head 77 F2
Cressy (TAS) 97 E6
Cressy (VIC) 92 A3
Creswick 92 B1
Crib Point 93 E4
Cridland Hill 21 F2

Croajingolong National Park 95 G3
Croker Island 10 D1
Crooble 44 A4
Crooked Creek 19 F2
Crooked River 94 B2
Crookwell 80 A5
Crookwell River 79 H4
Croppa Creek 44 A3
Croppies Point 97 F4
Crosbie River 21 F6
Crossley 91 F4
Crowdy Bay National Park 77 F3
Crowdy Head 77 F4
Crower 82 B5
Crows Nest 71 E1
Crows Nest Falls National Park 71 E1
Crowther 79 F3
Crowther Creek 79 F3
Croxton East 91 F2
Croydon (QLD) 19 G3
Croydon (WA) 22 D1
Cryon 43 G4
Crystalbrook 33 G5
Crystal Brook (QLD) 54 C2
Crystal Brook (SA) 67 F6
Cuballing 64 D1
Cudal 79 G1
Cuddapan 32 B5
Cuddell 78 A5
Cudgegong River 75 E4
Cudgelglomera Creek 19 G5
Cudgen 71 H5
Cudgera Creek 71 H5
Cudgewa Falls Campsite 87 H4
Cudgewa 87 H4
Cudgewa North 87 H4
Cudimera 62 C2
Cudmirrah 89 G2
Cue 37 E2
Culbin 64 D2
Culburra 82 B1
Culburra Beach 89 H1
Culcairn 87 F2
Culford 64 C1
Culgoa 85 E1
Culgoa Flood Plain National Park 43 F3
Culgoa River 43 G3
Cullen Bullen 80 C1
Cullendulla 89 F3
Cullen Point 21 E2
Cullivel 87 E1
Culloden 94 A3
Cullulleraine 49 G2
Culpataro 50 A2
Culpaulin 42 C6
Cultivation Shelter 84 B4
Cultowa 42 D5
Cumberland River Campsite 92 B5
Cumborah 43 G4
Cummins 68 B2
Cumnock 74 C6
Cundeelee Aboriginal Land 38 B5
Cunderdin 63 E5
Cungulla 56 C1
Cunnamulla 43 E2
Cunningar 79 F5
Cunningham 70 D3
Cunningham Channel 13 E1
Cunningham Highway 44 A3, 71 E3
Cunninghams Gap 71 E3
Cunyu 23 G6
Cuprona 96 C4

Curacoa Island 55 G5
Curban 74 D1
Curbur 36 C1
Curlewis 44 A5
Curlew Island 57 G6
Curnamona 67 H3
Currabubula 76 A1
Curranyalpah 42 D5
Currarong 89 H1
Currawang 80 A6
Currawarna 78 C6
Currawilla 32 B4
Currawinya 42 D3
Currawinya National Park 42 D3
Currie 96 C2
Currockbilly Mountain 89 F2
Currumbin 71 H4
Curtin Springs Roadhouse 30 A5
Curtis Island (QLD) 59 G5
Curtis Island (TAS) 53 E2
Curtis Island National Park 59 G4
Curumbenya Range 74 C6
Curyo 83 H2
Cuttabri 43 H5
Cutta Cutta Caves 13 F6
Cuttlefish Bay 69 E6
Cygnet 99 E4
Cythera 43 G1

D

Dadswells Bridge 84 C2
D'Aguilar Highway 61 F6
Daguragu 16 D2
Daguragu Aboriginal Land 16 D2
Dagworth 54 B3
Dahlonega 33 G3
Dahwilly 86 A1
Daintree 20 B1
Daintree National Park 20 B1
Dairy Creek 22 C6
Daisy Dell 96 C5
Daisy Hill 85 F6
Dajarra 31 H1
Dalaroo 62 C3
Dalbeg 56 C3
Dalby 60 D6
Dales Gorge 23 E3
Dalgety 88 C5
Dalgety Downs 22 D6
Dalgaranga 37 E2
Dalgaranga Hill 37 E2
Dalhousie Springs 31 E6
Dallachy 55 F4
Dallarnil 61 F3
Dalma Scrub 59 E4
Dalmeny 89 F4
Dalton 79 H5
Dalveen 70 D5
Dalwallinu 62 D2
Daly Heads 68 D4
Daly Range 12 C2
Daly River (NT) 12 B4
Daly River - Port Keats Aboriginal Land Trust
   12 A5
Dalyston 93 E5
Dalyup 47 F2
Daly Waters 17 F1
Dampier 22 C1
Dampier Archipelago National Park 22 C1
Dampier Downs 15 E4
Dampier Peninsula 14 D2

Dandaloo **74** A3
Dandaraga **37** F3
Dandaragan **62** C3
Dandenong **93** E3
Dandenong Park **56** B4
Dandenong Ranges **93** E3
Dandenong Ranges National Park **93** E3
Dangars Falls **72** B5
Dangarsleigh **72** B5
Danggali Conservation Park **49** F1
Dangin **63** F5
Dangore Mountain **61** E5
Daniels Well Station **22** D2
Danmor **62** C3
Dannevig Island **100** B6
Daradgee **55** F3
Darby Bay **100** B4
Darby River **100** B4
Darbys Falls **79** G3
Darbys Falls Observatory **79** G3
Dardadine **64** D2
Darda **37** H2
Dardanup **64** B3
Dargals Range **88** A4
Dargo **94** B2
Dargo River **94** B1
Darkan **64** D3
Darkan River **62** D6
Darke Peak **68** B1
Darkwood **73** E5
Darling Downs **70** A1
Darling Point **71** G2
Darling Range **97** G2
Darling Ranges **64** C2
Darling River **42** D5, **49** G2
Darlington (TAS) **99** G3
Darlington (VIC) **91** H3
Darlington Point **50** B3
Darnick **50** A1
Darnum **93** G4
Daroobalgie **79** F1
Darradup **64** B4
Darriman **94** A5
Darr River **32** D2
Dartmoor **90** D2
Dartmouth **87** G5
Dartmouth Reservoir **87** G5
Darwin **10** B3
Darwin River Dam **12** C2
Datchet Downs **32** A1
Davenport Creek **41** E2
Davenport Downs **32** B3
Davenport Murchison National Park **17** H6
Davenport River **28** B5
Davey Head **98** C4
Davey Point **92** D4
Davey River **98** C4
Davis River **23** G2
Dawesville **64** B1
Daw Island **47** H2
Dawson (SA) **67** G5
Dawson (VIC) **93** H3
Dawson Highway **58** B5, **59** F5
Dawson River **60** A3
Dayboro **71** G1
Day Dawn **37** E2
Daylesford **92** B1
Daymar **43** H3
Daysdale **87** E2
Deadman Hill **23** F4
Deakin **105** E6
Deal Island **53** F2

Deans Marsh **92** B4
Debesa **15** F3
Deception Bay **71** G1
Deddington **97** F6
Dederang **87** F5
Dee Lagoon **98** D2
Deep Bight **9** G4
Deep Creek **92** D2
Deep Creek Conservation Park **69** F5
Deepinghurst **63** E4
Deep Lead **85** D3
Deep River **64** D6
Deepwater **72** C2
Deepwater National Park **59** H6
Deep Water Point **15** E2
Deep Well **30** C3
Deeral **55** F2
Dee Why **81** E3
De Grey **14** B6
De Grey River **14** B6
Degulla **33** F2
Delamere (NT) **10** C6
Delamere (SA) **69** F5
Delamere Road **10** C6, **17** E1
Delegate **95** F1
Delegate River (NSW) **95** F1
Delegate River (VIC) **95** E1
Delicate Nobby **77** F2
Delissaville/Wagait/Larrakia Aboriginal Land Trust **12** B3
Dellyanine **64** D3
Delmore Downs **30** D2
Delny **30** D2
Deloraine **97** E5
Delta **57** E2
Delta Downs **19** F2
Delungra **72** A2
Denham **36** A1
Denham Island **18** D1
Denham Sound **36** A1
Denial Bay **40** C6
Deniliquin **86** B1
Denison **94** A4
Denison Range **98** D2
Denman **75** H5
Denmark **65** E6
Dennington **91** F4
Den of Nargun **94** B3
D'Entrecasteaux Channel **99** E5
D'Entrecasteaux National Park **64** C5
Depot Glen **42** B3
Depot Springs **37** G2
Depuch Island **22** D1
Derby (TAS) **97** G5
Derby (VIC) **85** G4
Derby (WA) **15** E3
Dereel **92** A2
Dergholm **82** D6
Deringulla **75** E1
De Rose Hill **30** C6
Derrinallum **91** H3
Derriwong **50** D1
Derry Downs **30** D1
Derwent **30** B2
Derwent Bridge **98** D1
Derwent Island **57** G5
Derwent River (NT) **28** B6
Derwent River (TAS) **99** E3
De Sailly Range **20** A1
Desault Bay **14** D4
Descartes Bay **90** D4
Desert Camp Conservation Park **82** B3

Desmond **47** E2
D'Estrees Bay **69** E6
Detention River **96** B4
Deua National Park **89** E4
Deua River **89** E3
Devenish **86** D4
Devil's Gullet **96** D6
Devil's Marbles Conservation Reserve **17** G5
Devonborough Downs **42** A6
Devoncourt **19** E6
Devonport **96** D4
Dewars Point **57** F4
De Witt Island **98** C5
De Witt Range **98** C4
Dharug National Park **81** E2
Dhupuma **11** H3
Dhurringile **86** B4
Diamantina Developmental Road **31** H1, **32** C5
Diamantina Gates National Park **32** B3
Diamantina River **31** H5, **32** A4
Diamond Beach **77** E4
Diamond Creek **56** C6
Diamond Head **77** F3
Diamond Mountain **75** H3
Diamond Well **23** F6
Diapur **83** E3
Diddleum Plains **97** F5
Diemals **37** G4
Digby **90** D2
Digby Peaks **32** A1
Diggers Rest **92** D2
Dilli Village **35** F5
Dillon Bay **65** H4
Dimboola **83** F4
Dimbulah **54** D2
Dingee **85** G4
Dingley Dell **63** E6
Dingo **58** D4
Dingo Beach **57** E3
Dingwall **85** G2
Dinner Plain **87** G6
Dinninup **64** D4
Dinoga **44** A4
Dinyarrak **82** D3
Dipperu National Park **58** C1
Direction Island **14** B2
Dirk Hartog **36** A1
Dirk Hartog Island **36** A1
Dirranbandi **43** G3
Disappointment Bay **96** C1
Disappointment Reach **22** A6
Disaster Bay (NSW) **95** H2
Disaster Bay (WA) **15** E2
Discovery Bay **90** C3
Dividing Range **36** D3
Dixalea **59** E5
Dixie (QLD) **21** G6
Dixie (VIC) **91** G4
Djuan **61** E6
Dlorah Downs **41** H6
Dneiper **30** D2
Dobbyn **19** E5
Docker River Road **26** B2
Doctor George Mountain **89** E6
Dodges Ferry **99** F4
Dog on the Tuckerbox, The **79** E6
Dollar **93** G5
Dolphin Island **22** C1
Don (QLD) **18** C5
Don (TAS) **96** D4
Donaghy's Hill Lookout **98** C1
Donald **85** E3

Donaldson **19** E5
Donaldson River **96** B5
Doncaster **93** E2
Dongara **36** C4
Dongolocking **65** E2
Donnelly River **64** C5
Donnybrook (QLD) **61** G6
Donnybrook (VIC) **92** D2
Donnybrook (WA) **64** B3
Donovans Landing **90** C3
Don River (QLD) **57** E3
Don River (QLD) **59** E5
Doodlakine **63** G4
Dooen **83** G4
Dookie **86** C4
Dooley Downs **22** D4
Doolgunna **23** F6
Doomadgee **18** D3
Doon Doon Aboriginal Land **16** A1
Doongmabulla **56** A6
Doorawarrah **22** B6
Dora Dora **87** G3
Doreen **43** H4
Dorisvale **12** D6
Dorre Island **22** A6
Dorrigo **73** E5
Dorrigo National Park **73** E5
Dorset Downs **64** D4
Double Island Point **61** G4
Double Lagoon **19** F2
Double Mountain **59** F2
Double Peak (QLD) **60** A1
Double Peak (TAS) **98** C3
Double Point (QLD) **21** F2
Double Point (QLD) **55** F3
Doubtful Bay **15** F1
Douglas **83** E5
Douglas Apsley National Park **97** G6
Douglas Creek **41** E2
Douglas Hot Springs Nature Park **12** D4
Douglas Point (SA) **67** E5
Douglas Point (SA) **90** B3
Douglas River **12** D4
Dover **99** E5
Dover Island **53** F2
Dowerin **63** E4
Downers Range **11** F5
Downside **78** C6
Dragon Rocks Nature Reserve **65** G1
Drake **71** E6
Drillham **60** B5
Dripstone **74** D5
Dromana **92** D4
Dromedary **99** E3
Drouin **93** F4
Drovers Cave National Park **62** B2
Druid Range **67** F3
Drumduff **19** H1
Drummond **85** H6
Drummond Point **68** A2
Drummond Range **33** G3
Drum Top **86** D5
Dryander National Park **57** E3
Dryandra Woodland **64** D2
Dry River **10** D6
Drysdale **92** C4
Drysdale Island **11** G2
Drysdale River (WA) **9** G6
Drysdale River Homestead (WA) **15** H1
Drysdale River National Park **9** G5
Dualling **65** F2
Duaringa **58** D5

Dubbo **74** C3
Dubbo Hill **88** B2
Dublin **69** F3
Duchess **19** E6
Ducie River **21** F2
Duck Creek **22** C3
Duck Point **100** B1
Duck River **96** B4
Dudgeon Point **57** F5
Dudinin **65** E1
Dudley Conservation Park **69** E6
Dugald River **19** E5
Duke Island **59** F1
Duke of Orleans Bay **47** G2
Dukes Highway **69** H6, **82** C2
Dukin **63** F3
Dulacca **60** A5
Dulacca West **60** A5
Dulbydilla **33** G6
Dulhunty River **21** E2
Dulkaninna **41** G3
Dululu **59** E5
Dumaresq River **70** A5
Dumbalk North **93** G5
Dumberning **64** D2
Dumbleyung **65** E2
Dumbleyung Lake **65** E2
Dumosa **85** E2
Dunalley **99** F4
Dunbar **19** G1
Dunbogan **77** F3
Duncan Road **16** B2
Duncombe Bay **77** G4
Dundas **71** F1
Dundas Nature Reserve **38** B6
Dundas Rocks **47** F1
Dundas Strait **10** C1
Dundee **72** C2
Dundubara Campsite **35** G3
Dundurrabin **73** E4
Dunearn **62** B3
Dunedoo **75** E3
Dunester **62** C1
Dungarvon **42** D3
Dunggir National Park **73** E6
Dungog **76** C5
Dungowan **76** B1
Dunkeld (NSW) **80** A2
Dunkeld (VIC) **84** B6
Dunk Island **55** F4
Dunk Island National Park **55** F4
Dunmara **17** F1
Dunmore **74** B5
Dunnstown **92** B2
Dunolly **85** F5
Dunoon **71** G6
Dunsborough **64** A3
Dunstable **58** A5
Dunterry **62** C5
Dunwich **71** H2
Durack River **16** A1
Duranillin **64** D3
Durba Springs **24** A3
Durham Downs **42** B1
Durham Ox **85** G3
Duri **76** A1
Durong **60** D5
Durras **89** F3
Durras Lake **89** F3
Durrie **32** A5
Dutchman, The **97** H2
Dutchmans Stern Conservation Park **67** E4

Dutson **94** A4
Dutton **69** G3
Dutton River **19** H5
Duyfken Point **21** E3
Dwarda **64** D1
Dwellingup **64** C1
Dynamite Bay **62** A2
Dynevor Downs **42** D2
Dysart (QLD) **58** B2
Dysart (TAS) **99** E3

E

Eagle Bay **46** A6
Eagle Bay Beach **64** A3
Eaglehawk Neck **99** G4
Eagle Heights **71** G3
Eagle Point **94** C3
Earaheedy **23** H5
Earlando **57** E3
East Alligator River **13** G2
Easter Group **36** B4
Eastern Group **47** H2
Eastern View **92** B4
East Gresford **76** C5
East Jindabyne **88** B5
East Kangaroo Island **97** G2
East Perth **105** H1
East Point **81** H5
East Sandy Point **97** F4
East Tamar Highway **97** E4
East Vernon Island **12** C1
Eastville (VIC) **85** G5
Eastville (WA) **65** E1
Eateringinna Creek **30** B6
Eaton **64** B3
Eatonsville **73** F3
Ebagoola **21** F5
Ebden **87** F4
Ebenezer Mount **87** F6
Ebor **72** D5
Ebor Falls **72** D5
Eccleston **76** B4
Echidna Chasm **16** B2
Echo Point **45** G4
Echuca **86** A3
Echunga **69** F4
Eclipse Island **65** F6
Eco Beach **14** D4
Edaggee **22** B6
Edah **37** E3
Eddington (VIC) **85** G5
Eddington (WA) **63** F6
Eddystone Point **97** H4
Eden **95** H1
Edenhope **82** D5
Eden Island **71** H3
Eden Vale **54** A3
Eden Valley **69** G3
Eden Valley Wineries **69** G3
Edgar Ranges **15** E4
Edgecombe Bay **57** E3
Edgeroi **44** A4
Edi **87** E5
Edith **80** B3
Edithburgh **69** E4
Edith Creek **96** B4
Edith Falls **13** E5
Edith River **13** E5
Edjudina **38** A4
Edkins Range **15** G1
Edmonton **55** F2

Edmund **22** C4
Edmund Kennedy National Park **55** F4
Edward Island **11** G5
Edward River (NSW) **50** A3
Edward River (QLD) **21** E5
Egera **56** A4
Egg Lagoon **96** C1
Eidsvold **60** D2
Eight Mile River **21** F6
Eighty Mile Beach **14** C5
Eildon **93** G1
Eildon Park **32** C3
Eimeo **57** F5
Einasleigh **54** B4
Einasleigh River **19** G3, **54** B4
Elabbin **63** G4
Elaine **92** B2
Elands **77** E3
El Arish **55** F3
Elbow Hill **68** C1
Elbow Valley **70** D4
Elcho Island **11** G2
Elderslie **99** E3
Eldon **99** F3
Eldon Bluff **98** C1
Eldorado **87** E4
Elephant Hide **84** C3
Eli Creek **35** G4
Elizabeth **69** F3
Elizabeth Beach **77** E5
Elizabeth Downs **12** B4
Elizabeth Town **96** D5
Eliza Point **99** E5
Elkedra **17** H6
Elkedra River **18** A6
Ella Bay National Park **55** F2
Ellalong **76** B6
Ellangowan **70** D3
Ella Vale **43** E3
Ellavalla **22** B6
Ellenbrae **15** H1
Ellendale (TAS) **98** D3
Ellendale (WA) **15** F3
Ellengail **62** B2
Ellen Peak **65** G4
Ellenvale **20** A5
Ellerslie (VIC) **91** G3
Ellerslie (WA) **64** D2
Ellerston **76** B3
Ellery Creek **28** C4
Ellery Creek Big-Hole **28** C3
Ellesford **62** C4
Elliminyt **92** A4
Ellinbank **93** F4
Elliot Bay **98** B4
Elliot Point **98** B4
Elliot Price Conservation Park **41** F2
Elliot Range **98** C2
Elliot River Campsite **92** A5
Elliott **17** G2
Elliott Heads **61** G2
Elliott Hill **98** B4
Ellis Beach **55** F1
Elliston **48** A2
Elmhurst **85** E6
Elmina **43** F1
Elmore (QLD) **19** G5
Elmore (VIC) **85** H4
Elong Elong **74** D3
Elphinstone (QLD) **57** E5
Elphinstone (VIC) **85** H6
El Questro **16** A1

Elserae **62** D1
Elsey National Park **11** E5
Elsmore **72** B3
El Trune **43** F5
Elvo **32** C3
Embley River **21** E3
Emby **43** G5
Emerald (QLD) **58** B4
Emerald (VIC) **93** E3
Emerald Beach **73** F4
Emerald Hill **44** A5
Emily & Jessie Gaps Nature Park **29** G5
Emily Bay **77** G6
Emily Creek **29** G5
Emita **97** G2
Emma Gorge **16** B1
Emmaville **72** C2
Emmet **32** D4
Empire Vale **73** H1
Emu Bay **68** D5
Emu Hill **63** G5
Emu Park **59** F4
Emu Plains **56** D4
Emu Springs **82** B1
Emu Vale **71** E4
Encounter Bay **69** F5
Endeavour **21** H6
Endeavour Bay **98** B3
Endeavour Strait **21** F1
Enderby Island **22** C1
Endyalgout Island **10** D2
Eneabba **62** B2
Eneabba Springs **62** B1
Enfield **92** B2
Engineer Range **98** C2
Enngonia **43** E3
Ensay **94** C2
Entrance, The **81** F2
Entrance Point **100** D1
Epenarra **17** H5
Eppalock **85** H5
Epping Forest **97** F6
Epsilon **42** A2
Eradu **36** C4
Erainia **66** C6
Erica **93** G3
Erigolia **78** A2
Erikin **63** G5
Erith Island **53** F2
Erldunda **30** C4
Erlistoun **38** A2
Ernabella (Pukatja) **30** B5
Ernest Giles Road **27** E6
Eromanga **32** C6
Erong Springs **22** D6
Errabiddy **22** D6
Errinundra **95** F2
Errinundra National Park **95** E2
Erskine Falls **92** B5
Erskine Island **59** H5
Erudina **67** H3
Escott **18** D3
Eskdale **87** G5
Esk **71** F1
Esk Main Road **97** F6
Esmeralda Farm **13** E4
Esmeralda **19** G4
Esperance **47** F2
Etadunna **41** G2
Ethel Creek **23** G3
Ethel River **23** E4
Ethel, Wreck of The **68** C5

Eton **57** F5
Ettamogah Wildlife Sanctuary **87** F3
Ettrick (NSW) **71** F5
Ettrick (WA) **14** B6
Euabalong **50** C1
Euabalong West **50** C1
Eubenangee Swamp National Park **55** F2
Euchareena **74** D6
Eucla **39** G5
Eucla National Park **39** G5
Eucumbene **88** B4
Eudunda **69** G2
Eugowra **79** F1
Euleilah **61** F1
Eulo **43** E2
Eumandah **43** G4
Eumundi **61** G5
Eumungerie **74** C3
Eungai Creek **73** E6
Eungella **57** E5
Eungella Dam **57** E5
Eungella National Park **57** E4
Eurack **92** A3
Euramo **55** F4
Eurardy **36** C3
Eurimbula National Park **59** H6
Euroa (VIC) **86** C5
Euroa (WA) **63** G5
Eurobin **87** F5
Eurobodalla **89** E4
Eurobodalla National Park **89** F4-5
Euroka **45** G5
Euroka Springs **19** F5
Eurombah Creek **33** H6, **60** A3
Eurong **35** F5
Eurongilly **78** D6
Eva Downs **17** H3
Evandale **97** F6
Evansford **85** F6
Evans Head **73** G1
Evans Lookout **45** F4
Evanson Point **21** G5
Eveleigh **54** B4
Evelyn Creek **40** D2
Evelyn Downs **40** D2
Evelyn Farm **65** F1
Eve Peak **21** G4
Everard Ranges **30** B6
Evercreech Forest Reserve **97** G5
Everton **87** E4
Ewan **55** F6
Ewaninga **30** C3
Ewlyamartup **65** E3
Exeter **80** C5
Exmouth **22** A3
Exmouth Gulf **22** A3
Expedition National Park **60** A2
Eyre Bird Observatory **39** E6
Eyre Creek **31** G5, H3
Eyre Developmental Road **31** H5
Eyre Highway **38** B6, **40** A5
Eyre Peninsula **68** A2

F

Fair Cape **21** G3
Fairfield **15** G3
Fairhaven Beach **92** B4
Fairholme **50** E2
Fairlight (NSW) **43** F5
Fairlight (QLD) **20** A1
Fairview Conservation Park **82** B4

Fairy Dell **86** A4
Fairy Hill **71** F6
Fairyland **60** C5
Falls Creek **87** G6
Falls Reserve **45** G3
Falmouth **97** H6
False Bay **67** E6
False Cape Bossut **14** D4
False Island Point **22** A3
False Orford Ness **21** F2
False Pera Head **21** E4
False Point **11** F2
Fanning River **56** B2
Fantome Island **55** G5
Faraway Hill **67** H6
Far Bald Mountain **88** B4
Farina **41** G4
Farleigh **57** F5
Farm Beach **68** A3
Farnham **74** D5
Farquhar Inlet **77** E4
Farrars Creek **32** B4
Farrell Flat **69** G2
Fassifern **71** E3
Faulconbridge **45** G2
Faure Island **36** B1
Fay's Bay **46** B5
Federal Highway **88** D1
Federation Peak **98** D4
Feilton **99** E3
Felton East **70** D2
Feluga **55** F3
Fentonbury **98** D3
Fergusson River **13** E5
Fermoy **32** C3
Fernbank **94** B3
Fernihurst **85** G3
Fern Tree **99** E4
Fernvale **71** F2
Ferries McDonald Conservation Park **69** G5
Field Island **13** F1
Fifield **50** D1
Fifteen Mile Creek **29** F6
Figtree Lake **35** F5
Finch Hatton **57** E5
Fine Flower **73** E2
Fingal **97** G6
Fingal Bay **76** D6
Finke **30** D5
Finke Bay **13** E1
Finke Gorge National Park **27** G3
Finke River **30** B4, C4
Finley **86** C2
Finniss **69** G5
Finniss River **12** B3
Finniss River Store **12** C3
Finniss Springs **41** F3
Finucane **14** A6
Fish Creek **93** G6
Fisher Bluff **96** B6
Fisherman Bay **69** E1
Fisherman Islands **71** H2
Fishermans Paradise **89** G2
Fishes Shelter **84** B4
Fish Point **85** G1
Fish River **12** C5
Fish River Reserve **12** C6
Fishy Point **81** G4
Fiskville **92** C2
Fitzgerald Bay **67** E5
Fitzgerald **98** D3
Fitzgerald River **65** H3

Fitzgerald River National Park **65** H3
Fitzmaurice Point **19** F2
Fitzmaurice River **10** B5
Fitzroy (NT) **10** C6
Fitzroy (VIC) **109** G1
Fitzroy Crossing **15** G3
Fitzroy Falls **80** C6
Fitzroy Island **55** F1
Fitzroy River (NT) **15** H2
Fitzroy River (QLD) **59** E4
Five Corners **43** F6
Five Mile Beach **100** D4
Five Mile Bluff **97** E4
Five Mile Road **100** C3
Flagstaff Hill **74** D6
Flat Top **32** B5
Flat Topped Bluff **96** A3
Fletcher Lake **49** G2
Fleurieu Peninsula **69** F5
Flinders **92** D5
Flinders Bay **64** B5
Flinders Chase National Park **68** C6
Flinders Group National Park **21** G5
Flinders Highway (QLD) **19** G6
Flinders Highway (SA) **68** A1
Flinders Island (QLD) **21** G5
Flinders Island (SA) **48** A2
Flinders Island (TAS) **97** G2
Flinders Peak **71** F3
Flinders Peninsula **11** G3
Flinders Ranges **67** G2
Flinders Ranges National Park **67** F2
Flinders River **19** F3-5
Flinton **44** A2
Floating Islands Reserve **91** H4
Flodden Hills **32** C4
Flora River **10** C5
Flora Valley **16** B3
Florence Creek **29** E2
Florence Falls **12** B3
Florentine River **98** D3
Florina **12** D6
Flowerdale (TAS) **96** C4
Flowerdale (VIC) **93** E1
Flowerpot **99** E4
Flying Fish Cove **14** B3
Flying Fish Point **55** F3
Flynn **93** H4
Foam Point **97** G3
Foelsche River **18** B1
Fog Bay **12** A3
Fog Creek **19** G4
Fogg Dam **12** D2
Folded Range **98** C4
Foleyvale **58** D4
Footscray **92** D2
Forbes **79** E1
Fords Bridge **43** E4
Fords Lagoon **69** H1
Forest **96** B3
Forest Creek **19** F4
Forest Den National Park **33** E2
Forester **97** G4
Forest Grove **64** A4
Forest Hill (NSW) **78** D6
Forest Hill (QLD) **71** E2
Forestier Peninsula **99** F4
Forest Reefs **79** H2
Forest Vale **33** G6
Forktown **94** C2
Formby Bay **68** D4
Forrest (ACT) **105** F6

Forrest (VIC) **92** A4
Forrest Beach **55** F5
Forrest Lakes **39** G3
Forrest River **9** H6
Forsayth **54** B4
Forster **77** E5
Forsyth Island **97** H3
Fortescue Bay **99** G4
Fortescue Falls **23** E3
Fortescue River **22** C2, **23** F2
Fortescue River Roadhouse **22** C2
Fort Grey **42** A3
Forth **96** D4
Fortis Creek National Park **73** F2
Fortress, The **84** B4
Fort Roger **19** E6
Forty Mile Scrub National Park **54** D4
Fossil Head **10** A5
Foster **93** G5
Fosterville **85** H5
Foul Bay **68** D4
Four Brothers **67** H4
Four Mile Creek **97** H6
Four Mile Hole Camping Area **13** E2
Fowlers Bay **40** B6
Fowlers Gap **42** B5
Fowlers Station **66** D2
Foxdale **57** E3
Foxhow **92** A3
Framlingham **91** G3
Frampton **79** E5
Frances **82** D4
François Péron National Park **36** A1
Frankford **97** E5
Frankford Road **97** E5
Frank Hann National Park **47** E1
Frankland **65** E5
Frankland Islands **55** F2
Frankland Range **98** C3
Frankland River (TAS) **96** A4
Frankland River (WA) **64** D6
Franklin **99** E4
Franklin-Gordon Wild Rivers National Park **98** C2
Franklin Harbour **68** D1
Franklin Harbour Conservation Park **68** D1
Franklin River **98** C2
Franklin Sound **97** H2
Frankston **93** E4
Fraser Bluff **96** D2
Fraser Island **61** H3
Fraser Range **38** B6
Frasers Creek **100** C5
Frazer River **15** E3
Frazier Downs **14** D4
Frederick Henry Bay **99** F4
Frederick Hills **11** G3
Frederickton **77** F1
Freeburgh **87** F5
Freeling **69** G3
Freemans Reach **80** D2
Freemans Waterholes **81** F1
Freestone **70** D4
Fregon **30** B6
Fremantle **62** C6
French Island **93** E4
French Island National Park **93** E4
Frenchmans Cap **98** C2
French Park **87** F1
Freshwater Camp **61** G4
Freshwater Cove **100** D1
Freshwater Creek **92** C4

Freshwater Point **57** F6
Frew Creek **41** E1
Freycinet National Park **99** G2
Friendly Point **21** G4
Frodsham's Pass **98** D3
Frogmore **79** G4
Frome Downs **67** H2
Frome River **41** G3
Fryerstown **85** H6
Frying Pan Creek **88** C4
Fulham **94** A4
Fullarton River **19** F6
Fullerton **80** A4
Fullerville **67** F5
Funnel Creek **58** C1
Funnel Mountain **58** A5
Furneaux Group **97** G2
Furneaux Lookout **97** H2
Furracabad **72** C3
Furze Point **21** F1

G

Gabbin **63** F3
Gabbyquoiquoi **63** E4
Gable End **94** A2
Gabo Island **95** H3
Gabyon **36** D3
Gadara **65** H4
Gaffneys Creek **93** G2
Gairdner River **65** G3
Galbraith **19** F1
Galga **69** H3
Galiwinku **11** G2
Gallipoli **18** C4
Gallipoli Beach **68** A3
Galloway Plains **59** F6
Galong **79** F5
Galore **78** B6
Galore Scenic Reserve **78** B6
Galston **81** E3
Galway Downs **32** C5
Gamboola **19** H2
Gammon Ranges **41** G4
Gammon Ranges National Park **67** H1
Ganmain **78** C5
Gantheaume Bay **36** B3
Gapuwiyak **11** G3
Garah **44** A3
Garawa Aboriginal Land Trust **18** B2
Garden, The **29** F4
Garden Island **62** C2
Garden Island Creek **99** E4
Gardens of Stone National Park **80** C1
Garden Vale **42** D4
Gardner Range **16** B4
Gardner River **64** C5
Garema **79** E2
Garfield **93** F4
Gargett **57** E5
Garie Beach **81** E4
Garland **79** H2
Garnpung Lake **49** H2
Garra **74** C6
Garrawilla **43** H5
Garrthalala **11** H3
Garry's Anchorage **35** F5
Garup **83** G4
Garvoc **91** G4
Gary Highway **24** C4
Gary Junction **24** C2
Gascoyne Junction **22** C6

Gascoyne River **22** B6, **23** F5
Gatcombe Head **59** G5
Gatton **71** E2
Gavial **59** F4
Gawler (SA) **69** F3
Gawler (TAS) **96** D4
Gawler Ranges **66** B4
Gayndah **61** E3
Geelong **92** C3
Geelvink Channel **36** B4
Geeralying **64** D2
Geeveston **99** E4
Gefn **63** G6
Geike Gorge National Park **15** G3
Gelantipy **94** D1
Gellibrand **92** A4
Gellibrand River **91** H5
Gelorup **64** B3
Gembrook **93** F3
Gemtree Caravan Park **29** E5
Genoa **95** G3
Genoa River **95** G2
Gentle Annie **87** H5
Geographe Bay **64** B3
Geographe Channel **22** A6
Geordie Bay **46** B5
George Bay **81** H6
George River **97** G5
Georges Plains **80** A2
Georgetown (QLD) **54** A4
Georgetown (SA) **69** F1
George Town **97** E4
Georgia Bore **24** A3
Georgica **71** G5
Georgina **18** C6
Georgina River **18** C4, **31** G1
Geraldton **36** C4
Gerang Gerung **83** F3
Geranium **55** G3
Gerara **43** F3
Gerard Community **49** F2
Gerogery **87** F3
Gerringong **80** D6
Gerroa **80** D6
Ghinghindah **60** B2
Gibb River **15** H1
Gibb River Aboriginal Land **15** H1
Gibb River Road **9** G6, **16** A1
Gibbs Siding **64** D3
Gibinbell **70** A4
Gibraltar Falls **88** C2
Gibraltar Range National Park **72** D2
Gibson Desert **24** C3
Gibson Desert Nature Reserve **24** D4
Gibson **47** F2
Gibson Steps **91** H5
Gidgea **22** B6
Gidgee **37** F2
Gidgegannup **62** D5
Gidgi Lakes **38** D3
Gidginbung **78** D4
Giffard **94** A5
Giffard West **94** A5
Gifford Creek **22** C4
Gilberton **54** B6
Gilbert River **19** G3
Gil Blas Point **61** F1
Gilen Creek **29** E5
Giles (Meteorological Station) **25** F4
Giles Creek **29** G3
Giles Memorial **41** E2

Gilgai **72** A3
Gilgandra **74** D2
Gilgering **63** E6
Gilgunnia **50** C1
Gilliat **19** F6
Gilliat River **19** F5
Gillieston **86** B4
Gilpeppee **32** B5
Gilroyd **36** C1
Gilston **71** G4
Gimbat **13** F4
Gimlet Park **63** G4
Ginawarra **62** C1
Gindalbie **38** A4
Gingin **62** C4
Gin Gin **61** F2
Gippsland Lakes Coastal Park **94** B4
Gipsy Point **95** G3
Giralia **22** B3
Giralia Range **22** A4
Girgarre **86** A4
Girgarre East **86** B4
Girilambone **43** F5
Girraween **62** C3
Girraween National Park **70** D6
Giru **56** C1
Gisborne **92** C1
Gladstone (NSW) **77** F1
Gladstone (QLD) **59** G5
Gladstone (SA) **67** F6
Gladstone (TAS) **97** G4
Gladstone (WA) **36** B1
Gladysdale **93** F3
Glainorie **65** F4
Glamorgan Vale **71** F2
Glass House Mountains **61** G6
Glastonbury **61** F5
Glebe **112** C1
Glen **37** E2
Glen, The **97** E5
Glenaire **91** H5
Glenaladale **94** B3
Glenalbyn **85** F4
Glen Alice **75** G6
Glen Avon **63** E3
Glenayle **24** A5
Glenbrook **45** G1
Glenburgh **22** C6
Glenburn **93** E1
Glencoe (NSW) **72** C3
Glencoe (QLD) **19** F2
Glencoe (SA) **90** B1
Glencoe (WA) **47** H2
Glendambo **66** B1
Glen Davis **80** C1
Glenden **56** D5
Glendevie **99** E4
Glendhu **54** D4
Glendon Brook **76** B5
Glendower Point **57** G6
Gleneagle **71** G3
Gleneagle Homestead **55** E4
Glenelg **69** F4
Glenelg Highway **90** C2, **91** G2
Glen Elgin **72** D2
Glenelg River **83** E6, **84** B3
Glenern **65** G2
Gleneva **56** C5
Glenfern **99** E3
Glen Florrie **22** C3
Glen Forbes **93** E5
Glen Garland **21** F5

Glengarry (TAS) **97** E5
Glengarry (VIC) **93** H4
Glengower **85** F6
Glengyle **31** H4
Glenhaughton **60** A2
Glen Helen **30** B3
Glen Helen Gorge **28** B4
Glen Helen Homestead **28** B4
Glen Hill **16** B1
Glenhope **43** F5
Glen Hope **42** C5
Glen Huon **99** E4
Glenhurst **63** G6
Gleniffer **73** E5
Glen Innes **72** C3
Glenisla **84** B4
Glenlee **63** G5
Glenluce **85** G6
Glenlyle **67** F3
Glenmaggie **93** H3
Glenmore **92** C2
Glenmorgan **60** A6
Glen of Palms **27** G2
Glenora (NSW) **19** G4
Glenora (SA) **42** D4
Glenora (WA) **69** H1
Glenorchy (SA) **41** H6
Glenorchy (VIC) **84** D2
Glenore **97** E6
Glenore Grove **71** E2
Glenorie **81** E3
Glenormiston **31** G2
Glenorn **38** A3
Glenorn Aboriginal Land **38** A3
Glenreagh **73** F4
Glenrock **58** A6
Glenrowan **86** D4
Glenroy **15** H2
Glen Ruth **55** E4
Glenthompson **84** C6
Glentromie **62** D3
Glen Valley **87** G6
Glenvar **63** E3
Glen Wills **87** G6
Gloucester **76** D4
Gloucester Island **57** E2
Gloucester River **76** C4
Glyde Point **12** C1
Glyde River **18** A1
Gnarabup Beach **64** A4
Gnaraloo **22** A5
Gnarlbine Rocks **37** H5
Gnarwarre **92** B3
Gnowangerup **65** F3
Goalen Head **89** E6
Goat Camp Creek **29** G3
Godfreys Creek **79** G4
Gogango **59** E4
Gogo **15** G3
Golconda **97** F5
Golden Beach **94** B4
Golden Valley **97** E6
Goldsmith Island **57** F4
Goldsworthy **14** B6
Golegumma Mountain **59** G6
Gol Gol **49** H2
Gollan **74** D4
Golspie **80** A4
Gongolgon **43** F4
Goobang National Park **74** C5-6
Gooch Range **22** B4
Goodenough Bay **15** E2

Goodingnow **37** E4
Goodna **71** G2
Goodooga **43** G3
Goodparla **13** E3
Goodradigbee River **88** C1
Goold Island **55** F4
Goolgowi **50** B2
Goolma **75** E4
Gooloogong **79** F2
Goolwa **69** F5
Goomadeer **13** H1
Goomadeer River **13** H1
Goomalling **63** E4
Goombalie **43** E4
Goombungee **70** D1
Goomburra **70** D3
Goomeri **61** E4
Goondah **79** G5
Goondiwindi **44** A3
Goongarrie **37** H4
Goongarrie National Park **38** A4
Goongerah Campsite **95** E2
Goonumbla **74** B6
Goorambat **86** D4
Gooram **86** C5
Goornong **85** H4
Goose Island **97** G2
Goovigen **59** E6
Gorae **90** D3
Gordon **92** B2
Gordon Dam **98** C3
Gordon Downs **16** B4
Gordon River (TAS) **98** D2-3
Gordon River (WA) **65** E4
Gordon River Road **98** C3
Gordon Splits **98** C3
Gordonvale **55** F2
Gore **70** C4
Gore Highway **70** A3
Gore Point **19** E2
Gorey **47** F2
Gorge Point **98** B2
Gormandale **93** H4
Gormanston **98** B1
Goroke **83** E4
Gorrie **10** D6
Goschen **85** F1
Gosford **81** F2
Gospers Mountain **80** D1
Gosse Bluff **28** C6
Gosses **66** A1
Gostwyck **72** B5
Goughs Bay **93** G1
Goulburn **80** A6
Goulburn River (NSW) **75** G4
Goulburn River (VIC) **86** B3
Goulburn River National Park **75** G4
Goulburn Valley Highway **86** B6
Goulburn Weir **86** B5
Goulds Country **97** G5
Gourdon Bay **14** D4
Govana **60** C6
Gove Peninsula **11** H3
Government House Lake **46** C6
Govett's Leap **45** F4
Gowrie **70** D2
Gowrie Park **96** D5
Goyder River **11** F3
Grabben Gullen **79** H5
Gracefield **65** E4
Gracemere **59** F4

Gracetown **64** A4
Gradgery **43** G5
Grafton **73** F3
Grafton Passage **55** G1
Grampians, The **83** G6
Grampians National Park **84** C4
Grampians Road **84** B1
Grampians Tourist Road **84** C4
Grampians Wineries **83** H6
Granite Belt Wineries **70** D5
Granite Downs **30** C6
Granite Island **100** C1
Granite Mountain **88** A3
Granite Peak **23** H5
Granites, The **37** D5
Granites Mine, The **16** D5
Granite Tor **96** C6
Grantham **71** E2
Grant Island **10** D1
Granton **99** E3
Grants Head **77** F3
Grantville **93** E5
Granville Harbour **96** A6
Granya **87** G3
Grassmere (NSW) **43** G2
Grassmere (VIC) **91** F4
Grass Patch **47** F2
Grasstree **57** F5
Grass Valley **63** E5
Grassville **69** H1
Grassy **96** C2
Grassy Harbour **96** D2
Grassy Island **57** E3
Gravesend **44** A4
Grawin (NSW) **43** G4
Grawlin (NSW) **79** E1
Gray **97** G6
Graytown **86** A5
Great Alpine Road **94** C1
Great Barrier Reef **34** C2
Great Barrier Reef Marine Park **21** G3, **34** C2
Great Basalt Wall National Park **20** B5
Great Central Road **25** E5, **38** C1
Great Dividing Range **50** C6, **51** E3
Great Dog Island **97** H2
Great Eastern Highway **63** F5
Great Forester River **97** F4
Great Glennie Island **100** A5
Great Keppel Island **59** G4
Great Lake **97** E6
Great Musselroe Bay **97** G4
Great Musselrose River **97** G4
Great Northern Highway **16** A3, **23** F5
Great Ocean Road **92** A5
Great Oyster Bay **99** G2
Great Palm Island **55** G5
Great Pine Tier **98** D1
Great Sandy Desert **15** F5
Great Sandy National Park **35** G3
Great Sandy Strait **35** G5
Great Southern Highway **65** E2
Great Victoria Desert **39** E1
Great Victoria Desert Nature Reserve **39** F3
Great Western **83** H6
Great Western Highway **80** B2
Great Western Tiers **96** C5
Greenbank (NT) **18** B1
Greenbank (QLD) **71** G3
Greenbushes **64** C4
Greendale **92** C2
Greenethorpe **79** F3
Green Head **62** A2

Green Hill **99** E2
Greenhill Island **10** C2
Greenhills **63** E5
Green Island **55** F1
Green Lake **84** B1
Greenly Beach **68** A3
Greenmount **70** D2
Greenock **69** G3
Greenough **36** C4
Greenough River **36** C3
Green Point **77** E5
Greens Beach **97** E4
Greensborough **93** E2
Greenvale (NSW) **43** F4
Greenvale (QLD) **54** D6
Greenville **65** E1
Greenways (SA) **69** H3
Greenways (SA) **82** B6
Greenwell Point **89** H1
Greenwood **64** B3
Gregory Creek **41** F3
Gregory Developmental Road **55** E6, **56** A4
Gregory Downs Hotel **18** D3
Gregory Highway **58** B3
Gregory National Park **10** C6, **16** C1
Gregory Range (QLD) **19** H4
Gregory Range (WA) **23** H1
Gregory River **18** D4
Gregory Springs **20** A5
Grenfell **79** F3
Grenville **92** B2
Gresford **76** C5
Greta (NSW) **76** B6
Greta (VIC) **86** D5
Greta South **86** D5
Greta West **86** D5
Gretna **99** E3
Grevillia **71** F5
Grey **62** B3
Greymare **70** D4
Grey Mountain **99** E4
Grey Peaks National Park **55** F2
Grey Range **42** B3, D1
Grey River **92** B5
Gridstone Bay **99** G2
Griffith **50** B3
Grimwade **64** C3
Grindal Island **68** B4
Grogan **79** E4
Grong Grong **78** B5
Groote Eylandt **11** H5
Grose River **45** F2, F4
Grose Valley **45** F4
Grove **99** E4
Grove Hill Hotel **12** D4
Growler Creek **100** C5
Gubara **13** G2
Gubatta **78** B1
Gudarra **38** A5
Guichen Bay **82** A5
Guilderton **62** C5
Guildford (TAS) **96** C5
Guildford (VIC) **85** G6
Gular **74** C1
Gulargambone **74** C1
Gulf Creek **44** A5
Gulf Developmental Road **19** F3, **54** A4
Gulf of Carpentaria **11** H5, **18** D1
Gulf St Vincent **69** E3
Gulgong **75** F4
Gulgurn Manja (Flat Rock) **84** C2
Gulnare **69** F1

Guluguba **60** B4
Guluwuru Island **11** H2
Gumble **74** C6
Gumbo **42** D3
Gumbo Gumbo Creek **42** D1
Gumeracha **69** G4
Gum Flat **68** A1
Gum Lagoon Conservation Park **82** B3
Gum Lake **49** H1
Gumlu **56** D2
Gumly Gumly **78** D6
Gums, The **60** B6
Gum Vale **42** B3
Gunalda **61** F4
Gunbar **50** B2
Gunbarrel Highway **24** B5, **25** E4
Gunbower **85** H2
Gunbower Creek **85** G2
Gundabloui **43** H3
Gundagai **79** E6
Gundaring **65** E2
Gundaroo **88** D1
Gundiah **61** F4
Gundillion **89** E3
Gundy **76** A3
Gunebang **50** C1
Gungal **75** H4
Gunlom (Waterfall Creek) Camping Area **13** F4
Gunnadorrah **38** D5
Gunnamatta Beach **92** D5
Gunnary **79** G4
Gunnedah **44** A5
Gunnewin **33** H6
Gunniguldrie **50** C2
Gunningbland **74** A6
Gunning **79** H6
Gunning Ridge **74** A6
Gunn Point **12** C1
Gunn Point Forestry Reserve **12** C1
Gunns Plains Cave **96** C5
Gunpowder **18** D5
Gunpowder River **18** D5
Gununa **18** D1
Gunyidi **62** C2
Gurig National Park **10** D1
Gurley **44** A4
Gurrundah **79** H5
Gutha **36** D4
Guthalungra **56** D2
Guthega Ski Field **88** B5
Guy Fawkes River **72** D4
Guy Fawkes River National Park **72** D3
Guyra **72** C4
Guyra River **72** C4
Gwabegar **43** H5
Gwydir Highway **43** H4, **73** E2
Gwydir River **43** H4, **73** A4
Gymbowen **83** E4
Gympie **61** F4

H

Haasts Bluff Aboriginal Land Trust **25** G3, **30** A3
Habana **57** F5
Hackney **111** E1
Haddon Corner **32** A5
Haddon Rig **74** B1
Haden **70** D1
Hadspen **97** E6
Hagley **97** E6
Hahndorf **69** G4
Halbury **69** F2

Hale River **30** D3
Half Tide **57** F5
Halfway Creek **73** F4
Halidon **49** F3
Halifax **55** F5
Halifax Bay **55** G6
Hallett **69** G1
Hallidays Point **77** E4
Halligan Bay **41** F2
Halls Creek **16** A3
Halls Gap **84** C3
Halton **76** C5
Haly Creek **61** E5
Hambridge Conservation Park **68** B1
Hamel **64** B2
Hamelin **36** B1
Hamelin Bay **64** A5
Hamelin Pool **36** B1
Hamersley **22** D3
Hamersley Gorge **23** E2
Hamersley Range **22** D2, **23** E3
Hamilton (SA) **30** D6
Hamilton (SA) **69** G2
Hamilton (VIC) **91** E2
Hamilton (TAS) **99** E3
Hamilton Creek **30** D6
Hamilton Downs **28** B2
Hamilton Downs Youth Camp **28** B1
Hamilton Gate **42** C3
Hamilton Highway **91** F2, **92** A3
Hamilton Island **57** F3
Hamilton Park **43** E4
Hamilton River **32** A2
Hamley Bridge **69** F3
Hammersley Lakes **63** H2
Hammond **67** F5
Hammond Downs **32** C5
Hammond **67** F5
Hammond Island **21** E1
Hampshire **96** C5
Hampton (NSW) **80** B2
Hampton (QLD) **71** E1
Hampton **45** F6
Hampton Tableland **39** E6
Hanging Rock **92** C1
Hannahs Bridge **75** F3
Hannan Lake **38** A5
Hann Range **30** B2
Hann River (QLD) **21** G6
Hann River (WA) **15** H2
Hann Tableland **55** E1
Hann Tableland National Park **55** E1
Hanson **69** G1
Hanson River **17** G6
Hanwood **50** B3
Happy Valley (VIC) **49** H3
Happy Valley (VIC) **94** A2
Happy Valley (QLD) **35** G4
Happy Valley Homestead **32** C2
Harcourt **85** G6
Harden **79** F5
Hardey River **22** D3
Harding Range **37** E3
Hardwicke Bay **68** D4
Harefield **78** D6
Harford **96** D5
Hargrave's Lookout **45** G5
Harrietville **87** F6
Harrington **77** E4
Harrismith **65** E1
Harrisville **71** F3
Harrow **83** E6

Harston **86** B4
Hartley **45** E5
Harts Range **30** D2
Hartz Mountains **98** D4
Hartz Mountains National Park **98** D4
Hartz Peak **98** C5
Harvest Home **56** B3
Harvey **64** B2
Harwood **73** G2
Haslam **40** C6
Haslewood Island **57** F3
Hassan Walls **45** E5
Hastings (TAS) **99** E5
Hastings (VIC) **93** E4
Hastings Caves **98** D5
Hastings Point **71** H5
Hastings River **77** E2
Hastings Valley Wineries **77** F2
Hatches Creek Mine **17** H6
Hatfield **50** A2
Hat Head **77** G1
Hat Head National Park **77** G1
Hathersay **63** E3
Hat Hill **45** F4
Hat Hill Road **45** F4
Hattah **49** G3
Hattah-Kulkyne National Park **49** G3
Hatton Vale **71** F2
Haughton River **56** C2
Havannah Island **55** G5
Havelock **85** F5
Haven **85** B1
Hawker **67** F3
Hawker Gatehouse **42** A3
Hawkesbury Heights **45** F1
Hawkesbury Road **45** G2
Hawkesbury River **80** D3
Hawkesdale **91** F3
Hawksbury Point **11** F2
Hawks Head Lookout **36** B3
Hawks Nest **76** D6
Hawkwood **60** C3
Hay **50** B3
Haycock Point **95** H1
Hayes **99** E3
Hayes Creek **12** D4
Hayman Island **57** F3
Hazel Park **93** G5
Hazlewood Pondage **93** G4
Headingly **18** C6
Head of Bight **40** A5
Headstone Point **77** F5
Healesville **93** F2
Healesville Wildlife Sanctuary **93** F2
Heart, The **94** A4
Heathcote **85** H5
Heathcote Junction **92** D1
Heathcote National Park **80** D4
Heathlands Ranger Station **21** F2
Heathlands Reserve **21** F2
Heathmere **90** D3
Hebel **43** G3
Hedley **93** H5
Heka **96** C5
Helena River **62** D6
Helensburgh **80** D4
Helen Springs **17** G3
Helenvale **20** B1
Helidon **71** E2
Hell Hole Gorge National Park **32** D5
Hell's Gate Roadhouse **18** C2
Hellyer **96** B3

Hellyer Gorge State Reserve **96** C5
Henbury **30** C4
Henbury Meteorite Craters Historic Reserve **30** B4
Hendersyde **86** B4
Hendon **70** D3
Henrietta **96** C4
Henri Freycinet Harbour **36** B1
Henty (NSW) **87** F2
Henty (VIC) **90** D1
Henty Dunes **98** B1
Henty Highway **83** G5, **90** D3
Henty Vale **64** D4
Hepburn Springs **92** B1
Herald Island **55** G6
Herbert Downs **31** H2
Herberton **55** E2
Herbert River **55** E4
Herbert Vale **18** C4
Herbert Wash **24** C5
Hermannsburg (Ntaria) **27** G2
Hermannsburg Aboriginal Land **28** C4
Hermidale **43** F6
Hermit Hill **41** F3
Heron Island **59** H4
Herrick **97** G5
Herschel Lake **46** B5
Hervey Bay **35** E4
Herveys Range **74** C5
Hesket **92** D1
Hester **64** C4
Hewart Downs **42** B3
Hewitt **55** F3
Heybrook **63** F6
Heyfield **93** H3
Heywood **90** D3
Hiawatha **93** G5
Hibbs Bay **98** B2
Hibbs Point **98** B2
Hidden Valley (NT) **17** F1
Hidden Valley (QLD) **55** F6
Hidden Valley Homestead **56** C4
Hideaway Bay **57** E3
Highbury (QLD) **19** H1
Highbury (WA) **64** D2
Highclere **96** C4
Highcroft **99** F4
Highfields **70** D1
Highgrove **61** E6
Highlands **86** B6
High Range **22** B4
High Rocky Point **98** B3
High Yellow Bluff **99** G4
Hildawn **63** E2
Hillard Head **98** C5
Hill End (NSW) **75** E6
Hill End (VIC) **93** G3
Hill Grange **67** G5
Hillgrove **72** C5
Hilliard Head **98** C4
Hillman **64** D2
Hillock Point (QLD) **55** G5
Hillock Point (SA) **68** D5
Hill River **62** B3
Hillside (WA) **23** F2
Hillside (WA) **62** C3
Hill Springs **22** B5
Hillston **50** B2
Hilltop **80** C5
Hill Top **89** G2
Hillview (QLD) **71** G4
Hillview (WA) **37** F1
Hillview (WA) **65** E6

Hiltaba **40** D6
Hinchinbrook Island **55** F4
Hinchinbrook Island National Park **55** F4
Hincks Conservation Park **68** B2
Hindmarsh Island **69** G5
Hines Hill **63** G4
Hinnomunjie **94** C1
Hinton **76** C6
Hirstglen **71** E3
Hivesville **61** E4
Hobart **99** E4
Hobartville **33** F3
Hobbs Head **100** D5
Hobbys Yards **80** A2
Hobgoblin **99** F1
Hockley **55** E1
Hoddles Creek **93** F3
Hodgson Downs **11** F6
Hodgson Downs Aboriginal Land **11** E6
Hodgson River **11** F5
Hogan Island **53** F2
Holbrook **87** G2
Holdfast Bay **69** F4
Holland Landing **94** B4
Holloway **64** D4
Holloway Point **97** G1
Hollow Tree **99** E3
Holly **65** E3
Hollydeen **75** H4
Holmwood **79** G2
Holowilena **67** G3
Holroyd River **21** E5
Holt Rock **46** D1
Holwell **97** E5
Homebush **57** F5
Home Hill **56** C2
Home Island **14** B2
Homeleigh **62** D2
Homestead **20** B6
Home Valley **9** H6
Honeymoon Bore **30** D1
Honeysuckle Range **88** B1
Honeysuckles, The **94** A5
Hooker Creek Aboriginal Land **16** D3
Hook Island **57** F3
Hook Peak **57** F3
Hook Point **35** F6
Hooley **23** E2
Hope Campbell Lake **38** B3
Hope Channel **96** A2
Hopetoun (VIC) **83** G1
Hopetoun (WA) **47** E3
Hopevale **21** H6
Hopkins Highway **91** G3
Hopkins Lake **25** F3
Hopkins River **85** D6
Horn Island **21** F1
Horn Point **100** D4
Hornsby **81** E3
Horrocks **36** C3
Horsburg Island **14** A2
Horse Mountain **71** F2
Horseshoe Bay **55** G6
Horseshoe Bend **30** C4
Horsham **83** G4
Horton River **44** A5
Hoskinstown **88** D2
Hotham Ranges **93** G5
Hotham Valley Tourist Railway **64** C1
Hotspur Island **57** H6
Houghton **69** F4
House Of Lords Mountain **79** G1

Houtman Albrolhos Islands **36** B4
Howard **61** G3
Howard Channel **12** C1
Howard Island **11** G2
Howard Springs **12** C2
Howard Springs Nature Reserve **12** C2
Howden **99** E4
Howes Valley **76** A6
Howlong **87** E3
Howqua **93** G1
Howqua River **93** G1
Hoyleton **69** F2
Huckitta **30** D2
Hughenden **20** A6
Hugh River **28** D2
Humbert River **16** D1
Hume Freeway **87** E4
Hume Highway **80** B5, **87** G2
Humps, The **63** H6
Humpty Doo **12** C2
Humula **87** H2
Hungerford **42** D3
Hungry Head Beach **73** F5
Hungry Knob **12** C6
Hunter **85** H4
Hunter Bay **81** G4
Hunter Island **96** A2
Hunter Passage **96** A3
Hunter Point **100** D1
Hunter River **76** A4, B5
Huntingfield **49** G2
Huntly **85** H5
Hunt Ranges **37** G5
Huon River **98** D4
Huon Valley Wineries **99** E4
Huonville **99** E4
Hurricane **20** A2
Hurstbridge **93** E2
Huskisson **89** G1
Hutt **36** C3
Hutton Creek **33** H6
Hyden **63** H6
Hyde Park **56** A5
Hyland Highway **93** H5
Hynam **82** C5
Hypurna **49** F2

Ibis Creek **56** B5
Icy Creek **93** G3
Ida Bay **99** E5
Idalia National Park **33** E4
Ida Valley **37** H3
Idracowra **30** C4
Iffley **19** F4
Ikoymarrwa Lookout **13** E4
Ikuntki (Haasts Bluff) **30** A3
Ikymbon River **10** B6
Ilbilbie **57** F6
Ilford **75** F6
Ilfracombe **33** E3
Illabo **78** D5
Illalong Creek **79** G5
Illamurta Bore **27** F4
Illamurta Springs **27** F4
Illawong **62** A1
Illbilla Creek **27** F4
Illbilla Spring **27** F4
Illeroo **66** D5
Illistrin **19** E5
Illowa **91** F4

Illpurla **27** F4
Iluka **73** G2
Ilyungmadja Point **11** H4
Imanpa Community **30** B4
Imbil **61** F5
Immarna **40** B4
Ince Bay **57** H6
Indarrie **62** D3
Indented Head **92** D3
Indiana **30** D2
Indian Head **35** G2
Indian Island **12** B2
Indian Island Forestry Reserve **12** B2
Indulkana **30** C6
Ingebyrah **88** B5
Ingham **55** F5
Inglewood (QLD) **70** B4
Inglewood (VIC) **85** G4
Inglewood (WA) **37** F2
Inglewood (WA) **62** C1
Inglis Island **11** H2
Inglis River **96** C4
Ingomar **40** D3
Injinoo **21** F1
Injune **33** H6
Inkerman **56** C2
Inkerman Homestead **19** F1
nman Valley **69** F5
Innamincka **42** A1
Innamincka Regional Reserve **42** A1
Inner Sister Island **97** G1
Innes National Park **68** D4
Innesowen **42** D5
Innesvale **10** C6
Innisfail **55** F3
Innisplain **71** F4
Innot Hot Springs **55** E3
Inorunie **19** G3
Inskip Point **35** F6
Interlaken **99** E2
Intermediate Hill **81** G5
Inverell **72** A2
Invergordon North **86** C3
Inverleigh **92** B3
Inverloch **93** F5
Inverness **62** B1
Inverway **16** C3
Investigator Strait **68** D5
Iona **49** H2
Iowna **37** E3
Ipolera **30** B3
Ipswich **71** F2
Irishtown **96** B3
Iron Baron **66** D6
Ironhouse Point **97** H6
Iron Knob **66** D5
Iron Range National Park **21** G3
Irrewillipe **92** A4
Irrunytju Aboriginal Land **39** F1
Irvinebank **55** E2
Irwin **36** C4
Irwin Inlet **65** E6
Irwin River **36** C4
Irymple **49** G2
Isaac River **58** B1
Isdell River **15** G2
Isisford **32** D4
Isla Gorge National Park **60** B2
Island Lagoon **66** C2
Islay Plains **33** G3
Isle Woodah **11** G4
Israelite Bay **47** H2

Isthmus Bay **65** F6
Ita Lake **50** A2
Ivanhoe (NSW) **50** A1
Ivanhoe (WA) **9** H6
Iwupataka **28** C2
Iwupataka Aboriginal Land **28** C1

Jabiru **13** F2
Jackadgery **73** E2
Jackie Junction **25** E5
Jack River **21** H6
Jacks Knob **21** F4
Jack Smith Lake **94** A5
Jackson **60** A5
Jacobs Well **71** H3
Jagumba Mountain **88** A3
Jakes Corner Beach **36** B3
Jallukar **85** D4
Jalna **63** E6
Jamberoo **80** D6
Jambin **59** E6
James Creek **18** D2
James Crossing **64** D3
James Price Point **14** D3
James Range **27** H3
James River **18** B5
Jamestown **67** F6
Jamieson **93** G1
Jamison Valley **45** H4
Jandakot **62** C6
Jandowae **60** D5
Jan Juc **92** C4
Jaraga **56** D3
Jardine River **21** F1
Jardine River National Park **21** F2
Jarklin **85** G3
Jarrahdale **64** B1
Jarrahmond **94** D3
Jarrahwood **64** B4
Jarring **65** F2
Jarrold Point **67** E6
Jay Creek **28** C1
Jeannie's Lookout **46** B6
Jecundars Park **62** D2
Jedburgh **32** D4
Jeedamya **37** H4
Jeetho **93** F5
Jenolan Caves **45** H6
Jenolan Caves Road **45** G6
Jenolan River **45** H6
Jenolan State Forest **45** G6
Jeogla **72** C5
Jeparit **83** F3
Jerangle **88** D3
Jerdacuttup **47** E2
Jericho **99** E2
Jerilderie **86** C1
Jerramungup **65** G3
Jerrawa **79** H6
Jerrys Plains **76** A5
Jerseyville **77** G1
Jervis Bay **89** G1
Jervois **31** E2
Jervois Range **31** E2
Jessamine Creek **32** D2
Jessie Creek **29** G5
Jessies Knoll **32** C2
Jetsonville **97** F5
Jewel Cave **64** A5
Jigalong **23** G3

Jigalong Aboriginal Land **23** G4
Jilakin Lake **65** F1
Jilakin Rock **65** F1
Jilbadji **62** C2
Jilliby **81** F2
Jillicambra Mountain **88** D4
Jimberlana **38** A6
Jimboomba **71** G3
Jimbour **60** D6
Jimenbuen **88** C6
Jim Jim Billabong **13** F3
Jim Jim Camping Area **13** F3
Jim Jim Creek **13** F3
Jim Jim Falls **13** G3
Jimma Range **61** F5
Jindabyne **88** B5
Jindare **12** D5
Jindera **87** F3
Jindivick **93** F3
Jindong **64** B4
Jingalup **64** D4
Jingellic **87** H3
Jingemarra **36** D2
Jinka **31** E2
Jip Jip Conservation Park **82** B3
Jitarning **65** F1
Jiwaranpa **16** C4
Johanna **91** H5
Johnburgh **67** F5
John Flynn Memorial **17** G4
Johnny Souey Cove **100** D2
Johnny Souey Track **100** D3
Johnsonville **94** C3
Johns River **77** F3
Jolimont **109** G5
Jomara **43** G3
Jondaryan **70** C1
Jondaryan Woolshed Complex **70** C1
Jones Lake **42** B5
Jordan River **99** E2
Josbury **64** D2
Joseph Bonaparte Gulf **9** H5, **10** A5
Josephine Falls **55** F2
Josephville **71** G4
Jubilee Downs **15** G3
Jubilee Lake **39** E3
Jubuk **63** F6
Judbury **99** E4
Juenburra **18** D6
Jugiong **79** F6
Julia Creek (QLD) **19** F5
Julia Creek (QLD) **19** F6
Juna Downs **23** E3
Junction Bay **11** E2
Junction View **71** E3
Junction Waterhole **27** G3
Jundah **32** C4
Jundee **23** G6
Junee **78** D5
Junee Reefs **78** D5
Jupiter Well **24** D2
Jura **63** G5
Jurien **62** B3
Jurien Bay **62** A3

Kaarimba **86** B3
Kaban **55** E3
Kabra **59** F4
Kadina **69** E2
Kadnook **83** E6

Kadungle **74** A5
Kaimkillenbun **60** D6
Kain **89** E3
Kairi **55** E2
Kajabbi **19** E5
Kakadu Highway **13** E3
Kakadu Holiday Village **13** F2
Kakadu National Park **10** D3
Kakadu National Park Headquarters & Bowali
    Information Centre **13** F2
Kakadu National Park Headquarters **10** D3
Kalabity **41** H6
Kalala **17** F1
Kalamunda **62** D6
Kalamurina **41** G1
Kalangadoo **90** B1
Kalannie **63** E2
Kalarka **58** D1
Kalbar **71** F3
Kalbarri **36** B3
Kalbarri National Park **36** B3
Kaleentha Loop **49** H1
Kalgan River **65** F5
Kalgoorlie-Boulder **38** A5
Kalimna **94** C3
Kalinga **21** G6
Kalkarinji **16** D2
Kalkaroo **42** A5
Kallala **31** H1
Kalli **37** E2
Kallioota **67** E3
Kalpowar **61** E1
Kalpowar Homestead **21** G6
Kaltukatjara (Docker River) **25** G4
Kalumbar Park **62** C2
Kalumburu **9** F5
Kalumburu Aboriginal Reserve **9** G5
Kaluwiri **37** G2
Kalyeeda **15** F4
Kamarah **78** B4
Kamaran Downs **31** H4
Kamarooka **85** H4
Kambalda **38** A5
Kamballan **64** C3
Kamilaroi **19** E4
Kanandah **38** D5
Kanangra-Boyd National Park **45** H6
Kanangra **64** D5
Kandanga **61** F5
Kandos **75** F6
Kangan **23** E1
Kangarilla **69** F4
Kangaroo Flat **76** D1
Kangaroo Island (SA) **68** C6
Kangaroo Island (TAS) **96** A3
Kangaroo Lake **85** G1
Kangaroo Mountain **79** F6
Kangaroo Point (QLD) **19** E2
Kangaroo Valley **80** C6
Kangiara **79** G5
Kanimba Valley **45** F5
Kaniva **82** D3
Kanowna Island **100** B6
Kanya **83** H5
Kanyaka **67** F4
Kanyapella **86** A3
Kapooka **78** C6
Kapunda **69** G3
Kara **42** B5
Karabine **63** E5
Karakin Lakes **62** B4
Karalundi **23** F6

Karara (QLD) **70** C4
Karara (SA) **37** E4
Karatta **68** D6
Karbar **37** E2
Karijini (Hamersley Range) National Park **23** E3
Karinga **62** D4
Karkoo **68** B2
Karlantijpa North Aboriginal Land Trust **17** E4
Karlantijpa South Aboriginal Land Trust **17** F5
Karlgarin **63** H6
Karlinka **41** H6
Karmona **42** B1
Karoola **97** E5
Karoonda **69** H4
Karpa Kora **49** H1
Karping **64** D1
Karragullen **62** D6
Karrakin **63** F5
Karratha **22** C1
Karratha Roadhouse **22** C1
Karridale Estate **64** A5
Kars **42** B6
Kars Springs **75** H3
Karte **49** F3
Karte Conservation Park **49** F3
Karuah **76** C6
Karumba **19** F2
Katamatite **86** C3
Katandra **86** C4
Katandra West **86** C3
Katanning **65** E3
Katapata Gap **30** B3
Kata Tjuta (The Olgas) **25** H5
Katherine **13** E6
Katherine Gorge **13** F5
Katherine Gorge Visitor Centre **13** F6
Katherine River **13** E6
Katiti Aboriginal Land Trust **25** H4, **30** A4
Katoomba **45** G4
Katunga **86** C3
Kawarren **92** A4
Kayrunnera **42** B4
Keduma River **45** H3
Keelbottom Creek **56** A1
Keep River **10** A6
Keep River National Park **10** A6
Keera **44** B4
Keeroongooloo **32** C5
Keith **82** B2
Kellatier **96** C4
Kellerberrin **63** F5
Kellevie **99** F3
Kellidie Bay Conservation Park **68** A3
Kelly Hill Caves Conservation Park **68** D6
Kelsey Creek **57** E3
Kelso **97** E4
Kelstern **62** C1
Kempsey **77** F1
Kempton **99** E3
Kendall **77** F3
Kendall River **21** E5
Kendenup **65** E5
Kenebri **43** H5
Kenilworth **61** F5
Kenmore **80** A6
Kennedy Developmental Road **20** A5, **32** A2
Kennedy **55** E4
Kennedy Highway **54** D5, **55** E1
Kennedy Range **22** B5
Kennedy Range National Park **22** B5
Kennedy River **21** G6
Kennedy Road **55** E1

Kennedy's Cottage **14** D3
Kenneth Range **22** D4
Kennett River **92** B5
Kensington **64** B1
Kentucky **72** B6
Keppel Bay **59** G4
Keppel Sands **59** F4
Keppoch **82** C4
Kerang East **85** G2
Kerang **85** G2
Kerein Hills **50** C1
Kergunyah **87** F4
Kergunyah South **87** F4
Keri **12** B3
Kernot **93** F5
Kernot Range **30** B4
Kerrabee **75** G4
Kerrs Creek **74** D6
Kerrydale **65** G2
Kerry **71** G4
Kersbrook **69** G4
Kersops Peak **100** D5
Ketchowla **67** G6
Kettering **99** E4
Kevington **93** G1
Kew **77** F3
Keyling Inlet **10** A5
Keyneton **69** G3
Keysbrook **64** B1
Khancoban **88** A4
Kiah **77** H2
Kialla **86** B4
Kiama **80** D6
Kiana **18** A2
Kiandra **88** B3
Kianga **60** B1
Kia-ora (NSW) **43** F4
Kia-Ora (SA) **69** H1
Kiata **83** F3
Kidman Way **43** E5, **50** B3
Kidson Track **14** D6
Kidston **54** C5
Kidston Goldmine **54** C5
Kielpa **68** B1
Kiewa **87** F4
Kiewa River **87** F5
Kiewa Valley Highway **87** F5
Kiki **69** H5
Kikoira **78** B1
Kilcoy **61** F6
Kilcunda **93** E5
Kilfeera **86** D5
Kilgour River **18** A2
Kilgowla Mountain **87** H1
Kilkivan **61** F4
Killagurra Springs (Well 17) **24** A3
Killara **37** F1
Killarney (NT) **17** E1
Killarney (VIC) **71** E4
Killiecrankie **97** G1
Kilmany **94** A4
Kilmore **92** D1
Kilto **14** D3
Kimba (QLD) **21** G6
Kimba (SA) **66** C6
Kimberley **96** D5
Kimberley Aboriginal Reserve **9** F5
Kimberley Downs **15** F3
Kimbiki **43** F5
Kimbriki **76** D4
Kinalung **42** B6
Kinchega National Park **42** B6

Kinclaven **38** D5
Kindarun Mountain **75** H6
Kingaroy **61** E5
King Edward River (NT) **9** F5
King Edward River (NT) **9** F6
Kingfisher Bay Resort & Village **35** F4
King George Falls **9** G5
King George River **9** G5
King George Sound **65** F6
King Island **96** C1
King Junction **19** H1
Kinglake **93** E2
King Lake **94** C3
Kinglake **93** E2
Kinglake National Park **93** E2
King Leopold Ranges **15** G3
King Point **81** G6
Kingoonya **66** A1
Kingower **85** F4
King Ranch **62** B2
King River (NT) **9** H6
King River (NT) **10** D5
King River (TAS) **98** B1
King River (VIC) **87** E5
King Rock **46** D1
Kingsborough **54** D1
Kings Canyon **30** A3
Kingscliff **71** H4
Kingscote **69** E5
Kings Creek Station **30** A4
Kingsdale **80** A6
Kings Highway **89** E2
King Solomon Cave **96** D5
King Sound **15** E2
Kings Plains National Park **72** B2
Kingsthorpe **70** D1
Kingston (ACT) **105** H6
Kingston (NI) **77** G6
Kingston (TAS) **99** E4
Kingston (VIC) **92** B1
Kingston OM **49** F2
Kingston SE **82** A4
Kingsvale **79** F4
King Valley **87** E5
Kinka **59** F4
Kinkuna National Park **61** F2
Kinrara **54** D4
Kirkalocka **37** E3
Kirkimbie **16** C3
Kirkstall **91** F3
Kirrama **55** E4
Kirup **64** C4
Kital **70** D3
Kitchcoolie **63** E4
Kiwirrikurra **25** E2
Klimpton **89** G1
Kneebone **10** A6
Knockrow **71** H6
Knorrit Flat **76** D3
Knowsley **85** H5
Koah **55** E1
Kodj Kodjin **63** F4
Koetong **87** G4
Kogan **60** C6
Kojonup **65** E3
Kokatha **66** A2
Kokerbin Rock **63** F5
Kolburn **62** C3
Kolendo **66** C4
Kolindale **65** E1
Koloona **44** B4
Komungla **80** A6

Kondinin **63** G6
Kondinin Lake **63** G6
Kondoolka **40** D6
Kongorong **90** B2
Kongwak **93** F5
Koojan Downs **62** C3
Kookynie **38** A3
Koolan Island **15** E1
Koolanooka Springs **36** D4
Koolatah **19** G1
Koolburra **21** G6
Koolburra Mountain **21** G6
Kooline **22** C3
Kooljaman **15** E2
Kooloonong **49** H3
Koolpinyah **12** C2
Koolyanobbing **37** G5
Koomooloo **69** H1
Koonalda Cave **39** H5
Koonalda **39** H5
Koonamore **67** H4
Koonda **86** C4
Koondrook **85** G1
Koongawa **66** B6
Koongie Park **16** A3
Koonmarra **37** E1
Koonoomoo **86** C2
Koonwarra **93** F5
Koonya (TAS) **99** F4
Koonya (WA) **62** C3
Kooralbyn **71** F4
Koorawatha **79** G3
Koorda **63** F3
Koordarrie **22** B3
Kooreh **85** E4
Kooringa **62** B2
Kooringal **71** H2
Koornalla **93** H4
Kooroocheang **85** G6
Kootingal **72** A6
Koo-Wee-Rup **93** E4
Korogoro Point **77** G1
Koroit **91** F4
Korong Vale **85** F3
Korora **73** F5
Korrelocking **63** F4
Korumburra **93** F5
Kosciuszko National Park **88** B3
Kotta **85** H3
Kotupna **86** B3
Koumala **57** F6
Koumala South **57** F6
Kowanyama **21** E6
Kow Swamp **85** H2
Koyuga **86** A3
Krambach **76** D4
Kroombit Tops National Park **59** F6
Krowera **93** F5
Kudardup **64** B5
Kuender **65** G1
Kukerin **65** F2
Kulgera **30** C5
Kulikup **64** D4
Kulin **65** F1
Kulliparu Conservation Park **48** A1
Kulnura **81** E1
Kulpara **69** E2
Kulpi **61** E6
Kulvegalinna Creek **40** D2
Kulyaling **64** D1
Kumarina Roadhouse **23** F5
Kumbarilla **60** C6

Kumbia **61** E5
Kunama **88** A2
Kundabung **77** F2
Kungala **73** F4
Kungara **69** H1
Kunghur **71** G5
Kunjin **63** G6
Kunmunya Aboriginal Reserve **15** F1
Kununoppin **63** F3
Kununurra **10** A6
Kuranda **55** F1
Kuri Bay **9** E6
Kuridala **19** E6
Kurinelli Mine **17** H5
Ku-Ring-Gai Chase National Park **81** E3
Kurlkuta Aboriginal Land **25** E3
Kurrajong Camping Ground **16** B2
Kurrajong **45** E1
Kurrajong Heights **45** E1
Kurri Kurri **76** B6
Kurrimine **55** F3
Kurundi **17** H5
Kururrungka Roadhouse **16** A5
Kuttabul **57** F5
Kwinana **62** C6
Kwobrup **65** F3
Kwolyin **63** F5
Kyabra **32** C6
Kyabra Creek **32** C5
Kyabram **86** B4
Kyalite **49** H3
Kyancutta **66** A6
Kybeyan Range **88** D5
Kybo **39** E5
Kyburra **56** D2
Kybybolite **82** D5
Kyeamba **87** H2
Kyeema Conservation Park **69** F5
Kylie **64** D3
Kyneton **92** C1
Kyno **62** C3
Kynuna **32** B1
Kyogle **71** F5
Kyong **33** F2
Kyvalley **86** B4
Kywong **78** B6

Laanecoorie **85** G5
Laanecoorie Reservoir **85** G5
Labelle Downs **12** B3
Labertouche **93** F3
Labillardiere State Reserve **99** E5
Labona **56** A6
Lacepede Bay **82** A5
Lachlan **99** E3
Lachlan Range **50** B2
Lachlan River **50** C1, **79** H5
Lacrosse Island **9** H5
La Cuesta **62** C1
Lady Barron **97** H2
Lady Bay **91** F4
Lady Elliot Island **34** D4
Lady Julia Percy Island **91** E4
Ladysmith **87** H1
Laggan **80** A5
Lagoon, The **81** G5
Lagoon Beach **81** G4
Lagoon Creek (QLD) **18** C2
Lagoon Creek (QLD) **33** F3
Lagoon of Islands **99** E1

La Grange Bay **14** C4
Lagrange **14** D4
Laguna Quays **57** E4
Laharum **84** B2
Lah-Arum **83** G5
Laheys Creek **75** E4
Laidley **71** E2
Lajamanu **16** D3
Lake Acraman **66** A4
Lake Ada **96** D6
Lake Aerodrome **23** H4
Lake Albacutya **83** F1
Lake Albert **69** G5
Lake Alexandrina **69** G5
Lake Altibouka **42** C4
Lake Amadeus **25** H4, **30** H4
Lake Anec **25** F3
Lake Annean **37** F1
Lake Argyle **16** B1
Lake Argyle Village **16** B1
Lake Arumpo **49** H2
Lake Augusta **96** D6
Lake Auld **24** B2
Lake Austin **37** E2
Lake Awoonga **59** G6
Lake Bael Bael **85** G2
Lake Baghdad **46** B5
Lake Baladjie **63** H3
Lake Ballard **37** H4
Lake Banksiadale **64** C1
Lake Barambah **61** E5
Lake Barlee **37** G3
Lake Barlee Homestead **37** F4
Lake Barracoota **95** H3
Lake Barrington **96** D5
Lake Bathurst **89** E1
Lake Bedford **24** B6
Lake Bellfield **84** C4
Lake Bennet **25** H2
Lake Bennett **12** C3
Lake Betty **15** H5
Lake Bindegolly National Park **42** D2
Lake Birrabeen **35** F5
Lake Blair **24** D4
Lake Blanche (SA) **41** H3
Lake Blanche (WA) **24** A2
Lake Boga **85** F1
Lake Bolac **84** D6
Lake Bonney **90** A2
Lake Boomanjin **35** F5
Lake Boonderoo **38** C5
Lake Boondooma **60** D4
Lake Bowarrady **35** G3
Lake Breaden **24** D5
Lake Bremer **24** B5
Lake Brewster **50** C2
Lake Brown **63** G3
Lake Buchanan (QLD) **33** F1
Lake Buchanan (WA) **24** B5
Lake Buchan **65** G2
Lake Buffalo **87** E5
Lake Bullen Merri **91** H4
Lake Buloke **85** E3
Lake Buninjon **84** D5
Lake Burbury **98** C1
Lake Burkanoko **43** E4
Lake Burley-Griffin **88** D1
Lake Burnside **24** A5
Lake Burragorang **80** C4
Lake Burrendong **75** E5
Lake Burrendong State Recreation Area **74** D5
Lake Burrumbeet **92** A1

Lake Cadibarrawirracanna **40** D2
Lake Callabonna **41** H3
Lake Camm **65** H1
Lake Campion **63** G3
Lake Carey **38** A3
Lake Cargelligo **50** C2
Lake Carmody **46** D1
Lake Carnegie **24** A6
Lake Carree **35** G2
Lake Cathie **77** F3
Lake Cave **64** A4
Lake Cethana **96** D5
Lake Charm **85** G1
Lake Chinokup **65** F2
Lake Chisholm Forest Reserve **96** B4
Lake Clifton **64** B2
Lake Cobb **24** D4
Lake Colac **92** A4
Lake Coleman **94** B4
Lake Colongulak **91** H3
Lake Condah **91** E3
Lake Condah Mission **91** E3
Lake Conjola **89** G2
Lake Coolmunda **70** B4
Lake Cooper **86** A4
Lake Cootharaba **61** G5
Lake Corangamite **91** H3, **92** A3
Lake Corringle **95** E3
Lake Cowal **78** D2
Lake Cowan **38** A6
Lake Crescent **99** E2
Lake Cressbrook **71** E1
Lake Cronin **47** E1
Lake Cullen **85** G1
Lake Cullivel **85** G1
Lake Curdlawidny **66** A1
Lake Curlip **95** E3
Lake Dalrymple **56** B3
Lake Darlot **37** H2
Lake Dartmouth **33** E6
Lake Deborah East **37** G5
Lake Deborah West **63** H2
Lake De Courcy **63** E2
Lake Dennis **16** B6
Lake Disappointment **24** A3
Lake Dora **24** A2
Lake Dove **96** C6
Lake Dundas **47** F1
Lake Dunn **33** F2
Lake Dutton **66** D3
Lake Echo **98** D2
Lake Eildon **86** C6
Lake Eildon National Park **93** G1
Lake Eliza **82** A6
Lake Elphinstone **56** D5
Lake Eppalock **85** H5
Lake Epsom **57** F6
Lake Eucumbene **88** B4
Lake Everard **66** A2
Lake Everard Homestead **66** A3
Lake Everard National Park **66** A2
Lake Eyre National Park **41** F2-3
Lake Eyre North **41** F2
Lake Eyre South **41** F3
Lake Farnell **95** F3
Lake Farnham **25** E4
Lake Fergus **98** D1
Lakefield **21** G6
Lakefield National Park **21** G5
Lake Finnis **66** D3
Lake Finniss **12** D1
Lake Fox **65** H1

Lake Frome **41** H4
Lake Frome Regional Reserve **41** H4
Lake Fyans **84** D3
Lake Gairdner (SA) **66** B3
Lake Gairdner (TAS) **96** C5
Lake Gairdner National Park **66** B2
Lake Galilee **33** F2
Lake Garawongera **35** F4
Lake George (NSW) **88** D1
Lake George (SA) **82** A6
Lake George (WA) **24** B2
Lake Giles **37** G4
Lake Gillen **24** C6
Lake Gilles **66** D5
Lake Gillies Conservation Park **66** C6
Lake Gilmore **47** F1
Lake Glenlyon **70** B6
Lake Glenmaggie **94** A3
Lake Gnarann **35** G3
Lake Gnarpurt **91** H3
Lake Goongarrie **37** H4
Lake Gordon **98** C3
Lake Grace **65** F2
Lake Greenly **68** A3
Lake Gregory (SA) **41** G2
Lake Gregory (WA) **16** A5
Lake Gregory (WA) **23** G6
Lake Gregory Aboriginal Land **16** A5
Lake Gulson **65** H1
Lake Hamilton **68** A2
Lake Hancock **24** C4
Lake Hanson **66** C1
Lake Harris **66** A2
Lake Hart **66** C2
Lake Harvey **63** F2
Lake Hazlet **25** F1
Lake Hillman **63** E2
Lake Hindmarsh **83** F2
Lake Hoar **24** B5
Lake Hope (SA) **41** H2
Lake Hope (WA) **47** E1
Lake Hume **87** G3
Lake Hurlsstone **46** D1
Lake Illawarra **80** D5
Lake Ilma **39** F3
Lake Ina **98** D1
Lake Innes **77** F3
Lake Jack Smith **94** A5
Lake Jasper **64** B5
Lake Jennings **35** F5
Lake Jindabyne **88** B5
Lake Johnston **47** E1
Lake Jones (WA) **15** H5
Lake Jones (WA) **24** B5
Lake Joy **65** G3
Lake Judd **98** D4
Lake Julius **18** D5
Lake Kajatabie **43** H2
Lake Keene **24** B5
Lake Keepit **44** A5
Lake Keepit State Recreation Area **44** A5
Lake Kerrylyn **23** G5
Lake King **65** H1
Lake King William **98** D2
Lake Koombekine **63** E4
Lake Koombooloomba **55** E3
Lake Lalbert **85** F1
Lakeland **20** B1
Lake Langan **15** H5
Lake Lea **96** C5
Lake Leaghur **49** H2
Lake Leake **99** G1

Lake Lefroy **38** A6
Lake Leslie **70** D4
Lake Lewis **30** B2
Lake Linlithgow **91** F2
Lake Lockhart **65** G2
Lake Lonsdale **84** D2
Lake Lucy **55** E5
Lake Lyell **45** E6
Lake MacDonald **25** F3
Lake MacFarlane **66** C3
Lake Machattie **31** H4
Lake Mackay **25** F2
Lake Mackay Aboriginal Land Trust **25** G1
Lake Mackenzie **96** D6
Lake Mackintosh **96** C6
Lake MacLeod **22** A5
Lake Macquarie **81** F1
Lake Magenta **65** H2
Lake Magenta Farms **65** H2
Lake Magenta **65** H2
Lake Maitland **37** H1
Lake Malata **68** A2
Lake Marabon **58** A4
Lake Margaret **98** B1
Lake Marmion **38** A4
Lake Marong **35** F1
Lake Mason **37** G2
Lake McKenzie **35** F4
Lake McLernon **15** H5
Lake Mendes **47** F2
Lake Meran **85** G2
Lake Meston **96** D6
Lake Milarup **65** H2
Lake Minan **62** D4
Lake Minigwal **38** B4
Lake Minker **35** G2
Lake Miranda **37** H2
Lake Modewarre **92** B4
Lake Moira **86** B2
Lake Mokoan **86** D4
Lake Monduran **61** E1
Lake Moondarra **18** D5
Lake Moore **63** E1
Lake Mountain Ski Field **93** F2
Lake Muck **42** A4
Lake Muir **64** D5
Lake Muirhead **84** D5
Lake Mulwala **86** D3
Lake Mungo **49** H2
Lake Murdeduck **92** B3
Lake Myrtle **96** D6
Lake Nabberu **23** G6
Lake Nagambie **86** B5
Lake Nash **18** C6
Lake Neale **25** H1
Lake Nenone **98** D1
Lake Nerramyne **36** C3
Lake Newell **24** D4
Lake Newland Conservation Park **48** A1
Lake Nichebulka **43** E4
Lake Noondie **37** G3
Lake Norman **98** D1
Lake Nuga Nuga **33** H5
Lake Oberon **80** B3
Lake O'Grady **63** F2
Lake Olive **96** D6
Lake Omeo **87** H6
Lake Owen **37** H4
Lake Pallarup **47** E2
Lake Parangana **96** D6
Lake Payanna **98** C1
Lake Pedder **98** C4

Lake Perserverance **71** E1
Lake Phillipi **31** G4
Lake Pieman **96** B6
Lake Pinganup **65** G3
Lake Pingrup **65** G2
Lake Pinjar **62** C5
Lake Preston **64** B2
Lake Proserpine **57** E3
Lake Pure (QLD) **42** B1
Lake Purrumbete **91** H4
Lake Reaside **38** A4
Lake Rebecca **38** A4
Lake Reeve **94** B4
Lake Repulse **98** D2
Lake Roe **38** B5
Lake Rosebery **96** C6
Lake Rotuli **96** D6
Lake Rowallan **96** D6
Lake Rowan **86** D4
Lake Rufus **98** C2
Lake Sappho **98** D1
Lake Seabrook **37** G5
Lakes Entrance **94** C3
Lake Sharpe **47** E1
Lakeside **37** E2
Lakes National Park, The **94** C4
Lake Somerset **61** F6
Lake Sorrell **99** E1
Lake St Clair (SA) **82** A6
Lake St Clair (TAS) **98** C1
Lake Stewart **42** A3
Lake Stubbs **65** G1
Lake Sunshine **23** G5
Lake Sylvester **18** A4
Lake Tandou **49** G1
Lake Tay **47** E2
Lake Teague **23** H6
Lake Terrinallum **91** H2
Lake Thomson **93** G3
Lake Throssel **38** C2
Lake Tiberias **99** F2
Lake Tinaroo **55** E2
Lake Torquinie **31** G4
Lake Torrens (SA) **67** E2
Lake Torrens National Park **67** E1
Lake Tutchewop **85** G1
Lake Tyers **94** D3
Lake Tyrel **49** H3
Lake Urana **50** B4
Lake Victoria (NSW) **49** G2
Lake Victoria (VIC) **94** B4
Lake Violet **37** G1
Lake Wabby **35** F4
Lake Wallambiry **63** F3
Lake Wanhar **35** G1
Lake Warrakatanna **41** H2
Lake Waukarlycarly **23** H1
Lake Way **37** G1
Lake Weering **92** A3
Lake Wellington **94** B4
Lake Wells **38** B1
Lake White **16** B6
Lake Wilderness **23** H4
Lake Will **96** C6
Lake Wills **16** B6
Lake Windabout **66** D2
Lake Windamere **75** F5
Lake Winifred **24** B2
Lake Wivenhoe **71** F1
Lake Wongitta **31** G3
Lake Woods **17** G3
Lake Woytchugga **42** C5

Lake Wuruma **60** D2
Lake Wyangala **79** H3
Lake Wynwyn **83** F4
Lake Yantara **42** B4
Lake Yindana **38** B5
Lake Yindarlgooda **38** A5
Lake Younghusband **66** B1
Lalbert **85** F1
Lal Lal **92** B2
Lalla Rookh **23** F1
Lambert Centre **30** D5
Lambina **30** C6
Lamboo **16** A3
Lameroo **49** F3
Lamington National Park **71** G4
Lancaster **86** B4
Lancefield **92** D1
Lancelin **62** B4
Lander River **17** E5, **30** B1
Landfall Point **21** E3
Land Mark **62** C4
Landor **22** D5
Landsborough (QLD) **61** G6
Landsborough (VIC) **85** E5
Landsborough Creek **33** E1
Landsborough (Matilda) Highway **19** E6, **33** F4
Langdon **19** G3
Langhorne Creek **69** G5
Langkoop **82** D5
Lang Lang **93** F4
Langleydale **49** H2
Langley **85** H6
Langlo River **33** E5
Langtree **50** B2
Langwarrin **93** E4
Lankeys Creek **87** H3
Lannercost **55** F5
Lansdale **43** F6
Lansdowne (NSW) **77** E3
Lansdowne (QLD) **33** F5
Lansdowne (WA) **15** H3
La Perouse **81** E4
Lapoinya **96** C4
Lappa **54** D2
Lara **92** C3
Larapinta Drive **28** C2-6
Laravale **71** F4
Lardner **93** F4
Largs Bay **69** F4
Lark Quarry Conservation Park **32** C2
Larpent **92** A4
Larras Lee **74** D6
Larrawa **15** H4
Larrey Point **14** A6
Larrimah **11** E6
Lascelles **83** H1
Lasseter Highway **30** A4
Latham **62** D1
Latrobe **96** D5
Latrobe Range **100** C4
Latrobe River **93** H4, **94** A4
Lauderdale **99** F4
Laughing Jack Lagoon **98** D1
Launceston **97** E5
Laura (QLD) **21** G6
Laura (SA) **67** F6
Lauradale **43** E4
Laura River **21** G6
Laurel Hill **88** A2
Laurieton **77** F3
Lauriston **85** H6
Lauriston Reservoir **92** C1

Lavers Hill **91** H5
Laverton (VIC) **92** D3
Laverton (WA) **38** A3
Laverton Downs **38** A3
Lavinia Nature Reserve **96** D1
Lavinia Point **96** D1
Lawlers **37** G2
Lawn Hill **18** C3
Lawn Hill Creek **18** C3
Lawn Hill National Park **18** C3
Lawnton **71** G1
Lawnvale **54** A4
Lawrence **73** F2
Lawrence Road **73** F2
Lawrenny **98** D2
Lawson **45** G3
Leading Hill **35** F4
Leadville **75** F3
Leander **43** F3
Learmonth (VIC) **92** A1
Learmonth (WA) **22** A3
Ledge Point (WA) **62** B4
Ledge Point (WA) **65** G5
Leeman **62** A2
Lee Point **12** C1
Leeton **78** A4
Leeuwin-Naturaliste National Park **64** A4-5
Leeville **71** F6
Lefroy **97** E4
Left Hill **21** F2
Legana **97** E5
Legendre Island **22** C1
Legerwood **97** G5
Legges Tor **97** F6
Legume **71** E4
Legune **10** A6
Leichardt **85** G5
Leichhardt Falls **19** E3
Leichhardt Highway **60** B2
Leichhardt River **19** E3
Leigh Creek **67** F1
Leinster **37** H2
Leinster Downs **37** H2
Leitchville **85** H2
Lemnos **86** C4
Lemont **99** F2
Len Beadell's Tree **25** G4
Lennonville **37** E2
Lennox Head **71** H6
Leonard Point **100** B4
Leonards **92** B1
Leongatha **93** F5
Leongatha South **93** F5
Leonora-Gwalia **37** H3
Leopold **92** C4
Leopold Downs **15** G3
Leopold River **15** H3
Lerderderg Gorge **92** C2
Lerderderg River **92** C2
Lerida **43** E6
Leschenault **64** B3
Leschenault Inlet **64** B3
Leslie Peak **31** H2
Lesueur National Park **62** B2
Lethbridge **92** B3
Leura **45** G4
Levendale **99** F3
Levuka **32** D2
Lewis Creek **16** B4
Lewisham **99** F3
Lexia **62** C5
Lexton **85** F6

Leyburn **70** C3
L'Haridon Bight **36** B1
Liawenee **96** D6
Liberal Well (Well 37) **24** C2
Licola **93** H2
Liddell **76** A5
Lidsdale **80** C2
Liena **96** D5
Lietinna **97** F5
Liffey **97** E6
Liffey Falls **97** E6
Lighthouse Point **100** D2
Lighthouse Track **100** C5
Lightning Ridge **43** G4
Liguanea Island **68** B4
Lilla Creek **30** C5
Lillimur **82** D3
Lilydale (SA) **49** E1
Lilydale (TAS) **97** F5
Lilydale (VIC) **93** E2
Lilyvale **21** G5
Limbla **30** D3
Limbunya **16** C2
Limeburners Creek **76** C6
Lime Lake **65** E3
Limerick **80** A4
Limestone Caves **70** A6
Limestone Gorge **16** D1
Limevale **70** B5
Limmen Bight **11** G5
Limmen Bight River **11** G6, **17** H1
Limmen Bight River Fishing Camp **11** G6
Lincoln Highway **68** B2
Lincoln National Park **68** B4
Lindeman Group **57** F4
Lindeman Island **57** F3
Lindenow **94** B3
Lindesay Highway **71** G3
Lind Lind National Park **95** F3
Lindsay Creek **30** D5
Lingi Point **10** C1
Lingnoonganee Island **19** E1
Linke Lakes **24** B6
Linton **92** A2
Linville **61** F6
Lipson **68** B3
Lipson Cove **48** C2
Lismore (NSW) **71** G6
Lismore (VIC) **91** H3
Lissadell **16** B2
Liston **70** D5
Listowel Downs **33** E5
Litchfield **83** H3
Litchfield National Park **12** C4
Litchfield Outstation **12** B4
Lithgow **80** C2
Littabella National Park **61** F1
Little Adolphus Island **21** F1
Little Armstrong Bay **46** B5
Little Billabong **87** H2
Little Desert Lodge **83** E4
Little Desert National Park **82** D4, **83** E4
Little Dip Conservation Park **82** A6
Little Lake **99** E1
Little Mount Finke **40** C5
Little Mulgrave **55** F2
Little Pine Lagoon **98** D1
Little Rame Point **95** G3
Little River **92** C3
Little River Falls Lookout **94** D1
Little Sandy Desert **23** G4, **24** B4
Little Swanport (TAS) **99** G2

Little Swanport River **99** F2
Little Topar Roadhouse **42** B5
Liveringa **15** F3
Liverpool **80** D3
Liverpool Range **75** H3
Liverpool River **13** H2
Lizard Island **21** H5
Lizard Island National Park **21** H5
Llanelly **85** G5
Llangothlin **72** C4
Llewellyn Bay **57** F6
Llowalong **94** A3
Loadstone **71** F5
Lobethal **69** G4
Loccota **97** G2
Loch Ard Gorge **91** H5
Lochcair **65** G1
Lochern National Park **32** C3
Loch **93** F4
Lochiel (QLD) **32** C4
Lochiel (SA) **69** F2
Lochinvar **76** B6
Loch Sport **94** B4
Lock **68** B1
Lockerbie **21** F1
Lockhart **78** B6
Lockhart River **21** G3
Lockington **85** H3
Locksley **80** B2
Lockwood **85** G5
Loddon River **85** G3
Loddon Valley Highway **85** G3
Lofty Range **23** F4
Logan (QLD) **71** G2
Logan (VIC) **85** F4
Loganholme **71** G3
Logan Lagoon **97** H2
Logan River **71** F4
Logan Village **71** G3
Logie Brae **86** C1
Lombadina **15** E2
Lombadina Aboriginal Land **15** E2
Lombadine Point **14** D2
Lomos **63** F6
London Bridge **91** G5
Lone Pine Koala Sanctuary **71** G2
Long Beach **89** F3
Long Flat **77** E2
Longford (TAS) **97** E6
Longford (VIC) **94** A4
Long Island (NT) **15** E2
Long Island (QLD) **57** F3
Long Island (QLD) **59** E1
Long Island (TAS) **97** G3
Longlea **85** H5
Longley **99** E4
Long Point (TAS) **97** G2
Long Point (TAS) **97** H6
Longreach (QLD) **32** D3
Longreach (WA) **62** C2
Longreach (WA) **65** H1
Longreach Bay **46** B5
Long Reef Point **81** E3
Longton **20** B6
Longwarry **93** F4
Longwood **86** B5
Lonnavale **98** D4
Lookout Hill **46** C6
Lookout Point (QLD) **21** H6
Lookout Point (WA) **65** G5
Lookout Rocks **100** B4
Looma **15** F3

Loongana **96** C5
Loop, The **36** B3
Loorana **96** C2
Lora Creek **40** D2
Lord Howe Island **81** H5
Lorella **11** G6
Lorinna **96** D5
Lorna Downs **32** A3
Lorna Glen **23** H6
Lorne **92** B5
Lornsleigh **56** B4
Lorquon **83** F3
Lorraine **19** E4
Lorrett Downs **32** A2
Lostock **76** B5
Lottah **97** G5
Lotus Vale **19** F2
Louisa Downs **15** H4
Louisville **99** G3
Louth **43** E4
Louth Bay **68** B3
Louth Island **68** B3
Lowan Conservation Park **69** H4
Lowanna **73** F4
Lower Acacia Creek **71** E4
Lower Barrington **96** D5
Lower Barry Creek Campsite **100** C2
Lower Beulah **96** D5
Lower Bucca **73** F4
Lower Creek **72** D6
Lower Glenelg National Park **90** D3
Lower Hunter Wineries **76** B6
Lower King **65** F6
Lower Light **69** F3
Lower Lila **43** E4
Lower Quipolly **75** H2
Lowesdale **87** E2
Low Head **97** E4
Lowlands **50** B1
Lowly Point **67** E6
Lowmead **61** E1
Lowood **71** F2
Low Point (CI) **14** B4
Low Point (WA) **22** A3
Low Rocky Point **98** B4
Lowther **45** F6
Loxton **49** F2
Lubeck **85** C1
Lucaston **99** E4
Lucinda **55** F5
Lucindale **82** B5
Lucknow **79** H1
Lucky Downs **54** D5
Lucy Creek **31** E2
Lucyvale **87** H4
Luddenham **80** D4
Ludlow **64** B3
Lue **75** F5
Lughrata **97** G2
Luina **96** B5
Luluigui **15** F3
Lulworth **97** E4
Lumholtz National Park **55** E4
Lunawanna **99** E5
Lurg **86** D5
Lurg Upper **86** D5
Luritja Road **30** B4
Luscombe **65** E4
Lyell Highway **98** C1, D2
Lymington **99** E4
Lymwood **96** C2
Lynchford **98** B1

Lynchs Creek **71** F5
Lyndavale **30** B5
Lyndhurst (NSW) **79** H2
Lyndhurst (SA) **41** G4
Lyndhurst (WA) **64** D5
Lyndoch **69** G3
Lyndon (WA) **22** B4
Lyndon (WA) **65** E4
Lyndon River **22** B4
Lynd Range **60** A2
Lynd River **54** B1, C3
Lynton Convict Ruins **36** B3
Lynwood **32** D5
Lyons **90** D3
Lyons River (WA) **22** C5
Lyonville **92** C1

M

Maaroom **35** E5
Maatsuyker Group **98** C5
Maatsuyker Island **98** C5
Mabel Creek **40** C3
Mabel Downs **16** B2
Macadam Range **12** A6
Macalister **60** D6
Macalister River **93** H2
Macarthur **91** E3
Macauley's Headland **73** F5
Mac Clark Conservation Reserve **30** D4
Macclesfield **69** G4
MacDonald River **75** H6
MacDonnell Ranges **30** B3
MacDonnell Ranges East **30** D3
Macedon **92** C1
Macintyre Creek **70** A4
Macintyre River **44** A3, **72** A1
Mackay **57** F5
Mackenzie Falls **84** C3
Mackenzie River (QLD) **58** C4, D4
Mackenzie River (VIC) **85** B1-2
MacKillop's Bridge **95** E1
Macknade **55** F5
Macksville **73** E6
Mackunda Creek **32** B2
MacLagan **61** E6
Maclean (NSW) **73** G2
Maclean (QLD) **71** G3
Maclean Bay **99** H1
Macleay Island **71** H2
Macleay River **72** C6, **77** F1
Macquarie Harbour **98** B2
Macquarie Pass National Park **80** D5
Macquarie River (NSW) **43** G5, **74** B2, **80** A3
Macquarie River (TAS) **97** E6, **99** F1
Macumba **41** E1
Macumba River **31** E6
Madigan **15** H5
Madoonga **37** E1
Madoonia Downs **38** B6
Madora **64** B1
Madura **39** E6
Mafeking Campsite **84** D5
Maffra (NSW) **88** C5
Maffra (VIC) **94** A3
Magela **13** G2
Maggea **49** F2
Maggieville **19** F2
Magnetic Island **55** G6
Magnetic Island National Park **55** G6
Magnetic Passage **55** H6
Magra **99** E3

Maguk Camping Area **13** F3
Mahanewo **66** C3
Maheno Beach **35** G4
Mahoneys Swamp **85** B6
Maiala National Park **71** F1
Maiden Gully **85** G5
Maidenwell **61** E6
Mailer Flat **91** F4
Maindample **86** D6
Maingon Bay **99** F5
Mainoru **11** F4
Main Range National Park **71** E3-4
Maitland (NSW) **76** C6
Maitland (SA) **69** E3
Maitland Downs **20** A1
Majorca **85** F6
Major Mitchell Plateau **84** C4
Majors Creek (NSW) **89** E2
Majors Creek (QLD) **56** B1
Malabar Hill **81** G4
Malagarga **32** C6
Malak Malak Aboriginal Land Trust **12** C4
Malanda **55** E2
Malay Road **11** H2
Malbom **19** E6
Malcolm **37** H3
Maldon **85** G6
Maleny **61** G6
Mallacoota **95** G3
Mallacoota Inlet **95** G3
Mallala **69** F3
Mallanganee **71** F6
Mallapunyah **18** A2
Mallee Cliffs National Park **49** H2
Mallee Highway **49** G3
Mallett **67** G6
Mallina **23** E1
Malmsbury **85** H6
Malmsbury Reservoir **85** H6
Malua Bay **89** F3
Malyalling **65** E1
Ma Ma Creek **71** E2
Mamukala Wetlands **13** F2
Manangatang **49** H3
Manangoora **18** B1
Manann Beach **35** G1
Manberry **22** B5
Manchester **43** G4
Mandalay **42** C5
Mandilla **38** A6
Mandora **14** C5
Mandorah **12** B2
Mandu Mandu Reef Campsite **22** A3
Mandurah **64** B1
Mandurama **79** H2
Maneroo Creek **32** D2
Manfred **36** D1
Mangalo **68** C1
Mangalore (TAS) **99** E3
Mangalore (VIC) **86** B6
Mangana **97** G6
Mangana Point **99** E5
Mangaroon **22** C4
Mangkururrpa Aboriginal Land **16** C5
Mangoplah **87** G1
Mangowine **63** G3
Mangrove Point (QLD) **61** G3
Mangrove Point (SA) **67** E6
Manguel Creek **15** E3
Manildra **74** C6
Manilla **44** A5

Manilla Homestead **49** G1
Maningrida **11** F2
Manja (Cave of Hands) **84** B4
Manjimup **64** C5
Manly (NSW) **81** E3
Manly (QLD) **71** G2
Manmanning **63** E3
Mannahill **41** H6
Mannanarie **67** F6
Manna Vale **65** F1
Manners Creek **31** G1
Manners Well **67** G1
Manning River **76** C3
Mann Ranges **25** G5
Mann River (NT) **11** E3
Mann River (QLD) **72** D3
Manns Beach **93** H6
Mannum **69** G4
Manoora **69** G2
Mansfield **86** D6
Manton **56** B1
Manton Dam **12** C3
Mantuan Downs **33** G4
Mantung **49** F3
Manuallaluk Aboriginal Land Trust **13** G5
Manumbar **61** F5
Manunda **67** H5
Manyallaluk **13** G5
Manyallaluk Aboriginal Land Trust **10** D4
Manypeaks **65** F5
Many Peaks **61** E1
Mapala **60** A1
Mapleton **61** G5
Mapoon **21** E2
Maragle Range **88** A3
Marakoopa Cave **96** D6
Maralinga (Restricted Area) **40** A4
Maralinga Tjarutja Aboriginal Land **39** H3, **40** A2
Maranalgo **37** E4
Maranboy **13** F6
Marandoo Mine **23** E3
Marangaroo **62** C5
Maranoa River **43** G1
Marathon **19** H6
Marbellup **65** F6
Marble Bar **23** F1
Marburg **71** F2
Marchagee **62** C2
Marchinbar Island **11** H1
Marcoola **61** G5
Marcus Beach **61** G5
Mardathuna Station **22** B5
Mardie **22** C2
Mardo **62** C3
Mardugal Camping Area **13** F3
Mareeba **55** E1
Marfield **50** A1
Margaret River (NT) **12** D3
Margaret River (NT) **15** H3
Margaret River (WA) **64** A4
Margaret River Homestead (NT) **15** H4
Margaret River Wineries **64** A4
Margate (QLD) **71** G1
Margate (TAS) **99** E4
Maria Island (NT) **11** G5
Maria Island (TAS) **99** G3
Maria Island National Park **99** G3
Mariala National Park **33** E6
Marian **57** F5
Marillana **23** F3
Marina Plains **21** G5
Marion Bay (SA) **68** D4

Marion Bay (TAS) **99** G3
Marion Downs **31** H3
Marjorie Bay **46** A6
Markwell **76** D5
Markwood **87** E4
Marla **40** C1
Marlborough **59** E3
Marlo **95** E3
Marloo Bay **35** G1
Marloo, Wreck of the **35** G2
Marmbulligan **17** H1
Marmor **59** F5
Marne Valley Conservation Park **69** G3
Marnhull **60** D5
Marnoo **83** H4
Marong **85** G5
Maroochydore **61** G6
Maroona **91** G1
Maroonah **22** C4
Maroondah Highway **86** C6, **93** E3
Maroon **71** F4
Maroon Dam **71** E4
Marqua **31** F2
Marra Aboriginal Land Trust **11** G5
Marrabel **69** G2
Marra **42** D5
Marrakai **12** D2
Marrakai Conservation Reserve **12** D2
Marrammarra National Park **81** E2
Marranup **64** C5
Marrar **78** C5
Marrawah **96** A3
Marrawah Beach **96** A3
Marree **41** G3
Marrilla **22** B4
Marron **22** B6
Marryat Creek **30** B5
Marsden **78** D2
Marsh, The **85** F1
Marshall Bay **97** G1
Marshall River **31** F3
Martindale **75** H5
Martins Washpool **82** A2
Martins Washpool Conservation Park **82** A2
Martins Well **67** G3
Martinup **65** F3
Marulan **80** B6
Marum Marum **91** F1
Marvel Loch **37** G6
Marwok Creek **11** E5
Maryborough (QLD) **61** G3
Maryborough (VIC) **85** F6
Mary Cove **46** B6
Maryfield **11** E6
Mary Island **15** E2
Maryknoll **93** F2
Maryland River **70** D5
Mary River Conservation Reserve **12** D1
Mary River (NT) **12** D2-3
Mary River (QLD) **61** F3
Mary River National Park **12** D2-3
Mary River Roadhouse **13** E4
Mary Springs **36** C3
Marysville **93** F2
Maryvale (NSW) **74** D4
Maryvale (NT) **30** C4
Maryvale **71** E3
Maryvale Roadhouse **31** H2
Masthead Island **59** H5
Mataranka **11** E5
Matheson **72** B2
Mathiesons **86** A4

Mathinna **97** G6
Mathoura **86** A2
Matilda Highway (Landsborough Highway) **33** F5
Matlock (VIC) **93** G2
Matlock (WA) **64** C2
Matong **78** B5
Mattawarrangala **67** G4
Maude (NSW) **50** A3
Maude (VIC) **92** B3
Maudsland **71** G3
Maunchel Spring **62** D2
Maupertuis Bay **68** C6
Mawbanna **96** B4
Mawson **63** E5
Maxwelton **19** G6
Mayanup **64** C4
Mayberry **96** D6
Maybrook **64** D3
Maydena **98** D3
Mayne River **32** B3
Mayrung **86** C1
Maytown **20** A1
Mazeppa National Park **33** G2
McAllister **80** A5
McArthur River **18** A1
McCoys Well **67** G5
McDouall Peak **40** D3
McDougalls Well **42** A5
McGuires Track **16** B5
McHugh Island **100** B6
McIlwraith Range **21** G4
McIvor Highway **85** H5
McKees Hill **71** G6
McKinlay **19** F6
McKinlay River (QLD) **19** F6
McKinlay River (NT) **12** D3
McLaren Creek **17** G5
McLaren Vale **69** F4
McLaren Vale Wineries **69** F4
McLoughlins Beach **94** A5
McMahons Creek **93** F2
McMahons Reef **79** F5
McMinn Creek **27** G5
McPhersons Pillar **24** D4
McQueens **62** B1
Meader Falls **96** D6
Meadow **36** B2
Meadowbank **54** D4
Meadowbank Lake **98** D3
Meadow Downs **67** G5
Meadows **69** F4
Meandarra **60** B6
Meander **96** D6
Meckering **63** E5
Meda **15** F3
Meda River **15** F2
Medlow Bath **45** G4
Medowie **76** C6
Medwin Point **14** B4
Meeberrie **36** D2
Meedo **22** B6
Meekatharra **37** F1
Meeline **37** F3
Meenaar **63** E5
Meena Murtee **42** C5
Meeniyan **93** F5
Meenjoro **62** D5
Meeragoolia **22** B6
Meerlieu **94** B4
Megalong **45** G5
Megalong Road **45** G5
Megalong Valley **45** G5

Megalong Valley Farm **45** G4
Megan **73** E5
Mehi River **43** H4
Meka **36** D2
Melaleuca Mine **98** C5
Melba Highway **93** F2
Melbourne **92** D3
Melbourne Airport **92** D2
Melita **37** H3
Mella **96** B3
Mellenbye **36** D4
Melrose (SA) **67** F5
Melrose (TAS) **96** D5
Melrose (WA) **37** H2
Melton (SA) **67** H4
Melton (VIC) **92** C2
Melton Mowbray **99** E2
Melton Reservoir **92** C2
Melville Caves **85** F4
Melville Island **10** B2
Memana **97** H2
Memerambi **61** E5
Mena Creek **55** F3
Menangina **38** A4
Menangle **80** D4
Mendleyarri **38** A4
Mendooran **75** E2
Mengha **96** B4
Menindee **42** B6
Menindee Lake **42** B6
Meningie **69** G5
Menzies **37** H4
Mepunga West **91** G4
Merah North **43** H4
Merapah **21** F4
Merbein **49** G2
Mercunda **69** H3
Mercury Passage **99** G3
Meredith **92** B2
Mereenie Loop Road **30** A3
Meri Camping Area **13** G2
Merilup **65** F2
Merimbula **95** H1
Merimbula Lake **95** H1
Meringo **89** F4
Meringur **49** G2
Merino **90** D2
Merluna **21** F4
Merolia **38** B3
Merredin **63** G4
Merriangaah Peak **88** C6
Merriang **87** E5
Merrigum **86** B4
Merrijig **86** D6
Merri Merrigal **78** A1
Merrimerriwa Range **50** B1
Merri River **91** F3
Merriton **69** F1
Merriwagga **50** B2
Merriwa **75** H4
Merry Beach **89** F3
Merrygoen **75** E2
Merrywinebone **43** H4
Mersey River **96** D5
Merton **86** C6
Mertondale **38** A3
Merty Merty **42** A2
Messent Conservation Park **82** A2
Messum Hill **21** F2
Metcalfe East **85** H6
Metcalfe **85** H6
Meteor Downs **58** B6

Metricup **64** A4
Metung **94** C3
Meunna **96** B4
Mewstone Rock **95** H1
Mia Mia (QLD) **57** E5
Mia Mia (VIC) **85** H6
Mia Mia (WA) **22** B4
Miandetta **43** F6
Michelago **88** D3
Middalya **22** B5
Middle Beach Campsite **13** E1
Middlecamp **42** B6
Middlecamp Hills Conservation Park **68** C1
Middlefield **74** A4
Middlegate **77** H5
Middle Island **47** G3
Middle Lake **85** G1
Middlemount **58** C2
Middle Park **19** H5
Middle Point **14** A4
Middle Rocks **35** G2
Middleton **32** B2
Middleton Creek **32** B2
Midge Point **57** E4
Midland Highway (TAS) **97** F6, **99** F1
Midland Highway (VIC) **86** D5, **92** B3
Midway Point **99** F3
Mid Western Highway **78** A2, **79** F3
Miena **98** D1
Milabena **96** C4
Mila **95** F1
Milang Roadhouse **67** G4
Milang **69** G5
Milarup **65** H2
Milawa **87** E4
Milbrulong **87** F1
Mildura **49** G2
Miles **60** B5
Mileura **37** E1
Milgun **23** E5
Milikapiti **10** B2
Miling **62** D3
Milingimbi **11** F2
Military Training Area (QLD) **61** G4
Military Training Area (WA) **15** F2
Milkshake Hills Forest Reserve **96** B4
Millaa Millaa **55** E3
Millaa Millaa Lookout **55** E2
Millaroo **56** C2
Millbillillie **37** G1
Millbong **71** F3
Millbrook Farm **65** F5
Mil Lel **90** C2
Millers Bluff **99** E1
Millers Creek (SA) **41** E3
Millers Landing **100** B2
Millfield **76** B6
Millgrove **93** F3
Millicent **90** A1
Millie **43** H4
Millijiddee **15** G4
Millijiddee Aboriginal Land **15** F4
Millmerran **70** B2
Milloo **85** H3
Millrose **23** H6
Mills Creek **32** D2
Millstream **22** D2
Millstream-Chichester National Park **22** D2
Millstream National Park **55** E3
Millthorpe **79** H2
Millungera **19** F5
Millwood **78** C6

Millyering Visitors' Centre **22** A3
Milly Milly **36** D1
Milman **59** F3
Milo **32** D5
Milparinga **65** G5
Milparinka **42** B3
Milray **20** B6
Milton (NSW) **89** G2
Milton (QLD) **59** G6
Milton Park **28** A3
Milvale **79** E4
Milyakburra **11** G4
Milyeannup **64** B5
Mimegarra **62** B4
Mimili **30** B6
Mimosa **78** C5
Mimosa Rocks National Park **89** E6
Minara **38** A3
Minarup **65** H4
Minbun **55** E2
Minburra **67** G4
Mincha **85** G2
Mindarabin **65** F3
Minden **71** F2
Minderoo **22** B3
Mindy **23** F3
Miners Rest **92** B1
Minerva Hills National Park **58** A5
Minetta **42** D4
Mingah Springs **23** F5
Minganooka **62** C2
Mingary **42** A6
Mingary Creek **42** A5
Mingela **56** B2
Mingenew **36** C4
Mingera Creek **18** C5
Mingoola **70** C6
Minhamite **91** F3
Minilya **22** A5
Minilya River **22** A5
Minilya Roadhouse **22** A5
Minimay **82** D4
Mininera **91** G2
Mininer **23** E4
Minjilang **10** D1
Minlaton **69** E4
Minmi **76** C6
Minnamoolka **54** D4
Minnie Creek **22** C5
Minnies **19** G3
Minnie Water **73** G3
Minnipa **66** A5
Minnivale **63** E4
Minore **74** C3
Mintabie **40** C1
Minyip **83** H4
Miram **83** E3
Miranda Bay **100** D3
Miranda Downs **19** G2
Mirani **57** F5
Mirboo **93** G5
Mirboo North **93** G5
Miriam Vale **59** G6
Mirikata **40** D3
Mirimbah **93** H1
Miriwinni **55** F2
Mirra Mitta Bore **41** G1
Mirrinyungu **17** E4
Mirrool **78** C4
Missabotti **73** E5
Mission Beach **55** F3
Mission River **21** E3

Mistake Creek (NT) **16** C2
Mistake Creek (QLD) **33** G2, **56** B6
Mistake Mountains **71** E3
Mitakoodi **19** E6
Mitchell **33** G6
Mitchell and Alice Rivers National Park **21** E6
Mitchell (Matilda) Highway **43** F1, **74** D6
Mitchell Falls **9** F5
Mitchell Plateau **9** F5
Mitchell Range **11** G3
Mitchell River (QLD) **20** A1, **21** E6
Mitchell River (VIC) **94** B3
Mitchell River (WA) **9** F6
Mitchell River National Park **94** B2
Mitchellstown **86** B5
Mitchellville **68** D1
Mitiamo **85** H3
Mitre **83** F4
Mitre Lake **83** F4
Mittagong **80** C5
Mitta Junction **87** F3
Mitta Mitta **87** G5
Mitta Mitta River **87** G4-6
Mittiebah **18** B3
Mittyack **49** H3
Moa Island **21** F1
Moama **86** A3
Modella **93** F4
Moe **93** G4
Moggs Creek **92** B4
Moglonemby **86** C5
Mogo **89** F3
Mogriguy **74** D3
Mogumber **62** C4
Moina **96** C5
Mokanab Island **21** F1
Mole Creek **96** D6
Mole River **70** C6, **72** C1
Molesworth **86** C6
Moliagul **85** F5
Mollerin Lake **63** F2
Molong **74** D6
Momba **42** C5
Monaro Highway **88** D3, **95** G1
Monaro Range **88** B4
Monarto **69** G4
Monarto Zoological Park **69** G4
Mona Vale **81** E3
Monbulk **93** E3
Moncrief Bay **69** E6
Mondrain Island **47** G3
Mondure **61** E4
Mondurup Peak **65** F4
Monegeetta **92** D1
Mongarlowe **89** E2
Mongers Lake **37** E4
Mongooburra **33** E2
Monkey Mia **36** B1
Monkira **32** A4
Mon Repos Beach **61** G2
Monstraven **19** F5
Montagu **96** A3
Montague Island **89** F5
Montague Range **37** G1
Montague Sound **9** E5
Montana **96** D6
Monteagle **79** F4
Montebello Islands **22** B1
Monte Christo **56** D3
Montecollina Bore **41** H3
Montejinni **17** E1
Montezuma Falls **96** B6

Manto **60** D1
Montville **61** G6
Mooball **71** H5
Mooculta **43** E4
Moogara **99** E3
Moogerale Dam **71** F3
Moogooree **22** C5
Moojebing **65** E3
Mooka **22** B6
Mooki River **75** H1
Moola Bulla **16** A3
Moolah **50** B1
Moolawatana **41** H4
Moolayember Creek **33** H5
Moolbong **50** B2
Mooleulooloo **42** A5
Mooloo Downs **22** C6
Mooloogool **23** F6
Mooloolaba **61** G6
Moolooloo **17** E1
Moolort **85** G6
Moolpa **50** A3
Moolpa **50** A3
Moomba **42** A2
Moombooldool **78** B3
Moonah Creek **18** D6
Moonambel **85** E5
Moonan Flat **76** B3
Moona Plains **76** D1
Moonaree **66** B3
Moonbi **72** A6
Moonbi Range **72** A6
Moondarewa **71** H3
Moondarra **93** G3
Moonford **60** D1
Moongobulla **55** F6
Moonie **44** A2
Moonie Highway **70** A1
Moonie River **43** H3, **70** A1
Moonijin **63** E3
Moonlight Flat **66** A6
Moonlight Head **91** H5
Moonlight Tank **83** E1
Moonmera **59** F4
Moon Point **35** F3
Moonta **69** E2
Moonta Bay **69** E2
Moorabbin **92** D3
Mooraberree **32** A5
Moorabool Reservoir **92** B2
Moorabool River **92** B2
Moora **62** C3
Moora Downs **65** G2
Mooralla **85** A5
Moora Moore Reservoir **84** C4
Moorarie **23** E6
Moore **61** F6
Moore Park **61** F1
Moore River **62** C4
Moore River National Park **62** C4
Mooreville **96** C4
Moorilda **80** A2
Moorilurrup **65** F5
Moorine Rock **63** H4
Mooringa **64** D4
Moorland **77** E3
Moornanyah Lake **50** A1
Moorooduc **92** D4
Moorook **49** F2
Mooroongga Island **11** F2
Mooroopna **86** B4
Mooroopna North **86** B4

Moort-Lea **65** G3
Moorumbine **64** D1
Mooyouee Peaks **60** B4
Moppin **44** A3
Moralana **67** F3
Moranbah **58** B1
Moranding **86** A6
Morangarell **78** D3
Morangup **36** D6
Morangup Nature Reserve **62** D5
Morapoi **37** H4
Morass, The **89** E1
Morawa **36** D4
Morchard **67** F5
Morden **42** B4
Moree **44** A4
Morehead River **21** G6
Moreland Downs **42** D3
Morella **32** D2
Moresby **55** F3
Moreton Bay **71** G1
Moreton Island **71** H1
Moreton Island National Park **44** D2, **71** H1
Morgan **69** H2
Morgan River **9** F6
Morgan Vale **49** F1
Moriac **92** B4
Morialpa **67** H4
Moriarty **96** D5
Moriarty Point **97** H3
Morisset **81** F1
Morkalla **49** F2
Morney **32** B5
Mornington **92** D4
Mornington Island **18** D1
Mornington Peninsula **92** D4
Mornington Peninsula Freeway **92** D4
Mornington Peninsula National Park **92** C4
Moroak **11** E5
Morongla Creek **79** G3
Morpeth **76** C6
Morreldale **63** E6
Mortlake **91** G3
Morton National Park **89** F1
Morundah **78** A5
Moruya **89** F4
Moruya Heads **89** F4
Morven (QLD) **33** G6
Morven (VIC) **87** G2
Morwell **93** G4
Morwell National Park **93** G5
Morwell Open Cut Mine **93** G4
Mosquito Point **21** F3
Mossgiel **50** A1
Mossman **20** B2
Moss Vale **80** C5
Mossy Point **89** F3
Motpena **67** F2
Moulamein **50** A3
Moulting Lagoon **99** G1
Moulyinning **65** F2
Mount Abbot **56** D2
Mount Aberdeen National Park **56** D3
Mount Abrupt (Mount Murdadjoog) **84** B6
Mount Abundance **43** H1
Mount Acheron **58** A6
Mount Adolphus Island **21** F1
Mount Adrah (NSW) **50** D4
Mount Adrah (QLD) **56** D3
Mount Aggie **40** D1
Mount Agnew **96** B6
Mountain Of Light **67** F1

Mountain River **99** E4
Mountain Valley **13** H5
Mount Aitken **92** D2
Mount Alaric **12** B3
Mount Alberga **30** C6
Mount Aldis **60** A1
Mount Alexander (NT) **11** H3
Mount Alexander (QLD) **54** D2
Mount Alexander (QLD) **71** G4
Mount Alexina **86** B6
Mount Alford (QLD) **71** F4
Mount Alford (SA) **41** F3
Mount Alfred **31** G3
Mount Alice **40** D1
Mount Alma (QLD) **59** F5
Mount Alma (TAS) **98** C1
Mount Alone **17** H6
Mount Aloysius **25** F5
Mount Amhurst **16** A3
Mount Anderdon **9** E6
Mount Anderson **43** E1
Mount Anderson Aboriginal Land **15** F3
Mount Andrew **57** E5
Mount Andrews **40** D1
Mount Angus (QLD) **54** D2
Mount Angus (VIC) **87** E6
Mount Anna **41** E2
Mount Anne **98** D4
Mount Anstey **99** F2
Mount Aplin **32** A1
Mount Arapiles **83** F4
Mount Ararat **83** H6
Mount Archie **16** C3
Mount Arckaringa **40** D1
Mount Arden **67** E4
Mount Arid **47** G2
Mount Armstrong **10** C5
Mount Arrowsmith (NSW) **42** B4
Mount Arrowsmith (TAS) **98** C2
Mount Arthur **87** G6
Mount Asplenium **71** E4
Mount Atherton (QLD) **59** F3
Mount Atherton (QLD) **61** F4
Mount Augusta **99** F1
Mount Augustus **22** D5
Mount Avoca **85** E6
Mount Bagara (Mount Victory) **84** C3
Mount Baines **16** D2
Mount Bains **99** F3
Mount Bajimba **72** D1
Mount Baldhead **94** C2
Mount Balfour **96** A5
Mount Ball **58** A3
Mount Barker (QLD) **59** G4
Mount Barker (SA) **69** G4
Mount Barker (WA) **65** F5
Mount Barker Lookout **65** F5
Mount Barkly **30** B1
Mount Barloweerie **36** D2
Mount Barmoya **59** F3
Mount Barnett **15** G2
Mount Barnett Aboriginal Land **15** H2
Mount Barney **71** F4
Mount Barney National Park **71** F4
Mount Barren **99** E5
Mount Barry **40** D2
Mount Bartle Frere **55** F2
Mount Barton **16** D3
Mount Barwolla **10** B5
Mount Basedow **13** F3
Mount Bassett **43** H1
Mount Bates **77** G4

Mount Battery (VIC) **86** D6
Mount Battery (VIC) **94** B1
Mount Baw Baw **93** G3
Mount Baw Baw Alpine Village **93** G3
Mount Beau Brummell **71** E3
Mount Beauty (QLD) **54** C2
Mount Beauty (VIC) **87** F5
Mount Beckworth **92** A1
Mount Beenak **93** F3
Mount Beerwah **61** G6
Mount Behn **16** B2
Mount Bellalie **32** C6
Mount Bella Vista **56** D3
Mount Bellevue (QLD) **56** A3
Mount Bellevue (VIC) **86** D5
Mount Benambra **87** G5
Mount Benarige **61** F3
Mount Benjonney **56** C2
Mount Bennet **17** E6
Mount Bennett **12** B3
Mount Bentley **55** G5
Mount Bepcha **84** B4
Mount Bernard **86** B6
Mount Bertha **96** B5
Mount Besley **16** C2
Mount Bethune **98** D3
Mount Big Ben **87** F4
Mount Bindegolly **42** D2
Mount Bindo **80** B3
Mount Bingara **42** D2
Mount Bingeringo **56** A5
Mount Birnie **32** A1
Mount Birregun **94** B1
Mount Bishop **100** B4
Mount Black (QLD) **33** G5
Mount Black (VIC) **86** A5
Mount Blackwood **97** E6
Mount Blomford **94** A2
Mount Blue Rag **94** B1
Mount Blunt **33** F4
Mount Bobbara **79** F5
Mount Bobs **98** D5
Mount Bodumba **70** C3
Mount Boebuck **87** H5
Mount Boggola **23** E4
Mount Bogong **87** G5
Mount Bohle **56** A3
Mount Bonner **11** H2
Mount Booka Booka **32** C2
Mount Boolbun South **20** B1
Mount Booroomen **60** A1
Mount Boothby **82** A1
Mount Boothby Conservation Park **82** A1
Mount Boppy **43** E6
Mount Borium **54** B5
Mount Borradaile **13** G1
Mount Boulder (NT) **12** B5
Mount Boulder (VIC) **100** C5
Mount Bowen **95** E1
Mount Bowes **98** D3
Mount Bowman **12** D6
Mount Boyd **33** G6
Mount Brenanah **85** F4
Mount Briggs **12** C5
Mount Brockman (WA) **22** D3
Mount Brockman (NT) **13** G2
Mount Brogden **78** A3
Mount Brookes **32** D4
Mount Brooks **41** F4
Mount Brougham **40** C1
Mount Brown (NSW) **42** B3
Mount Brown (NT) **17** H1

Mount Brown (QLD) **19** F5
Mount Bruce **23** E3
Mount Bruno **86** D4
Mount Bruny **99** E5
Mount Bryan **69** G1
Mount Buangor **91** H1
Mount Buckaroo **75** F5
Mount Buck **95** E3
Mount Budawang **89** F2
Mount Buffalo **87** F5
Mount Buffalo National Park **87** E5
Mount Bullaganang **70** C5
Mount Buller **93** H1
Mount Buller Alpine Village **93** H1
Mount Bullioh **87** G4
Mount Bundey **12** D2
Mount Burges **37** H5
Mount Burrabaranga **70** C4
Mount Burramboot **86** A4
Mount Burrell **12** C4
Mount Burrowa **87** H4
Mount Burt **94** C1
Mount Bute **92** A2
Mount Bygalorie **78** B1
Mount Caernarvon **67** G2
Mount Caledon **11** H3
Mount Callanan **13** F4
Mount Camel **86** A5
Mount Cameron (TAS) **97** G4
Mount Cameron (VIC) **85** F6
Mount Cameron West **96** A3
Mount Campbell **30** A1
Mount Cann **95** F3
Mount Canobolas **79** H1
Mount Canterbury **20** A6
Mount Capo Goleburra **32** C2
Mount Carbine **20** B2
Mount Cardwell **54** D3
Mount Carey **25** G2
Mount Carlyle **95** H3
Mount Carmel **56** C5
Mount Carnage **37** H5
Mount Carnarvon **33** H5
Mount Caroline **18** D3
Mount Carter **21** F4
Mount Castle **71** E3
Mount Castletower National Park **59** G6
Mount Cattley **96** C5
Mount Celia **38** B4
Mount Challenger **57** E3
Mount Challicum **91** H1
Mount Chappell Island **97** G2
Mount Charles (NT) **16** C5
Mount Charles (WA) **37** E2
Mount Charon **58** A6
Mount Chaucer **90** D4
Mount Chrisp **11** F5
Mount Clark (QLD) **54** A4
Mount Clark (TAS) **99** E2
Mount Claude **96** D5
Mount Clear Campground **88** C3
Mount Clere **23** E5
Mount Cleveland **96** B5
Mount Cobbler **92** B2
Mount Cockburn (NT) **25** G5
Mount Cockburn (NT) **25** H2
Mount Coghlan **16** B3
Mount Cole **91** H1
Mount Colong **80** C4
Mount Combabula **60** A4
Mount Compass **69** F5
Mount Concord **86** C6

Mount Connor (Artula) **30** A5
Mount Coolon **56** C5
Mount Cooparinna **25** H6
Mount Cooper (QLD) **56** B3
Mount Cooper (QLD) **59** E6
Mount Cooper (VIC) **87** G5
Mount Coopracambra **95** G2
Mount Cordeaux **71** E3
Mount Coriaday **75** G6
Mount Coricudgy **75** G6
Mount Counsel **98** C5
Mount Crocker **58** C4
Mount Crompton **17** E1
Mount Crowther **79** F3
Mount Crozier **49** G3
Mount Cudgewa **87** G4
Mount Cunninghame **94** B4
Mount Currie **25** H4
Mount Cuthbert (SA) **30** B5
Mount Cuthbert (WA) **19** E5
Mount Dalrymple (QLD) **56** C2
Mount Dalrymple (QLD) **57** E5
Mount Daly **12** C2
Mount Damper **66** A6
Mount Danbulan **55** E1
Mount Dandenong **93** E3
Mount Daniels **13** E4
Mount Darcy **54** A4
Mount Dare **30** D5
Mount Darling (NSW) **79** G3
Mount Darling (VIC) **93** H1
Mount Darwin **98** B2
Mount Datson **32** A2
Mount Davenport (NT) **25** H2
Mount Davenport (SA) **30** A5
Mount David **13** F5
Mount Davidson (NT) **16** D5
Mount Davidson (SA) **67** G3
Mount Davy **32** C2
Mount Dawson **58** D5
Mount Deddick **95** E1
Mount Delegate **95** F1
Mount Delusion **94** B2
Mount Demipique **58** B3
Mount Dempsey **10** B6
Mount Denison **30** B1
Mount Denmarsh **95** F2
Mount Desolation **20** A6
Mount Despair **93** F1
Mount Dewalla **42** D2
Mount Didjun Cassel **85** D4
Mount Difficult **83** G5
Mount Difficult Range **84** C3
Mount Difficulty **94** B3
Mount Dillingen **58** B1
Mount Disappointment **93** E1
Mount Disaster **15** F2
Mount Dixon (NSW) **79** H6
Mount Dixon (NT) **30** D1
Mount Djoandah **94** B2
Mount Domville **70** B3
Mount Donaldson **96** B5
Mount Donna Buang **93** F2
Mount Doran **92** B2
Mount Dot **32** B4
Mount Douglas (NT) **12** D3
Mount Douglas (QLD) **32** C2
Mount Dove **99** G2
Mount Dow **94** C2
Mount Dromedary **99** E3
Mount Drummond (NT) **18** C3
Mount Drummond (SA) **68** A2

Mount Drummond (VIC) **84** C2
Mount Dryander **57** E3
Mount Dryden **84** C3
Mount Duckworth **64** A4
Mount Duff **30** C5
Mount Duffy **93** G2
Mount Duguid **30** B5
Mount Duncan **16** C1
Mount Dundas **91** E1
Mount Durand **12** C3
Mount Dutton **68** A3
Mount Duval **72** B4
Mount Easton **93** G2
Mount Eba **66** A1
Mount Eba Roadhouse **41** E4
Mount Ebenezer **30** B4
Mount Ebenezer Roadhouse **30** B4
Mount Ebsworth **13** F5
Mount Eccles (VIC) **91** E3
Mount Eccles (VIC) **93** F4
Mount Eccles National Park **91** E3
Mount Eckersley **90** D3
Mount Eclipse **11** F5
Mount Edward **30** A3
Mount Egerton **23** E5
Mount Elephant (QLD) **20** B2
Mount Elephant (VIC) **91** H3
Mount Elephant (VIC) **94** D2
Mount Elizabeth (VIC) **94** C2
Mount Elizabeth (WA) **15** G1
Mount Eliza (LHI) **81** G4
Mount Eliza (VIC) **92** D4
Mount Ellery **95** E2
Mount Ellison **12** D4
Mount Elmo **87** G5
Mount Elvire **22** D2
Mount Elvire Homestead **37** G4
Mount Ely **56** C4
Mount Emerald **55** E2
Mount Emily **33** G5
Mount Emlyn **70** C3
Mount Emu (VIC) **87** E5
Mount Emu (VIC) **87** G5
Mount Emu (VIC) **92** A2
Mount Emu Creek **91** H2
Mount Emu Plains **20** A5
Mount Erebus **59** F5
Mount Erica **93** G3
Mount Erip **92** A2
Mount Ernest **15** H5
Mount Esk (QLD) **54** C5
Mount Esk (QLD) **71** F1
Mount Esther **30** C1
Mount Etingimbra **31** E5
Mount Etna Caves National Park **59** F4
Mount Euee **40** D2
Mount Eumamurrin **33** H6
Mount Evelyn **13** G4
Mount Everard (SA) **30** B5
Mount Everard (SA) **95** F3
Mount Everard (WA) **24** C5
Mount Evernden **80** A2
Mount Eward **30** C2
Mount Ewen **94** B2
Mount Exmouth **74** D1
Mount Falconer **30** C5
Mount Faraday **33** G5
Mount Farewell **25** H1
Mount Farmer **37** E2
Mount Farquharson **16** C3
Mount Farrenden **56** A3
Mount Farrington **12** B3

Mount Feathertop (QLD) **18** A1
Mount Feathertop (VIC) **87** F6
Mount Felix **13** F5
Mount Field National Park **98** D3
Mount Field West **98** D3
Mount Figg **17** G5
Mount Finke **40** C4
Mount Finniss **12** C3
Mount Fitton Outstation **41** H4
Mount Flat Top **57** E4
Mount Flemming **12** D5
Mount Flincham **98** C2
Mount Florance **22** D2
Mount Forbes **25** H3
Mount Foelsche **12** C3
Mount Forestier **99** F4
Mount Fort Bowen **19** F5
Mount Fort William **61** E1
Mount Francis **42** D2
Mount Frankland (TAS) **96** A5
Mount Frankland (WA) **64** D6
Mount Frankland National Park **64** D5
Mount Franklin (ACT) **88** B2
Mount Franklin (TAS) **99** E1
Mount Franklin (VIC) **92** C2
Mount Fraser (VIC) **87** H6
Mount Fraser (WA) **23** E6
Mount Frazer **30** A5
Mount Freda **10** C5
Mount Frederick (NT) **16** C5
Mount Frederick (TAS) **98** D4
Mount Frederick (VIC) **84** C4
Mount Frederick Aboriginal Land **16** C5
Mount Freeling (NT) **30** B2
Mount Freeling (SA) **41** H4
Mount Freycinet **99** G2
Mount Funnel **57** F6
Mount Furner **11** F5
Mount Gairdner **66** B4
Mount Gambier **90** B2
Mount Gar (Mount Difficult) **84** C2
Mount Gardiner (NT) **13** E4
Mount Gardiner (NT) **58** D3
Mount Garnet **54** D3
Mount Gascoyne **22** D5
Mount Gawler **69** G4
Mount Geharty **68** D1
Mount Gellibrand **92** A4
Mount George (NSW) **76** D4
Mount George (NT) **13** E4
Mount Gerald **31** G3
Mount Gertrude **10** C6
Mount Giblin **98** C3
Mount Gibson **63** E1
Mount Giles (NT) **13** E5
Mount Giles (NT) **28** B4
Mount Gilruth **13** G3
Mount Gingera **88** C2
Mount Gipps **42** B5
Mount Glenroy **56** C3
Mount Glorious **71** F1
Mount Goodberry **33** E3
Mount Goodwin **10** A5
Mount Goondicum **61** E2
Mount Gordon **40** C1
Mount Gordon Mine **18** D4
Mount Gosse **10** C6
Mount Gould **23** E6
Mount Gould Lockup **23** E6
Mount Gower **81** G6
Mount Goyder **12** D2
Mount Granya **87** G4

Mount Grayling **17** G3
Mount Green **12** B4
Mount Greenly **68** A3
Mount Greenmantle **58** A2
Mount Greenwood **12** A4
Mount Gregory (NT) **10** C6
Mount Gregory (QLD) **56** B6
Mount Gregory (VIC) **93** G2
Mount Grenfell **43** E5
Mount Grenfell Historic Site **43** E5
Mount Grey **63** G3
Mount Grundy **30** D5
Mount Guenevere **30** D3
Mount Guide **31** F2
Mount Gunn **12** C3
Mount Gunnadorah **32** D6
Mount Gunson **66** D2
Mount Guouogang **80** C3
Mount Hakea **30** D4
Mount Hal **32** A5
Mount Hale **37** E1
Mount Hall (NT) **17** G3
Mount Hall (QLD) **58** A5
Mount Hallon **71** E1
Mount Hamilton (VIC) **91** G2
Mount Hamilton (VIC) **94** D1
Mount Hammond **30** B2
Mount Hardey **63** E5
Mount Hardy **30** A1
Mount Harriet (NT) **11** E5
Mount Harriet (SA) **30** A6
Mount Harry Marsh **56** C5
Mount Hart (NT) **15** F2
Mount Hart (VIC) **94** A1
Mount Hartwood **88** C1
Mount Harvey **13** F5
Mount Hawke **62** D2
Mount Hawker **17** G3
Mount Hay **59** E4
Mount Hazelton **96** A5
Mount Heemskirk **96** B6
Mount Helen (QLD) **32** B1
Mount Helen (QLD) **59** F5
Mount Helen (VIC) **92** B2
Mount Helena **56** A4
Mount Helpman **54** B5
Mount Henry **99** G1
Mount Herbert North **40** D1
Mount Hermannsburg **27** F2
Mount Herring **50** C1
Mount Hesperus **98** C4
Mount Hess **57** E5
Mount Hickey **86** B6
Mount Hiltaba **66** A4
Mount Hood **94** C2
Mount Hoare **25** G6
Mount Hobbs **99** F3
Mount Hodgson (NT) **16** D1
Mount Hodgson (QLD) **33** H5
Mount Hogarth (NT) **10** C5
Mount Hogarth (NT) **31** F1
Mount Holberton **32** C2
Mount Holder **12** B5
Mount Hollister **22** A3
Mount Hollowback **92** B1
Mount Hooghly **85** F5
Mount Hooper **13** F1
Mount Hope (NSW) **50** B1
Mount Hope (QLD) **56** B5
Mount Hope (QLD) **58** B6
Mount Hope (QLD) **58** C6
Mount Hope (SA) **68** A2

Mount Hope (VIC) **85** H2
Mount Hopeful (QLD) **59** F5
Mount Hopeful (VIC) **94** C2
Mount Hopeless (SA) **41** H3
Mount Hopeless (VIC) **94** C1
Mount Horeb **88** A1
Mount Horror **53** F4
Mount Horsfall **93** G3
Mount Hotham **85** F6
Mount Hotham Ski Field **85** G6
Mount Hotspur **33** G6
Mount House **15** G2
Mount Howe **30** C5
Mount Howitt (QLD) **32** B6
Mount Howitt (VIC) **93** H1
Mount Howship **13** G2
Mount Hoy **58** A3
Mount Humboldt **98** C2
Mount Hump **94** A2
Mount Hunter **100** D1
Mount Hurford **20** A1
Mount Hurley **94** B2
Mount Hutton **33** G5
Mount Hutton Homestead **33** H6
Mount Huxley **98** B1
Mount Hyland **72** D4
Mount Hypipamee National Park **55** E2
Mount Ida **86** A5
Mount Idamea **31** G2
Mount Ininji **10** B6
Mount Illbillee **30** B6
Mount Imlay **95** H2
Mount Imlay National Park **95** G2
Mount Inglis **58** B6
Mount Intrepid **42** B2
Mount Irvine **45** E3
Mount Isabel **31** E3
Mount Isa **18** D6
Mount Jack **21** H6
Mount Jackson **63** H1
Mount James **22** D5
Mount James Aboriginal Land **22** D5
Mount Jane **40** D6
Mount Jeffcott **85** E3
Mount Jenkins **25** G5
Mount Jersey **95** E2
Mount Jerusalem **96** D6
Mount Jess **49** G3
Mount Joe **17** H1
Mount John **42** A5
Mount Johns **12** B3
Mount Johnston **30** D2
Mount Jordan **54** C5
Mount Jowlaenga **15** E3
Mount Jukes **98** B1
Mount Julian **57** E3
Mount Kandanga **61** F5
Mount Kaputar National Park **44** A5
Mount Karamu **98** C5
Mount Kaye **95** F2
Mount Keith **37** G2
Mount Kent **94** A2
Mount Keppler **12** C3
Mount Kerang **85** F3
Mount Kerford **97** H3
Mount Killawarra **86** D4
Mount Killiecrankie **97** G1
Mount Kimon **16** C2
Mount Kincaid **90** D3
Mount King **56** C3
Mount Kingston **30** C5
Mount King William I **98** C2

Mount King William II **98** C2
Mount King William III **98** C2
Mount Kinross **92** A2
Mount Kintore **25** H6
Mount Kokeby **63** E6
Mount Koldonera **42** D2
Mount Kolendo **66** C4
Mount Kooyoora **85** F4
Mount Korong **85** F4
Mount Kosciuszko **88** A5
Mount Kukpalli **10** B6
Mount Labouchere **23** E5
Mount Lagani **10** B6
Mount Lamb **18** A4
Mount Lambell **13** F5
Mount Lambert **58** A6
Mount Lambie **80** B2
Mount Landsborough **32** D2
Mount Lane **58** A6
Mount Lang (QLD) **54** D4
Mount Lang (VIC) **84** C4
Mount La Perouse **98** D5
Mount Laptz **15** H3
Mount Larcom **59** G5
Mount Larrie **30** A2
Mount La Touche **31** H2
Mount Latrobe **100** C4
Mount Lawson **87** G3
Mount Lee **98** B3
Mount Lefroy **62** B1
Mount Leichhardt **30** B1
Mount Leisler **25** G3
Mount Leonard (NT) **10** C6
Mount Leonard (VIC) **100** B4
Mount Lesueur **62** B2
Mount Leura **58** A3
Mount Leventhorpe **97** H2
Mount Lewis (NSW) **43** E6
Mount Lewis (TAS) **98** B3
Mount Lidgbird **81** H5
Mount Liebig **30** A2
Mount Lindsay (SA) **25** H6
Mount Lindsay (WA) **65** E5
Mount Lindsey (NSW) **80** C5
Mount Lion (NSW) **71** F5
Mount Lion (QLD) **59** F4
Mount Liptrap **93** F6
Mount Litchfield **12** B4
Mount Little **57** E2
Mount Livingstone (TAS) **96** B6
Mount Livingstone (VIC) **94** C1
Mount Lofty **69** F4
Mount Lofty Range **69** F4
Mount Lonarch **85** E6
Mount Lonsdale **33** G6
Mount Loudon **56** C4
Mount Louisa (QLD) **56** C2
Mount Louisa (TAS) **98** D5
Mount Lovick **93** H1
Mount Lowe **71** E3
Mount Lubra **84** C4
Mount Lucas **42** C2
Mount Lucy **30** C2
Mount Luke **36** D2
Mount Lukin **20** A1
Mount Lyall **55** E6
Mount Lyell **98** B1
Mount Lyell Brown **25** H3
Mount Lyndhurst **41** G4
Mount Mabel **12** C3
Mount Macartney **57** E4
Mount Macedon **92** C1

Mount Macintosh **59** E5
Mount Mackersey **85** A5
Mount Macleay **33** G5
Mount Macquarie **79** H2
Mount Madden **47** E2
Mount Magnet **37** E3
Mount Maiden **38** A2
Mount Maiyu **16** C3
Mount Major **86** C4
Mount Malakoff **56** A3
Mount Malua **40** D1
Mount Manaman **56** C5
Mount Manara **42** C6
Mount Mann (NT) **25** G5
Mount Mann (NT) **30** C1
Mount Marathon **19** E5
Mount Marcella **61** E4
Mount Margaret (VIC) **100** D2
Mount Margaret (QLD) **19** E5
Mount Margaret (QLD) **54** C6
Mount Margaret (QLD) **60** D1
Mount Margaret (SA) **41** E2
Mount Margaret Roadhouse **32** C6
Mount Margaret Track **100** D2
Mount Maria (QLD) **70** C1
Mount Maria (TAS) **99** G3
Mount Marie **12** B3
Mount Marion **58** C1
Mount Marlow **32** D4
Mount Marquette **55** F3
Mount Marsh **73** F2
Mount Martha **92** D4
Mount Martin (QLD) **57** F5
Mount Martin (VIC) **87** G5
Mount Marulan **80** B6
Mount Marumba **11** F4
Mount Mary (NT) **16** C1
Mount Mary (QLD) **32** B3
Mount Mary (SA) **69** H2
Mount Mary (VIC) **87** F6
Mount Massie **55** F2
Mount Masson **13** E4
Mount Mattingley **83** F1
Mount Maurice (TAS) **97** F5
Mount Mawson **98** D3
Mount McAlister **80** A5
Mount McCall **98** C2
Mount McConnell **56** B3
Mount McConnell Roadhouse **56** B4
Mount McCormack **21** H6
Mount McDonald **58** A5
Mount McEvoy **32** D3
Mount McGuire **57** E3
Mount McIver (QLD) **32** D6
Mount McIver (VIC) **87** E6
Mount McKinlay **67** G1
Mount McLachlan **13** E4
Mount McLeod **94** D2
Mount McMaster **54** C4
Mount Mee **61** F6
Mount Meg **86** D4
Mount MeHarry **23** E3
Mount Mein **25** G3
Mount Melaleuca **98** C5
Mount Mercer **92** B2
Mount Meredith **96** B5
Mount Merlin **32** A1
Mount Merrick **27** G3
Mount Methwin **13** G5
Mount Mica **58** A3
Mount Michael **18** C6
Mount Milford **42** B2

Mount Milson **58** A2
Mount Minerva **58** B5
Mount Misery (NSW) **78** B4
Mount Misery (QLD) **60** C3
Mount Misery (QLD) **55** E2
Mount Misery (SA) **68** A2
Mount Misery (TAS) **99** E4
Mount Mistake (NT) **10** C5
Mount Mistake (QLD) **71** E3
Mount Mistake (NT) **12** D6
Mount Mitchell **85** F6
Mount Moffatt **19** E5
Mount Molangul **61** E1
Mount Moliagul **85** F5
Mount Molloy **55** E1
Mount Molongo **88** D2
Mount Monger **38** A5
Mount Monster **82** B3
Mount Monster Conservation Park **82** B3
Mount Moobi **76** A4
Mount Moore **59** G5
Mount Moornambool **85** D5
Mount Morgan (NSW) **88** C3
Mount Morgan (QLD) **59** F5
Mount Moriac **92** B4
Mount Morphett **17** G6
Mount Morris (NT) **25** G2
Mount Morris (QLD) **42** B2
Mount Moss **60** B2
Mount Mott **13** G6
Mount Mueller **98** D3
Mount Mulgrave **20** A1
Mount Mulligan **54** D1
Mount Mulyah **42** D4
Mount Munro **97** H3
Mount Murchison (NSW) **42** C5
Mount Murchison (TAS) **96** C6
Mount Murchison (WA) **36** D1
Mount Muriel **12** C5
Mount Murray **99** G3
Mount Murray **25** H3
Mount Murrungowar **95** E3
Mount Mystery **30** C6
Mount Nancar **12** C5
Mount Nangar **79** G1
Mount Napier (NT) **16** C2
Mount Napier (VIC) **91** E2
Mount Narayen **60** C3
Mount Nardi **71** G5
Mount Narra Narra **87** G3
Mount Narryer **36** C1
Mount Nebo **71** F2
Mount Needham **10** C6
Mount Nelse **87** G6
Mount Nelson **91** F1
Mount Newman **23** F3
Mount Nicholas **97** G6
Mount Nicholls **98** C5
Mount Nicholson **60** A1
Mount Nicker **25** H2
Mount Ninmaroo **32** A2
Mount Nolan **56** A3
Mount Noorat **91** G3
Mount Norfolk **96** A5
Mount Norgate **100** C5
Mount Norman **19** H5
Mount Norna **19** E6
Mount Norold **98** C4
Mountnorris Bay **10** D2
Mount Northampton **33** F4
Mount Northcote **17** E2
Mount Nor'west **41** F4

Mount Nott **66** B5
Mount NowaNowa **94** D3
Mount Nunniong **94** D1
Mount Oberon **100** C5
Mount Observatory (QLD) **58** A3
Mount Observatory (VIC) **49** G3
Mount Ochtertyre **87** E3
Mount O'Connell **59** E3
Mount Octy **30** C1
Mount Oliphant **30** A3
Mount Olive (NSW) **76** B5
Mount Olive (NSW) **81** E2
Mount Olympus **98** C1
Mount Ophir **87** E3
Mount Ord **15** G2
Mount Organ **60** A4
Mount Orso **61** F3
Mount Osborne **12** D4
Mount Osmund **98** B3
Mount Ossa (QLD) **57** F4
Mount Ossa (TAS) **96** C6
Mount Oweenee **55** E6
Mount Oxide **18** D4
Mount Oxide Mine **18** D4
Mount Oxley **43** F4
Mount Padbury **23** E6
Mount Palgrave **22** C4
Mount Panorama **58** B6
Mount Panton **16** C2
Mount Paqualin **12** D4
Mount Parker **16** B2
Mount Parkinson **17** F6
Mount Parnassus **59** F3
Mount Parslow **94** B1
Mount Partridge **13** F3
Mount Patricia **17** E6
Mount Patterson **23** G6
Mount Paul **99** G2
Mount Peake (NT) **10** C6
Mount Peake (NT) **17** F6
Mount Pearce **12** D6
Mount Pearse **96** C5
Mount Pearson **97** G5
Mount Peddington **45** F4
Mount Peebles **30** D5
Mount Peel **10** B3
Mount Pelion **57** F4
Mount Pelion West **96** C6
Mount Pellinore **30** D3
Mount Pendergast **87** H6
Mount Penny West **99** E1
Mount Penrhyn **40** D3
Mount Permain **10** D2
Mount Perry **61** E2
Mount Perseverance **71** E1
Mount Peter **99** G1
Mount Philip **71** E3
Mount Phillip **22** C5
Mount Phillips **25** G4
Mount Philp **19** E6
Mount Phipps (QLD) **59** F3
Mount Phipps (VIC) **94** B1
Mount Picton **98** D4
Mount Pitt **77** G4
Mount Pleasant (QLD) **20** A5
Mount Pleasant (QLD) **56** D3
Mount Pleasant (SA) **69** G4
Mount Pleasant (VIC) **86** D5
Mount Pleasant (VIC) **87** E6
Mount Pleasant (NT) **12** C4
Mount Pollux **98** D5
Mount Poole (NSW) **42** B3

Mount Poole **54** C3
Mount Poole Roadhouse **95** G2
Mount Poondinna **39** H1
Mount Porepunkah **87** F5
Mount Porter **13** E4
Mount Portwine **33** G4
Mount Prara **43** E1
Mount Ptilotus **16** D5
Mount Puckapunyal **86** A6
Mount Putardi **30** A3
Mount Pyrton **22** D2
Mount Ragged **47** H2
Mount Ragless South **67** E4
Mount Ramsay (QLD) **59** E6
Mount Ramsay (VIC) **100** C4
Mount Ramsay (TAS) **96** B5
Mount Rankin **58** A1
Mount Raoul **99** F5
Mount Rawlins **17** F6
Mount Razorback **28** B5
Mount Read **96** B6
Mount Redan **56** A3
Mount Redcap **54** C4
Mount Redhead **60** D3
Mount Redshirt **59** F5
Mount Redvers **25** G2
Mount Reid (NT) **17** E3
Mount Reid (TAS) **99** E2
Mount Remarkable (QLD) **19** E5
Mount Remarkable (QLD) **54** C6
Mount Remarkable (SA) **67** F5
Mount Remarkable (WA) **16** A2
Mount Remarkable Homestead **38** A3
Mount Remarkable National Park **67** E5
Mount Remus **96** C6
Mount Rennie (NT) **17** F6
Mount Rennie (NT) **25** G3
Mount Rescue **82** C2
Mount Rescue Conservation Park **82** B2
Mount Reynard **93** H2
Mount Reynolds **30** C5
Mount Richardson **20** B6
Mount Richmond (NSW) **71** E6
Mount Richmond (VIC) **90** D3
Mount Richmond National Park **90** D3
Mount Riddock **29** E3
Mount Ringwood **12** D3
Mount Ripple **98** C4
Mount Robe **42** A5
Mount Robert **30** A5
Mount Rodinga **30** D4
Mount Roland **96** D5
Mount Romulus **96** C6
Mount Roper **11** F5
Mount Rose **16** C2
Mount Rosea **84** C4
Mount Ross **12** D3
Mount Roundback **100** D2
Mount Rourke **32** B1
Mount Rouse **91** F2
Mount Royal **76** B4
Mount Roy **42** D2
Mount Rufus **98** C1
Mount Ruskin **90** C3
Mount Russell **25** H2
Mount Ryan **21** F5
Mount Saddleback **97** G5
Mount Sainthill **31** E2
Mount Samuel **17** G4
Mount Samuel Lookout **24** D5
Mount Sandiman **22** C5
Mount Sandman **16** D1

Mount Sanford **16** D2
Mount Sarah (SA) **30** D6
Mount Sarah (VIC) **94** A1
Mount Sargood **25** G4
Mount Sassafras **87** H5
Mount Saunders **13** E4
Mount Schanck **90** B2
Mount Scholfield **58** A4
Mount Scoria **60** C1
Mount Scott Conservation Park **82** B4
Mount Scrumlo **76** B4
Mount Seale **17** E2
Mount Searcy **12** B4
Mount Seaview **76** D2
Mount Sedgwick **98** B1
Mount Sellars **10** B6
Mount Selma **93** H2
Mount Selwyn **88** B3
Mount Serle **67** G1
Mount Seymour **99** F2
Mount Shadwell **91** G3
Mount Shanahan **94** C1
Mount Shannon **42** B4
Mount Sharples **55** E4
Mount Shaugh **82** D1
Mount Shaugh Conservation Park **82** D2
Mount Shaw **94** C1
Mount Shepherd **13** F6
Mount Shillinglaw (NT) **17** G3
Mount Shillinglaw (QLD) **42** C2
Mount Singapore **100** D1
Mount Singleton (NT) **25** H1
Mount Singleton (SA) **37** E4
Mount Sircom **54** A4
Mount Sir Thomas **39** G1
Mount Skene **25** G4
Mount Skinner **30** C1
Mount Skipper **32** B2
Mount Smith **12** C4
Mount Solitaire **17** E5
Mount Sonder **28** B4
Mount Sorell **98** B2
Mount Spencer **61** F6
Mount Spode **99** E3
Mount Sprent **98** C3
Mount Spring **88** D1
Mount Squire **30** C4
Mount Stafford **30** B1
Mount Stanley (TAS) **96** C2
Mount Stanley (VIC) **87** F4
Mount Stapylton **84** C2
Mount Statham **94** D1
Mount Stavely **84** D6
Mount Steadman **61** E3
Mount Steiglitz **18** C3
Mount Sterculia **58** A6
Mount Stevens **16** D1
Mount Stewart **94** D1
Mount Stirling (NT) **30** C1
Mount Stirling (VIC) **93** H1
Mount St John (TAS) **97** G6
Mount St John (VIC) **87** H4
Mount Stone **56** B4
Mount Stott **30** D1
Mount Stow **13** F5
Mount Strathbogie **86** D6
Mount St Mungo **66** A4
Mount Strzelecki **17** G6
Mount Stuart **22** C3
Mount Stuckey (Numbargulme) **21** H6
Mount Sturgeon (Mount Wurgarri) **84** B6
Mount Styx **98** D3

Mount Sugarloaf (QLD) **56** D4
Mount Sugarloaf (QLD) **58** B6
Mount Sugarloaf (VIC) **85** H5
Mount Sugarloaf (VIC) **87** H4
Mount Sugarloaf (VIC) **94** C2
Mount Sullivan **17** E1
Mount Sunday **58** A6
Mount Sunrise **56** A3
Mount Surprise **54** C4
Mount Swan **30** D2
Mount Sylvia **71** E2
Mount Tabletop **94** B1
Mount Tabor **33** G5
Mount Talbot (QLD) **54** B4
Mount Talbot (VIC) **84** A2
Mount Tallyho **42** B2
Mount Tambo **94** C1
Mount Tamborine **71** G3
Mount Tanami **16** C5
Mount Tanglefoot **93** F2
Mount Tanjil **93** G3
Mount Tanner **97** G1
Mount Tara **94** D3
Mount Tarampa **71** F2
Mount Tarana **80** B2
Mount Tarley **31** H3
Mount Tarrangower **85** G6
Mount Tawonga **87** F5
Mount Taylor (NSW) **79** F1
Mount Taylor (VIC) **94** B3
Mount Taylor (VIC) **95** E1
Mount Tempest **71** H1
Mount Tennyson **95** F2
Mount Terrible **93** G1
Mount Terrick Terrick (Mitiamo Rock) **85** H3
Mount Tewoo **61** F5
Mount Thackeray **84** B4
Mount Theo **17** E6
Mount Thomas **12** C4
Mount Thomson **94** B2
Mount Thorley **76** A5
Mount Tianjara **89** F1
Mount Tietkens **31** F2
Mount Timbertop **93** H1
Mount Timothy **82** B1
Mount Timothy Homestead **82** C1
Mount Toby **16** C2
Mount Todd **13** E5
Mount Tolmer **12** B3
Mount Tomah **45** E3
Mount Tomah Botanic Gardens **45** E3
Mount Tom Price **23** E3
Mount Toobier **58** D1
Mount Topps **30** C1
Mount Torbreck **93** G1
Mount Torrens **69** G4
Mount Townsend **88** A5
Mount Towrang **80** B6
Mount Tozer **21** F3
Mount Tracey **16** C5
Mount Trafalgar (QLD) **56** A3
Mount Trafalgar (WA) **9** E6
Mount Treachery **30** B1
Mount Trioda **30** D4
Mount Tucker **30** A3
Mount Turnbell **17** E6
Mount Turner (NT) **31** E2
Mount Turner (QLD) **54** A4
Mount Tymn **12** C3
Mount Typo **87** E6
Mount Tyson **70** C2
Mount Ulandra **79** E5

Mount Unbunmaroo **32** A2
Mount Unicorn **87** H4
Mount Urah **61** F4
Mount Useful **93** H3
Mount Vandyke **90** D3
Mount Vereker **100** C3
Mount Vergemont **32** C3
Mount Vernon **23** E4
Mount Vero **96** B5
Mount Vetters **38** A5
Mount Victor **67** H4
Mount Victoria (NSW) **95** H3
Mount Victoria (NSW) **45** F5
Mount Victoria (QLD) **19** E3
Mount Victoria (SA) **67** H4
Mount Victory Bagara **83** G6
Mount Victory Road **84** B2
Mount View **87** E6
Mount Vista **56** D4
Mount Vite Vite **91** H2
Mount Vivian **41** E4
Mount Waddikee **40** D1
Mount Wallace **92** C2
Mount Walsh National Park **61** E3
Mount Wandoo **58** A5
Mount Wanganderry **80** C5
Mount Wanungara **71** G4
Mount Warburton **16** D1
Mount Warby **86** D4
Mount Warning **71** G5
Mount Warning National Park **71** G5
Mount Warrawolong **81** E1
Mount Warrenmang **85** E6
Mount Watson **17** E3
Mount Wayo **80** A5
Mount Webb **25** F2
Mount Wedge (NT) **30** B2
Mount Wedge (TAS) **98** D3
Mount Wee Jasper **88** C1
Mount Weejort **91** H1
Mount Weld (TAS) **98** D4
Mount Weld (WA) **38** A3
Mount Weldon **60** A2
Mount Wellington **99** E4
Mount Weribone **60** A6
Mount Werong **80** B4
Mount West Wall **16** B3
Mount Westwood **42** B5
Mount Whinham **25** H5
Mount Whitestone **71** E2
Mount Whyalla **66** D5
Mount Wickham **16** C2
Mount Widderin Caves **91** H2
Mount Widderin **91** H2
Mount Wilkin **58** A1
Mount William (TAS) **97** H4
Mount William (VIC) **84** D4
Mount William National Park **97** H4
Mount William Range **84** C5
Mount Williams **17** E2
Mount William Swamp **84** D5
Mount Willieray **17** G3
Mount Willoughby **40** C1
Mount Wills **87** G6
Mount Wilson (NSW) **45** E3
Mount Wilson (VIC) **100** C5
Mount Windajong **17** F6
Mount Windarra **38** A3
Mount Windeyer **33** F4
Mount Windsor **56** A3
Mount Windsor Homestead **32** B3

Mount Winnecke **16** D4
Mount Winter **25** H3
Mount Wittenoom **36** D2
Mount Wombat **86** C5
Mount Woneeala **32** A4
Mount Wood **42** B3
Mount Woods **12** C3
Mount Woodcock **17** G4
Mount Woodhouse **18** D6
Mount Woodward **30** A5
Mount Wooldridge **31** F2
Mount Woowoolahra **42** A5
Mount Worcester **94** B1
Mount Worth **93** F4
Mount Wudinna **66** A6
Mount Wudjub-guyun (Hollow Mountain) **84** C2
Mount Yaamba **59** F3
Mount Yengo **76** A6
Mount York **45** E5
Mount Yorke **87** F5
Mount Young **97** G5
Mount Yuelamu **30** A1
Mount Zeehan **96** B6
Mount Zeil **28** A5
Mount Zero (QLD) **55** F6
Mount Zero (VIC) **84** C2
Moura **59** E6
Mourilyan **55** F3
Mouroubra **37** E4
Mowanjum **15** E3
Mowla Bluff **15** E4
Moyhu **87** E5
Moyle River **12** A5
Moyston **83** H6
Muccan **14** B6
Muchea **62** C5
Muckadilla **43** H1
Muckaty **17** G3
Mudall **43** F6
Mudamuckla **40** C6
Mudgee **75** F5
Mudgeegonga **87** F5
Mudgeeraba **71** H4
Mudginberri **13** F2
Mud Island **71** H2
Mueller Creek **30** C2
Mueller Range **16** A3
Muggleton **60** A4
Muggon **36** C1
Muirella Park Camping Area **13** F2
Muirs Highway **65** E5
Muja **64** C3
Mukinbudin **63** G3
Mulbring **76** B6
Mulga Downs **23** E2
Mulga Park **30** A5
Mulgaria **41** F4
Mulgathing **40** C4
Mulga View **67** G1
Mulgoa **45** H1
Mulgoa Road **45** H1
Mulgul **23** E5
Mulka **41** G2
Mullaley **44** A5
Mullaloo **62** C5
Mullalyup **64** C4
Mullaway **73** F4
Mullawoolka Basin **42** D4
Mullengandra **87** G3
Mullengudgery **74** A1
Muller Creek **29** E5
Mullewa **36** C3

Mulligan Creek **31** G2
Mulligans Mountain **88** B6
Mullimburra Point **89** F4
Mullion Creek **74** D6
Mullmullang Caves **39** F5
Mullumbimby **71** H5
Muloorina **41** F3
Mulureen **63** F5
Mulurulu Lake **49** H1
Mulwala **86** D3
Mulyie **14** B6
Mulyungarie **42** A5
Mumballup **64** C3
Mumbleberry Lake **31** G4
Mumblebone **74** A1
Mumbulla Mountain **89** E5
Mummulgum **71** F6
Munbinia **37** E3
Muncoonie Lake East **31** G4
Muncoonie Lake West **31** G4
Mundabullangana **23** E1
Mundaring **62** D5
Mundaring Reservoir (Helena Reservoir) **62** D6
Mundaring Weir **62** D6
Mundoora **69** E1
Mundora Downs **62** C4
Mundowdna **41** G3
Mundrabilla **39** F6
Mundrabilla Roadhouse **39** F6
Mundubbera **60** D3
Mundulla **82** C3
Mungabroom **17** H3
Mungallala **33** G6
Mungana **54** C1
Mungari **38** A5
Mungaroona Range Nature Reserve **23** E2
Mungedar **62** C3
Mungerannie Hotel **41** G2
Mungeribar **74** B3
Mungeroo Knobs **32** A3
Mungery **74** B4
Mungilli Aboriginal Land **24** C5
Mungindi **43** H3
Mungkan Kandju National Park **21** F4
Mungkarta Aboriginal Land Trust **17** G5
Munglinup **47** F2
Mungo **49** H2
Mungo National Park **49** H2
Munmarlary **13** F2
Munmorah State Recreation Area **81** F2
Munro **94** B3
Munro Bight **99** G5
Muntadgin **63** H5
Munyabla **87** F2
Munyaroo Conservation Park **66** D6
Muradup **64** D3
Muralgarra **37** E3
Murchison **86** B5
Murchison Dam **96** C6
Murchison Downs **37** F1
Murchison East **86** B5
Murchison Highway **96** C5
Murchison House **36** B3
Murchison River (TAS) **96** C6
Murchison River (WA) **23** E6, **36** C3
Murchison Settlement Roadhouse **36** D2
Murdinga **68** B1
Murdoch Point **21** H5
Murdong **65** E3
Murdunna **99** F4
Murgenella (Ranger Station) **10** D2
Murgenella Creek **10** D2

Murgheboluc **92** B3
Murgon **61** E4
Murgoo **36** D2
Murkaby **69** H1
Murninnie **66** D6
Murnpeowie **41** G3
Murphys Creek **71** E1
Murrabit **85** G1
Murrabrine Mountain **89** E5
Murramarang Coast Beach **89** F3
Murramarang National Park **89** F3
Murranji Aboriginal Land **17** F2
Murranji **17** F2
Murrawal **75** E1
Murray Bridge **69** G4
Murray Creek **58** D1
Murray Downs **17** H6
Murray Hill **14** A4
Murray Lagoon **68** D6
Murray Mouth **69** G5
Murray River (Bulyong Island) National Park **49** F2
Murray River (Katarapko) National Park **49** F2
Murray River (NSW/VIC/SA) **49** H3, **69** H3
Murray River (WA) **64** C1
Murray-Sunset National Park **49** G3
Murray Town **67** F5
Murray Upper **55** F4
Murray Valley Highway **85** G2, **87** E3
Murrayville **49** F3
Murrindal **94** D2
Murringo **79** F4
Murroon **92** A4
Murrumbateman **79** G6
Murrumbidgee River **50** B3, **88** C2
Murrumbidgee Wineries **78** A3
Murrumburrah **79** F5
Murrum **37** E3
Murrungower **95** E3
Murrurundi **76** A3
Murtoa **83** G4
Murweh **43** F1
Murwillumbah **71** H5
Musgrave **21** G5
Muswellbrook **76** A4
Mutarnee **55** F6
Mutchilba **55** E2
Mutooroo **42** A6
Muttaburra **33** E2
Muttama **79** E5
Muttama Hill **79** E5
Mutton Bird Island **81** H5
Mutton Bird Point **81** H5
Mutton Hole **19** F2
Myalla **96** C4
Myall Creek **66** D5
Myall **42** D5
Myall Lakes National Park **76** D5
Myalup **64** B2
Myamyn **91** E3
Myers Flat **85** G5
Mylestom **73** F5
Myola **19** F4
Mypolonga **69** G4
Myponga **69** F5
Myrniong **92** C2
Myroodah **15** F3
Myrrhee **86** D5
Myrtlebank **94** A4
Myrtleford **87** E3
Myrtle Scrub **76** D2
Myrtle Springs **41** G4
Myrtleville **80** B5

Mysia **85** F3
Mystic Park **85** F1
Myuna **43** F3

N

Nabageena **96** B4
Nabarlek **13** G1
Nabawa **36** C3
Nabiac **77** E4
Nabowla **97** F5
Nackara **67** G5
Nadgee Nature Reserve **95** H2
Nagambie **86** B5
Nagoorin **59** G6
Nala **99** F2
Nalangil **92** A4
Nalbarra **37** E3
Nalkain **63** F3
Nallan **37** E2
Nalya **63** F6
Namadgi National Park **88** C2
Namatjira Drive **28** B4
Nambi **38** A3
Nambour **61** G5
Nambrok **94** A4
Nambucca Heads **73** F6
Nambung **62** B3
Nambung National Park **62** A3
Namoi River **43** G4, **44** A5
Namtjira Drive **30** B3
Nana Glen **73** F4
Nananbinia **47** H1
Nanango **61** E5
Nancy Cove **46** B6
Nandaly **49** H3
Nandewar Range **44** A5
Nandi **60** D6
Nandowrie Needle **58** A5
Nanga **36** B1
Nangar National Park **79** G1
Nangiloc **49** G3
Nangus **79** E6
Nangwarry **90** C1
Nanneella **86** A4
Nannine **37** F1
Nannup **64** B4
Nanson **36** C4
Nantawarrinna **67** G1
Nantilla **42** D4
Nanutarra Roadhouse **22** C3
Napier Broome Bay **9** F5
Napier Downs **15** F2
Napier **93** H5
Napier Range **15** G2
Napoleons **92** B2
Nappa Merry **42** A1
Napperby (NT) **30** B2
Napperby (SA) **67** F6
Napranum **21** E3
Napunyah **42** D4
Naracoopa **96** D2
Naracoorte **82** C5
Naracoorte Caves Conservation Park **82** C5
Naradhan **78** A1
Naraling **36** C3
Narangba **71** G1
Narbethong **93** F2
Nardoo (NSW) **42** A4
Nardoo (QLD) **18** D4
Nardoo - Burketown Road **19** E3
Nareeb **91** F2

Narembeen **63** G5
Naringal **91** G4
Narioka **86** B3
Narlingup **64** D4
Narloo **36** D3
Nar Nar Goon **93** F4
Narndee **37** F3
Narooma **89** F5
Narrabarba **95** H2
Narrabri **44** A5
Narracan **93** G4
Narrandera **78** B5
Narrandera Range **78** B4
Narran Lake **43** G4
Narran River **43** G3
Narrapumelap **85** D6
Narrawa **79** H5
Narrawong **90** D3
Narrayarra **62** B1
Narridy **69** F1
Narrien **33** G3
Narrien Range National Park **33** G3
Narrina **67** G1
Narrogin **64** D2
Narromine **74** B3
Narrow Neck (NSW) **45** H4
Narrow Neck (WA) **46** A6
Narrung **69** G5
Narwietooma **28** A4
Narwinbi Aboriginal Land Trust **18** A1
Naryilco **42** B2
Nashdale **79** H1
Nassau River **19** F1
Nathalia **86** B3
Nathan River **11** G6
Natimuk **83** F4
National Park **98** D3
Native Companion Creek **33** G4
Native Gap Conservation Reserve **30** C2
Native Point **12** B2
Natone **96** C4
Nattai National Park **80** C4
Natte Yallock **85** F5
Naturaliste Channel **22** A6
Navarre **85** E5
Nayook **93** F3
N'Dhala Gorge Nature Park **29** G4
Neale Junction **38** D2
Neale Junction Nature Reserve **38** D2
Neales Creek **40** D1
Nearie Lake **49** G1
Nebine River **43** F2
Nebo **57** E6
Nebo Creek **57** E5
Neckaboo Range **42** D6
Neds Beach **81** G4
Neds Creek **23** F6
Neds Knob **12** C4
Neerabup National Park **62** C5
Neerim **93** F3
Neerim South **93** F3
Neeworra **43** H3
Negri River **16** C2
Neika **99** E4
Neiliabublica **15** G3
Neilrex **75** E2
Nelia **19** G6
Nelia Ponds **19** G6
Nelligen **89** F3
Nelson **90** C3
Nelson Bay **90** D4

Nelson Bay River **96** A4
Nelson Lagoon **89** E6
Nelsons Bay **76** D6
Nemingha **76** B1
Nene Valley **90** B2
Nepabunna **67** G1
Nepean Bay **69** E5
Nepean Island **77** G6
Nepean River **80** D4
Nerang **71** H4
Nerang Cowal **78** D1
Neranwood **71** G4
Nerimbera **59** F4
Nerren Nerren **36** B2
Nerriga **89** F1
Nerrigundah **89** E4
Nerrima **15** F4
Netherby **83** E2
Nethercote **95** H1
Nettlegoe Lake **42** B6
Neurea **74** D5
Neutral Junction **17** G6
Nevertire **74** A2
Neville **79** H2
New Bamboo **21** G5
Newborough **93** G4
Newbridge (NSW) **80** A2
Newbridge (VIC) **85** G5
New Brighton **71** H5
Newbury **92** C1
Newcastle **81** G1
Newcastle Bay **21** F1
Newcastle Creek **17** G2
Newcastle Range **54** B4
Newcastle Waters **17** F2
New Chum **42** D4
New Crown **30** D5
Newdegate **65** G2
New Dixie **21** F6
Newell Highway **44** A3, **50** B3
New England Highway **61** E6, **72** B5, **76** A5
New England National Park **72** D5
New Forest **36** C2
New Gisborne **92** C1
Newham **92** D1
New Harbour **98** C5
Newhaven (NT) **30** A2
Newhaven (VIC) **93** E5
New Italy **73** G1
Newland Head Conservation Park **69** F5
Newlands **64** C3
Newlands Coal Mine **56** D5
Newlyn **92** B1
Newman **23** F3
Newman's Rocks **38** B6
Newmerella **94** D3
New Mollyan **75** E2
New Norcia **62** D4
New Norfolk **99** E3
New River Lagoon **98** D5
Newry (NT) **16** C1
Newry (VIC) **94** A3
Newrybar **71** H6
New Springs **23** G6
Newstead **85** G6
New Strathearn **42** A5
New Strathgordon **21** F5
Newton Boyd **72** D3
Newtown **92** A2
New Year Island **96** C1
Ngamadjidj (Cave of Hands) **84** C2
Ngarkat Conservation Park **82** C1

Ngkala Rocks **35** G2
Nguiu **10** B2
Ngukurr **11** F5
Nhill **83** E3
Nhulunbuy **11** H2
Niagara Dam **38** A4
Niangala **76** C1
Nicholson (VIC) **94** C3
Nicholson (WA) **16** B3
Nicholson Range **36** D2
Nicholson River (NT) **16** B3
Nicholson River (QLD) **18** D3
Nicholson River (VIC) **94** C2
Nickol Bay **22** C1
Nicol Island **11** H4
Nietta **96** C5
Nightcap National Park **71** G5
Nildottie **69** H3
Nile **97** F6
Nillup **64** B5
Nilpena **67** F2
Nilpinna **41** E2
Nimbin **71** G5
Nimbuwah **13** G1
Nimingarra **14** B6
Nimmitabel **88** D5
Nindigully **43** H3
Nine Mile Beach **77** E4
Nine Mile Lake **42** C5
Ninety Mile Beach **94** A5, D3
Ningaloo **22** A4
Ningaloo Marine Park **22** A3
Ningbing **9** H6
Ninghan **37** E4
Nipan **60** B1
Nippering **65** E2
Nirranda **91** G4
Nisbet Range **32** B3
Nita Downs **14** D5
Nitmiluk (Katherine Gorge) National Park **13** F5
Nive River **33** F5
Nob, The **33** E4
Nobbies Lookout **56** D2
Nobbies, The **92** D5
Nobby **70** D3
Nobles Nob Mine **17** G5
Nob Point **21** H6
Noccundra **42** C2
Nocholeche **42** D4
Noland Bay **97** E4
Nomans Lake **65** E2
Nome **56** C1
Nonning **66** C5
Noojee **93** G3
Nookanellup **65** E3
Nookawarra **36** D1
Noonama **42** D4
Noonamah **12** C2
Noonbinna **79** G3
Noondoonia **38** C6
Noongal **36** D3
Noongar **63** H4
Noonkanbah **15** F4
Noonkanbah Aboriginal Land **15** F3
Noonyereena Hill **23** F6
Nooramunga Marine & Coastal Park **93** H6
Noorat **91** G3
Noosa Heads **61** G5
Nooyeah Downs **42** C2
Noradjuha **85** A1
Norah Head **81** F2
Nords Wharf **81** F1

Noreena Downs **23** G2
Norfolk **18** C4
Norfolk Bay **99** F4
Norfolk Island **77** H5
Norie **37** F1
Norley Range **42** D1
Norman Bay **100** B5
Normanby **21** H6
Normanby Range **59** E2
Normanby River **21** G5
Norman Island **100** B4
Norman Point **100** B5
Norman River **19** F3
Normanton **19** F3
Normanville **69** F5
Nornakin **63** G6
Nornalup **64** D6
Norring Lake **65** E3
Norseman **47** F1
North Adelaide **111** E5
Northam **63** E5
Northampton **36** C3
North Bay **81** G4
North Bay Point **21** H5
North Branch **70** C1
Northbridge **105** E5
North Bruny Island **99** E4
Northcliffe **64** C5
North Dandalup **64** B1
North East Point (CI) **14** B3
North East Point (QLD) **59** G2
Northern Highway **85** H5, **92** D1
Northern Plateau **14** B4
Northern Road **45** H1
North Goulburn Island **11** E2
North Haven **77** F3
North Head (LHI) **81** G4
North Head (QLD) **61** G3
North Head (TAS) **98** C4
North Head Homestead **54** A5
North Hobart **112** A3
North Island (NT) **11** H6
North Island (WA) **36** B3
North Keeling Island **14** A1
North Keppel Island **59** G4
North Lagoon **14** A2
North Melbourne **108** B1
North Molle Island **57** F3
North Muiron Island **22** A2
North Mulga **41** H4
North Point (QLD) **59** G5
North Point (TAS) **96** B3
North Point (WA) **46** B5
North Red Bluff **59** E2
North Rothbury **76** B6
North Scottsdale **97** F5
North Shields **68** B3
North Star **44** A3
North Stradbroke Island **71** H3
North Tamborine **71** G3
Northumberland Islands **57** G6
North Well **66** A1
North West Cape **22** A3
North West Coastal Highway **22** B4
North West Island **59** H4
North West Point **14** A3
North West Vernon Island **12** C1
Northwood **86** B6
Norton Summit **69** F4
Norwin **70** C2
Notting **63** G6

Nourlangie **13** F2
Nowa Nowa **94** D3
Nowendoc **76** C2
Nowingi **49** G3
Nowley **43** H4
Nowra **89** G1
Nubba **79** F5
Nubeena **99** F4
Nucha Lake **42** B5
Nugadong **62** D2
Nugent **99** F3
Nuggetty **85** G5
Nullagine **23** F2
Nullagine River **23** G1
Nullarbor **40** A5
Nullarbor National Park **39** H5
Nullarbor Plain **39** E5
Nullarbor Regional Reserve **39** H5
Nullarbor Roadhouse **40** A5
Nullawarre **91** G4
Nullawil **85** E2
Numbugga **89** E6
Numbulwar **11** G5
Numeralla **88** D4
Numeralla River **88** D4
Numery **30** D3
Numil Downs **19** F5
Numinbah Valley **71** G4
Numurkah **86** C3
Nunamara **97** F5
Nundle **76** B2
Nundora **42** B4
Nundroo Roadhouse & Hotel **40** B5
Nungarin **63** G4
Nuntherungie **42** B5
Nuriootpa **69** G3
Nut, The **96** B3
Nutwood Downs **11** F6
Nuyts Archipelago Conservation Park **40** C6
Nuytsland Nature Reserve **47** H2
Nyabing **65** F3
Nyah **49** H3
Nyamup **64** C5
Nyanda Downs **65** G3
Nyang **22** B4
Nychum **54** C1
Nye Bay **98** B4
Nyinpinti Point **11** G5
Nymagee **43** E6
Nymbi Binderay National Park **73** E4
Nymboida **73** E4
Nymboida National Park **73** E2
Nymboida River **73** E3
Nyngan **43** F6
Nyngynderry **42** C6
Nyora **93** F4

○

Oakbank **49** F1
Oak Beach **55** E1
Oakdale (NSW) **80** C4
Oakdale (QLD) **57** F5
Oakdale (SA) **68** A2
Oakden Hills **66** D3
Oakenden **57** F5
Oakey **70** D1
Oakey Creek **75** F2
Oakhurst **63** E4
Oakland **64** C3
Oaklands (NSW) **86** D2
Oaklands (WA) **62** C1

Oakover River 14 C6, 23 G2
Oaks, The (QLD) 80 D4
Oaks Fire Trail, The 45 H2
Oaks Homestead, The (QLD) 59 F3
Oaks Homestead, The (QLD) 54 C5
Oakvale 49 F1
Oak Valley 54 C6
Oakwood 99 F4
Oatlands 99 F2
Oban 18 D6
Obanpark 62 C3
Oberne 87 H1
Oberon 80 B3
Oberon Bay 100 C5
Oberon Point 100 B5
Obley 74 C5
O'Briens Creek Gemfields 54 B3
OBX Creek 73 E3
Ocean Beach (TAS) 98 B1
Ocean Beach (WA) 65 E6
Ocean Grove 92 C4
Ocean Shores 71 H5
Ochre Pits 28 B4
Ockley 65 E1
Oenpelli 13 G1
Officer Creek 30 B6, 40 B1
Ogmore 59 E2
Olary Creek 42 A6
Olary 41 H6
Old Adaminaby 88 B4
Old Andado 30 D5
Old Bar 77 E4
Old Beach 99 E3
Old Bonalbo 71 E5
Old Cork 32 B2
Old Delamere 10 C6
Oldfield River 47 E2
Old Glenroy 56 C3
Old Grevillia 71 F5
Old Halls Creek 16 A3
Old Herbert Vale 18 C4
Old Junee 78 D5
Old Koomooloo 69 H1
Old Mans Head 99 E2
Old May Downs 18 D5
Old Mornington Cattle Station 15 H3
Old Mount Bundey 12 D2
Old Oakden Hills 66 D2
Old Onslow 22 B2
Old Parakylia 41 E4
Old Port Davey Track 98 C4
Old Station Well 27 G2
Old Strathgordon 21 E5
Old Tallangatta 87 G4
Old Warrah 76 A2
Old Warriedar 37 E4
Old Woodleigh 36 B1
Old Wooroona 18 C5
Olga Gorge (Tatintjawiya) Walk 26 B6
Olga River 98 C3
Olinda 75 G6
Olive Creek 21 F3
Olive Grove 67 E5
Oliver's Hill Gun Emplacement 46 B6
Olympic Dam 41 F4
Olympic Highway 87 F2
Olympic Way 79 E5
Omeo 94 C1
Omeo Highway 87 G5
Omicron 42 B2
One Arm Point 15 E2
O'Neill Point 31 E4

One Tree 50 A2
One Tree Hill 62 B1
Ongerup 65 G3
Ongeua Creek 29 E4
Onoto 32 C3
Onslow 22 B2
Oobagooma 15 F2
Oodla Wirra 67 G5
Oodnadatta 40 D1
Oodnadatta Track 30 D6, 41 E3
Ooldea 40 A4
Ooldea Range 40 A4
Oolloo 12 C5
Ooma Creek 79 F2
Oonah 96 C5
Ooratippra 31 E1
Ooratippra Aboriginal Land Trust 31 E1
Ootann 54 D2
Opalton 32 C3
Ophir 80 A1
Ophthalmia Range 23 E3
Ora Banda 37 H5
Orange 79 H1
Oranmeir 89 E3
Oraparinna 67 G2
Orara River 73 F3
Oratunga 67 F2
Orbost 94 D3
Orchid Beach 35 G2
Ord River 16 B3
Ord River Nature Reserve 9 H6
Orford (TAS) 99 G3
Orford (VIC) 91 E3
Orford Ness 21 F2
Organ Pipes National Park 92 D2
Orielton 99 F3
Orient 42 C2
Orientos 42 B2
Ormeau 71 G3
Ormiston Creek 28 B4
Ormiston Gorge 28 B4
Ormley 97 G6
Orpheus Island 55 G5
Orpheus Island National Park 55 G5
Orroral Campground 88 C3
Ororoo 67 F5
Orroroo 67 F5
Osbornes Flat 87 F4
O'Shanassy River 18 C4
Osmaston 97 E6
Osmington 64 B4
Osterley 98 D2
OT Downs 17 H1
Otford 80 D4
Ottleys River 70 A5
Otway National Park 92 A5
Otway Ranges 92 A5
Oudabunna 37 E4
Oulnina Park 41 H6
Ourimbah 81 F2
Ournie 87 H3
Ouse 98 D2
Ouse River 99 E1
Outalpa 41 H6
Outer Sister Island 97 H1
Outtrim 93 F5
Ouyen 49 G3
Ovens 87 F5
Ovens River 86 D3, 87 F5
Overlander Roadhouse 36 B1
Owen Downs 42 C3
Owen 69 F3

Owens Gap 76 A3
Owen Springs 28 C1
Oxenford 71 H3
Oxenhope 20 B6
Oxers Lookout 23 E3
Oxley (NSW) 50 A2
Oxley (VIC) 87 E4
Oxley Highway 72 A6
Oxley River 71 G5
Oxleys Peak 75 H3
Oxley Wild Rivers National Park 72 C6
Oyster Bay 69 E4
Oyster Cove 99 E4
Oyster Point 71 H2

P

Pacific Highway 71 H4, 76 D6
Pacific Palms 77 E5
Packsaddle Roadhouse 42 B4
Padburys Station 62 B2
Paddy 22 B5
Padgee 64 D5
Padthaway 82 C4
Padthaway Conservation Park 82 C4
Pains Island 18 D2
Pajinka Wilderness Lodge 21 F1
Pakenham 93 E3
Pakenham Upper 93 E3
Palana 97 G1
Palen Creek 71 F4
Palgarrup 64 C4
Pallamallawa 44 A4
Pallarenda 55 G6
Pallinup 65 F4
Pallinup River 65 F4
Palm Beach (NSW) 81 E3
Palm Beach (QLD) 71 H4
Palm Cove 55 F1
Palm Creek 27 F3
Palmer Point 55 F2
Palmer River (NT) 27 E6
Palmer River (QLD) 19 H1, 20 A1
Palmers Island 73 G2
Palmerston 12 C2
Palmer Valley 30 C4
Palmerville 20 A1
Palm Islands 55 G5
Palm Passage 55 H5
Palm Valley Campground 27 F2
Palmview 61 G6
Palparara 32 B4
Paluma 55 F6
Paluma Range 55 F6
Paluma Range National Park 55 F6
Palumpa 12 A6
Pambula 95 H1
Pambula Beach 95 H1
Pampas 70 C2
Panama, Wreck of the 35 F1
Pan Ban 49 H1
Pandanus Creek 54 C6
Pandappa Conservation Park 67 G6
Pandappa 67 G6
Pandie Pandie 31 H5
Pankie 62 D3
Panmure 91 G4
Pannawonica 22 C2
Panorama Point Lookout 45 E1
Pantapin 63 F5
Pantijan Aboriginal Reserve 15 F1
Pantijan 15 F1

Panton River 16 B3
Pappinbarra 77 E2
Papunya 30 A2
Papunya Road 25 H3, 30 A2
Paraburdoo 22 D3
Parachilna 67 F2
Paradise Valley Campsite 92 A5
Parakeet Bay 46 B5
Parakylia 41 E4
Paratoo 67 H5
Parattah 99 F2
Pardoo 14 B6
Pardoo Roadhouse 14 B6
Parham 69 F3
Paringa 42 B5
Parkers Point 46 B6
Parkerville 62 D5
Parkes (NSW) 74 B6
Parkes (ACT) 105 F4
Parkeston 65 F2
Parkhurst 59 F4
Park Ridge 71 G3
Parkside 97 H5
Parkville 76 A3
Parndana 68 D6
Parndana Conservation Park 68 D6
Parnella 97 H5
Paronella Park 55 F3
Paroo 23 G6
Paroo Overflow 42 C5
Paroo Range 18 D5
Paroo River 42 D3, 43 E1
Parramatta 81 E3
Parrawe 96 C5
Parry Harbour 9 F5
Parrys Bay 97 G2
Parry's Lagoon Nature Reserve 9 H6
Parsons Range 11 G4
Partacoona 67 F4
Partridge Island 99 E5
Paruna 49 F3
Pascoe River 21 F3
Passage Island 97 H3
Passchendeele 62 C1
Pata 49 F3
Patchewollock 49 G3
Paterson 76 C6
Patersonia 97 F5
Paterson River 76 B4
Patho 85 H3
Pathungra 32 A2
Patriachs, The 97 H2
Pawleena 99 F3
Pawtella 99 F2
Paxton 76 B6
Payne Bay 98 C4
Paynes Crossing 76 A6
Paynes Find 37 E4
Paynesville 94 C3
Peaceful Bay 65 E6
Peak Alone 89 E5
Peak Charles 47 F1
Peak Charles National Park 47 F1
Peak Crossing 71 F3
Peak Downs Highway 58 B1
Peake Creek 41 E2
Peak Eleanora 47 F1
Peake Telegraph Station 41 E2
Peak Hester 23 E2
Peak Hill (NSW) 74 B5
Peak Hill (WA) 23 F6
Peak Range 58 B2

Peak Range National Park **58** B2
Peak View **88** D4
Pearcedale **93** E4
Pearce Point **10** A5
Pearl Bay **59** F2
Pearl Beach **81** E3
Pearl Point **95** E3
Pearson Island **48** A2
Peases Lookout **57** E5
Peats Ridge **81** E2
Pebble Point **91** H5
Pebbly Beach **22** A3
Pechey **71** E1
Peebinga Conservation Park **49** F3
Peedamulla **22** C2
Peedamulla Aboriginal Land **22** B2
Peegull Waterhole & Caves **38** C2
Peel **80** B1
Peel Inlet **64** B1
Peel Island **71** H2
Peel River **76** B1
Peelwood **80** A4
Peeramon **55** E2
Peera Peera Poolanna Lake **31** F6
Pegarah **96** C2
Pekina **67** F5
Peko Mine **17** G4
Pelham **99** E3
Pelican Creek **54** A2
Pelican Spit **18** B1
Pelorus Island **55** G5
Pelsaert Island **36** B4
Pelverata **99** E4
Pemberton **64** C5
Pembrooke **77** F2
Penarie **49** H3
Pender Bay **14** D2
Penguin **96** D4
Penguin Head **89** H1
Peninsula **64** C4
Peninsula Developmental Road **21** F4
Penna **99** F3
Penneshaw **69** E5
Penola **82** C6
Penong **40** B6
Penrith **80** D3
Penrith Island **57** H5
Penrose **80** B6
Penshurst **91** F2
Pentecost Downs **16** A1
Pentland **20** B6
Peppimenarti **12** A5
Pera Channel **11** G2
Pera Head **21** E3
Percival Lakes **24** B1
Percy Islands **57** H6, **59** F1
Peregian Beach **61** G5
Perenjori **62** C1
Perforated Point **59** G2
Pericoe **95** G1
Peri Lake **42** C5
Peringillup **65** E4
Perisher Blue Ski Field **88** B5
Perisher Village **88** B5
Perkins Bay **96** B3
Perkins Island **96** B3
Perkolilli **38** A5
Pernatty **66** D2
Pernatty Lagoon **66** D3
Peron **36** A1
Peron Island North **12** A3
Peron Island South **12** A3

Perpendicular Peak **54** A5
Perponda **69** H4
Perrinvale **37** G3
Perry Bridge **94** B4
Perry's Lookdown **45** F4
Perseverance **71** E1
Perth (TAS) **97** E6
Perth (WA) **62** C6
Perth City **105** F3
Perthville **80** A2
Perup River **64** D4
Peterborough (SA) **67** G6
Peterborough (VIC) **91** G5
Petermann Aboriginal Land Trust **25** G4
Petermann Ranges **25** G4
Petford **54** D2
Petita **42** C4
Petrel Point **95** G4
Petrie **71** G1
Pettit **79** E6
Phelp River **11** F4
Phillip Creek **27** G4
Phillip Island **93** E5
Phillip Point **46** C5
Phillips Hill **99** E4
Phillips Range **15** G2
Phillips River **47** E2
Phoques Bay **96** C1
Piallaway **76** A1
Piatree Waterhole **31** G3
Piawaning **62** D3
Picaninny Bore **16** C5
Piccaninny Point **97** H6
Pickertaramoor **10** B2
Picnic Bay (VIC) **100** B4
Picnic Bay (QLD) **55** G6
Picnic Beach **55** F5
Picnic Rocks Surf Beach **97** H4
Picola **86** B3
Picton **80** D4
Picton River **98** D5
Piebald Mountain **59** E5
Pieman Head **96** A6
Pieman River **96** B6
Piemonte **55** E2
Pierre Springs (Well 6) **23** H5
Pigeon Box Mountain **88** D5
Pigeon House Mountain **89** F2
Pike Creek **70** C6
Pikedale **70** C5
Pillar Valley **73** F3
Pilliga **43** H5
Pilot, The **88** A6
Pilot Range **87** F4
Pilton **70** D3
Pimba **66** C2
Pimbee **22** B6
Pimpama **71** G3
Pimpara Lake **42** B4
Pimpinio **83** F4
Pinbarren **61** G5
Pincally **42** B4
Pinch Mountain **88** B6
Pindabunna **37** F4
Pindar **36** D3
Pinda Springs **67** G1
Pindi Pindi **57** E4
Pine Creek (SA) **67** G6
Pine Creek (NT) **13** E4
Pine Gap **29** G6
Pinegrove **36** C3
Pine Lake (NSW) **42** C1

Pine Lake (VIC) **84** B1
Pine Mountain (NSW) **79** G3
Pine Mountain (QLD) **59** F2
Pine Mountain (VIC) **87** H3
Pine Mountains (QLD) **57** E6
Pine Peak Island **57** H6
Pine Point **69** E3
Pine Ridge **75** H2
Pine Ridge Homestead **42** B4
Piners Peak **98** C4
Pinery **69** F3
Pine Valley **49** F1
Pingandy **22** D4
Pingaring **65** G1
Pingelly **64** D1
Pingrup **65** G3
Pinjarra **64** B1
Pinjin **38** B4
Pinkawillinie Conservation Park **66** B5
Pinkilla **32** D6
Pink Lake **83** F3
Pinnacle **57** E5
Pinnacle Knob **31** H1
Pinnacle Mountain **58** A6
Pinnacles **59** E6
Pinnacles, The **62** B3
Pinnacles Homestead **37** G2
Pinnacles, The **35** G3
Pinnacles Bore **29** F5
Pinnacles Desert **62** B3
Pinnaroo **49** F3
Pinwernying **65** E3
Pioneer **97** G5
Pipalyatjara **25** G5
Pipers Brook **97** F4
Pipers Landing Ground **80** A1
Piper's River **97** E4
Pippingarra **14** A6
Pirron Yallock **92** A4
Pitarpunga Lake **49** H3
Pitcairn **67** G6
Pithara **62** D2
Pitjantjatjara Aboriginal Land **30** A6
Pittong **92** A2
Pittsworth **70** C2
Pitt Town **80** D3
Pituri Creek **31** G2
Planet Creek **58** C6
Planet Downs Homestead (QLD) **18** D3
Planet Downs Homestead (QLD) **32** B5
Platypus Bay **35** F2
Playa Lakes **31** F6
Pleasant Hills **87** F1
Pleiades, The **98** C3
Plenty Highway **30** C2
Plenty River **30** D2, **31** F3
Pleystowe **57** F5
Plumbago **67** H4
Plum Mountain **18** D6
Plumridge Lakes **38** D3
Plumridge Lakes Nature Reserve **38** C3
Pmere Nyente Aboriginal Land **31** E3
Pmere Ulperre Ingwemirnw Arletherre Aboriginal Land **31** E5
Poatina **97** E6
Poeppel Corner **31** G5
Point Addis **92** C4
Point Alexander **11** H3
Point Ann **47** E3
Point Annie **68** C4
Point Austin **19** E2
Point Avoid **68** A3

Point Bailly **99** G2
Point Bell **40** B6
Point Blackbourne **77** H5
Point Blaze **12** A3
Point Bolingbroke **68** B3
Point Bristow **11** G2
Point Brown **40** C6
Point Burrowes **19** E2
Point Charles **47** E3
Point Cloates **22** A4
Point Culver **47** G6
Point D'Entrecasteaux **64** C6
Point Dover **47** H6
Point Farewell **13** F1
Point Fowler **40** B6
Point Franklin **92** A6
Point Grant **92** D5
Point Henry **65** H4
Point Hicks **95** F4
Point Hillier **65** E6
Point Hughes **69** E2
Point Hunter **77** G6
Point Irwin **65** E6
Point Jenny **12** A3
Point Lookout **71** H2
Point Malcolm **47** H2
Point Margaret **68** C4
Point Marsden **69** E5
Point Maud **22** A4
Point Moore **36** B4
Point Murat **22** A3
Point Nepean **92** C4
Point Nuyts **64** D6
Point Pass **69** G2
Point Pearce Aboriginal Land **68** D3
Point Plomer **77** F2
Point Quobba **22** A5
Point Reynolds **69** E6
Point Riley **69** E2
Point Roadknight **92** B4
Point Ronald **91** G5
Point Ross **77** G6
Point Salvation Aboriginal Land **38** C2
Point Samson **22** D1
Point Sinclair **40** B6
Point Sir Isaac **68** A3
Point Stephens **12** C1
Point Stuart **13** E1
Point Stuart Coastal Reserve **13** E1
Point Tinline **69** E6
Point Torment **15** E2
Point Vincent **77** F4
Point Vivian **98** D5
Point Waters **12** B2
Point Well **67** G2
Point Westall **48** A1
Point Whidbey **48** A3
Point Yorke **68** D4
Pokartaroo **43** H4
Police Mountain **33** G2
Police Point **99** E4
Pollappa **21** F5
Polly's Lookout **31** H2
Polocara **42** D5
Pomborneit **91** H4
Pomona **61** G5
Pomonal **84** D4
Pompeys Pillat **16** B1
Pondalowie Bay **68** C4
Pontville **99** E3
Poochera **40** D6
Poolaijelo **82** D6

Poole **97** H4
Poona **35** E6
Poona National Park **61** G3
Pooncarie **49** H1
Poopelloe Lake **42** D6
Pootnoura Creek **40** C2
Poowong **93** F4
Poowong East **93** F4
Popanyinning **64** D1
Popiltah **49** G1
Popiltah Lake **49** G1
Porcupine Gorge National Park **20** A5
Porcupine Range **67** G6
Porepunkah **87** F5
Pormpuraaw **21** E5
Porongurup **65** F5
Porongurup National Park **65** F5
Porpoise Bay **46** B6
Port Adelaide **69** F4
Port Albert **93** H6
Port Alfred **69** E3
Port Alma **59** F5
Portarlington **92** C3
Port Arthur **99** F4
Port Augusta **67** E5
Port Bradshaw **11** H3
Port Broughton **69** E1
Port Campbell **91** G5
Port Campbell National Park **91** H5
Port Clinton **69** E2
Port Darwin **12** C2
Port Davey **98** C5
Port Davis **67** E6
Port Denison **62** A1
Port Douglas **20** B2
Port Elliot **69** F5
Porters Retreat **80** B3
Port Esperance **99** E5
Port Fairy **91** F4
Port Franklin **93** G6
Port Germein **67** E6
Port Gibbon **48** C2
Port Gregory **36** B3
Port Hedland **14** A6
Port Hughes **69** E2
Port Hunter **81** G1
Port Huon **99** E4
Port Julia **69** E3
Port Kenny **48** A1
Portland (NSW) **80** B1
Portland (VIC) **90** D4
Portland Bay **90** D4, **91** E4
Portland North **90** D4
Portland Roads **21** G3
Port Latta **96** B3
Port Lincoln **48** B3
Port MacDonnell **90** B3
Port Macquarie **77** F2
Port McArthur **11** H6
Port Minlacowie **68** D4
Port Musgrave **21** E2
Port Neill **48** C2
Port Phillip **92** D3
Port Pirie **67** E6
Port Rickaby **68** D3
Port Roper **11** G5
Portsea **92** D4
Port Smith **14** C4
Port Sorell **96** D4
Port Stephens **76** D6
Port Victoria **68** D3
Port Vincent **69** E4

Port Wakefield **69** F2
Port Welshpool **93** G6
Potato Point **89** F4
Pot Boil Point **97** H2
Pot Jostler Creek **32** B2
Pottsville **71** H5
Poverty Knob **19** E3
Powell Creek **32** D5
Powell Creek Outstation **17** G3
Powelltown **93** F3
Powlathanga **56** A2
Powlett River **93** E5
Poyungan Rocks **35** F4
Poyungan Valley **35** F4
Pozieres **70** D5
Prairie **20** A6
Prairie Homestead **42** D1
Prairie Downs **23** F4
Prairie Peak **32** D2
Pratten **70** D3
Precipitous Bluff **98** D5
Premaydena **99** F4
Premer **75** G1
Premier Downs **38** D4
Prenti Downs **24** B6
Preolenna **96** C4
Preservation Island **97** G3
Preston Beach **64** B2
Preston **96** C5
Pretty Gully **71** E6
Prevelly Park **64** A4
Price **69** E3
Price Mountain **59** E2
Prime Seal Island **97** G2
Primrose Sands **99** F4
Prince Frederick Harbour **9** E6
Prince Of Wales Island **21** E1
Prince Of Wales Range **98** C2
Prince Regent Nature Reserve **9** E6
Prince Regent River **9** E6, **15** G1
Prince William Henry Bay **81** G5
Princes Freeway **92** C3
Princes Highway **69** F1, **90** C2, **91** G4
Princess Charlotte Bay **21** G5
Princess Hills **55** E4
Princess Margaret Rose Caves **90** C2
Princetown **91** H5
Prion Bay **98** D5
Priors Knob **12** C5
Priory **97** G5
Professor Range **96** B6
Prominent Pillar **30** D4
Proserpine **57** E3
Prospect **19** G4
Prosser River **99** F3
Proston **61** E4
Proudhoe Island **57** G6
Prungle **49** H2
Puckapunyal **86** A6
Puckapunyal Military Area **86** A6
Puddingpan Hill **21** F2
Pudman Creek **79** G5
Puffing Billy Tourist Railway **93** E3
Pularumpi **10** B2
Pulchera Lake **31** G3
Pulgamurtie **42** B4
Pullaboka **79** E2
Pullagaroo **37** E4
Pulpit Rock **45** F4
Pul Pul **13** F4
Punchmirup **65** E3
Pungalina **18** B1

Punsand Bay Resort **21** F1
Purcells Lake **50** B1
Pureba Conservation Park **40** D6
Purfleet **77** E4
Purga **71** F2
Purlewaugh **75** F1
Purnanga **42** C4
Purnim **91** G4
Purnong **69** H4
Purnululu (Bungle Bungle) National Park **16** B3
Purple Downs **66** D1
Puttapa **67** F1
Pyalong **86** A6
Pyara **62** C2
Pyengana **97** G5
Pyramid **56** C4
Pyramid Hill **85** G3
Pyramid Lake **47** E2
Pyrenees, The **85** E5
Pyrenees Highway **85** E6
Pyrenees Wineries **85** E5
Python Pool **22** D2

Q

Quaalup **65** H4
Quaama **89** E5
Quaggy Mountain **60** C2
Quail Island **59** E1
Quairading **63** F5
Quambatook **85** F2
Quambone **43** G5
Quamby **19** E5
Quamby Brook **97** E6
Quanbun **15** G3
Quandary **78** C4
Quandialla **79** E3
Quandong **42** B6
Quangallin **65** E2
Queanbeyan **88** D2
Queens Beach **57** E2
Queenscliff **92** C4
Queens Channel **10** A5
Queens Lake **77** F3
Queenstown **98** B1
Queen Victoria Rock Nature Reserve **37** H6
Queen Victoria Spring Nature Reserve **38** B4
Queerearrup Lake **65** E3
Quforty **64** B2
Quilberry **43** F1
Quilpie **32** D6
Quinalow **60** D6
Quindanning **64** C2
Quinns Rocks **62** C5
Quinyambie **42** A4
Quirindi **76** A2
Quobba **22** A5
Quoin Island **10** A5
Quokka Stop **46** B6
Quondong Vale **49** F1
Quongup **64** C4
Quorn **67** E4

R

Rabbit Flat Roadhouse **16** D5
Rabbit Island (QLD) **57** F4
Rabbit Island (VIC) **100** D3
Radio Hill Lookout **23** E3
Radio Telescope **74** B6
Raglan (QLD) **92** A1
Raglan (VIC) **91** H1

Raglan **59** F5
Raglan Range **98** C1
Railton **96** D5
Rainbow **83** F2
Rainbow Beach **61** G4
Rainbow Flat **77** E4
Rainbow Gorge **35** F4
Rainbow Valley Conservation Reserve **30** C3
Rainsby **33** E1
Ralph Illidge Sanctuary **91** G4
Raminea **99** E5
Ramingining **11** F3
Ramornie **73** E3
Ranceby **93** F4
Rand **87** E2
Ranelagh **99** E4
Ranford **64** C1
Ranga **97** H2
Ranges Valley **32** B1
Ranken River **18** B5
Rankins Springs **78** A2
Rannes **59** E5
Rantyirrity Point **11** G4
Rapid Bay **69** F5
Rappville **73** F1
Rason Lake **38** C3
Ratcatchers Lake **42** C6
Rathdowney **71** F4
Rattlesnake Island **55** G6
Rattlesnake Point **20** B1
Ravensbourne **71** E1
Ravensbourne Creek **33** E4
Ravensbourne National Park **71** E1
Ravenshoe **55** E3
Ravensthorpe **47** E2
Ravenswood (QLD) **56** B2
Ravenswood (VIC) **85** G5
Ravenswood (WA) **64** B1
Ravenswood South **85** G5
Ravensworth **76** A5
Rawbelle River **60** C1
Rawdon Vale **76** C4
Rawlinna **38** D5
Rawlinna Hill **99** G1
Rawlinson Range **25** E4
Rawson **93** G3
Raymond Falls **94** D2
Raymond Island **94** C3
Raymond Terrace **76** C6
Raymore **32** C6
Ray Range **98** C5
Raywood **85** G4
Recherche Bay **99** E5
Redbank **85** E5
Redbank Creek **28** B5
Redbank Gorge **28** B5
Redcliffe (QLD) **71** G1
Redcliffe (SA) **69** H1
Red Cliffs (QLD) **21** F2
Red Cliffs (VIC) **49** G2
Redesdale **85** H6
Red Hands Cave **45** G1
Redhill **69** F1
Red Hill (VIC) **92** D4
Red Hill (WA) **22** C2
Red Hills **96** D5
Red Knob Outstation **38** A3
Redland Bay **71** H2
Red Lily Billabong **13** F2
Red Man Bluff **84** C4
Red Mountain **58** B1
Redpa **96** A4

Red Point (LHI) **81** H6
Red Point (QLD) **21** H5
Red Range **72** C3
Red River **19** G2
Red Rock **73** F4
Reece Dam **96** B6
Reed's Lookout **84** C3
Reedy Creek (QLD) **60** A2
Reedy Creek (SA) **82** B5
Reedy Creek (VIC) **93** E1
Reedy Lake **86** A5
Reedy Marsh **97** E5
Reef Point **59** F2
Reefton **50** D3
Reekara **96** C2
Reevesby Island **68** C3
Refrigerator Bore **16** D6
Refuge Cove **100** D5
Regatta Point **98** B1
Reid **105** H2
Reid River **56** B2
Rekuna **99** F3
Relbia **97** F6
Remarkable Cave **99** F4
Remlap **63** F2
Remuera **63** E5
Renison Bell **96** B6
Renmark **49** F2
Renner Springs **17** G3
Rennie **86** D2
Reola **42** C4
Repulse Bay **57** F4
Repulse Island **57** F4
Retreat (QLD) **32** C5
Retreat (TAS) **97** F5
Reynella **69** F4
Reynolds River **12** C4
Rheban **99** G3
Rheola **85** F4
Rhymie **69** F2
Rhyndaston **99** F2
Riana **96** C4
Ribblesdale **65** G2
Richardson Range **21** F2
Richardson River **83** H4
Rich Avon **83** H4
Richlands **80** B4
Richmond (NSW) **80** D2
Richmond (QLD) **19** G6
Richmond (TAS) **99** F3
Richmond Downs **43** H1
Richmond Range National Park **71** F6
Richmond River **71** F5
Rickeys **63** E5
Riddells Creek **92** D1
Ridgelands **59** F4
Ridgley **96** C4
Ringarooma **97** G5
Ringarooma Bay **97** G4
Ringarooma River **97** G5
Ringwood Beef Road **29** G4
Ringwood **30** D3
Rip, The **92** C4
Ripplebrook **93** F4
Ripponhurst **91** E3
Risdon Vale **99** E3
Risk, The **71** F5
Rita Island **56** D1
River Clayton **41** G3
River Clyde **99** E2
River Derwent **99** E3
Riveren **16** D3

River Forth **96** D5
River Heads **35** E4
Riverina **37** H4
Riverina Highway **86** B1
River Leven **96** C5
Riverside **110** C3
Riverslea **94** A4
Riversleigh **18** D4
River Tamar **97** E5
Rivoli Bay **90** A1
RM Point **56** D2
Roaring Meg Campsite **100** C6
Roaring Meg Creek **100** C6
Robbins Island **96** B3
Robbins Passage **96** A3
Robe **82** A5
Robe River **22** C2
Robertson **80** C5
Robertson Range **23** G3
Robertstown **69** G2
Robin Hood **54** B5
Robinson Range **23** E6
Robinson River (QLD) **18** B1
Robinson River (WA) **15** F2
Robinvale **49** H3
Robinvale Wineries **49** H3
Rochester **86** A4
Rochford **92** D1
Rock, The **87** G1
Rockdale **65** E6
Rocket Lake **49** G3
Rock Flat **88** D5
Rockhampton **59** F4
Rockhampton Downs **17** H4
Rock Hill, The **87** G1
Rockingham **64** B1
Rockingham Bay **55** F4
Rocklands Reservoir **84** A4
Rocklea Homestead (WA) **22** D3
Rocklea Homestead (WA) **65** F1
Rockley **80** A2
Rock Nature Reserve, The **87** G1
Rockybar **60** C3
Rocky Bay **46** A6
Rocky Bluff **73** F4
Rocky Creek **44** A4
Rocky Dam **70** A6
Rocky Gully **65** E5
Rocky Hall **95** G1
Rocky Mountain **56** A6
Rocky Point (CI) **14** B3
Rocky Point (NI) **77** F6
Rocky Point (QLD) **59** H6
Rocky River (NSW) **72** B5
Rocky River (SA) **68** C6
Rocky Valley Reservoir **87** G6
Rodondo Island **53** E2
Roebourne **22** D1
Roebuck Bay **14** D3
Roebuck Plains **14** D3
Roebuck Roadhouse **14** D3
Roe Creek **28** B1
Roe River **9** F6
Roger River **96** B4
Rokeby (TAS) **99** F4
Rokeby (VIC) **93** F4
Rokewood **92** A3
Roland **96** D5
Rolleston **58** B6
Rollingstone **55** G6
Roma **43** H1
Roma Peak **57** E3

Romsey **92** D1
Rookhurst **76** D3
Rookwood **54** C1
Rooney Point **35** F1
Roper Bar **11** F5
Roper Creek (QLD) **58** C3
Roper Creek (NT) **13** G6
Roper Highway **11** E5
Roper River **11** F5
Ropers Peak **60** A1
Roper Valley **11** E5
Roscommon **43** F4
Roseberth **31** H5
Rosebery **96** B6
Rosebrook **91** F4
Rosebud (QLD) **19** E6
Rosebud (VIC) **92** D4
Rosedale (QLD) **61** F1
Rosedale (VIC) **93** H4
Rosedale Homestead **33** F3
Rosella **57** F5
Rosemary Island **22** C1
Rosenthal **76** D5
Rose River **11** G4
Roses Gap Road **84** C2
Rosevale (QLD) **71** E3
Rosevale (TAS) **97** E5
Rosewood (NT) **16** B1
Rosewood (QLD) **71** F2
Roseworthy **69** F3
Roslyn **80** A5
Rossarden **97** G6
Rossbridge **91** G1
Ross Mount **34** D6
Ross River **29** G4
Ross River Dam **56** B1
Rossville **20** B1
Rotamah Island **94** C4
Rotamah Island Bird Observatory **94** C4
Roto **50** B1
Rottnest Island **62** B6
Rouchel Brook **76** B4
Round Head **57** F4
Round Hill **88** C6
Round Mountain (QLD) **21** G4
Round Mountain (QLD) **32** B4
Round Mountain (QLD) **58** A6
Round Mountain (QLD) **59** E4
Round Point (QLD) **21** F2
Round Point (QLD) **21** G4
Rowena **43** H4
Rowsley **92** C2
Roxby Downs **66** D1
Roxby Downs Homestead **66** C1
Roxby Island **68** C3
Royal George **99** G1
Royalla **88** D2
Royal National Park **81** E4
Roy Hill **88** D2
Royston **62** D2
Royston Head **68** C4
Royston Range **93** F1
Rubicon **93** F1
Rubicon River **96** D5
Ruby **93** F5

Ruby Gap Nature Park **29** F2
Ruby Plains **16** A4
Rubyvale **58** A3
Rudall **68** C1
Rudall Conservation Park **68** C1
Rudall River National Park **23** H2, **24** A2
Ruffy **86** C6
Rugby **79** G4
Rugby Range **98** C4
Ruined Castle **45** G4
Rukenvale **71** F5
Rules Beach **61** F1
Rum Jungle **12** C3
Rumula **20** B2
Running Stream **75** F6
Running Waters **27** G4
Running Water Yard **27** G4
Runnymede **99** F3
Rupanyup **83** H4
Rupanyup North **83** H4
Rupert Point **96** A5
Rushworth **86** A4
Russell Falls **98** D3
Russell Island **71** H3
Russell Range **47** G2
Russell River National Park **55** F2
Rutherglen **87** E3
Rutland Plains **21** E6
Ryan Well Historic Reserve **30** C2
Rydal **80** B2
Ryde **81** E3
Rye **92** D4
Rye Park **79** G5
Rylstone **75** F6

S

Sabina Point **59** F2
Sabine **70** D1
Sacred Canyon **67** G3
Saddleworth **69** G2
Safety Beach **92** D4
Saint Andrews **93** E2
Saint Helens **91** E3
Saint Leonards **92** D4
Saint Patricks River **97** F5
Sale **94** A4
Salisbury (NSW) **76** C4
Salisbury (VIC) **83** F3
Salisbury Island **47** H3
Sallys Flat **75** E6
Salmon Bay **46** B6
Salmond River **16** A1
Salmon Gums **47** F1
Salmon Point **46** B6
Salt Creek (SA) **82** A2
Salt Creek (VIC) **91** G3
Salt Lake (VIC) **92** A4
Salt Lake, The (NSW) **42** B4
Salt Lakes **62** A2
Saltwater River **99** F4
Samford **71** G2
Samson Well **69** H2
Sanctuary Cove **71** H3
Sanctuary Point **89** G1
Sandalwood **49** F3
Sand Bay **57** F5
Sandfire Roadhouse **14** C5
Sandfly **99** E3
Sandford **90** D1
Sandgate **71** G1
Sandhill Lake **85** F2

Sandigo 78 B5
Sandon Bluffs 73 G3
Sandover Highway 30 C2
Sandover River 30 D1, 31 E1
Sandpatch Point 95 G3
Sandringham 31 H3
Sandspit River Reserve 99 F3
Sandstone 37 F2
Sandy Bight 47 G2
Sandy Blight Junction 25 G2
Sandy Camp 43 G5
Sandy Cape (QLD) 35 G1
Sandy Cape (TAS) 96 A5
Sandy Creek 87 F4
Sandy Flat 72 D1
Sandy Hill 70 D6
Sandy Hollow 75 H4
Sandy Point (NSW) 89 E1
Sandy Point (QLD) 61 G3
Sandy Point (VIC) 93 G6
Sandy Point (WA) 62 A2
Sanford River 36 D2
San Remo (QLD) 64 B1
San Remo (VIC) 93 E5
Santa Teresa 30 C3
Santa Teresa Aboriginal Reserve 29 H4
Sapphire (NSW) 72 B2
Sapphire (QLD) 58 A4
Sarina Beach 57 F5
Sarina 57 F5
Sassafras (NSW) 89 F1
Sassafras (TAS) 96 D5
Saunders Beach 55 G6
Saunders Creek 16 B3
Savage River 96 B5
Savernake 86 D2
Sawtell 73 F5
Saxby Downs 19 G5
Saxby River 19 F3, G5
Sayers Lake 49 H1
Scaddan 47 F2
Scarborough 62 C6
Scarborough Point 71 G1
Scarsdale 92 A2
Scawfell Island 57 G4
Sceale Bay 48 A1
Schouten Island 99 G2
Schouten Passage 99 G2
Scone 76 A4
Scoria 60 C1
Scorpion Bight 39 E6
Scorpion Springs Conservation Park 82 C1
Scott Creek 10 C5
Scott National Park 64 B5
Scotts Creek 91 G4
Scottsdale 97 F5
Scotts Head 73 F6
Scottville 56 D3
Scrubby Range 36 D1
Seabird 62 B4
Seacombe 94 B4
Sea Elephant 96 D2
Sea Elephant Bay 96 D2
Seaford 69 F4
Seaforth 57 F4
Sea Lake 83 H1
Seal Bay Conservation Park 68 D6
Sealers Cove 100 D4
Sealers Cove Track 100 C5
Sealers Creek 100 C4
Seal Point 96 C2

Seal Rocks (NSW) 77 E5
Seal Rocks (VIC) 92 D5
Searcy Bay 48 A1
Searles Point 81 G4
Seaspray 94 A5
Seaton 93 H3
Seaview 93 F4
Seaview Range 55 E5
Sebastian 85 G4
Sebastopol 78 D5
Secret Harbour 64 B1
Secure Bay 15 F2
Sedan 69 G3
Sedgeford 33 F4
Sedgwick 85 H5
Seemore 62 B4
SE Freeway 69 G4
SE Hyden 65 G1
Seisia 21 F1
Selbourne 97 E5
Sellers Lagoon 97 H2
Sellheim 56 B2
Selwyn 32 A1
Selwyn Range 32 A1
Separation Creek 92 B5
Serpentine (VIC) 85 G4
Serpentine (WA) 64 B1
Serpentine Chalet 28 C3
Serpentine Creek 85 F2
Serpentine Dam 64 C1
Serpentine Gorge 28 C3
Serpentine Lake 46 B6
Serpentine Lakes 39 G2
Serpentine National Park 64 B1
Serra Range 84 C5
Serviceton 82 D3
Settlement Creek 18 C2
Settlement, The 14 B3
Seven Emu 18 B1
Seven Mile Beach National Park 80 C6
Seventeen Seventy 59 H6
Seventy Mile Mountain 56 A3
Seventy Mile Range 56 A3
Severnlea 70 D5
Severn River 70 C6, 72 B1
Seville 93 E3
Seymour 86 B6
Shackerston 65 H3
Shackleton 63 F5
Shadforth 79 H1
Shady Camp 12 D2
Shallow Inlet 100 A1
Shallow Inlet Marine & Coastal Park 100 A1
Shannon 64 D5
Shannon Lodge & Campsite 64 D5
Shannon National Park 64 D5
Shannons Flat 88 C3
Shark Bay (NT) 10 B2
Shark Bay (WA) 22 A6
Shark Bay Marine Park 36 A1
Sharp Point 21 F1
Shaw Island 57 F4
Shaw River 23 F1
Shay Gap 14 B6
Sheep Hills 83 G3
Sheffield 96 D5
Sheila 18 D6
Shelbourne 85 G5
Shellbourne Bay 21 F2
Shelford 92 B3
Shellback Island 100 A3
Shelley 87 G4

Shelley Beach Head 73 G2
Shellharbour 80 D6
Shelly Beach 99 G3
Shelter Cove 100 D1
Shenandoah 17 G1
Sheoak Hill Conservation Park 68 C1
Shepparton 86 B4
Sheringa 68 A2
Sherlock 22 D1
Shinfield 57 F6
Shoal Bay 12 C1
Shoal Cape 47 F2
Shoalhaven Heads 80 D6
Shoalhaven River 89 E2
Shoalwater Bay 59 F2
Shoalwater Bay Military Training Area 59 F2
Shoemaker Point 98 D5
Shooters Hill 80 B3
Shoreham 92 D4
Shovelanna Hill 23 G3
Shutehaven 57 F3
Shuttleton 43 E6
Shuttleworth 33 F2
Siam 66 C5
Siccus River 67 H3
Sidings Springs Observatory 43 G5
Silkwood 55 F3
Silvan Reservoir 93 E3
Silver City Highway 42 B4, 49 G1
Silver Plains 21 G5
Silverspur 70 B5
Silverton 42 A6
Simpson 91 H4
Simpson Desert Conservation Park 31 G5
Simpson Desert National Park 31 G4
Simpson Desert Regional Reserve 31 F6, 41 F1
Simpsons Bay 99 E5
Simpsons Gap 29 G6
Simson 85 F5
Single Peak 60 A1
Singleton (NSW) 76 B5
Singleton (NT) 17 G6
Sir Edward Pellew Group 11 H6
Sir Graham Moore Island 9 F4
Sir John Cape 97 G3
Sir John Falls 98 C2
Sir William Thompson Range 21 F3
Sisters, The (NSW) 79 E6
Sisters, The (QLD) 31 H3
Sisters, The (QLD) 33 E2
Sisters, The (QLD) 54 B4
Sisters, The (VIC) 84 C4
Sisters, The (VIC) 91 G3
Sisters Beach 96 C4
Sisters Creek 96 C4
Six Foot Trail Track 45 H6
Skipton 91 H2
Skirmish Point 71 H1
Skywatch Observatory 75 E1
Slacks Creek 71 G2
Slade Point 57 F5
Slashes Creek 32 A2
Sleaford Bay 68 B4
Slogan Downs 56 A3
Smeaton 92 B1
Smiggin Holes 88 B5
Smithburn River 19 F2
Smithson Bight 14 A4
Smiths Range 18 D4
Smithton 96 B3
Smithtown 77 F1
Smithville House 42 A4

Smoky Bay 40 C6
Smythesdale 92 A2
Snake Island 93 H6
Snake Range National Park 58 A5
Snake Valley 92 A2
Snapper Island 20 B1
Snapper Point 73 G1
Snelling Beach 68 D5
Snow Hill 99 G1
Snow Road Wineries 87 E4
Snowtown 69 F2
Snowy Mountains 88 A5
Snowy Mountains Highway 88 B3
Snowy Range (TAS) 98 D3
Snowy Range (VIC) 93 H1, 94 A1
Snowy River 88 B5, 94 D2
Snowy River National Park 95 E1
Snug 99 E4
Snug Cove 68 C5
Soda Valley 20 A6
Sofala 75 F6
Soldiers Mountain 79 G2
Soldiers Point 76 D6
Solway Downs 19 G5
Somers 93 E4
Somerset 96 C4
Somerset Dam 61 F6
Somerville 93 E4
Sorell 99 F3
Sorrento (VIC) 92 D4
Sorrento (WA) 62 C5
Soudan 18 B5
South Alligator River 13 F3
South Alligator River Crossing 10 D3
South Arm 99 F4
Southbank 108 C5
South Brisbane 110 A6
Southbrook 70 D2
South Bruny Island 99 E5
South Bruny Island National Park 99 E5
South Cape Bay 98 D6
South Coast Highway 65 G5, H3
South Coast Range 95 G1
South Coast Track 98 D5
South East Cape 98 D6
South East Forests National Park 95 G1
South-East Point 100 D6
Southend 90 A1
Southern Central Reserve Aboriginal Land 24 D5
Southern Cross 37 G6
Southern Hills 47 G1
Southern Ocean East Drive 47 E3
Southern Plateau 14 B4
South Esk River 97 F5-6
South Forest 96 B3
South Galway 32 B5
South Gap 67 E3
South Gippsland Highway 93 E3, 94 A5
South Goulburn Island 11 E2
South Head 54 A5
South Island 14 B2
South Johnstone 55 F3
South Keeling Islands 14 A2
South Kumminin 63 G6
South Lagoon 14 A2
South Melbourne 108 C6
South Mission Beach 55 F3
South Molle Island 57 F3
South Mount Cameron 97 G4
South Muiron Island 22 A2
South Nanango 61 E6
South Point (NT) 11 H5

South Point (VIC) **100** C6
Southport (QLD) **71** H4
Southport (TAS) **99** E5
South Riana **96** C5
South Springfield **97** F5
South Stradbroke Island **71** H3
South West Cape **98** C5
South Western Highway **64** C5
South West Island **11** H6
South West National Park **98** D4
South-West Point **100** B6
South West Rocks **77** G1
South West Vernon Island **12** C1
Southwood **44** A2
Southwood National Park **44** A2
South Wyola **63** F5
Sovereign Hill **92** B2
Spalding **69** F1
Spalford **96** D5
Spargo Creek **92** B1
Sparkes Lookout **100** B4
Speculation Lake **42** B6
Spencer Gulf **68** D2
Spencer Range **13** G1
Spicers Creek **75** E4
Spicers Peak **71** E4
Spiky Bridge **99** G2
Spilsby Island **48** C3
Spinifex Mountain **19** G4
Spion Kopje **93** F3
Spiro Range **98** D5
Split Rock **18** C5
Spoonbill **19** F5
Sprent **96** D5
Spreyton **96** D5
Spring Beach **99** G3
Springbrook **71** G4
Springbrook National Park **71** G4
Spring Creek (NT) **18** B1
Spring Creek (QLD) **32** A3
Spring Creek (QLD) **70** D3
Spring Creek (WA) **16** B2
Spring Creek Homestead **54** C5
Springdale **78** D4
Springfield (NSW) **43** G1
Springfield (QLD) **32** C5
Springfield (TAS) **97** F5
Spring Gully Conservation Park **69** F2
Springhill **20** A1
Spring Hill **110** B1
Springhurst **87** E4
Spring-Mount Conservation Park **69** F5
Springsure **58** B5
Springton **69** G3
Springvale **16** A3
Springwood **45** G2
Squaretop **60** D6
Squeaky Beach **100** B5
Staaten River **19** G1
Staaten River National Park **19** G2
Staceys Bridge **93** H5
Staghorn Flat **87** F4
Stake Hill **64** B1
St Albans **81** E2
Stamford **32** D1
Stanage **59** E1
Stanage Point **59** E1
Stanborough **72** A3
Stanbroke **31** H1
Standley Chasm **28** C1
Stanhope **86** A4
Stanley (TAS) **96** B3

Stanley (VIC) **87** F4
Stanley Point **97** G1
Stanley River **61** F6
Stannifer **72** B3
Stannum **72** C1
Stansbury **69** E4
Stanthorpe **70** D5
Stanwell **59** F4
Stanwell Park **80** D4
Stapylton **71** G3
Starcke National Park **21** H6
Starfish, The **98** C3
Stark Bay **46** A6
St Arnaud **85** E4
Star River **55** F6, **56** A1
Starvation Boat Harbour **47** E3
Staten River National Park **54** A1
Staughton Vale **92** C3
Stavely **85** D6
Staverton **96** D5
Stawell **83** H6
Stawell River **19** G5
St Bees Island **57** G5
St Clair **76** B5
St Columba Falls **97** G5
Steavensons Falls **93** F2
Steels Point **77** H5
Steep Point **36** A1
Steiglitz **92** B3
Stenwood **64** C2
Stephens Creek **42** B6
Stephensons Falls **92** A5
Steppes **99** E1
Stevenson Creek **30** C5
Stewart Island **35** E5
Stewart River **21** G5
St James **86** D4
St George **43** H2
St George Ranges **15** G4
St Georges Basin **89** G1
St Georges Head **89** G2
St Germains **86** B3
St Helens **97** H5
St Helens Beach **57** F4
St Helens Point **97** H5
Stingray Point **12** B2
Stirling (NT) **30** C1
Stirling (QLD) **19** F2
Stirling (SA) **69** F4
Stirling Dam **64** C2
Stirling Range **65** F4
Stirling Range Caravan Park **65** F4
Stirling Range National Park **65** F4
St Kilda **92** D3
St Kilda Junction **100** D3
St Lawrence **58** D2
St Mary Peak **67** F3
St Marys **97** G6
Stockdale **94** B3
Stockinbingal **79** E4
Stockwell **69** G3
Stockyard Point **59** G3
Stokehall Downs **62** B3
Stokes Bay (SA) **68** D5
Stokes Bay (WA) **15** E2
Stokes Inlet National Park **47** F2
Stokes Point **96** C2
Stokes Range **10** B6
Stonehenge (NSW) **72** C3
Stonehenge (QLD) **32** C4
Stonehenge (TAS) **99** F2
Stone Hut **67** F6

Stone Island **57** E3
Stones Crossing **21** E3
Stoneyford **91** H4
Stonor **99** F2
Stony Head **97** E4
Stony Point **93** E4
Stony Range **41** F4
Storeys Creek **97** G6
Storm Bay **99** F4
Stormlea **99** F4
Stowport **96** C4
St Pauls Dome **97** G6
St Pauls River **97** F6
St Peter Island **40** C6
Strachan **64** D5
Stradbroke **94** A4
Stradbroke West **94** A4
Strahan **98** B1
Strangways River **11** E6
Strangways Telegraph Station **41** E3
Stratfield **62** C1
Stratford (NSW) **76** D4
Stratford (VIC) **94** A3
Strathalbyn (QLD) **56** C3
Strathalbyn (SA) **69** G5
Stratham **64** B3
Strathaven **21** F5
Strathblane **99** E5
Strathbogie (NSW) **72** B2
Strathbogie (QLD) **56** C3
Strathbogie (VIC) **86** C5
Strathbogie Ranges **86** C6
Strathburn **21** F5
Strath Creek **93** E1
Strathdickie **57** E3
Strathdickie North **57** E3
Strathfieldsaye **85** H5
Strathgordon **98** C3
Strathkellar **84** B6
Strathleven **19** H1
Strathmay **21** F5
Strathmerton **86** C3
Strathmore **19** G3
Strathpark **54** A6
Streaky Bay (SA) **40** C6
Streaky Bay (SA) **48** A1
Streatham **91** H2
Strelley **14** A6
Stretton **65** E1
Strickland Bay (WA) **15** E2
Strickland Bay (WA) **46** A6
Strickland **98** D2
Stroud **76** D5
Stroud Road **76** C5
Strzelecki **93** F4
Strzelecki Highway **93** G4
Strzelecki National Park **97** H2
Strzelecki Peaks **97** H2
Strzelecki Ranges **93** F4
Strzelecki Regional Reserve **41** H2
Strzelecki Track **41** H3
Stuart **56** B1
Stuart Bay **48** C3
Stuart Creek (SA) **41** E3
Stuart Highway **10** D5, **30** C4, **66** D2
Stuart Memorial **17** G4
Stuart Mill **85** E5
Stuart Range **40** D3
Stuart River **61** E4
Stuarts Point **73** F6
Stuarts Well **30** C3
Stuart Town **74** D5

Stubbings Point **14** B4
Sturt Bay **68** D4
Sturt Creek **16** B4
Sturt Highway **69** G3, **78** B6
Sturt Meadows **37** H3
Sturt National Park **42** B3
Sturt Vale **49** F1
St Valentines Peak **96** C5
St Vidgeon **11** F5
Subiaco **62** C6
Sublime Point **45** G4
Sugarloaf Passage **81** G4
Sugarloaf Rock **64** A3
Suggan Buggan **88** A6
Suggan Buggan Range **88** A5
Sulphur Creek **96** C4
Sultana Point **69** E4
Summer Mountain **61** F5
Summit, The **70** D5
Sunbury **92** D2
Sunday Creek **17** F1
Sunday Island **93** H6
Sundown National Park **70** C6
Sundown Point **96** A4
Sunny Creek **41** E2
Sunnyside **70** D6
Sunraysia Highway **83** H1, **92** A1
Sunvale **62** D4
Suplejack **16** C4
Surat **43** H1
Surat Developmental Road **60** A6
Surbiton **33** F3
Surfers Paradise **71** H4
Surprise Mountain **60** A2
Surveyors Bay **99** E5
Surveyors Lake **50** A1
Susan River **35** E4
Sussex **43** E5
Sussex Inlet **89** G1
Sutherlands **69** G2
Sutton **88** D1
Sutton Grange **85** H6
Suttor River **56** D5
Svenor Point **98** B4
Swain Reefs **34** D1
Swamp Point **10** A5
Swan Bay **92** C4
Swan Haven **51** F4
Swan Hill **49** H4
Swan Island **97** G4
Swan Lake **95** F3
Swan Lake Camp **90** D3
Swan Marsh **91** H4
Swan Point **15** E2
Swanpool **86** D5
Swanport **69** G4
Swan Reach (SA) **69** H3
Swan Reach (VIC) **94** C3
Swan Reach Conservation Park **69** H3
Swan River (TAS) **99** G1
Swan River (WA) **62** C6
Swansea (NSW) **81** F1
Swansea (TAS) **99** G2
Swan Valley Vineyards **62** D5
Swanwick **99** G2
Sweers Island **18** D2
Swifts Creek **94** C1
Swim Creek Plains **12** D1
Swim Creek Rainforest Reserve **13** E2
Sydenham Inlet **95** F3
Sydney **81** E4
Sydney Bay **77** G6

Sydney Harbour National Park **81** E3
Sydney Island **18** D1
Synnot Range **15** G2

Taabinga **61** E5
Taarblin Lake **65** E2
Tabba Tabba **23** E1
Tabbimoble **73** G1
Tabbita **50** B2
Table Head **98** B2
Tableland **15** H2
Tablelands Highway **18** A3
Table Mountain (QLD) **56** D3
Table Mountain (TAS) **99** E2
Tabletop (WA) **24** B2
Tabletop (WA) **37** F3
Table Top (NSW) **87** F3
Table Top (NT) **13** G3
Tabletop Mountain **88** A1
Tabletop Range **12** B3
Tabratong **74** A3
Tabulam **71** E6
Tacking Point **77** F3
Taggerty **93** F1
Tahara **91** E2
Tahmoor **80** D4
Tahune Forest Reserve **98** D4
Tailem Bend **69** H5
Taincrow **37** E2
Takone **96** C4
Talaroo **54** B4
Talawa **97** G5
Talawanta **19** E3
Talbingo **88** B2
Talbingo Reservoir **88** B2
Talbot **85** F6
Talbot Bay **15** E1
Talbots Lagoon **96** C5
Talbragar River **75** F3
Taldora **19** F4
Talga River **23** F1
Talgarno **87** G3
Talia (SA) **48** A1
Talia (WA) **64** C3
Talisker **36** C1
Tallabung Mountain **79** E2
Tallalara **42** D5
Tallangallook **86** C6
Tallangatta **87** G4
Tallangatta East **87** G4
Tallaringa Conservation Park **40** C2
Tallaroo Hot Springs **54** B4
Tallarook **86** B6
Tallawana Track **23** H3, **24** A3
Tallebudgera **71** H4
Tallering **36** D3
Tallering Peak **36** C3
Tallong **80** B6
Tallygaroopna **86** C3
Talmalmo **87** G3
Talwood **44** A3
Tamala **36** B2
Tamala Park **46** A1
Tamarang **75** G2
Tamar Hills **63** F6
Tamar Valley **97** E5
Tambar Springs **75** G1
Tambellup **65** E4
Tambo **33** F5
Tambo Crossing **94** C2

Tamboon **95** F3
Tamboon Inlet **95** F3
Tamborine **71** G3
Tamborine Mountain **71** G3
Tambo River **94** C2
Tambo Upper **94** C3
Tamleugh North **86** C4
Tamleugh West **86** C4
Tammarin Rock **63** G4
Tammin **63** F5
Tamworth **76** B1
Tanami Desert **16** D5
Tanami Downs **16** C5
Tanami Mine **16** C5
Tanami Road **30** B2
Tanami Track **16** D6, **30** A1
Tanbar **32** B5
Tangadee **23** F5
Tangalooma Resort **71** H1
Tangambalanga **87** F4
Tangmangaroo **79** G5
Tangorin **33** E1
Tanja **89** E6
Tanjil Bren **93** G3
Tanjil South **93** G4
Tannum Sands **59** G5
Tannymorel **71** E4
Tansey **61** E4
Tantangara Reservoir **88** B3
Tantanoola **90** B2
Tantanoola Caves **90** B2
Tantawangalo Mountain **88** D6
Tanumbirini **17** H1
Tanunda **69** G3
Tapio **49** G2
Tara (QLD) **60** C6
Tara Homestead (NSW) **42** D5
Tara Homestead (NSW) **50** C1
Taradale **85** H6
Tarago **93** F3
Tarago Reservoir **93** F3
Taralga **80** B5
Tarampa **71** F2
Taranna **99** F4
Taravale **55** F6
Tarcoola **40** D4
Tarcoon **43** F4
Tarcowie **67** F6
Tarcutta **87** H1
Taree **77** E4
Tarella **42** C5
Targa **97** F5
Tarin Rock **65** F2
Tarin Rock Nature Reserve **65** F2
Tarlee **69** G3
Tarlo **80** B5
Tarlo River National Park **80** B5
Tarlton Downs **31** F2
Tarlton Downs Aboriginal Land **31** F2
Tarlton Range **31** F2
Tarmoola **37** H3
Tarnagulla **85** F5
Tarong National Park **61** E6
Taroom **60** B3
Taroona **99** E4
Tarpeena **90** B1
Tarrabool Lake **17** H3
Tarra-Bulga National Park **93** H5
Tarraleah **98** D2
Tarranyurk **83** F3
Tarraville **93** H5
Tarrawingee **87** E4

Tarrington **91** E2
Tarwilli **64** D3
Tarwin Lower **93** F5
Tarwin River East Branch **93** F5
Tarwong **50** A2
Tarzali **55** E2
Tasman Head **99** E5
Tasman Highway **97** F5, **99** G2
Tasman Island **99** G5
Tasman Peninsula **99** G4
Tate River **54** C2
Tatham **71** G6
Tathra **89** E6
Tathra Head **89** E6
Tathra National Park **62** B1
Tatong **86** D5
Tatura **86** B4
Tatyoon **91** G1
Tawonga **87** F5
Tawonga South **87** F5
Tayan Peak **75** G6
Taylor Island **68** B4
Taylors Arm **73** E6
Taylors Beach **55** F5
Taylors Flat **79** H4
Taylors Lake **84** C1
Tea Gardens **76** D6
Teano Range **23** E5
Ted's Beach **98** C3
Teepookana Forest Reserve **98** B1
Teesdale **92** B3
Teetulpa **67** H5
Tego **43** F3
Telegraph Point **77** F2
Telegraph Station **17** G4
Telford **86** D3
Telopea Downs **82** D2
Telowie Gorge Conservation Park **67** F6
Temma **96** A4
Temora **78** D4
Tempe Downs **27** E5
Temple Bay **21** F3
Temple Court **76** A3
Templeton **19** G3
Templeton River **18** C6
Tenindewa **36** C3
Ten Mile Lake **23** G5
Tennant Creek **17** G4
Tennyson **85** H3
Tenterden **65** E4
Tenterfield **72** D1
Terang (VIC) **91** G4
Terang (WA) **62** C4
Teridgerie **43** H5
Termeil **89** F2
Terminal Lake **23** G4
Tero Creek **42** C4
Terowie **67** G6
Terrigal **81** F2
Territory Wildlife Park **12** C2
Teryaweynya Lake **42** C6
Teryawynia **42** C6
Tewantin **61** G5
Tewinga **73** E6
Tewkesbury **96** C4
Texas **70** B5
Texas Downs **16** B2
Texas Homestead **33** F3
Thackaringa **42** A6
Thalaba **80** A4
Thallon **43** H3
Thane **70** C3

Thanes Creek **70** C3
Thangoo **14** D4
Thangool **59** F6
Thargomindah **42** D2
Theda **9** G5
Theodore **60** B1
Theresa Creek **58** A3
Theresa Creek Dam **58** A2
Thevenard **40** C6
Thevenard Island **22** B2
Thirlestone **33** F1
Thirlmere **80** C4
Thirlmere Lakes National Park **80** C4
Thirroul **80** D5
Thistle Island **68** B4
Thologolong **87** G3
Thomas Bay **14** D2
Thomas Island **57** F4
Thomas Mountains **32** B4
Thomas River **22** D5
Thomson Bay **46** C5
Thomson River (QLD) **32** D3
Thomson River (VIC) **93** H3, **94** A4
Thoona **86** D4
Thornborough Homestead (QLD) **54** D1
Thornborough Homestead (QLD) **60** A5
Thornhill **33** H6
Thornton (QLD) **71** E3
Thornton (VIC) **93** F1
Thornton Beach **20** B1
Thorntonia **18** D4
Thornton Peak **20** B1
Thorpdale **93** G4
Thredbo **88** A5
Thredbo Village **88** A5
Three Brothers, The **32** B4
Three Hummock Island **96** B2
Three Knobs **17** H1
Three Mile Beach **100** D2
Three Mile Point **100** D2
Three Pioneers, The **42** D2
Three Rivers **23** F5
Three Sisters (VIC) **45** G4
Three Sisters, The (QLD) **18** D6
Three Springs **62** B1
Three Thumbs **99** G3
Threeways **17** G4
Thrings Channel **12** B2
Throssel Range **23** H2
Thrushton National Park **43** G2
Thuddungra **79** E3
Thulimbah **70** D5
Thulloo **78** B2
Thundelarra **37** E4
Thurburn Bluff **9** H5
Thurles Park **32** C4
Thurlga **66** B4
Thurloo Downs **42** C3
Thurra River **95** F3
Thursday Island **21** E1
Thylungra **32** D6
Tia River **76** D1
Tiaro **61** F4
Tiarra **50** B1
Tibbuc **76** D3
Tibooburra **42** B3
Tichborne **74** B6
Tickalara **42** B2
Tickera Bay **69** E1
Tickera **69** E1
Tickeroo **62** C4
Tidal River **100** B5

Tielta **42** A5
Tieri **58** B3
Tieyon **30** C5
Tilba Tilba **89** E5
Tilmouth Well Roadhouse **30** B2
Tilpa **42** D5
Tilpal **59** E3
Tiltagoonah **42** D5
Timbarra **94** D2
Timbarra River (NSW) **72** D2
Timbarra River (VIC) **94** C3
Timber Creek **10** B6
Timberfield **37** H5
Timboon **91** G4
Timmering **86** A4
Timor **85** F5
Timor Sea **10** A3
Tinamba **94** A3
Tinaroo Falls **55** E2
Tin Can Bay **35** F6
Tindarey **83** E5
Tinderbox **99** E4
Tinderry **42** D1
Tinderry Peak **88** D3
Tingaringy **88** B6
Tingha **72** B3
Tingoora **61** E5
Tin Mine Cove **100** C1
Tin Mine Track **100** D1
Tinonee **77** E4
Tinsmith Island **57** F4
Tintaldra **87** H3
Tintinara **82** B2
Tin Tin Lake **49** H2
Tipperary **12** C4
Tipton **70** C1
Tirita **42** B5
Tirrannaville **80** A6
Titania Creek **100** C4
Ti-Tree (NT) **30** C1
Ti-Tree (NT) **30** C1
Tiverton **67** H5
Tiwi Aboriginal Land Trust **10** B2
Tjirrkarli Aboriginal Land **24** D5
Tjukayirla Roadhouse **38** C1
Tnorala (Gosse Bluff) Conservation Reserve **28** C5
Tobermorey **31** G1
Tobin Lake **24** C1
Tobys Knob **60** B4
Tocumwal **86** C2
Todd Glen **27** G2
Todd River (NT) **30** C3, D3
Todd River Homestead (NT) **29** H4
Todmorden **30** D6
Togari **96** A4
Togganoggera **89** E3
Tolga **55** E2
Tolmie **86** D6
Tomahawk **97** G4
Tomahawk River **97** G4
Tomakin **89** F3
Tomaree National Park **76** D6
Tombstone Rocks **62** B3
Tomerong **89** G1
Tomingley **74** B4
Tomoo **43** G1
Tom Price **23** E3
Toms Cap **93** H5
Tone River **64** D4
Tongala **86** A3
Tonganah **97** F5
Tongio West **94** C1

Tongo Lake **42** C4
Tongue Point **100** B4
Tongy **43** G1
Tonkoro **32** C3
Toobanna **55** F5
Toobeah **44** A3
Tooborac **86** A6
Toodyay **62** D5
Toogong **79** G1
Toogoolawah **61** F6
Toogoom **61** G3
Toolakea **55** G6
Toolamba **86** B4
Toolamba West **86** B4
Toolangi **93** E2
Toolbrunup **65** F4
Toolbrunup Peak **65** F4
Tooleybuc **49** H3
Toolibin **65** E2
Toolleen **86** A5
Toologie **48** B2
Toolondo Reservoir **85** A2
Toolonga Nature Reserve **36** C2
Tooloom National Park **71** E5
Tooma **88** A3
Toomba **20** B5
Toompine **42** D1
Tooms Lake **99** F2
Toona Gate **42** B3
Toonboro Mountain **61** E1
Tooncatchyin Creek **41** G3
Toongabbie **93** H4
Toongi **74** C4
Toonpan **56** B1
Toonumbar **71** E5
Toonumbar National Park **71** E5
Tooradin **93** E4
Toora **93** G5
Toorale **43** E4
Tooraweenah **74** D1
Toorbul **71** G1
Toorloo Arm **94** D3
Tootool **87** F1
Tootra **62** D3
Toowoomba **70** D2
Top Hut **49** H2
Topiram **93** F4
Top Springs **17** E1
Torbanlea **61** G3
Torbay **65** F6
Torbay Head **65** F6
Torndirrup National Park **65** F6
Toronto **81** F1
Torquay **92** C4
Torrens Creek (QLD) **20** A6
Torrens Creek (QLD) **33** E1
Torrington **72** C2
Tor Rock **13** G1
Torrumbarry **85** H3
Torsdale **59** E6
Torwood **54** B2
Tottenham **43** F6
Toukley **81** F2
Towallum **73** F4
Towamba **93** G1
Towera **22** B4
Towerhill Creek **33** E1
Tower Hill State Game Reserve **93** F4
Townsend Creek **17** E2
Townshend Island **59** F2
Townson **71** E3
Towns River **11** F5

Townsville **55** G6
Towong **87** H4
Towrana **22** C6
Towrang **80** B6
Trafalgar **93** G4
Tragowel **85** G2
Trangie **74** B3
Trans-Australian Railway **38** C5
Traralgon **93** H4
Traralgon South **93** H4
Travellers Lake **49** G1
Travellers Rest Lake **98** D1
Trawalla **92** A1
Trawool **86** B6
Trayning **63** F3
Traysurin **65** F1
Trebonne **55** F5
Tree Point **10** A4
Tree Top Walk **64** D6
Trefoil Island **96** A3
Trelega **49** G2
Trentham **92** C1
Trephina Creek **29** F4
Trephina Gorge **30** D3
Trephina Gorge Nature Park **29** G4
Tresco **85** F1
Trevallyn **76** C5
Trevallyn Homestead **42** D5
Trewalla **32** C4
Trewilga **74** B5
Triabunna **99** G3
Trial Harbour **96** B6
Triangle Cliff **35** F2
Trillbar **23** E6
Trinity Bay **55** F1
Trinity Beach **55** F1
Triplet Falls **92** A5
Troopers Creek **84** C2
Troubridge Point **69** E4
Trowutta **96** B4
Trundle **74** A5
Trunkey Creek **80** A3
Truro **69** G3
Tryon Island **59** H4
Tuan **35** E6
Tubbul **79** E4
Tucabia **73** F3
Tuckanarra **37** E2
Tuena **79** H3
Tuen **43** F2
Tuggerah Lake **81** F2
Tugun **71** H4
Tulendeena **97** F5
Tullah **96** C6
Tullamore **74** A4
Tullaroop Reservoir **85** F6
Tullibigeal **78** B1
Tully **55** F3
Tumanmang Mountain **88** D3
Tumbarumba **88** A3
Tumblong **79** E6
Tumbulgum **71** H4
Tumby Bay **68** B3
Tummaville **70** C2
Tumoulin **55** E3
Tumut (NSW) **88** B1
Tumut (WA) **62** C4
Tumut River **88** B3
Tunbridge **99** F2
Tuncurry **77** E4
Tundulya **43** E5
Tungamah **86** D3

Tunnack **99** F2
Tunnel **97** F5
Tunnel Creek National Park **15** F3
Tura Beach **95** H1
Turallin **44** B2
Turee Creek **23** E4
Turill **75** F3
Turingal Head **89** E6
Turipa **62** C2
Turkey Beach **59** H6
Turkey Creek (Warmun) **16** B2
Turkey Island **35** E5
Turlee **49** H2
Turner **16** B3
Turner River **23** E1
Turners Beach **96** D4
Turners Marsh **97** E5
Turon River **75** E6
Tuross Head **89** F4
Tuross Lake **89** F4
Tuross River **89** E4
Turrawan **44** A5
Turriff **83** G1
Turtle Head Island **21** F1
Turtle Point **10** A5
Tuyali **62** B3
Tweed Heads **71** H4
Tweed River **71** G5
Twelve Apostles, The **91** H5
Twelve Mile **75** E4
Twilight Cove **39** E6
Twin Falls **13** F3
Twin Lakes **49** G1
Twin Peaks (QLD) **21** H5
Twin Peaks (WA) **36** D2
Twins, The (NT) **31** E4
Twins, The (SA) **40** D4
Twofold Bay **95** H2
Two Mile Flat **75** E4
Two Mile Waterhole Camping Area **13** E2
Two Peoples Bay **65** G6
Two Peoples Bay Nature Reserve **65** F6
Two Rivers **32** A2
Two Rocks **62** C5
Two Wells **69** F3
Tyaak **93** E1
Tyabb **93** E4
Tyagarah **71** H5
Tyalgum **71** G5
Tycannah **44** A4
Tyenna **98** D3
Tyers **93** H4
Tyers Junction **93** G3
Tylden **92** C1
Tylers Pass **28** B5
Tyndale **73** G2
Tynong **93** F4
Tyntynder Homestead **49** H3
Tyrendarra **91** E3
Tyrendarra East **91** E3
Tyringham **73** E4

U

Uarbry **75** F3
Uaroo **22** B3
Ubirr Lookout **13** G1
Ucharonidge **17** G2
Udialla **15** E3
Ukalunda **56** C4
Uki **71** G5
Ulamambri **75** E1

Ulan **75** F4
Ulenia Lake **42** B4
Ulind **75** F2
Ulladulla **89** G2
Ullawarra **22** C4
Ullawarra Aboriginal Land **22** C4
Ullina **85** G6
Ulmarra **73** F3
Ulong **73** E4
Ultima **85** E1
Uluru (Ayers Rock) **30** A5
Uluru-Kata Tjuta National Park **30** A4
Ulverstone **96** D4
Umaralla Mountain **88** D4
Umbakumba **11** H4
Umbeara **30** C5
Umberatana **41** G4
Umberumberka Reserve **42** A5
Umbrawarra Gorge Nature Park **12** D5
Undara Volcanic National Park **54** C4
Undera **86** B4
Underwood **97** F5
Undilla **18** C4
Undoolya **29** G5
Undulla **60** B6
Ungarie **50** C2
Ungarra **48** B2
Ungowa **35** F5
Unicup Lake **64** D5
Uno **66** C5
Upotipotpon **86** C4
Upper Blessington **97** F5
Upper Castra **96** D5
Upper Coliban Reservoir **92** C1
Upper Esk **97** G5
Upper Freestone **71** E4
Upper Horton **44** A5
Upper Hunter Wineries **75** H5
Upper Manilla **44** A5
Upper Myall **76** D5
Upper Natone **96** C5
Upper Scamander **97** G6
Upper Stone **55** F5
Upper Swan **62** D5
Upper Tallebudgera **71** G4
Upper Tenthill **71** E2
Upper Widgee **61** F4
Upper Yarra Reservoir **93** G2
Upstart Bay **56** D2
Uraidla **69** F4
Urala **22** B2
Uralla **44** B5
Urana **87** E1
Urandangi **31** G1
Urangan **35** E4
Urangeline East **87** F1
Uranquinty **87** G1
Urapunga **11** F5
Urapuntja **30** D1
Urbenville **71** E5
Urisino **42** D4
Urunga **73** F5
Useless Loop **36** A1
Ussher Point **21** F2
Utah Lake **42** D4
Uxbridge **99** E3

V

Vale, The **50** A2
Vale Lookout **45** F1

Valencia Creek **94** A3
Valentine Plains **59** F6
Valla **73** F6
Valla Beach **73** F6
Valley of the Giants **64** D6
Vanderlin Island **11** H6
Van Dieman Gulf **10** C2
Van Lee **54** B3
Vanrook **19** G2
Vanrook Creek **19** F1
Vansittart Bay **9** F5
Vansittart Island **97** H2
Van Spoult Head **21** E1
Varley **65** H1
Vasey **83** F6
Vashon Head **10** C1
Vasse **64** B4
Vasse Highway **64** B4
Vaughan Springs **25** H1
Vectis South **85** A1
Veitch **49** F3
Veldt, The **42** B4
Vena Park **19** F3
Vennachar Point **68** C6
Venus Bay **93** F5
Vereker Lookout **100** B3
Vereker Range **100** B3
Vergement Creek **32** C3
Vernon Point **35** E3
Verona Sands **99** E4
Vesper **93** G3
Victor Harbor **69** F5
Victoria Downs **56** A3
Victoria Highway **10** C6, **16** C1
Victoria Lake **42** C6
Victoria Pass **45** F5
Victoria Point **71** H2
Victoria Range **84** B5
Victoria River **10** B6, **16** D2
Victoria River Crossing **10** C6
Victoria River Downs **10** D1
Victoria Vale **19** G4
Victoria Valley (VIC) **84** B5
Victoria Valley (TAS) **98** D2
Victoria Valley Road **84** B5
Victory Downs **30** B5
Vimy **59** E5
Vincentia **89** G1
Vincents Hill **99** F2
Violet Town **86** C5
Violet Vale **21** G5
Violet Valley Aboriginal Land **16** A2
Vivian Well **41** E4
Vivien **37** H2
Vivonne Bay **68** D6
Vivonne Bay Conservation Park **68** D6
Vlaming Head **22** A3
Vooden Point **21** G4
Vrilya Point **21** E2

W

Waaia **86** B3
Waanyi/Garawa Aboriginal Land **18** B3
Wabricoola **67** H5
Wadbilliga National Park **88** D5
Waddamana **99** E1
Wadderin **63** G5
Waddikee **66** C6
Waddy Point **35** G2
Wadeye (Port Keats) **10** A5
Wadjemup Hill **46** B6

Wadnaminga **41** H6
Wagerup **64** B2
Waggaboonya Range **18** D5
Wagga Wagga (NSW) **78** C6
Wagga Wagga (WA) **37** E3
Wagin **65** E2
Wagon Flat **83** E2
Wagoora **57** E4
Wagra Mountain **87** G3
Wagurunguru Aboriginal Land **16** C1
Wahgunyah **87** E3
Wahring **86** B5
Wahroonga **22** B6
Waigen Lakes **39** G1
Waikerie **69** H2
Wail **83** F4
Wairuna **55** E4
Waite Creek **30** C2
Waite River **30** D2
Wakaya Aboriginal Land Trust **18** A5
Wakooka **21** H5
Wakool **85** H1
Wakool River **85** G1
Walabanba Hills **30** B1
Walbundrie **87** F2
Walcha **72** B6
Walcott Inlet **15** F1
Waldburg **22** D5
Waldburg Range **23** E5
Waldegrave Island **48** A1
Walebing **63** G3
Walgett **43** G4
Walgoolan **63** H4
Walgra **31** G1
Walgun **23** G3
Walhalla **93** H3
Walhalla Goldfields Railway **93** H3
Walkamin **55** E2
Walkaway **36** C4
Walken River **11** G4
Walker Channel **96** A3
Walker Island **96** A3
Walkers Lookout **97** H2
Walkerston **57** F5
Walkerville **93** F6
Wallabadah **19** G3
Wallabi Group **36** B4
Wallaby Point **96** A2
Wallace **92** B2
Wallacedale **91** E2
Wallace Rockhole **30** B3
Wallace Rockhole Aboriginal Community **27** H3
Wallacia **80** D3
Wallaga Lake National Park **89** E5
Wallagaraugh River **95** G2
Wallal Downs **14** C5
Wallaloo **83** H5
Wallaman Falls **55** F5
Wallan **92** D1
Wallangarra **70** D6
Wallangra **72** A1
Wallareenya **23** E1
Wallaroo **69** E2
Wallaroo Bay **48** C2
Wallatinna **40** C1
Walla Walla **87** F2
Wallendbeen **79** E5
Wallerawang **80** C2
Wallerberdina **67** F3
Wallhollow **18** A2
Walli **79** G2
Walling Rock **37** H4

Wallis Lake **77** E5
Walloon **71** F2
Walls Lookout **45** F4
Walls of Jerusalem National Park **96** D6
Wallumbilla **60** A5
Walma **65** H1
Walmer **74** D5
Walpeup **49** G3
Walpole **64** D6
Walpole-Nornalup National Park **64** C6
Walsall **64** B4
Walsh River **54** C1
Walungurru **25** G3
Walwa **87** H3
Walyunga National Park **62** D5
Wamberra **49** G2
Wambiana **56** A3
Wambidgee **79** E6
Wamboin **43** F5
Wamoon **78** A4
Wamuran **71** G1
Wanaaring **42** D4
Wanarra **62** D1
Wanbi **49** F3
Wandarrie **37** E2
Wanderer River **98** B3
Wandering **64** D1
Wandiligong **87** F5
Wandoan **60** B4
Wandong **92** D1
Wando Vale (QLD) **20** A5
Wando Vale (VIC) **90** D1
Wandsworth **72** B3
Wanerie Farm **62** C4
Wanganella **50** A3
Wangan **53** F3
Wangangong **50** C1
Wangara **62** C5
Wangaratta **87** E4
Wangary **68** A3
Wanggoolba **35** F4
Wangi **12** D1
Wangi Wangi **81** F1
Wangoom **91** F4
Wanilla **68** B3
Wanna **22** D4
Wanna Lakes **39** F2
Wannamal **62** C4
Wanneary **62** D3
Wannon **91** E2
Wannon River **84** A5, **91** E2
Wannon Swamp **84** B6
Wantabadgery **78** D6
Wanyanmera Point **11** H3
Wappinguy **75** H4
Warakurna Aboriginal Land **25** F4
Warakurna Roadhouse **25** F4
Warambie **22** D1
Waranga Basin **86** B4
Waranga Western Channel **83** H2, **85** G4
Waratah (NSW) **43** F4
Waratah (TAS) **96** B5
Waratah Bay **100** A3
Warbreccan **32** C4
Warburton (NT) **25** E6
Warburton (VIC) **93** F3
Warburton Aboriginal Land **25** E5
Warburton Creek **41** G1
Warburton Range **25** E6
Warcowie **67** F3
Wardang Island **48** C2
Wardarlea Bay **11** H3

Wardell **73** G1
Warden Head **89** G2
Ward River **33** F6
Wards River **76** D4
Wareek **85** F5
Warenda **32** A2
Warge Rock **74** A4
Warialda **44** A4
Warialda Rail **44** A4
Warkton **75** E1
Warkworth **76** A5
Warmga **60** D6
Warncoort **92** A4
Warners Bay **81** F1
Warnertown **67** F6
Warnga Point **11** G2
Warooka **68** D4
Waroona **64** B2
Warra **60** C6
Warra Homestead **32** A2
Warrabah National Park **72** A5
Warracknabeal **83** G3
Warraderry **79** F2
Warragoon **86** D2
Warragul **93** F4
Warrah Creek **76** A2
Warrak **85** E6
Warrakimbo **67** F3
Warrakoo **49** F2
Warrakunta Point **11** G5
Warral **76** A1
Warral Island **21** E1
Warralong **14** B6
Warrambine **92** B3
Warramboo (SA) **66** A6
Warramboo (WA) **62** C4
Warramuggan **63** F3
Warrananga **49** G2
Warrawagine **23** G1
Warraweena Sanctuary **67** G1
Warrayure **84** B6
Warrego Highway **33** G6, **70** C1
Warrego River **33** F5, **43** E3
Warrell Creek **73** E6
Warren **74** B2
Warrenbayne **86** C5
Warrenben Conservation Park **68** D4
Warren National Park **64** C5
Warren River **64** C5
Warrenup **65** F6
Warren Vale **19** E3
Warriedar **37** E4
Warrill Creek **71** F3
Warrill View **71** F3
Warrimoo **45** G1
Warringa **96** C5
Warrinilla **43** G4
Warrion **92** A4
Warri Warri Gate **42** B3
Warrnambool **91** F4
Warrock Homestead **90** D1
Warrong **91** F3
Warroora **22** A4
Warrumba Range **79** F3
Warrumbungle National Park **75** E1
Warrumbungle Ranges **75** F1
Wartaka **66** D5
Wartook **84** B2
Wartook Reservoir **83** G6
Warumungu Aboriginal Land Trust **17** H4-5
Warwick **70** D4

Warwick Downs **18** C6
Washpool National Park **72** D2
Wasleys **69** F3
Watarrka National Park **30** A3
Watchem **83** H3
Waterbank **14** D3
Waterfall **80** D4
Waterfall Bay **99** G4
Waterfall Way, The **73** E5
Waterford **71** G3
Waterhouse Island **97** G4
Waterhouse Point **97** G4
Waterloo (NT) **16** C1
Waterloo (TAS) **99** E4
Waterloo (VIC) **92** A1
Waterloo (WA) **64** B3
Waterloo Bay **100** D5
Waterloo Point **100** D5
Waterloo Point Surf Beach **99** G2
Watermill Creek **77** G5
Water Park Point **59** F3
Watervale **69** F2
Watheroo **62** C2
Watheroo National Park **62** C2
Wathumba Campsite **35** G2
Watson River **21** E4
Watsons Creek **72** A5
Watson Taylors Lake **77** F3
Watsonville **55** E2
Wattamondara **79** G3
Wattle Island **100** C6
Waubra **92** A1
Wauchope (NSW) **77** F2
Wauchope (NT) **17** G5
Waurn Ponds **92** C4
Wave Hill **16** D2
Waverley Downs **42** D3
Waverley Gate **42** D3
Waverney **32** B5
Wave Rock **63** H6
Wayatinah **98** D2
Wayatinah Lagoon **98** D2
Waychinicup National Park **65** G5
Wearyan River **18** B1
Wedderburn **85** F4
Weddin Mountain Range **79** E2
Weddin Mountains National Park **79** E3
Wedge Bay **99** F4
Wedge Island **62** B4
Wedin **65** E2
Wednesday Island **21** F1
Weeaproinah **92** A5
Weebo **37** H2
Weebubbie Cave **39** G5
Weedina Creek **41** E2
Wee Jasper **88** C1
Weelarrana **23** G4
Weelhamby Lake **36** D4
Weemelah **43** H3
Weerangourt **91** E2
Weerite **91** H4
Weetah **97** E5
Weetaliba **75** F2
Weethalle **78** B2
Wee Waa **43** H4
Weipa **21** E3
Weir River **70** A2
Weirs Farm **62** C1
Weismantels **76** D5
Weja **78** C1
Welbourn Hill **40** C1
Welbungin **63** F3

Welcome Stranger Monument **85** E5
Weldborough **97** G5
Weld Range **37** E2
Weld River **98** D4
Weld Springs (Well 9) **23** H5
Welford Lagoon **32** D5
Well 1 **37** G1
Wells 2-4A **23** G6
Well 5 **23** H5
Well 6 (Pierre Springs) **23** H5
Well 7-8 **23** H5
Well 9 (Weld Springs) **23** H5
Well 10-12 **23** H5
Well 13-16 **24** A4
Well 17 (Killagurra Springs) **24** A3
Well 18-22 **24** A3
Well 23-26 **24** B3
Well 27-30 **24** B2
Well 31-36 **24** C2
Well 37 (Liberal Well) **24** C2
Well 38-42 **24** D1
Well 43 **15** H6
Well 49 **15** H5
Well 50 (dry) **16** A5
Wellcamp **70** D2
Wellesley Islands Aboriginal Land **18** D1
Wellingrove **72** C2
Wellington (NSW) **74** D4
Wellington (SA) **69** G5
Wellington Caves **74** D5
Wellington Dam **64** C3
Wellington Mill **64** B3
Welltree **12** B3
Welshpool **93** G5
Wengenville **61** E6
Wenlock River **21** F3
Wenonah Head **73** F5
Wentworth **49** G2
Wentworth Creek **45** F3
Wentworth Falls **45** G3
Wernadinga **19** E3
Werribee **92** D3
Werribee River **92** C2
Werrikimbe National Park **77** E1
Werrimull **49** G2
Werrington **54** B6
Werris Creek **44** A6
Wertaloona **67** H1
Wesley Mountain **88** B4
Wessel Islands **11** G2
West Baines River **10** A6, **16** C1
West Barwon Dam **92** A5
West Bay **68** C6
West Branch **93** F5
Westbrook **70** D2
Westbury **97** E6
West Cape **48** C3
West Cape Howe National Park **65** E6
Westdale **63** E6
West End **46** A6
Western Cove **69** E5
Western Creek (NT) **10** D6
Western Creek (TAS) **96** D6
Western Freeway **92** C2
Western Highway **83** E3, **91** H1
Western Junction **97** F6
Western Motorway **45** G1
Western Plains Zoo **74** C4
Western Port **93** E4
Western River **32** C2
Western River Conservation Park **68** D5
Western River Cove **68** C5

West Group **47** F3
Westgrove **33** H5
West Hill National Park **58** D1
West Island (CKI) **14** A2
West Island (NT) **11** H6
West MacDonnell National Park **28** B4
West Melbourne **108** A2
Westmere **91** G2
West Montagu **96** A3
Westmoreland **18** C2
West Mount Barren **65** H4
Westonia **63** H4
West Perth **105** F6
West Point (SA) **68** B4
West Point (TAS) **96** A4
West Portal **98** D4
West River **47** E2
West Sandy Point **97** E4
West Takone **96** C4
West Tamar Highway **97** E5
Westvale **62** D4
Westwood **59** E4
West Wyalong **50** C2
Weymouth **97** F4
Weymouth Bay **21** G3
Whalers Way **68** A4
Wharparilla **86** A3
Wharton **47** G2
Wheeo **79** H5
Whetstone **70** A4
Whian Whian State Forest **71** G5
Whim Creek **22** D1
Whiporie **73** F2
Whisky Bay **100** B4
Whistler Point **96** C1
Whitby **62** D6
White Cliffs (NSW) **42** C5
White Cliffs (WA) **38** B2
White Flag Lake **37** H5
Whitefoord **99** F2
White Hills **97** F6
White Horse Gap **27** F5
White Lake (VIC) **83** E5
White Lake (WA) **23** H5
Whitemark **97** G2
White Mountains National Park **20** A6
White Rock **55** F1
White Springs **23** E2
Whitewood **32** D1
Whitfield **87** E5
Whitsunday Island **57** F3
Whitsunday Islands National Park **57** F3
Whitsunday Passage **57** F3
Whitsundays, The **57** F3
Whittata **66** D3
Whittlesea **93** E2
Whitton **78** A4
Whorouly **87** E5
Whorouly South **87** E5
Whroo Historic Reserve **86** A5
Whyalla **67** E6
Whyalla Conservation Park **67** E5
Whymlet **40** D4
Whynot **56** C5
Whyte River **96** B5
Whyte-Yarcowie **67** G6
Wialki **63** G2
Wiangaree **71** F5
Wickepin **65** E1
Wickham **22** D1
Wickham River **16** D1
Wickliffe **91** G2

Wide Bay Highway **61** F4
Widgee Downs **43** F3
Widgee Mountain **61** F5
Widgiemooltha **38** A6
Widgiewa **78** A6
Wigton Island **57** G4
Wilberforce **80** D2
Wilby **86** D3
Wilcannia **42** C5
Wildman River **13** E2
Wilga **64** C3
Wilga Downs **43** E5
Wilga Mia Ochre Mine **37** E1
Wilgaroon **43** E5
Willandra National Park **50** B1
Willare Bridge Roadhouse **15** E3
Willatook **91** F3
Willaura **85** D6
Willawarrin **77** F1
Willbriggie **50** B3
Willeroo **10** C6
William Bay **65** E6
William Bay National Park **65** E6
Williambury **22** B4
William Creek **41** E2
Williams **64** D2
Williamsford **96** B6
Williams Island **68** B4
Williams River (NSW) **76** C6
Williams River (QLD) **19** F6
Williamstown (SA) **69** G3
Williamstown (VIC) **93** D3
Williba **49** G1
Willippa **67** G3
Willouran Range **41** G3
Willowdene **86** B4
Willow Grove **93** G4
Willowie **67** F5
Willowra **17** F6
Willows Gemfields **58** A4
Willow Tree **76** A2
Willow Waters **67** F3
Wills Creek **31** H1
Wills Developmental Road **19** F5
Willunga **69** F5
Willung **93** H4
Wilmington **67** F5
Wilmot **96** D5
Wilpena **67** F3
Wilpena Creek **67** G3
Wilpena Pound **67** F3
Wilpoorinna **41** G4
Wilroy **36** D3
Wilson Bay **46** A6
Wilson Island **59** H4
Wilson Range **100** C5
Wilson River (NSW) **42** C1
Wilson River (NSW) **77** E2
Wilson River (WA) **16** A2
Wilsons Promontory **53** E2
Wilsons Promontory Marine Park **100** A3
Wilsons Promontory National Park **100** C4
Wilton **80** D4
Wilton River **11** F4
Wiltshire **96** B3
Wiluna **37** G1
Wimmera Highway **83** E5, **85** H5
Wimmera River **83** F4, H5
Winchelsea **92** B4
Winchelsea Island **11** H4
Windalle **42** B6
Windara **42** D5

Windellama **89** E1
Windera **61** E4
Winderie **22** C6
Windermere **92** A1
Windeyer **75** E5
Windidda **24** A6
Windidda Aboriginal Land **24** A6
Windimurra **37** F3
Windjana Gorge National Park **15** F3
Windjingayr Aboriginal Outstation **15** F2
Windorah **32** C5
Window on the Wetlands **12** D2
Windside **65** E2
Windsor (NSW) **80** D3
Windsor (SA) **69** F3
Windy Corner **24** C3
Windy Harbour **64** C6
Windy Hill **65** H3
Windy Saddle **100** C4
Windy Spring **62** C1
Wingadee **43** G5
Wingan Inlet **95** G3
Wingan River **95** G3
Wingate Mountains **12** B6
Wingeel **92** B3
Wingelinna Aboriginal Land **25** F5
Wingellina **25** G5
Wingello **80** B6
Wingen **76** A3
Wingham **77** E4
Winiam **83** E3
Winingarra Aboriginal Land **16** C6
Winkleigh **97** E5
Winnathee **42** A3
Winning **22** B4
Winninowie Conservation Park **67** E5
Winslow **91** F3
Wintinna **40** C1
Winton (QLD) **32** C2
Winton (VIC) **86** D4
Wirlyajarrayi Aboriginal Land **17** F6
Wirrabara **67** F6
Wirraminna **66** C2
Wirrealpa **67** G2
Wirrengren Plain **49** G3
Wirrimah **79** F3
Wirrinya **79** E2
Wirriwa **43** G3
Wirrula **40** D6
Wiseleigh **94** C3
Wisemans Ferry **81** E2
Wishbone **65** F2
Wistow **69** G4
Witchcliffe **64** A4
Witchelina **41** G4
Withcott **70** D2
Witjira National Park **31** E5
Wittenoom **23** E2
Wivenhoe **96** C4
Wodonga **87** F3
Wogarl **63** H5
Wogarno **37** E3
Wog Wog Mountain **95** G1
Wog Wog River **95** G1
Wokalup **64** B2
Wokingham Creek **32** C1
Woko National Park **76** C3
Wolabler Mountain **74** C6
Wolca **61** E2
Woleebee **60** B4
Wolfe Creek Crater National Park **16** A4
Wolfram **54** D2

Wollar **75** G4
Wollemi National Park **75** H5, **80** D1
Wollengambie River **45** E4
Wollogorang **18** C2
Wollombi **76** A6
Wollomombi **72** C5
Wollomombi Falls **72** C5
Wollondilly River **80** B6
Wollongbar **71** G6
Wollongong **80** D5
Wollun **72** B6
Wolseley **82** D3
Wolumla **95** H1
Wolumla Peak **95** H1
Wolvi **61** G4
Wombat **79** F4
Wombelano **83** E5
Wombeyan Caves **80** B4
Womboota **86** A2
Wombungi **10** C5
Wompah Gate **42** B3
Wonanggatta River **94** A1
Wonboyn Lake **95** H2
Wondagee **22** B4
Wondai **61** E5
Wondalga **88** A2
Wonderland Range **84** C4
Wondinong **37** F2
Wondoola **19** F3
Wonga **20** B1
Wongalara Lake **42** D5
Wongalea **50** B2
Wongalee **20** A6
Wongamine **62** D5
Wongan Hills **62** D3
Wonganoo **37** H1
Wongarbon **74** D4
Wongawal **24** A6
Wongawallan **71** G3
Wongoondy **36** C4
Wonnaminta **42** B4
Wonoka **67** F3
Wonthaggi **93** E5
Wonwondah North **85** B2
Wonwron **93** H5
Wonyip **93** G5
Woodanilling **65** E3
Woodbourne **92** B2
Woodbridge **99** E4
Woodburn **73** G1
Woodbury **99** F2
Woodchester **69** G4
Woodenbong **71** F5
Woodend **92** C1
Woodford (QLD) **61** F6
Woodford (NSW) **45** G2
Woodgate **61** G2
Woodgate National Park **61** G2
Woodglen **94** B3
Woodhill **71** G3
Woodhouse **91** F2
Woodhouselee **80** A5
Wood Island **15** F1
Woodlands (WA) **23** E5
Woodlands (WA) **64** A4
Woodlands (WA) **64** C3
Woodleigh (VIC) **93** F4
Woodleigh (WA) **36** B1
Woodmurra Creek **41** E1
Wood Point **69** E1
Woodsdale **99** F3
Woodside (SA) **69** G4

Woodside (VIC) **94** A5
Woodside Beach **94** A5
Woodside East **94** A5
Woodside North **93** H5
Woods Lake **99** E1
Woods Point **93** G2
Woods Quoin **99** E2
Woodstock (NSW) **79** G2
Woodstock (QLD) **56** B1
Woodstock (VIC) **85** G5
Woodstock Homestead **43** E4
Wood Wood **49** H3
Woody Head **73** G2
Woolamai **93** E5
Woolamba **67** H6
Woolaning School **12** B3
Wool Bay **69** E4
Woolbernup Hill **47** E3
Woolbrook **72** A6
Wooleen **36** D2
Woolgangi **69** H1
Woolgoolga **73** F4
Woolgorong **36** D3
Woolibar **38** A5
Wooli **73** G3
Woolla Downs **30** C1
Woolner **12** D1
Woolnorth **96** A3
Woolnorth Point **96** A3
Woolomin **76** B1
Wooloongabba **71** G2
Woolshed Falls **87** E4
Woolshed Mountain **61** E6
Woolsthorpe **91** F3
Wooltana **41** H4
Woomargama **87** G3
Woombye **61** G6
Woomelang **83** H1
Woomera **66** C2
Woomera Prohibited Area **66** C1
Woorabinda **58** D5
Wooramel **36** B1
Wooramel River **22** B6
Woorarra **93** G5
Wooreen **93** F5
Woori Yallock **93** F3
Woorim **71** H1
Woorlba **47** H1
Woorndoo **91** G2
Wooroloo **62** D5
Wooroolin **61** E5
Wooroona **18** C5
Wooroonook **85** E3
Wooroonooran National Park **55** F2
Woorragee **87** F4
Wootton **76** D5
Wooyung **71** H5
Worbody Point **21** E4
Woree **55** F1
Worsley **64** C3
Wotjalum Aboriginal Land **15** E2
Wowan **59** E5
Woy Woy **81** E2
Wreck Island **59** H4
Wreck Point **14** A1
Wrotham Park **54** C1
Wubin **62** D2
Wudinna **66** A6
Wujal Wujal **20** B1
Wulgulmerang **94** D1
Wundowie **62** D5
Wunghnu **86** C3

Wungong Dam 62 D6
Wunkar 49 F2
Wunura Store 18 B5
Wurdibuloc Reservoir 92 B4
Wurung 19 E4
Wutul 61 E6
Wyaaba Creek 19 F1
Wyalkatchem 63 F4
Wyalong 78 C3
Wyanbene Caves Mountain 89 E3
Wyandotte 54 D5
Wyandra 43 F1
Wyan 73 F1
Wyanga 74 B4
Wyangala 79 G3
Wyangala Waters State Recreation Area 79 H3
Wycheproof 85 E3
Wychitella 85 F3
Wycliffe Well 17 G6
Wydgee 62 C5
Wyee 81 F1
Wyelangta 92 A5
Wye River 92 B5
Wylds Craig 98 D2
Wylie Creek 70 D5
Wyloo 22 C3
Wymah 87 G3
Wynbring 40 C4
Wyndham (NSW) 95 G1
Wyndham (WA) 9 H6
Wynnum 71 G2
Wynsmith Hills 96 B5
Wynyangoo 37 F2
Wynyard 96 C4
Wyole Lake 39 H3
Wyong 81 F2
Wyperfeld National Park 83 E1
Wyralinu Hill 38 B6
Wyreema 70 D2
Wyrrabalong National Park 81 F2
Wyuna 86 B3
Wyuna Downs 43 F5
Wyuna East 86 B3
Wy Yung 94 C3

X

Xantippe 63 E2

Y

Yaamba 59 F3
Yaapeet 83 F1
Yabba North 86 C3
Yabba South 86 C4
Yabooma Island 11 F2
Yacka 69 F1
Yackandandah 87 F4
Yadlamalka 67 E4
Yakabindie 37 G2
Yalangur 70 D1
Yalardy 36 C1
Yalata Aboriginal Land 40 A5
Yalbalgo 22 B6
Yalboroo 57 E4
Yalbarrin 63 G5
Yalboroo 57 E4
Yalbra 22 D6
Yalgogrin 78 B2
Yalgoo 36 D3
Yalgorup National Park 64 B1
Yallalong 36 C2

Yallaroi 44 A3
Yallata Roadhouse 40 B5
Yalla-Y-Poora 91 H1
Yalleroi 33 F4
Yallingup 64 A4
Yallock 42 D6
Yallourn North 93 G4
Yallourn Open Cut Mine 93 G4
Yalpara 67 G5
Yalpirakinu Aboriginal Land Trust 30 A2
Yalymboo 66 D3
Yamarna 38 B2
Yambacoona 96 C1
Yamba 73 G2
Yambah 29 E6
Yamberra Mountains 10 B5
Yambira Mountain 79 F2
Yambuk 91 E4
Yanac 83 E2
Yanakie 100 A1
Yanakie Beach 100 B1
Yancannia 42 C4
Yancannia Range 42 C4
Yanchep 62 C5
Yanchep National Park 62 C5
Yanco 78 A4
Yanco Glen 42 B5
Yandal 37 H2
Yandama 42 B3
Yandaran 61 F1
Yandeyarra 23 E1
Yandeyarra Aboriginal Land 23 E2
Yanderra 80 C5
Yandil 37 G1
Yandilla (NSW) 43 E5
Yandilla (QLD) 70 C2
Yandina 61 G5
Yandoit 85 G6
Yangan 71 E4
Yaninee 66 A5
Yankalilla Bay 69 E5
Yankaninna 41 G4
Yankee Jack Lake 35 F5
Yannarie River 22 B4
Yannathan 93 F4
Yannergee 75 G1
Yanneri Lake 23 G4
Yanrey 22 B3
Yantabangee 42 C4
Yantabulla 43 E3
Yantara 42 B4
Yaouk Peak 88 C3
Yappar River 19 F3
Yaraka 32 D4
Yaramulla 54 D4
Yarck 86 C6
Yardea 66 A4
Yarding 63 G5
Yaringa 36 B1
Yarlarweelor 23 E6
Yaroomba 61 G5
Yarra 80 A6
Yarrabah 55 F1
Yarrabandai 74 A6
Yarrabubba 37 F2
Yarra Creek 96 C2
Yarraden 21 F5
Yarra Glen 93 E2
Yarragon 93 G4
Yarra Junction 93 F3
Yarraloola 22 C2
Yarralumla 105 E5

Yarraman (NSW) 75 G2
Yarraman (QLD) 61 E6
Yarramba 42 A5
Yarram 93 H5
Yarrangobilly 88 B2
Yarrangobilly Caves 88 B3
Yarranlea 70 C2
Yarra Ranges National Park 93 G2
Yarra River 93 E2
Yarras 77 E2
Yarra Valley Wineries 93 E2
Yarrawalla South 85 G3
Yarrawin 43 F4
Yarrawonga 86 D3
Yarrawonga Point 57 G6
Yarra Yarra Lakes 62 C1
Yarrie 14 C6
Yarrowitch 76 D2
Yarrowmere 33 F1
Yarrowyck 44 B5
Yarwun 59 G5
Yass 77 E2
Yass River 79 G6
Yatala 71 G3
Yathong Cliffs 35 F3
Yathong 50 B1
Yatina 67 F5
Yatteyattah 89 G2
Yea 93 E1
Yealering 65 E1
Yearinan 43 H5
Yednalue 67 F4
Yednia 61 F6
Yeeda 15 E3
Yeelanna 68 B2
Yeelirrie 37 G2
Yeenunga 32 D5
Yelarbon 70 A4
Yeldulknie Conservation Park 68 C1
Yelka 42 B4
Yellabinna Regional Reserve 40 C5
Yellowdine 37 G6
Yellow Rock 45 G1
Yelma 23 H6
Yeltacowie 66 D2
Yelta Lake 49 G1
Yelvertoft 18 D5
Yenadine 63 E5
Yenda 78 A3
Yengo National Park 76 A6, 81 E1
Yeodene 92 A4
Yeo Lake 38 C2
Yeo Lake Nature Reserve 38 C2
Yeoval 74 C5
Yeppoon 59 F4
Yerecoin 62 D3
Yerilla 60 C3
Yerong Creek 87 G1
Yerrinbool 80 C5
Yetman 70 A5
Yidney Rocks Cabins 35 F4
Yidney Scrub 35 F4
Yimkin 43 E5
Yindi 38 B4
Yingualyalya Aboriginal Land 16 C4
Yinnar 93 G4
Yinnetharra 22 C5
Yirrkala 11 H2
Yolla 96 C4
Yongala 67 G6
Yoongarillup 64 B4
Yorana 64 B3

York 63 E5
Yorke Peninsula 69 E2
Yorketown 69 E4
York Plains 99 F2
York Sound 9 E6
Yornaning 64 D1
Yoting 63 F5
Youangarra 37 F3
Youanmi Downs 37 F3
Youanmite 86 C3
Youndegin 63 F5
Young 79 F4
Younghusband Peninsula 69 G5, 82 A3
Young River 47 E2
Youngs 65 E6
Youno Downs 37 F1
Youraling 63 E6
Yourambulla 67 F3
You Yangs Forest Reserve 92 C3
Yowah 43 E2
Yowah Creek 43 E2
Yowerdabbie 62 C3
Ytiniche 62 C2
Yudnapinna 66 D4
Yuelamu 30 B1
Yuendumu 30 A1
Yuin 36 D3
Yuinmery 37 F3
Yulara 30 A4
Yuleba 60 A5
Yulecart 91 E2
Yule Point 55 E1
Yule River 23 E1
Yuluma 78 A6
Yumali 69 H5
Yumbarra Conservation Park 40 C5
Yuna 36 C3
Yundamindra 38 A3
Yungaburra 55 E2
Yunkanjini Aboriginal Land Trust 25 H2, 30 A1
Yunta 67 H5
Yuraygir National Park 73 G3
Yuulong 91 H5

Z

Z-Bend Gorge 36 B3
Zeehan 96 B6
Zeehan Highway 96 B6
Zig Zag Railway 45 E5
Zumstein Recreation Park 84 B3
Zuytdorp Nature Reserve 36 B2